3.3.77

THE
ENGLISH CRAFT GILDS

STUDIES IN THEIR PROGRESS
AND DECLINE

AMS PRESS

NEW YORK

THE
ENGLISH CRAFT GILDS

STUDIES IN THEIR PROGRESS
AND DECLINE

✦

By STELLA KRAMER, Ph. D.

Author of "The English Craft Gilds
and the Government"

COLUMBIA UNIVERSITY PRESS

NEW YORK ∽ 1927

Library of Congress Cataloging in Publication Data

Kramer, Stella, 1870-1936.
    The English craft gilds.

    Reprint of the 1927 ed. published by Columbia
University Press, New York.
    Bibliography: p.
    Includes index.
    1. Gilds—England—History. I. Title.
HD6460.K82   1976   338.6'32'0942   70-153335
ISBN 0-404-03777-1

Reprinted with permission of Columbia University Press

From the edition of 1927, New York
First AMS edition published in 1976
Manufactured in the United States of America

AMS PRESS INC.
NEW YORK, N. Y.

PREFACE

The three studies relating to the history of the English gilds which are discussed in this volume have grown out of an earlier investigation into the relations commonly supposed to have existed between the English government and the craft gilds, entitled "The English Craft Gilds and the Government," and published in 1905 as a doctoral dissertation in Studies in History, Economics and Public Law, edited by the Faculty of Political Science of Columbia University.

Despite its shortcomings, the critics were kind enough to welcomes this first study of the English gilds, and one of them, writing in The English Athenaeum under date of April 14, 1906, expressed the hope that it might be enlarged and carried forward. That hope coincided with my own, and has its fulfilment in the present volume.

"The Amalgamation of the English Trades and Handicrafts," the first study in the present volume, discusses a movement that followed closely upon the rise of individual gilds. This was one, seemingly, in such contradiction to the spirit of the age which called for the separation of gild interests, as to warrant a detailed inquiry into the causes of their amalgamation. Why the crafts were allowed to unite when the sentiment of the times favored their separation seemed a mystery worthy to be unravelled.

"The Conflict between the Trades and Handicrafts," the subject of the second study, aside from its interest to most students of gild history, led frequently to their amalgamation, and therefore needs to be taken into account in an investigation into the causes of the amalgamation movement. Besides, conflict played an important rôle not only in the rise and progress of the gilds but in their decline as well, and so has a place in a detailed account of English gild history.

The third study, as its title implies, has to do with the final acts in the history of the gilds. This aspect of the subject has for me an especial interest because its investigation virtually corroborated the conclusions reached in my earlier work, namely, that adverse government legislation or repression played comparatively little part in bringing about the end of the English gilds. The conclusion still seems warranted, that, when borough interests could no longer be best conserved by the preservation of craft companies, the companies had to go. That stage, as the present discussion tends, doubtless, to prove, was not reached simultaneously for all the gilds even in the same borough or corporate town.

iii

The student, interested in the fate of the gild merchant, may
find in the material relating to York, which is cited in this volume,
proof that the York gild merchant had ceased to function earlier
than one might have supposed from the evidence of gild merchant
activity extant in other communities. The "Register of the Freemen of the City of York from the City Records," a volume published by the Surtees Society as early as 1897, but which had been
overlooked in searching for material for my first study, shows how
comparatively short-lived was the activity of the gild merchant of
York. Conceded by King John in 1200 to the citizens of York,
by 1272, the gild merchant was evidently not functioning even as
the agency for registering the names of the freemen who were
then being admitted into the civic fold. Beginning with 1272 the
names of those who "intraverunt Libertatem civitatis" of York
were recorded annually in "Freemen's Rolls" along with the name
of the officiating mayor. (Vol. 96, pp. 86–213.) In addition "a
book of diverse memoranda concerning the city of York," edited
by Miss Maud Sellers as Vols. 120 and 125, of the Surtees Society
Publications, contains the ordinances which were drawn up by the
different craft gilds in the city from the early years of the fourteenth century, until, with the founding of the mercers' gild in
1357, the process, by which, apparently as early at least as 1272,
the gild merchant of York was yielding its place and powers in the
community to the civic authority and to the rising craft and merchant gilds, seems to have been virtually completed.

                                           STELLA KRAMER.
New York, October, 1926.

CONTENTS

STUDY ONE

The Amalgamation of the English Trades and Handicrafts

I

The Causes of the Amalgamation of the Mercantile Crafts

II

The Causes of the Amalgamation of the Handicrafts

III

CONCLUSION—THE SIGNIFICANCE OF THE AMALGAMATION MOVEMENT

IV

STUDY. TWO

The Conflict Between the Trades and Handicrafts

STUDY THREE

The End of the English Craft Gilds

I

Loss by the Gilds of the Power to Enforce Their System Particularly of Apprenticeship

Loss of Gild Power of Search

II

Some Last Acts of the Gilds

III

SUMMARY AND CONCLUSION—THE CAUSES OF THE END OF THE GILDS

IV

THE AMALGAMATION OF THE ENGLISH TRADES AND HANDICRAFTS [1]

I

In 1363, because of "the great mischiefs which have happened as well to the King as to the great men and commons of that the merchants called grocers do ingross all manner of merchandise vendible and suddenly do enhance the price of such merchandise within the realme," putting it to sale "by covin and ordinance made betwixt them," it was enacted by parliament that thereafter "no English merchant shall use no ware nor merchandise . . . but only one which he shall choose betwixt this and the feast of Candlemas next coming." And as a corollary it was further ordained "that artificers, handicraft people, hold them every one to one mystery which he shall choose betwixt this and the said feast of Candlemas, and two of every craft shall be chosen to survey that none use other craft than the same which he hath chosen." [2] To students of gild history this parliamentary measure [3] is extremely significant, first of all, because it shows the immense strides taken by industrial organisation since the days of the gild merchant's régime. That once favoured association was evidently superseded in its own sphere of activity by the craft gilds which had risen into ascendancy. The act has an additional significance for our subject, because it clearly shows that a distinct merchant class had differentiated itself from the handicraft, and as we gather one of its number, the grocers, had already come into collision with

[1] Part of this study was published in *The English Historical Review* of January and April, 1908, under the title "The Amalgamation of the English Mercantile Crafts."

[2] 37 Edward III. c. 5, 6. "And such as have other wares or merchandises in their hands," continues the act, "than those that they have chosen, may set them to sale before the feast of the nativity of Saint John next ensuing; and if any do the contrary of this Ordinance in any point and be thereof attainted in the manner as hereafter followeth, he shall forfeit against the King the merchandise which he hath so used against this Ordinance; and moreover shall make a fine to the King according to the quantity of the trespass."

[3] *Rotuli Parliamentorum*, vol. ii, p. 278, records the response given this petition. "It is accorded that no English merchant use ne merce ne Marchandie p lui mes soulement une quelle il vorra betwixt the next Feast of Chandelme," etc.

the trading rules of the times. It appears that in 1345,[4] but eighteen years before the passage of this act, the London pepperers, canvas dealers, and spicers—a group of trades under the leadership doubtless of the pepperers, a gild of considerable standing in the community [5]—succeeded in combining their gild fortunes,[6] and used them to so good purpose as to earn for them, as we learn from the above-quoted act, the name of grocers. In sanctioning this alliance the powers in authority gave public evidence that they were not inclined to place any great obstacle in the way of these merchants, who by amalgamating did their utmost to check the tendency of the times to insist upon a too rigid division of labor. It is of special importance, therefore, to notice at this point that simultaneously with the emergence of a distinct class of English merchants, a most significant fact in English social history, we find that they had initiated a new movement in industrial association. This we know as the amalgamation of the English crafts.

But in spite of the grocers' misdeeds, which were sufficiently obnoxious to provoke parliamentary censure, at a time when they were very influential in public affairs,[7] nevertheless they succeeded in obtaining within a year a repeal of so much of the act as had aimed at restricting them to the use of but one kind of merchandise.[8]

---

[4] At that time it was agreed "by assent that no one shall be of the Fraternity unless he be of good condition and of their mistery That is to say Pepperer of Sopers Lane, canvas dealer of the Ropery, or spicer of Chepe or other person of their mystery in whatever part he may live." Kingdon. *The Worshipful Company of Grocers*, pt. i. p. 9.

[5] We find the "Gilda piperariorum" among the nineteen gilds in London amerced as "adulterine" in the later years of King Henry II. *The Great Roll of the Pipe*, vol. xxix, p. 153. As early as 1316 the pepperers had become known as "the good folk of Sopereslane," from which centre they apparently regulated the sale of eastern produce: extract from *Letter-book E*, fol. 53; Kingdom. *Worshipful Company of Grocers*, pt. i, p. i. A "Grossarius" of Sopers' Lane is mentioned in city records in 1310. *Ibid.*, Preface, p. vii.

[6] By 1365 the society seems to have reckoned apothecaries among its members, as is evident from an entry in its records telling how on November 20, of that year twelve surveyors were elected by the mystery of "Grossariorum Piperariorum et appotecariorum," six of whom dwelt in "Sopereslane," two in the "Ropery," two in "Chepe" and two in "Bokeleresbery." *Ibid.* p. 7. Also *Letter Book G.* p. 204. In 1373, the "Compaygne des Grossers" boasted a membership of one hundred and twenty-four persons. Kingdon, *op. cit.*, Introduction, p. xviii.

[7] Miss Alice Law, in an article on "The English Nouveaux-Riches in the Fourteenth Century" (*Trans. Royal Historical Soc.*, n.s., vol. ix., p. 70), calls attention to the significance of the relation which the union of the pepperers and spicers bears to the failure of the Bardi and Peruzzi, the king's Florentine bankers, which had occurred just four months before. She claims that the object of their incorporation was doubtless to qualify as a large banking establishment. It may indeed be that by taking the place of the Italian bankers these London merchants secured royal support in their ambitious mercantile projects.

[8] 38 Edward III. c. 11. "To that which was ordained at the last Parliament of living and of apparel, and that no English merchant should use but one merchandise; It is ordained, That all people shall be as free as they were (at all ancient times) before the said Ordinance . . . and that all mer-

Merchants, however, were still to remain a class apart from handicrafstmen, and those who had not already done so hastened to secure a royal charter protecting them in their special monopoly. In this way the London fishmongers,[9] vintners and drapers took their place side by side with the grocers, mercers and the rest of the greater metropolitan trading companies previously founded; and the majority of the twelve great livery companies were now firmly established.

Let us consider, then, in what form of organisation these merchants were usually to be found. Whereas London and certain of the larger boroughs were able to support gilds of special merchants, or in some instances organisations which were limited to dealers in but two or three or possibly four species of trades, as was the case apparently at certain epochs in Bristol,[10] Beverley,[11] Oxford,[12] and Tewkesbury,[13] the great majority of English towns encouraged but one organisation for their pure traders. Thus from the later fourteenth or the early fifteenth century consolidated mercers' and merchant companies, comprising often the local grocers, haber-

chants as well aliens as denizens, may sell and buy all manner of merchandizes, and freely carry them out of the realm, paying the customs and subsidies thereof due." See *Letter Book G.* p. 186.

[9] In 1271 there is mention of the community of the fishmongers. By 1290 it seems to have numbered eighty-nine members who subscribed five hundred marks with which to purchase pardon for forestalling and like misdemeanours. Before the first quarter of the following century had elapsed a number of these fishmongers, at a certain court or "Halimot" held amongst themselves, had determined that they alone should have the selling of fish in the city and at a higher price than was customary, contrary to the regulations made for the common good. Unwin, *Gilds and Companies of London,* pp. 39–40, quoted from the *Chronicles of the Mayors and sheriffs,* 175. On July 12, 1364, came the incorporation of the fishmongers, followed three days later by that of the vintners and of the drapers respectively. *Letter-book G.* pp. 169, 167, 174. See also *Calendar of Close Rolls,* 38 Edward III., pp. 74–5, 1910. From the preamble of the letters patent conceded to the fishmongers the year following the passage of the act of 1363, it would seem as if these merchants had been instrumental in securing its enactment. After reciting the clause of the statute which required merchants to follow only their own branch of trade, the document proceeds to tell how it had been shown to the king in council (presumably by the fishmongers) that "all sorts of people as well non-freemen and aliens as freemen of other mysteries" engrossed the greatest part of the fish brought to the fairs in those parts of the kingdom where fish was sold, thereby raising the price of that commodity so that the fishmongers could no longer profitably deal in it: Herbert, *Twelve Great Livery Companies,* vol. ii, p. 20. Not that the fishmongers adhered strictly to their own business. The king evidently had cause to suspect them of reaching out for outside trade. For scarcely two weeks after issuing the letters patent giving them the monopoly of the fish business he bade the city's mayor summon all the men of the mistery of fishmongers who were of the liberty of the Halmote and inquire on oath as to those fishmongers who had meddled in another trade contrary to the "Statute made in the last Parliament." *Letter-book G,* p. 168.

[10] *Little Red Book,* vol. ii, p. 51.
[11] *Beverly Town Documents (Selden Society),* p. 74.
[12] Turner, *Records of Oxford,* p. 331.
[13] Bennett, *Hist. of Tewkesbury,* p. 199.

dashers, ironmongers, apothecaries, goldsmiths and sometimes even drapers, were growing up at York,[14] Shrewsbury,[15] Newcastle-upon-Tyne,[16] Dublin,[17] Southampton,[18] Coventry,[19] Kingston-upon-Hull,[20] Scarborough,[21] Lincoln,[22] Leominster,[23] Northampton,[24] Gloucester,[25] Rye,[26] Bath,[27] Worcester,[28] Hereford,[29] Kendal,[30] Lynn Regis,[31] Guildford,[32] Warwick,[33] Winchester,[34] Chester,[35] Nottingham,[36] Salisbury,[37] Durham,[38] Norwich,[39] Sandwich,[40] Derby,[41] Lichfield,[42] Morpeth,[43] Doncaster,[44] Carlisle,[45] Alnwick,[46] Preston,[47] Wells,[48] Banbury,[49] Bridgnorth,[50] Leeds,[51] Uttoxeter,[52] Youghal,[53] Chiches-

[14] Drake, *Eboracum*, vol. i. p. 321.
[15] *Shropshire Archaeol. and Nat. Hist. Soc. Trans.*, vol. viii. p. 269.
[16] *The Merchant Adventurers of Newcastle-upon-Tyne* (Surtees Soc.), xciii., p. 1.
[17] Egerton MS. B. M. 1765, *Corporation Records, City of Dublin*, f. 10.
[18] Davies, *History of Southampton*, p. 275.
[19] *Coventry Leet Book*, pt. ii. p. 545.
[20] Lambert, *Two Thousand Years of Gild Life*, p. 158.
[21] Hinderwell, *History of Scarborough*, p. 172.
[22] *Hist. MSS. Comm. Rep.*, xiv, app. viii, p. 30.
[23] Townsend, *Leominster*, p. 70.
[24] *Records of the Borough*, vol. ii, p. 279.
[25] Fosbrooke, *Hist. of Gloucester*, p. 404.
[26] *Hist. MSS. Comm. Rep.*, xii, app. iv, p. 55.
[27] King and Watts, *Municipal Records*, p. 45.
[28] Green, *Hist. of Worcester*, vol. ii. p. 42.
[29] Johnson, *Ancient Customs of Hereford*, p. 118.
[30] *Hist. MSS. Comm. Rep.*, x, app. iv, p. 300.
[31] *Archaeologia*, vol. 24, p. 325. Gurney, *Extracts from Proceedings of the Corporation* of Lynn Regis.
[32] *Surrey Archaeol. Collections.* Stevens, *Records and Plate of the Borough of Guildford*, vol. ix, p. 321.
[33] Kemp, The *Black Book of Warwick*, p. 139.
[34] Bailey, *Transcripts from Municipal Archives of Winchester*, p. 68. The records of Winchester and of other boroughs such as Coventry, Southampton, Lincoln, Guildford, and Lynn Regis, give us no specific information concerning their mercers' societies, so that we cannot tell how far they represented amalgamations of different species of trading crafts. We have no reason, however, to suppose that the mercers' companies recorded in these six communities differed materially from those established in the other boroughs.
[35] *Harleian MS.* 2054, f. 56.
[36] *Records of the Borough*, vol. iv. p. 311.
[37] Hoare, *History of Modern Wilts*, vol. vi. p. 475.
[38] Fordyce, *Hist. of Durham*, vol. i. p. 345.
[39] *Records of the City of Norwich*, vol. ii. p. 383.
[40] *Additional MSS. B. M.*, 27462.
[41] *Derbyshire Archaeol. and Nat. Hist. Soc. Journ.* vol. xv. p. 113.
[42] *Trans. Royal Hist. Soc.*, n. s., vol. vii, p. 109.
[43] Mackenzie, *Northumberland*, vol. ii. p. 192.
[44] *Records of the Borough*, vol. iv. p. 204.
[45] *Municipal Records of Carlisle*, p. 89.
[46] Tate, *History of Alnwick*, vol. ii. p. 321.
[47] Abram, *Memorials of the Preston Guilds*, p. 41.
[48] *Parl. Papers*, vol. 24. p. 1368.
[49] Beasley, *Hist. of Banbury*, p. 477.
[50] Skeel, *English Historical Review*, April, 1920, pp. 244–7.
[51] Wardell, *Hist. of Leeds*, p. 34.
[52] Redfern, *Hist. of Uttoxeter*, p. 291.
[53] *Council-Book*, p. 435.

ter,[54] Richmond,[55] Pontefract,[56] Ripon,[57] and Evesham.[58] In certain of the smaller towns, towards the latter part of the sixteenth and the succeeding century, all the crafts were being drawn into definite gild groups, the number of which was determined by the authorities. In these instances the company headed by the general traders included not only merchants but occasionally different handicrafts as well. The mercantile fraternities favoured at Gateshead,[59] Dorchester,[60] Reading,[61] Maidstone,[62] Ipswich,[63] St. Albans,[64] Kingston-upon-Thames,[65] Gravesend,[66] Buckingham,[67] Axbridge,[68] Andover,[69] Abingdon,[70] Ludlow,[71] Devizes,[72] Wallingford,[73] and Faversham[74] are interesting examples of this type. We are on the whole justified, therefore, in assuming that by the middle of the sixteenth, or the beginning of the seventeenth century, an amalgamated company of mercers and ordinary merchants, more or less comprehensive in character, became a practically universal institution in the English boroughs.

[54] Dallaway, *Hist. of Western Sussex*, Chichester, vol. i. p. 164.
[55] *History of Richmond*, printed by T. Bowman, p. 121.
[56] *Collections towards a Hist. of Pontefract*, vol. i. The Booke of Entries, p. 375.
[57] Harrison, *Ripon Millenary Record*, p. 48.
[58] May, *History of Evesham*, p. 341.
[59] *Supplement to Northern Notes & Queries. Records of the Gateshead Company.* Transcribed and edited by Mr. Edwin Dodds, 1907.
[60] Hutchins, *History of County of Dorset*, edited by Shipp and Hodson, vol. ii. p. 338.
[61] *Hist. MSS. Comm. Rep.* xi. app. vii. p. 224.
[62] Russell, *Hist. of Maidstone*, p. 310.
[63] Wodderspoon, *Memorials of Ipswich*, p. 174.
[64] *St. Albans Charters*, p. 7.
[65] *Genealogical Magazine*, vol. iii, p. 342.
[66] Cruden, *History of Gravesend*, p. 194.
[67] Willis, *History of Buckingham*, p. 166.
[68] *Hist. MSS. Comm. Rep.*, iii. app. p. 303.
[69] *Wilts. Archaeol. and Nat. Hist. Soc. Mag.*, vol. xxi. p. 306. Although the mercers seem most frequently to have given their name to these large federations, in many localities the haberdashers, grocers or even drapers enjoyed that distinction. Andover, for instance, encouraged her mercantile trades and various handicrafts to incorporate themselves as the haberdashers.
[70] *Selections from the Municipal Chronicles*, p. 159. The members of this great trading society were united under the patronage of the grocers. Moreover, according to an account of various specimens of tokens which were circulated by tradesmen of many of the smaller Yorkshire towns at the Restoration, the grocers of Cranswick, Hatfield, Heptonstall, Kilham, Sheffield, Skipton and Wakefield had evidently given their name to the commercial company established within the boundaries of those towns: Smith, *Old Yorkshire*, vol. v, pp. 122–134.
[71] *Journ. Brit. Archaeol. Assoc.* vol. xxiv, p. 327. By 1710 Ludlow had incorporated a curious combination of federated trades as the Stitchmen's Company.
[72] *Wilts. Archaeol. and Nat. Hist. Soc. Mag.*, vol. iv. p. 161.
[73] Hedges, *History of Wallingford*, vol. ii. p. 234. This is an instance where the drapers held together a large combination of trades and handicrafts.
[74] *Kent Archaeol. Soc. Trans.*, vol. ix. p. lxviii.

In connexion with the English merchant companies we have to consider those which the haberdashers formed apart from the general traders. It is true that very frequently the haberdashers merged their gild interests in the general mercantile fraternities, but they did not always thus lose their separate identity. In some instances they formed on their own account an association in conjunction with other naturally connected trades. Even the London haberdashers, who for a long time were content to keep their own gild, finally followed the example of amalgamation set them by the grocers, and in the very beginning of the sixteenth century absorbed the hatters' and the cappers' gilds.[75] On the other hand, in the smaller boroughs the haberdashers appear to have joined with the hatters, cappers and occasionally with the feltmakers, in forming gilds in which the last-named trades retained their identity, as appears from accounts from such places as Bristol,[76] Exeter,[77] Kendal,[78] and Ripon,[79] although doubtless similar gilds existed also in many other towns. Chester seems to have varied the customary arrangement by incorporating together the haberdashers and the skinners.[80] In the communities which supported only a limited number of gilds the haberdashers instead of the mercers gave occasionally their name to the complex trading company. The haberdashers' company of Andover, for example, one of the three large gilds in that town, included the milliners, grocers, innholders, vintners, bakers, brewers, smiths, cappers, hatmakers, barbers, painters and glaziers.[81]

[75] Herbert, *Twelve Great Livery Companies*, vol. ii. p. 537.
[76] Latimer, *Annals of Bristol in the Seventeenth Century*, p. 26.
[77] *Western Antiquary*, vol. iv. p. 188.
[78] *Boke of Record*, p. 67.
[79] *Millenary Record*, p. 65. By 1662 the haberdashers and feltmakers had apparently admitted the saddlers and joiners to membership in their gild. In that year we find the town issuing a decree to the gild to devise new orders and regulations for the government of its members.
[80] *Municip. Corp. Comm. Rep.*, 1835, p. 2633. Traces of a consolidated gild of haberdashers and brewers are found in the records of Gloucester's gild history. Walford, *Gilds*, p. 113. In 1729 Shrewsbury seems to have supported a haberdashers' company. Hibbert, *Influence and Development of English Gilds*, p. 100.
[81] *Wilts. Archaeol. and Nat. Hist. Soc. Trans.*, vol. xxi, p. 306. To these were added in 1715, surgeons, wheelwrights, cutlers, comb and pipe makers, plumbers and ironmongers. Gross, *Gild Merchant*, vol. ii. p. 349. The haberdashers of small wares were sometimes called milliners (millianers) from their dealing in commodities imported chiefly from Milan: Herbert, *op. cit.* vol. ii, p. 533.
The Dorchester haberdashers appear to have divided themselves into two camps, the haberdashers of small wares securing membership in the mercers' company, while the haberdashers of hats joined forces with the clothiers' company. Hutchins, *History of Dorset*, vol. ii. p. 338. A tankard bearing the arms of the Haberdashers' Company, under date of 1620, is still preserved at Guildford. Williamson, *Guildford in the Olden Time*, p. 33. It is quite probable that this company then represented an association composed of different trades and handicrafts. Whether incorporated separately as Merchant "Taylors" or in company with drapers, tailors evidently ranked as merchant and traders.

The drapers likewise, instead of joining the mercers' association, combined sometimes in a close union with kindred occupations. Of this nature were the gilds of drapers and tailors established at York,[82] Oxford,[83] Northampton,[84] Rye,[85] Durham,[86] Doncaster,[87] Pontefract,[88] Warwick,[89] Devizes,[90] or that at Tewkesbury [91] which included the dyers as well. Occasionally as at Chester [92] and Hereford,[93] the drapers and hosiers found it to their advantage to form a gild alliance. We notice, too, that the drapers sometimes gave their name to one of the complex trading associations which later developed in the smaller communities, as in the case of one of the four companies found at Ipswich [94] and Kingston-upon-Thames [95] or of one of the three at Devizes,[96] Axbridge [97] and Andover.[98] The membership of the drapers' company, which towards the close of the seventeenth century appears to have been the one trading gild permitted at Wallingford,[99] in Berkshire, was more complex.

The industrial crafts soon followed the example set them by the merchants and consolidated their forces. While the state soon repealed as much of the act of 1363 as had forbidden the merchants to trade in more than one line of goods, it left intact the clause which confined the handicrafts to their chosen craft; [100] and before long it brought into play in a specific industry the same principle of isolating the crafts. For the year 1390 witnessed the passage of another act which declared that "for as much as diverse shoemakers and cordwainers use to tan their leather and sell the same falsely tanned, also make shoes and boots of such leather not well tanned and sell them as dear as they will to the great deceit of the poor commons," no shoemaker or cordwainer should thereafter use the "craft of tanning nor tanner the craft of shoemaking." [101] The state was thoroughly in earnest, apparently, in its

[82] Drake, *Eboracum*, vol. i. p. 321.
[83] Turner, *Records of Oxford*, p. 333.
[84] *Records*, vol. ii, p. 295.
[85] *Hist. MSS. Comm. Rep.* xiii. app. iv. p. 59.
[86] Fordyce, *Hist. of Durham*, vol. i. p. 345.
[87] *Records*, vol. iv. p. 204.
[88] *The Booke of Entries*, p. 19.
[89] *The Black Book*, p. 117.
[90] *Wilts. Archaeol. and Nat. Hist. Soc. Mag.*, vol. iv. p. 160.
[91] Bennett, *History of Tewkesbury*, p. 199. At Ripon in 1662 the drapers headed a company which included the dyers, apothecaries, and barbersurgeons. *Millenary Record*, p. 65.
[92] *Harleian MS.*, 1996, f. 9.
[93] *Hist. MSS. Comm. Rep.* xiii. iv. p. 300.
[94] Wodderspoon, *Memorials of Ipswich*, p. 174.
[95] *Genealog. Mag.*, vol. iii. p. 342.
[96] *Wilts. Archaeol. and Nat. Hist. Soc. Trans.*. vol. iv. p. 162.
[97] *Hist. MSS. Comm. Rep.* iii, app. p. 303.
[98] *Wilts. Archaeol. and Nat. Hist. Soc., Trans.* vol. xxi. p. 306.
[99] Hedges, *Hist. of Wallingford*, vol. ii. p. 234.
[100] 38 Edward III. c. 11.
[101] 13 Richard II. c. 12. "He that doth contrary to this Act," continues the statute, "shall forfeit to the King all his leather so tanned and all his Boots and Shoes so wrought and shall be ransomed at the King's pleasure

desire to protect the English people from poorly made footgear. To that end it continued to reiterate through succeeding centuries the same sentiment. Gradually it carried the war into the camp of other leather workers such as the curriers and even the butchers, since they too were concerned in cutting leather.[102] Yet in the face of this positive command, one meets in local archives frequent mention of united gilds of tanners and shoemakers or of curriers and cordwainers. Chester [103] and Canterbury,[104] for instance, both furnish evidence of consolidated tanners' and shoemakers' gilds, and Exeter,[105] Boston,[106] Sandwich,[107] Morpeth,[108] Kendal,[109] Ripon,[110] Lichfield,[111] Salisbury [112] and Kinsale [113] of combinations of curriers and cordwainers. Ludlow went further in incorporating along with these two handicrafts, local fellmongers and tanners.[114]

While the tanners or curriers and shoemakers were thus uniting their gild forces, another group of leather workers naturally bound together by intimate trade relations in their turn joined the movement. Gilds of skinners and glovers are found to have existed in York,[115] Exeter,[116] Shrewsbury,[117] Alnwick,[118] Newcastle,[119] Doncaster,[120] Morpeth,[121] Carlisle [122] and Preston.[123] Sometimes, too these unions became more complex and included workers in other

notwithstanding any Charter or Patent made to the contrary, which if there be any, the King wills that they be utterly annulled and holden for none."

[102] 2 Henry VI, c. 7; 1 Henry VII, c. 5; 19 Henry VII, c. 19; 5 Eliz. c. 1; James I. c. 22.

[103] Morris, *Chester*, p. 410.

[104] *Rep. Hist. MSS. Com.* vol. lx. p. 175. Also Civis, *Canterbury*, No. xx.

[105] *Western Antiquary*, vol. iv. p. 187.

[106] Thompson, *Boston*, p. 158.

[107] Boys' *Sandwich*, p. 697.

[108] *Parliamentary Papers*, vol. 25, p. 1628.

[109] *Rep. Hist. MSS. Com.* vol. x, App. iv, p. 312.

[110] *Millenary Record*, p. 49.

[111] Harwood, *Lichfield*, p. 354.

[112] Hoare, *Wiltshire*, vol. vi. p. 381.

[113] *Council-Book*, p. 176.

[114] Parl. Papers, vol. 26, p. 2803. Occasionally tanners joined forces with a craft that used a different branch of the leather industry. For instance, the tanners of Northampton established a gild in company with local whittawyers (Borough Records, vol. ii, p. 295), and at Salisbury with the bridle-makers. (Hoare, *Hist. of Wiltshire*, vol. vi. p. 455.)

[115] Drake, *Eboracum*, vol. i, p. 322. At one time an organisation composed of fifteen glovers, a dozen tanners and four parchment makers seems to have existed in York. *Memorandum Book*, p. 82. also xlviii.

[116] *Western Antiquary*, vol. iv. p. 187. Also Izache, *Exeter*, p. 85.

[117] *Trans. Shrop. Archaeol. & Nat. Hist. Soc.*, vol. x, p. 40. By 1769 the gild of glovers and skinners included pointmakers, pursers, fell-mongers, leathersellers and parchment-makers.

[118] Tate, *Hist. of Alnwick*, vol. ii. p. 333.

[119] Brand, *Hist. of Newcastle*, vol. ii. p. 315.

[120] *Records*, vol. iv, p. 25.

[121] Hodgson, *Morpeth*, pp. 66–7. In 1604 this company annexed the butchers.

[122] *Munic. Records*, p. 209.

[123] Abram, *Memorials of Preston Guilds*, p. 99.

crafts as well. The Lincoln company of glovers and skinners increased its membership in 1562 by admitting the girdlers, pinners, pointers, scriveners and parchment makers.[124] The same two crafts at Durham [125] amalgamated in 1628 with the saddlers and the upholsterers and at Kendal [126] with the surgeons, scriveners, barbers, parchment and point-makers. On the other hand the glovers elsewhere frequently figured in gilds apart from the skinners. The London [127] glovers, for instance, joined the leather-sellers' company which included in addition, the white-tawyers, pursers and pouchmakers; somewhat similar combinations were incorporated at Worcester,[128] Tewkesbury,[129] Bristol,[130] Canterbury,[131] Chester,[132] Boston,[133] Ripon,[134] Preston, Lancaster, Liverpool, Manchester and various other places.[135] Aside from their membership in the large leather companies, the saddlers occasionally joined with some other leather craft in forming a small union. The saddlers and curriers at Chester,[136] the saddlers and shoemakers at Stratford-on-Avon,[137] and the saddlers, glovers and white-tawyers of Lichfield [138] combined in gilds of this nature. Large groups made up of all the leather crafts were also taking their place as one of the stated number of gilds permitted within the corporate limits in Reading,[139] Ipswich,[140] Dorchester,[141] Maidstone,[142] Andover,[143] Abingdon,[144] Axbridge [145]

[124] *Hist. MSS. Com. Rep.*, Lincoln, p. 57.
[125] Fordyce, *Hist. of Durham.*
[126] *Hist. MSS. Com. Rep.*, x, app. iv, p. 312.
[127] Black, *Hist. of London Leathersellers*, pp. 124–6.
[128] Green, *Hist. of Worcester*, vol. ii. p. 42.
[129] Bennett, *Tewkesbury*, p. 199.
[130] Latimer, *Annals of the 17th century*, p. 217.
[131] *Hist. MSS. Com. Rep.*, ix, p. 175.
[132] *State Papers Domestic*, 1669, No. 27. Also *Harleian MSS.*, 2054, 6.
[133] Thompson, *Boston*, p. 159.
[134] *Millenary Record*, p. 65.
[135] *Trans. Lancashire & Cheshire Archaeol. Soc.*, vol. x, p. 6. At Salisbury the glovers, collar-makers and sieve-makers established a gild. Hoare, *Wiltshire*, vol. vi, p. 475.
[136] *Parl. Papers*, vol. xxvi, p. 2636.
[137] *Hist. MSS. Com. Rep.*, ix, p. 292.
[138] Harwood, *Lichfield*, p. 569.
[139] *Hist. MSS. Com. Rep.*, xi, app. vii, p. 224. The tanners' and leathersellers' company held together Readings' leather crafts.
[140] Wodderspoon, *Memorials*, p. 174. The shoemakers' company was the only one of the four established at Ipswich in later Tudor times which appears to have restricted its membership to those who used similar materials.
[141] Hutchins, *Hist. of County of Dorset*. Edit. by *Shipp & Hodson*, vol. ii. pp. 338–9. The shoemakers and skinners gave their name to this gild.
[142] Russell, *Hist. of Maidstone*, p. 310. This was known as the cordwainers' company.
[143] *Wilts. Archaeol. & Nat. Hist. Soc. Mag.*, vol. xxi, p. 306. The crafts eligible to membership in this society of leathersellers were tanners, saddlers, glovers, pewterers, braziers, shoemakers, curriers, collar-makers, butchers, chandlers, dyers and upholsterers.
[144] *Selections from Records of the Borough*, p. 160. According to the record "all such Freemen as shall use or exercise any of the trades of tanners, cordwayners, corryers, glovers, p'chtm'tmakers, leathersellers, collar-makers, cutlers, sadlers and ropemakers shalbe sorted and severed to make upp the

and Devizes,[146] although the groups incorporated in the four last-named places did not confine their membership to leather crafts. It appears, then, that among the crafts concerned with leather industries, there were practically four different sorts of amalgamations, those of tanners or curriers and cordwainers; of skinners and glovers; of leathersellers which included makers of different leather goods; and the large companies, established in the smaller communities by gathering together all the leather crafts.

The men interested in the metal crafts seem to have joined the movement betimes, the Bristol [147] gild composed of farriers, smiths, cutlers and "lockyers" furnishing in 1403 the earliest details available of an association of metallers of any proportions. A few years later the records of York account for a union of the first-named crafts, the marshals—or farriers as they are usually designated—and the smiths.[148] In 1436 Coventry [149] records disclose the existence of a combine of the smiths, brakemen, girdlers and cardwire-drawers, and about a dozen years later, Norwich vouche: for a somewhat similar group composed of smiths, bladesmiths, locksmiths and lorimers.[150] By 1451, London seems to have sanctioned a gild of pinners, wireworkers and girdlers,[151] and by 1462, Scarborough one of blacksmiths and wire-makers.[152] By the last decade of the century, a group composed of "Smyths," cutlers, pewterers, "ffounders," cardmakers, girdlers, "Headworkers," wire-drawers and spurriers had taken its place among the local gilds at Chester.[153] However, by the middle of the sixteenth century the movement appears well grounded among the metal workers practically everywhere. London at that time was maintaining an amalgamation of blacksmiths and spurriers [154] while later still the authorities encouraged local braziers and armourers to form a company.[155] Canterbury [156] and Shrewsbury [157] alike offer evidence of combina-

Company of skynners, and shalbe called the Company of Skynners and their Fellowes."

[145] *Hist. MSS. Com. Rep.*, vol. iii, app. p. 303. There are no details given of this, the leathermen's gild.

[146] *Wilts. Archaeol. & Nat. Hist. Soc. Trans.*, n. s., vol. iv, p. 162. The members of this society organised themselves as the leathersellers.

[147] *Little Red Book*, vol. ii, p. 181.

[148] *Antiquary*, vol. ii, p. 105. As early as 1307 in York "at the askyng the girdlers and revettours and all that longes to that crafte" received permission to set up a gild. *Memorandum Book*, i, p. 180. By 1387 there seems to have been another combine consisting of ten "sporiers" and five "lorymers." *Ibid.*, p. 101.

[149] *Leet-book*, pt. i, p. 181.

[150] *Records of the Borough*, vol. ii, p. 280.

[151] Smythe, *History of the Girdlers' Company*, p. 47.

[152] Hinderwell, *History of Scarborough*, p. 172.

[153] *Journal Architectural, Archaeological & Historic Society for County and City of Chester & North Wales*, n. s., vol. xx, p. 5.

[154] Hazlitt, *The London Livery Cos.*, p. 372.

[155] *Ibid.*, p. 355.

[156] Civis, *Canterbury*, no. xxi, Supplement. Also *Econ. Journal*, vol. x, p. 410.

[157] *Reliquary*, vol. iii, p. 63.

tions made up of smiths and armourers. But for the most part in boroughs like Lincoln,[158] Hereford,[159] Norwich,[160] Gloucester,[161] Newcastle,[162] Kendal,[163] Salisbury,[164] Beverley,[165] Chester,[166] Durham,[167] Lichfield,[168] Doncaster [169] and Kinsale,[170] large combinations of local metal workers were the rule. Occasionally some community had annexed to her metal group other diverse crafts as well. Kingston-upon-Hull,[171] for example, permitted the musicians, stationers, bookbinders and basket-makers to affiliate with the metal crafts, while at Boston,[172] Exeter,[173] Morpeth,[174] Gloucester [175] and Lancaster [176] the gilds of metal workers boasted the saddlers in their membership.

In addition to these miscellaneous companies, different groups often merged themselves together under the name of cutlers, ironmongers, smiths or hammermen. Thus the celebrated cutlers' company in Hallamshire [177] seems to have included the closely allied crafts of bladesmiths and sheathers as did the cutlers' company of London [178] and York.[179] In the smaller boroughs cutlers were sufficiently influential, apparently to head one of the stated number of corporations organized later in the movement. A good example of this type of organisation was the cutlers and bellfounders' company of Reading.[180] When the ironmongers did not establish gilds of their own as they seem to have done at London,[181] York,[182] Nottingham,[183] Northampton,[184] Worcester [185] and Leeds,[186] they either

[158] *Hist. MSS. Com. Rep.,* xiv, app. viii, p. 57.
[159] *Hist. MSS. Com. Rep.,* xiii, app. iv, p. 319.
[160] Madders, *Rambles in an Old City,* p. 230.
[161] *Hist. MSS. Com. Rep.,* xii, p. 427.
[162] Walford, *Gilds,* p. 199.
[163] *Hist. MSS. Com. Rep.,* x, app. iv, p. 312.
[164] Hoars, *Wiltshire,* vol. vi, p. 475.
[165] *Hist. MSS. Com. Rep.,* Beverley, p. 102.
[166] *Parl. Papers,* vol. 26, p. 2632.
[167] Fordyce, *Durham,* vol. i, p. 345.
[168] Harwood, *Lichfield,* pp. 355, 569.
[169] *Records,* vol. iv, pp. 29, 95.
[170] *Council-Book,* p. 176.
[171] Lambert, *Two Thous. Years of Gild Life,* p. 262.
[172] Thompson, *Boston,* p. 159.
[173] *Western Antiquary,* vol. iv, p. 188.
[174] Hodgson, *Morpeth,* p. 66. Also *Parl. Papers,* vol. 25, p. 1628.
[175] Fosbrooke, *Gloucester,* p. 404. Also *Trans. Bristol & Gloucestershire Archaeol. Soc.,* vol. 13, p. 264.
[176] Simpson, *Hist. of Lancaster,* p. 275, note.
[177] Hunters' *Hallamshire,* p. 151, 165.
[178] Riley, *Memorials of London,* p. 567.
[179] *Memorandum Book,* i, p. 136.
[180] Walford, *Gilds,* p. 91. At Dublin local cutlers are found associated with diverse other crafts, such as painter-stainers and "staconers." *Egerton MS, B. M.,* no. 1765, f. 152.
[181] Noble, *History of London Ironmongers,* p. 20.
[182] *Memorandum Book,* pt. xxxvii.
[183] *Records of the Borough,* vol. v, p. 303.
[184] *Borough Records,* vol. ii, p. 279.
[185] Green, *Worcester,* vol. ii, p. 42.
[186] Wardell, *Hist. of Leeds,* p. 34.

became prominent members of a town's mercantile organisation as in Shrewsbury,[187] Chester,[188] Buckingham,[189] Doncaster,[190] Preston,[191] Durham,[192] Derby,[193] Pontefract[194] and Abingdon,[195] or else they joined the large societies organised in common by the metal crafts. In such towns as Dorchester,[196] Banbury[197] and Evesham,[198] the ironmongers were of sufficient standing to give their name to the all-inclusive metallers' company fostered within town limits. When the smiths did not join the general association of metal workers, they too, at times, formed a company among themselves. Alnwick,[199] for instance, had a society of blacksmiths and whitesmiths, Newcastle,[200] one of goldsmiths, blacksmiths, farriers, anchorsmiths and lock or whitesmiths. Carlisle[201] and Durham[202] both record the blacksmiths, whitesmiths, silversmiths and goldsmiths working together as one society. Still other communities, notably Ludlow,[203] Wells,[204] Hedon,[205] and Youghal[206] made their metal crafts famous under the name of hammermen, although those organisations did not always confine their membership to metal workers; Ludlow's hammermen held together an extremely large body of building crafts. Axbridge varied the gild arrangement still more, giving the name of firemen to her group,[207] one of three fraternities then permitted within her boundaries, while Ipswich,[208] curiously enough, had her metal crafts indiscriminately mixed up with many others under the patronage of the tailors. Certainly the gilds of metal workers did not hesitate to fall in with the general tendency toward consolidation,

In the early fifteenth century the craftsmen in the building crafts, had at least in some places, consolidated their corporate interests.[209] In fact York seems to have sanctioned two combina-

---

[187] *Shrop. Archaeol. & Nat. Hist. Soc. Trans.,* vol. viii, p. 269.
[188] *Harleian MS. B. M.,* 2054, f. 56.
[189] Willis, *Hist. of Buckingham,* p. 166.
[190] Tomlinson, *Hist. of Doncaster,* p. 329.
[191] Abram, *Memorials of Preston Guilds,* p. 41.
[192] Fordyce, *Hist. of Durham,* vol. i, p. 345.
[193] *Derbyshire Archaeol. & Nat. Hist. Soc. Journ.,* vol. xv, p. 113.
[194] *Collections,* vol. i, *The Booke of Entries,* p. 375.
[195] *Select. from Records,* p. 159. The ironmongers at Abingdon were reckoned among the "Fellowes" of the grocers' company, the organisation which included the town's ordinary traders.
[196] Hutchins, *Dorset,* vol. ii, p. 338.
[197] Beasley, *Hist. of Banbury,* p. 477.
[198] May, *Hist. of Evesham,* p. 341.
[199] Tate, *History of Alnwick,* vol. ii, p. 321.
[200] *Archaelogia Aeliana,* vol. xv, iii, p. 398.
[201] *Municipal Records of Carlisle,* p. 134.
[202] Fordyce, *History of Durham,* vol. i, p. 345.
[203] *Shropshire Archaeol. & Nat. Hist. Soc. Trans.,* vol. xi, p. 291.
[204] *Parl. Papers,* vol. 24, p. 1368.
[205] Boyle, *Hedon,* xcii, app. Note T.
[206] *Council-Book,* p. 457.
[207] *Hist. MSS. Com. Rep.,* iii, app. p. 303.
[208] Woodderspoon, *Memorials of Ipswich,* p. 174.
[209] Archdeacon Cunningham believed that local authorities did not encour-

tions, one of local tilers and plasterers and another of painters, stainers and gold-beaters.[210] By the middle of the century, Shrewsbury records a gild of carpenters and tilers, which at one time and another admitted local brickmakers, bricklayers and plasterers within its folds.[211] During this same period, Newcastle encouraged a combination of bricklayers and plasterers and there were doubtless similar societies elsewhere. The reign of King Charles II found Dublin [212] supporting such a combination, while the plasterers of Bristol had affiliated with the local tilers.[213] In London from the later sixteenth century, in addition to a union of bricklayers and tilers [214] there was formed one of painter-stainers [215] and another of joiners and carvers or ceilers [216] as they called themselves. By that time too, the joiners and carvers of Chester [217] had joined gild forces although most frequently the joiners figured as joint partners in a gild with the carpenters, as proved to be the case at York,[218] Worcester,[219] Newcastle,[220] Durham,[221] Boston,[222] Alnwick,[223] and Lancaster.[224] In two other instances, notably Gloucester [225] and Scarborough,[226] the joiners and coopers combined their gild forces.

age the building crafts to establish gilds at all. *Growth of Eng. Industry & Commerce,* vol. i, p. 96, note. Yet it is recorded that as early as 1356 London helped the city masons to organise a union. At that date the mayor summoned all the good folks of the trade to appear before him in order that he might "have from them good and due information how their trade might be best ordered and ruled profitably to the common people." The mayor had been led to take this step because "divers dissensions and disputes have been moved in the said city between the masons who are hewers on the one hand and the light masons and setters on the other, because their trade has not been regulated in due manner by the government of folks in their trade in such form as other trades are." Riley, *Memorials,* p. 280. Suffice it to say that the masons secured their gild as did the tilers, the carpenters and the other building crafts not alone in the metropolis but in most other boroughs. By 1375 Norwich supported a gild of carpenters and Lincoln one of tilers (Smith, *English Gilds,* p. 184). The carpenters in Northampton (*Liber Custumarum,* p. 43), the masons in Newcastle and Worcester had a gild; so did local brick-layers and coopers. Green, *Worcester,* vol. ii, p. 42. Kingston-upon-Hull records list separate gilds established by the carpenters, joiners and coopers. There seems little reason to suppose that master builders neglected to safeguard their industrial interests by organising themselves.

[210] *Reliquary,* vol. iii, p. 634. *Memorandum Book,* I, pp. 149, 164.
[211] Walford, *Gilds,* pp. 203-4.
[212] *Egerton, MSS. B. M., Dublin Corporation Records,* p. 200.
[213] *Additional MSS.,* 28000 f. ii.
[214] *Municipal Corp. Commis.,* 1837, vol. 25, p. 191.
[215] Herbert, *Twelve Great Livery Cos.,* vol. i, p. 175.
[216] *Municipal Corp. Commis. Rep.,* 1837, vol. 25, p. 201.
[217] Morris, *Chester,* p. 403.
[218] Drake, *Eboracum,* vol. i, p. 322.
[219] Smith (Toulmin), *English Gilds,* p. 208.
[220] Walford, *Gilds,* p. 201.
[221] Fordyce, *Durham,* vol. i, p. 345.
[222] Thompson, *Boston,* p. 159.
[223] Tate, *Alnwick,* vol. ii, p. 321.
[224] *Parl. Papers,* vol. 25, p. 1599.
[225] *Brit. & Glouc. Archaeol. & Nat. Hist. Soc. Trans.,* vol. xiii, p. 264.
[226] *Rep. Record Com.,* vol. vii, p. 483 (1837). At Coventry in 1667 the

Occasionally, as happened in Pontefract,[227] the various building crafts divided themselves into two camps, the workers in wood, the wrights or carpenters, bowyers, coopers, "patewners," turners, sawyers and "sewers" forming one combination and the bricklayers, masons, plasterers and slaters another. Usually, however, during this later period, large federations of the various building trades were being organised at boroughs like Newcastle,[228] Lincoln,[229] Chester,[230] Exeter,[231] Kingston-upon-Hull,[232] Kendal,[233] Durham,[234] Dublin [235] and Youghal.[236] We discover occasionally societies of builders which included other trades as well. The building crafts of Gateshead [237] admitted the local saddlers, bridlers, trunk-makers and even distillers to membership in their society. The boroughs which grouped all their trades within a limited number of organisations often distributed local builders through one or sometimes even two of these. The Reading cutlers' and bellfounders' company [238] to which reference has already been made, included local building crafts, as did the drapers' company at Devizes [239] and the fishmongers' at Dorchester.[240] Two of the four combines registered in Ipswich [241] show local groups of builders among the rest. Thus, in the drapers' company are found the joiners, carpenters, freemasons, bricklayers and tylers, and in the tailors' the plumbers, coopers, glaziers and turners. The hammermens' society in Ludlow, as already indicated, comprised all the building crafts.[242]

Records which establish an early date for the amalgamation of the different crafts concerned in the making of cloth are few and far between. Aside from a Coventry gild composed of shearmen, "taylours" and walkers, dating from King Richard's day,[243] the fifteenth century is well advanced before we find evidence that the movement had taken hold of the men engaged in the different processes of making cloth. These vouch. for an association of

carpenters and wheelwrights are on record as belonging to the same gild. Coventry *MS. Muniments.*

[227] *Booke of Entries,* p. 372.
[228] Brand, *Hist. of Newcastle,* vol. ii, p. 355.
[229] *Hist. MSS. Com. Rep.,* xiv, app. viii, p. 60.
[230] Morris, *Chester,* p. 453.
[231] *Devon. Assoc. for Advancement of Science,* vol. v, p. 120.
[232] Lambert, *Two Thous. Yrs.,* p. 272.
[233] *Hist. MSS. Com. Rep.,* x, app. iv, p. 312.
[234] Fordyce, *Durham,* vol. i, p. 345.
[235] *Journ. Royal Society of Antiquaries of Ireland,* vol. 35, pt. iv, p. 321.
[236] *Council-Book,* p. 457.
[237] *Parl. Pap.,* vol. 25, p. 1525.
[238] *Hist. MSS. Com. Rep.,* xi, app. vii, p. 224.
[239] *Wilts. Archaeol. & Nat. Hist. Soc. Trans.,* n.s., vol. iv, p. 162.
[240] Hutchins, *Dorset,* vol. ii, p. 338.
[241] Wodderspoon, *Memorials,* p. 174.
[242] *Parl. Pap.,* vol. 26, p. 2802.
[243] *The Leet Book,* pt. i, p. 246. In 1448 the Leet ordered the walkers, "severed from the Crafte of Taillours at the desire of the seid walkers as appereth by their peticion filed in the seid lete . . . and also by agrement of the Taillours as ther appereth." *Ibid.,* p. 234.

fullers and dyers in Newcastle-upon-Tyne,[244] of weavers and fullers in Oxford [245] and Exeter,[246] of fullers and shearmen in York,[247] and of clothworkers and shearmen [248] in Shrewsbury. In 1444 the records of Ipswich prove that the clothworkers, drapers, dyers and shearmen together formed one of the twelve groups which in that year took part in the Corpus Christi procession, but they yield no specific information concerning the economic relations of the different members in the group.[249] The century of the Tudors, however, brings evidence that the same forces that drew the crafts together in the other handicrafts had taken hold of the clothmakers in London,[250] Northampton,[251] Gloucester,[252] Warwick,[253] Durham,[254] Worcester,[255] Kendal,[256] Ipswich,[257] Leominster [258] and still later in Bury St. Edmunds,[259] Nottingham,[260] Southampton,[261] Lichfield,[262] Chester,[263] Coventry,[264] Shrewsbury,[265] Newbury,[266] Alnwick,[267] Salisbury [268] and Leeds.[269] Many of the other boroughs evidently failed to keep the membership of their associations of clothworkers confined to these craftsmen. For instance, the Doncaster [270] weavers, walkers, shearmen and dyers had the linendrapers and upholsterers as gild associates while the Lancaster [271] weavers, fullers and dyers were jumbled together with the gardeners and the sellers of salt. Still more heterogeneous was a company formed at Gateshead [272] of the dyers, fullers, blacksmiths, locksmiths, cutlers, joiners and carpenters and one at Morpeth

[244] Brand, *History of Newcastle-upon-Tyne,* vol. ii, p. 320.
[245] *Calendar of Patent Rolls,* 1907, vol. iii, pt. i, p. 347.
[246] *Devonshire Assoc. for Advancement of Science,* vol. v, p. 120.
[247] *Memorandum Book,* ii, p. 159.
[248] Fretton, *Memorials of Coventry,* p. 19.
[249] Wodderspoon, *Memorials of Ipswich,* p. 165.
[250] Herbert, *Twelve Grt. Liv. Cos.,* vol. ii, p. 654.
[251] *Borough Records,* vol. ii, p. 288.
[252] Fosbrook, *Hist. of Gloucester,* p. 404.
[253] *Black Book,* p. 71.
[254] *Parl. Pap.,* vol. 25, p. 1512.
[255] Green, *Worcester, app.* iv, no. xvi, lxxi.
[256] *Hist. MSS. Com. Rep.,* x, app. iv, p. 312.
[257] Wodderspoon, *Memorials,* p. 198. Also *Lansdowne MS. B.M.* 162, f. 195.
[258] Townsend, *Leominster,* p. 73.
[259] *Hist. MSS. Com. Rep.,* xiv.
[260] *Records of the Borough,* vol. v, p. 147.
[261] Davies, *Hist. of Southampton,* p. 275.
[262] Harwood, *Lichfield,* p. 570.
[263] *Hist. MSS. Com. Rep.,* viii, p. 403.
[264] *Coventry Muniments,* MS. Book of the "Taylors" and Clothworkers.
[265] Fretton, *Memorials of Coventry,* p. 19.
[266] *Hist. of Newbury,* p. 306.
[267] *Parl. Papers,* vol. 25, p. 1416.
[268] Hoare, *Wiltshire,* vol. vi, p. 475.
[269] Wardell, *Hist. of Leeds,* pp. 29, 34, 70.
[270] *Borough Records,* vol. ii, p. 288.
[271] *Parl. Papers,* vol. 25, p. 1599.
[272] *Gentleman's Magazine,* 1862, Preface. Quoted also in *Supplement to Northern Notes and Queries,* Newcastle-upon-Tyne, 1907.

which comprised the fullers, dyers, carvers, hatters and wrights.[273] Among the towns which from the later sixteenth century on supported only a few large companies, Reading [274] alone seems to have managed to preserve her clothiers' and clothworkers' company for the clothing trades. Dorchester's [275] clothiers' company was forced to admit various other trades and the Ludlow [276] cloth workers secured a place in the stitchmen's company.

Amalgamation seems not to have played a great rôle among the victualling crafts until the very end of Tudor times. Even then their unions were limited to two or three of the several branches of the art. Boston [277] and Newcastle-upon-Tyne [278] at that time were both supporting combinations of bakers and brewers. Ripon,[279] however, had sanctioned a union of bakers and inn-holders and a little later "upon due consideration had," Youghal thought it "fit that there shall be a yeeld of Innkeepers and Victuallers to the number of twelve within this Town at the election" of the "Maior." [280]   In Gloucester [281] there was a gild of innholders and cooks while a similar combination formed in Chester, included local victuallers as well.[282]   Kendal for her part had her innholders, alehouse-keepers and tipplers establish one company and her butchers and fishermen another.[283]   The borough of Salisbury [284] records an associated company of cooks and tallow chandlers and Lichfield one of butchers and chandlers.[285]   But the great majority of cities and corporate towns preferred, seemingly, to confine local bakers, brewers and dealers in food-stuffs generally to their own gild. However, when all the crafts of a community were compelled to join forces, dealers in food-stuffs had, apparently, to fall in line with the rest.   In these instances, some effort seems to have been made to associate the different victualling crafts.   In 1622 Norwich evidently favoured this arrangement, in allotting to the fishmongers, fishermen, vintners, "bochers" and cooks, one of the dozen companies which were organized in that year in the city.[286]   Boroughs

---

[273] *Parl. Papers,* vol. 25, p. 1628.
[274] *Hist. MSS. Com. Rep.,* xi, app. vii, p. 224.
[275] Hutchins, *Dorset,* vol. ii, p. 338.
[276] *Journ. Brit. Archaeol. Assoc.,* 1868, vol. 24, p. 328. One of the five companies registered at Evesham in King Charles II's day, was known as the clothworkers.
[277] Thompson, *History of Boston,* p. 159.
[278] Walford, *Gilds,* p. 191. In St. Albans the bakers and brewers had annexed local butchers. This appears from the record of a "Court" held in the borough on October 17, 1586, when the wardens of the company asked to "have until the next Court" to bring in their accounts. *St. Albans, Charters,* p. 14.
[279] *Millenary Record,* p. 65.
[280] *Council-Book,* p. 12.
[281] Walford, *Gilds,* p. 113.
[282] Morris, *Chester,* p. 411.
[283] *Hist. MSS. Com. Rep.,* x, app. iv, p. 312.
[284] Hoard, *Wiltshire,* vol. vi, p. 475.
[285] Harwood, *Lichfield,* pp. 356, 569.
[286] *Records of the Borough,* vol. ii, p. 383.

of the rank of Reading,[287] Maidstone [288] and Kingston-upon-Thames,[289] each supported a federated company composed exclusively of these craftsmen, although the Dorchester [290] fishmongers' company as we have noted, included besides the victuallers, groups of various building crafts. The grouping of the crafts in Ipswich [291] was especially disorderly as regards the victualling crafts, for it is necessary to search through three of the four companies to find them all. Then, too, the victualling crafts were often reckoned among the members of the mercers' companies. We find this arrangement in Devizes in Wiltshire,[292] when the craft grouping called for only three associations. The victuallers were also influential enough to give their name to one of the two companies which in Gravesend [293] and St. Albans [294] survived the middle of the seventeenth century. The single associations fostered in Faversham [295] and Wallingford [296] naturally included local dealers in food supplies.

Besides the industrial combinations which group themselves respectively as leather, metal, building, clothing and victualling companies, there were several small associations which have a place in the amalgamation movement. One such was the union of the bowyers and fletchers, the medieval bow and arrow makers who followed callings important enough in most boroughs of that epoch to attain to corporate rank. At an early date London [297] and York [298] publish unions of bowyers and fletchers and the records of Chester [299] and Shrewsbury [300] testify at a later date to consolidations of these workers which embraced in addition coopers and stringers. In the smaller boroughs, however, bowyers and fletchers took their place along with many other crafts in one of the large combines which were sponsored by the authorities. In Kendal,[301] for instance, they amalgamated with the metal crafts, and in Beverley with the wood workers, while in Ipswich,[302] St. Albans [303] and Devizes [304] they are recorded among the members of the mercers' companies.

[287] *Hist. MSS. Commis. Rep.,* xi, app. vii, p. 224.

[288] Russell, *History of Maidstone,* p. 310. This was one of five corporations which are recorded in the annals of the borough in the reign of Queen Elizabeth.

[289] *Genealogical Magazine,* vol. iii, p. 342.

[290] Hutchins, *Dorset,* vol. ii, p. 338.

[291] Wodderspoon, *Memorials,* p. 174.

[292] *Wilts. Archaeol. & Nat. Hist. Soc. Trans.,* n. s., vol. iv, p. 162.

[293] Cruden, *Hist. of Gravesend,* pp. 194–5.

[294] *St. Albans Charters,* p. 7.

[295] *Kent Archaeol. Soc. Trans.,* vol. ix, p. lxviii.

[296] Hedges, *Hist. of Wallingford,* vol. ii, p. 234.

[297] Herbert, *Twelve Great Liv. Cos.,* vol. i, p. 175.

[298] Drake, *Eboracum,* vol. i, p. 322.

[299] Morris, *Chester,* p. 572.

[300] *Shropshire Archaeol. & Nat. Hist. Soc. Trans,* vol. xi, p. 154.

[301] *Hist. MSS. Com. Rep.,* x, app. iv, p. 312.

[302] Wodderspoon, *Memorials,* p. 174.

[303] *St. Albans Charters,* p. 7.

[304] *Wilts. Archaeol. & Nat. Hist. Soc. Trans.,* n. s., vol. iv, p. 162.

The gilds of barber-surgeons represent a second type of small combination common to most English boroughs and corporate towns. London,[305] York,[306] Bristol,[307] Norwich,[308] Exeter,[309] Canterbury,[310] Salisbury,[311] Windsor,[312] Cork[313] and Dublin[314] all furnish evidence of their unions. Even these gildsmen, however, could not always preserve their gild intact. The barber-surgeons of Kingston-upon-Hull[315] extended the courtesy of their organisation to local peruke-makers and those of Kinsale[316] to the apothecaries. In Shrewsbury, the barber-surgeons and peruke-makers elected not only apothecaries, but wax and tallow chandlers to membership in their company.[317] In Chester,[318] Newcastle-upon-Tyne[319] and Sandwich[320] barber-surgeons had enough in common with the chandlers to make a joint union feasible. Again, barber-surgeons were sometimes compelled to seek membership in associations which included wholly unrelated crafts. In Lancaster,[321] for example, they are on record as united with the plumbers, glaziers, saddlers, whitesmiths and cutlers, and in Ripon[322] with drapers, dyers and apothecaries. Barber-surgeons in company with the scriveners, glovers, skinners, parchment and point makers made up one of the twelve companies which, in 1578, were listed in the records of Kendal.[323] In places like Ipswich,[324] Dorchester[325] and Devizes,[326] the barber-surgeons lost their gild identity and attached themselves

---

[305] *Annals of Barber-Surgeons*, pp. 23, 56.
[306] *Antiquary*, vol. vi, pp. 154–5.
[307] Latimer, *17th Century Annals*, p. 239.
[308] *Antiquary*, vol. 36, p. 274.
[309] *Western Antiquary*, vol. iv, p. 188.
[310] *Economic Journal*, vol. x, p. 404.
[311] Hoare, *Wiltshire*, vol. vi, p. 475.
[312] Tighe & Davis, *Annals of Windsor*, vol. i, p. 652.
[313] *Council-Book*, p. 512.
[314] *Journal Royal Soc. of Antiquaries of Ireland*, 5th series, vol. 33, pt. iii, p. 219.
[315] Lambert, *Two Thousand Years*, p. 357.
[316] *Council-Book*, p. lxx.
[317] *Shropshire, Archaeol. & Nat. Hist. Soc. Trans.*, vol. v, p. 265.
[318] *Hist. MSS. Com. Rep.*, viii, p. 403.
[319] Brand, *Newcastle*, vol. ii, p. 341.
[320] Boys, *Sandwich*, p. 678.
[321] *Parl. Papers*, vol. 25, p. 1599.
[322] *Millenary Record*, p. 65.
[323] *Hist. MSS. Com. Rep.*, x, app. iv, p. 312.
[324] Wodderspoon, *Memorials of Ipswich*, p. 174. At Ipswich, however, the two groups were evidently not incorporated in the same society, the barbers being registered with the tailors and their associates and the surgeons with the drapers.
[325] Hutchins, *Dorset*, vol. ii, p. 338.
[326] *Wilts. Archaeol. & Nat. Hist. Soc. Trans*, n. s., vol. iv, p. 162. There were of course other combinations, such for instance as that maintained by the London horners, who in 1557 confessed to having had associated with them city "bottellmakers" for "a hundred fourscore nine yeares and nine months wrytten the last daie of November" of that year. *MSS. Book of the Horners' Co.*, exhibited by the Rev. H. G. Rosedale, *Proceedings of the Society of Antiquaries of London*, 1910, p. 9.

probably as a last resort, to one of the miscellaneous craft companies which were fostered in those communities.

This concludes our survey of the different types of amalgamated gilds which were formed by the English trades and handicrafts. The gilds established by the mercantile crafts fall, for the most part, into three main divisions, according as these crafts associated themselves under the patronage of the mercers and merchants, the haberdashers or the drapers. While the London merchants, the pepperers, canvas dealers and spicers were the first of the gilds to combine their forces, the merchants of the provincial cities and corporate towns were not slow in following their lead. Indeed, in many cases they carried the plan of association much further, and established trading companies comprising practically all the ordinary dealers of their particular town. In the smaller communities the movement was developed still further, the traders enlarging the membership of their gilds, until they included many different handicrafts. Finally, in at least two communities—namely, Faversham and Wallingford—the mercantile fraternity became so comprehensive as to include within its ranks not only all the merchants, but all the local handicrafts as well.

While the amalgamations entered into by the industrial crafts fall, in the main, into five different gild groups which represent the leather, metal, building, clothworking and the victualling industries, respectively, there were additional associations maintained in common by crafts like the bowyers and fletchers and the barber-surgeons, which have been considered by themselves. It seems true that the trend toward consolidation took hold first among the mercantile groups, but it soon commended itself to the handicrafts; the victuallers alone, so far as we can judge, were debarred from an early exercise of the privilege of association.

II

THE CAUSES OF THE AMALGAMATION OF THE MERCANTILE CRAFTS

We have thus far sketched a bare outline of the rise and progress among the English trades and handicrafts of the movement towards amalgamation. It is in place next to inquire into the conditions in the English economic scheme which made the movement possible, in order that we may determine the causes which underlay its growth.

So far as the records furnish evidence the movement was started in 1345 when three groups of London merchants united to form the grocers' company and by their union contrived to work so much mischief to the public at large in eighteen years, by engrossing all manner of merchandise and by enhancing the price of their wares, as to call forth a parliamentary measure restricting the merchants as a class in their commercial operations. We have, however, to look further afield to discover why the state found it expedient to bind the handicrafts to their chosen craft. But we need not go outside London to perceive that the authorities were obliged to do something to allay the general discontent which had arisen because craftsmen were everywhere disregarding their neighbours' peculiar rights. The London handicrafts were seething with discontent. As we shall see, time and again the town council tried to keep the peace among the disaffected craftsmen by defining in gild ordinance the duties peculiar to each craft. This condition of affairs sufficiently explains why parliament in the act of 1363 included provisions which aimed at checking the aggressions of the crafts on one another's special field. Yet while state and municipality alike insisted that townsmen should keep within their separate spheres of industry, consolidated companies were springing up both among trades and handicrafts. Where, then, shall we seek for the explanation of this tendency towards amalgamation? Was the repealing act too late? Had the grocers already too well pointed out to their fellow-merchants the larger opportunities for commercial expansion which they might all enjoy by amalgamating with each other? To be sure the action of the grocers, who were the first of the gilds to profit by permission to amalgamate, had provoked the act of 1363, in which parliament, by requiring English merchants to "use no ware or merchandise" except the particular one which they should publicly select, directly forbade the grocers to do what had been made possible for them when, only eighteen years before, they

20

had been allowed to establish their organisation. The important point, however, is that the attention of the state was at this time directed against the monopolising practices of an amalgamated gild of merchants and that the act of 1363 was deliberately aimed against them. Albeit the superior commercial advantages enjoyed by the London companies made separate gilds of general traders possible and doubtless profitable, the purely merchant trades in the other English centres were compelled for the most part to combine their gild interests. Thus the merchants' and mercers' companies became one of the most, if not the most, important of all the gilds in the localities which fostered their growth. Shrewsbury supplies the first account of consequence we have of the internal economy of this species of gild.[1] The first articles of incorporation, issued in 1480,[2] are indubitably based on a much earlier foundation, and show that the organisation which contained the mercers, goldsmiths, and ironmongers had developed solely for the purpose of regulating in the interest of its members the conditions for the purchase and sale of the articles handled by them. We learn from their by-laws [3]

[1] The earliest book of the company apparently begins in 1424-5 in the third year of King Henry VI, with a record of the names of the "Brethren received and incorporated," together with the amount of the fine each was assessed upon his admission. *Trans. Shropshire Archaeol. & Nat. Hist. Soc.,* vol. viii, pp. 269, 300.

[2] At this time the gild appears as a developed corporation; its members were undoubtedly guilty of practising the abuses characteristic of gildsmen of the period. Indeed, from the preamble of the charter which King Edward IV conferred upon the "craftes of Mercers Ironmongers and Goldesmythes occupied undre One Gylde and Frat'nite" in the twentieth year of his reign, one might infer that the gildsmen had petitioned for incorporation solely to reform one of the more serious of the abuses, namely that of charging apprentices excessive fines for entry into the gild: *Trans. Shropshire Archaeol. & Nat. Hist. Soc.,* vol. viii, p. 270.

[3] It is surprising to find this Shrewsbury mercers' company already in 1424-5 receiving new members who were practising various other occupations. Besides a number of goldsmiths, that year's calendar registers a taverner, a capmaker, a farrier, several cardmakers, a "flecher," a smith, several shearmen, a draper and a furbisher. What do such entries signify? Why are townsmen who are neither mercers, nor goldsmiths, nor ironmongers permitted to join the company to exercise presumably their own branch of industry? It is true that by 1515 the company speaks of its membership as composed of pewterers, founders, cardmakers, and cappers as well as the three other trades, but this by no means accounts for the presence of the many other craftsmen just enumerated. Furthermore, we come upon some curious entries which prove that new members were permitted upon the payment of a double fine to exercise more than one calling at a time. For example, the year 1477-8 contains the following entries: "Geffrey Powys with Cappers only, makyng of capps, bying of capps, and sellyng of capps, fine xxs. If he use any other trade then xxs. more." In the twentieth year of the reign of Henry VIII: "Robert Lee p'ntes to Willm Edwards mercer and capper made freeman for xxs." It is an ordinary occurrence to find an item stating that a capper becomes a member "with cappers only," or that a man is made a freeman with "pewterers crafte only," or with "goldsmiths only." Obviously the company was careful to restrict new members to the use of their immediate branch of industry unless they would pay an additional fee

that if a person absented himself from the celebration of the Corpus Christi festival, because of his attendance at the Coventry fair or elsewhere, in order "to buy or sell," he was to pay a fine. Searchers were appointed to take care that "anything appertaining to the said crafts" should "be boght and solde" in the town, and that franchises should "be able, sufficient, and lawful." These supervisors were also empowered to "make serche uppon the Occupyers of the said Crafte within the Town . . . that none of theym occupie any false Balaunce Weight or measures, wherebie the Kynges People in any wise myght be hurt or dysseyved," on pain of forfeiting the balances and paying a fine. Nor should any person belonging to the gild, on pain of forfeit, sell or "make to be solde any maner of merchaundyce or ware belongyng to said Craftes or eny of theym purposely standing in the stretys, hyghe Way or pawment ,of the said town for to have better sale then eny of Combrethyrn or make noe boothes uppe Boordes Rackes or eny other suche instrument without theyre Bulkes but onelie in tyme of Fayre." So well, too, did the Shrewsbury organisation demonstrate its worth as a civil institution that from time to time it received recruits from other trades, until by the early sixteenth century it numbered among its members pewterers, founders, cardmakers and cappers.[4]

We are fortunate in possessing at this distance of time details of this associated mercantile company. Very often we have to

---

for further privileges. See *Trans. Shropshire Archaeol. & Nat. Hist. Soc.,* vol. viii, pp. 300–11, for the list of members chronicled in the records of this gild. As late as 1665 we find a townsman of Buckingham receiving the freedom of the local mercers' company, which at that time included ironmongers among various other trades, upon the understanding that he was "to follow the trade of an ironmonger." Six years later a brother of this man was also admitted to membership in the society "to follow only ye trade of an ironmonger." Noble, *History of the London Ironmongers' Company,* p. 5. The fifteenth-century account of the associated mercers' company of Shrewsbury gains an additional interest from the fact that by 1208, fully two centuries earlier, the old gild merchant had become nothing more than an organisation for enrolling the names of those who were admitted into the fold. For instance, one of these early "Rotulus" in the possession of the borough corporation contains a list of those who are "de Gilda Mercatorum in burgo Salopie." It looks very much as if the mercers' company was established to take the place of the gild merchant among the general traders of Shrewsbury. See my *English Craft Gilds and the Government* for an account of the relation between the gild merchant and the craft gilds in Leicester, pp. 21–26. The Rev. C. H. Drinkwater has published the thirteenth- and fourteenth-century rolls of the Shrewsbury gild merchant in the *Trans. Shropshire Archaeol. & Nat. Hist. Soc.,* 2nd ser., vols. ii and iii, and 3rd ser., vols. iii and iv. Unfortunately Mr. Drinkwater discusses these gild merchant rolls under the title "The Merchants' Gild of Salop or Shrewsbury," which, in the light of the existence of the fifteenth-century associated mercers' gild we are concerned with, is misleading and apt to lead to the confusion of the two species of gild. As we shall see handicraftsmen were admitted to membership in the gild founded by the mercers of York in the fourteenth century.

[4] *Trans. Shropshire Archaeol. & Nat. Hist. Soc.,* vol. viii, pp. 271–286. It is noteworthy that whereas handicraftsmen were openly admitted to membership, the company's records indicate that it concerned itself only with the purely commercial affairs of its members.

depend upon the most fragmentary evidence to convince us that similar societies were performing similar functions elsewhere. At Southampton,[5] for instance, in 1468, the mercers' craft levied fines upon an alien mercer "for that he went with his fardell up and down the town hawking his wares," contrary to the rules of the mercers' gild, and about the same period the Nottingham mercers supervised the sale of their wares by hawkers.[6] The Northampton records, however, give us the clearest idea of the purpose which a mercers' company served in a community in the later Elizabethan period. The society included at that time the mercers, haberdashers, linendrapers, grocers, apothecaries, upholsterers, and salters, besides "tryers of honye and waxe"—in all, nine different branches of trade.[7] The town experienced so much trouble in controlling the freemen of those occupations that it was forced at last to assert its authority by requiring them to meet lawfully thereafter at St. Katharine's Hall "without any confederecie, conspiracie, mutinee, or tumulte." It also ordered that no "foreigne chapman or unfranchised person" should sell within the town "anie drinckinge glasses or woollen cardes," and that no persons whatsoever not being free of the said town should sell to any foreigner or unfranchised person any kind of merchandise or wares pertaining to those trades within the town. It would be extremely interesting to know certainly the occasion of this stringent order, and to learn why these townsmen had been holding tumultuous meetings. It looks very much as if their gild rules had been for some reason in abeyance, and that the members had held an indignation meeting with the view of compelling the town to uphold the authority of the merchants' gild. From this time onward there is plenty of evidence bearing on the specific object of these associated mercantile fraternities.[8]

---

[5] Davies, *Hist. of Southampton*, p. 275.

[6] *Records of the Borough*, vol. iii, p. 104.

[7] *Borough Records*, vol. ii, pp. 276-7.

[8] According to an extant register of Minutes and Accounts dating from 1655–1772, a company composed of mercers, linen-drapers, woollen-drapers, and merchant taylors of the "ancient port" of Sandwich was incorporated in the first year of the reign of Queen Elizabeth with special rights to control local trade to the exclusion of Englishmen who were not freemen of the port. *Additional MSS. B. M.* no. 27, 462. In Leominster, at this time, local mercers, taylors and drapers together formed one of the five associated "occupacons" on record as paying an annual fine of xxd. to the chamberlains of the borough at Michaelmas. Townsend, *Leominster*, p. 70.

At Warwick, the borough records of 1575 show the municipality issuing a "declaracyon of the constitucyons Ordynaunces and decrees of the misteryes and crafts of mercers haburdasshers Grocers and Fishmongers . . . from henceforth justly and truly to be observid fulfilled and kept of them and eury of them and their Successors." Among these "Ordynaunces" we find one stipulating that no "forrener of the said Artes or crafts" should in "any wise uppon the market dayes holden in the said borough tyll over his or their heades or make any back shewe in any parte of the markett place (except it be in the boothe halle). And if they or any of them doo contrary to this ordynaunce to forfeyt for evry tyme to the master and wardens the some Ten Shillings." The "Maister" and wardens might also lawfully "enter the

Valuable testimony to the importance attached to amalgamations of traders both by municipal and gild authorities in the seventeenth century is furnished by the publication of the ordinances of the Lichfield mercers' company. In the early part of that century the city had received letters patent granting it, among various things, permission to make laws forbidding non-freemen to retail within its precincts any wares or merchandise except victuals, and to keep any shop or use any trade or manual art without being specially licensed for the purpose by the bailiffs. Accordingly, after the bailiffs and their brethren had duly considered how "mightilie decayed" the estate of the "Mercers, Grocers, Lynnen Drapers, Woollen Drapers, Silkemen, Hosiers, Salters, Apothecaries, and Haberdashers of small wares" appeared to be, not only for want of good orders for the better governing of the trades, but also "for that many strangers and young men which haue not served their apprentishipps within the said Cittie and manie other which haue shifted abroad in the Countrie and haue not orderlie served any apprentishipp in any one place haue hither repaired and sett vpp all or some of the aforesaid trades," they devised certain ordinances which should guide the tradesmen for the future in the sale of their commodities. The master and wardens of the company were granted authority to "enter from tyme to tyme into any house or howses, shop or shopps of any of the offenders," and "to take and carrie away goodes or chattells of everie such offender and the same to detayne and keepe to the vse of the said company vntill the forfeiture and forfeitures for which they or any of them shalbe so taken shalbe trewlie paid." They were also given power to supervise "all weights and measures as are used by any of the said Company and the same to trie by the King's standard." [9] The

houses shoppes closes or ffields within this borough or liberties of any such offender or offenders and there to take some parte of his goods and catalles in the name of a distres and the same to deteyne until such tyme as he or they haue paid the money or somes so forfeytid or lost by breaking any the said orders or agreaments:" *Black Book,* pp. 139–43. Although we cannot positively say that the Windsor mercers, drapers, haberdashers, and grocers were ever actually associated in a gild, we know that upon "Informacion" furnished in 1576 by townsmen using those occupations "of the great decay and poverty already growen by reason that forraine Retaylers" were allowed to come into the borough upon market days, the authorities decided to ordain "for a law" that from henceforth no "Draper Mercer Haberdasher Hatseller Grocer petty chapman or other Retailer and Victualler of all sorts (the like whereof are not made or traded in this Towne only excepted) shall shew or sell upon the Market (except faire dayes) any of the before mentioned wares:" Tighe and Davis, *Annals of Windsor,* vol. i, p. 642. At Durham, in 1591 the associated mercers, grocers, haberdashers, ironmongers and salters "found falte" with at least four persons "for sellinge wares beinge not free" of their company. In addition, their records list the "expenses" incurred by five members "for charges in the lawe for disobedyence of our corporacione." Thompson, *Minute-Book and Papers* formerly belonging to the Mercers' Company. *Archaeologia Aeliana, 3rd Ser.,* vol. xix, p. 214. (*Society of Antiquaries Pub.*)

[9] *Trans. Royal Hist. Soc.,* n. s., vol. vii, pp. 110–119. One of the orders promulgated in 1612 by the Salisbury traders' association, comprising then

seventeenth century by-laws of the Lichfield mercers follow, seem-ingly, pretty much the same direction as the fifteenth-century set given to the Shrewsbury corporation. Another example may serve to bridge the gap between the ac-counts of the Shrewsbury company and those of the Lichfield com-pany, and may help to explain why in the later period it was thought necessary to emphasise the particular rights of the town's ordinary traders. This is the Preston mercers' company, which included in 1628 the drapers, grocers, salters, ironmongers, and haberdashers of the borough. In that year the members based their petition to the town council for incorporation upon the failure of alien traders to obey not only a statute [10] of the previous century which had forbidden countrymen to "sett on saile or sell by retaile any manner of woollen cloth, linen cloth, mercery wares, haberdasherye wares, grocery wares or saltery wares except it bee in open Faires," but also the Elizabethan statute of apprentices, which had required that craftsmen should serve an apprenticeship of seven years preliminary to mastership in any trade. Notwithstanding these enactments the complaint avers, "divers handicraftsmen and servants at husbandry leaving their own occupations seeking not only to live easily but rather idly, had taken upon them within this town of Preston to set up and live by trade of buying and selling of divers wares and

merchants, grocers, apothecaries, goldsmiths, drapers, upholsterers, and em-broiderers, authorised the wardens, with the assistance of one or two of the "antient and most discreet of every trade" of the company, to "view, see, and search the wares, Merchandise, weights and measures of every brother and sister of the company" and to fine those whom they should find using unlaw-ful wares, weights and measures: Hoare, *Hist. of Modern Wiltshire*, vol. vi, p. 340.

[10] 1 & 2 Philip and Mary, c. 7; see Abram *Memorials of Preston Guilds*, p. 41. Archdeacon Cunningham seems to have missed the point in connexion with these mercers' organisations. He presents the laws of the Lichfield com-pany, which in the seventeenth century appears to him to be a new institu-tion, as typical of the ordinances which were made for industrial regulation in the seventeenth century contrasted with the ordinances of three centuries earlier. The great contrast which Dr. Cunningham finds in the tone of the two centuries' rules is that in the later period they have to do not with the making of goods, but with the condition of goods as sold. He fails to notice that the Lichfield company contained merchants only, whose sole concern was naturally the condition of goods as sold. Nor, as we have shown, did their laws differ in any respect from those issued by a similar society which existed at least two centuries earlier at Shrewsbury. That gilds which con-cerned themselves with the supervision of the quality of materials and the process of manufacture still existed Dr. Cunningham himself proves in telling how, in the later sixteenth and the following century, the Lichfield tailors, the saddlers, the smiths, and the dyers were all doing business organised sep-arately as of old. See *Trans. Royal Hist. Soc.*, n. s., vol. vii, pp. 109-11 for these ordinances of the Lichfield mercers. Professor Ashley, on the other hand, quotes the Preston mercers' society to show that the one purpose of the gild system, so far as it survived from the seventeenth century on, was, to use his own words, "the protection of the interests of the craftsmen of the several localities by ensuring to them a monopoly of the industry of their own town:" *Economic History*, vol. ii, p. 164. Yet the Preston consolidation of 1628 was also one of mere traders.

merchandise contrary to the law." [11] There was nothing new in complaints that strangers were coming into corporate towns to sell their wares, but the practice must have grown apace to warrant the central government in interfering to strengthen the authority of the municipalities over their own commercial concerns.

We have quoted at considerable length from the records of these three mercantile societies in order to show that they existed in the seventeenth century with precisely the same duties and functions as in the fifteenth.[12] The only appreciable difference seems to be that the membership even of the Shrewsbury company had increased considerably by the early sixteenth century,[13] which, no doubt, may be taken as testimony to the fact that townsmen who

---

[11] In 1662 members of this "Companie" after seriously considering the question of closing their shops earlier than had been customary, decided finally not to keep them open after "eight of the clock betwixt the 25 of March and the 25 of Sept. and after six of the clock betwixt ye 25 of Sept. and the 25 of March." Hardwick, *Hist. of Preston*, p. 286.

[12] At Ripon in 1622 the mayor, aldermen, and assistants in council assembled delegated to two of the aldermen the duty of summoning "their Company of Grocers and Mercers," in order that they might "consider how to reduce themselves" and "to propose what new Rules or Orders" might "be necessary for the better Regulation" of the company. *Millenary Record,* p. 65. In 1674 the Derby executive body still "thought fitt" to "constitute, make, and create the Mercers, Apothecaryes, Grocers, Ironmongers, Uphoulsters, and Milliners of this Burrough into a Company . . . finding by experience that the erecting of Companies and Societies for the Inspection and Regulating of trade and Commerce was the best way to avoid "fraudes and deceipts in the way of trade," which tend "much to the impoverishinge and damage of just and honest dealers." And in order that thereafter there might be "noe fraud or deceit used in any of the said trades to the dishonour of this Burrough," it was decreed that the company's wardens, "as often as they shall see occasion," should "enter into the shopps and Warehouses of any person or persons useinge any of the said trades . . . to attest, assay, and try theire weights and Measures and theire goods, Wares, and Merchandizes whether the same be good merchantable and vendible." *Derbyshire Archaeol. and Nat. Hist. Soc. Journ.*, vol. xv, pp. 118–231. During this same time the mercers of Buckingham refused to make free of their company any "strange or forrein p'son . . . to the intent to sell or utter any kind of wares usually solde by any artificer before such time as every such" person shall have paid for his freedom the sums specified by the company. Noble, *Hist. of the Ironmongers' Company of London*, p. 5. As late as 1700, the mayor and burgesses of Pontefract unanimously agreed that the "Merchants, Grocers, Ironmongers, Chirurgeons, Apothecaryes, Tallow Chandlers, habbadashers of hatts and small Wares, and Linnen Drapers Inhabiting and residing within the Burrough" might be made one company. Their wardens too were "to search and try all weights and measures in the shopps, warehouses, and sellers of every or any of the said Company." Any one of the company who should "refuse or deny to be searched or doe interrupt the searcyers in the discharge of their duty" was to forfeit for "every default the sume of five pounds." *The Booke of Entries*, pp. 375–8. In 1734 the corporation of Youghal issued a new charter to a local company of merchants and mercers, their old charter which was dated 1656, "being for many years past disused and silent." *Council-Book*, p. 435.

[13] In Elizabethan days the Shrewsbury mercers were admitting members "to exercise the onlye science of Poticarye and Grocerye." *Trans. Shropshire Archaeol. and Nat. Hist. Soc.*, vol. viii, p. 314.

may earlier have been able to maintain gilds of their own had finally been obliged to give them up and seek membership in the general trading company.[14]

It may be questioned how far the different trades represented in the larger mercantile associations had, previously to their incorporation in the general society, maintained separate gilds. It is evident that the Newcastle merchant company, the records of which emerge about 1477, claimed as their "brethren" in 1659 "as well Drapers as Mercers and Boothmen," and although these three groups had long before the latter date joined with other merchants in forming one gild, they had originally made up three of the dozen single gilds registered in the city in 1342.[15] There is reason to believe, too, that the consolidated mercers', drapers' and grocers' company recorded in 1612 at Nottingham had not always included all three trades, since the records show that in 1484 the drapers were maintaining a separate organisation and exercising the rights customary to gilds of the period.[16] Mr. Hodgson says also that the whole tenor of the old books of the Morpeth merchants' and 'taylors' company shows that "privately" they were two distinct crafts, although united for civic purposes.[17] Such evidence argues strongly for earlier separate incorporation. From all accounts the collective gilds of merchants established in the less important towns were built up by joining together one after another the various gilds of established standing. For example, at St. Albans in 1587 we find the drapers and mercers united in a single company and taking every precaution to preserve to the fullest degree the commercial

[14] This seems to have been the fate of the cappers of Shrewsbury who prior to 1515 had apparently supported their old gild. In sanctioning the ordinances drawn up by local mercers in that year, the bailiffs of the borough acknowledge having examined ordinances recited as well in this "composicion" as in another "ordeyned for good Rule and order to be used among the Combretherne of Cappers" within the "Towne of Shrouesbury, and Franchises of the same unyte and associate of old tyme nowe passed to the Wardeyns and Combretherne of Mercers, Ironmongers Goldesmythes, Peauterers, Founders and Cardemakers unyte also and occupyed under oone style and fraternite within the same Town and franches." *Ibid.*, p. 284. The cappers of Shrewsbury may have renounced their gild so as to reduce expenses, a reduction which was rendered necessary by the going out of fashion of caps and the coming in of felt hats. At about this same time the cappers of Chester confessed to being in "grete dekaye." Morris, *Chester*, p. 435. Later parliament evidently attempted ·to help arrest the decay of the cap trade by enacting a law which bade almost every person in the kingdom above the age of six years wear caps again. 13 Elizabeth, c. 19.

[15] *The Merchant Adventurers of Newcastle-upon-Tyne, Surtees Society Publications*, vol. 93, pp. 280, 76, 24.

[16] *Records of the Borough*, vol. iii, p. 5; vol. iv, p. 311.

[17] The brethren of this company drew up a set of bylaws in 1524 "for the sustentation of their crafts according to such liberties, ordinances and statutes as were granted by Lord Dacre of Gilsland." Half of the fines assessed for breaches of these laws were to go to Lord Dacre and half to the company's chest. Hodgson, *History of Morpeth*, p. 1. Later the company is on record as including barbers, wax-makers, carvers and sheathers. *Parl. Papers*, vol. 25, p. 1628.

rights which had long before been conferred upon its members. Yet not quite a century later both the drapers and the mercers, with a host of minor crafts, had become members of an extremely heterogeneous society, representing then just half the trades and handicrafts of the town.[18] Undoubtedly the men engaged in all the trades which later swelled the ranks of the mercantile fellowships had previously either maintained individual unions or had been partners of long standing in some limited group of closely allied crafts.

On the other hand, there can be no doubt that these gilds of merchants did not all originate in exactly the same way. Naturally the traders of the considerable boroughs and large towns were more numerous and had ampler opportunities to prosper commercially than those who dwelt in the small boroughs. The city merchants could therefore often either maintain single gilds, or gilds which were limited to but two, or possibly three, different groups of closely connected trades, when the country merchants found it difficult to support a single organisation for all. Then, too, the merchant companies often lost a section of their members who withdrew when they wanted to set up a gild of their own. We know that in Beverley in 1446 [19] there was a company composed of the merchants, mercers [20] and drapers who were using stringent measures to uphold their monopoly, and compelled any person who "newly sets up shop as a master," after having served a proper apprenticeship, to make a yearly payment toward the common expenses of the gild.[21] Half a century later, however, in 1493, we find this company about to dissolve. The mercers and merchants established themselves in one company,[22] while the drapers, "newly

18 Gibbs, *Corporation Records*, p. 16. Also *St. Albans Charters*, p. 19.
19 After diligently inspecting the bylaws drawn up by this gild, the twelve keepers of Beverley ordered them to be registered and forever observed. *Beverley Town Documents* (Selden Soc.), p. 74.
20 The mercers are on record in 1390, fully half a century earlier, *Ibid.*, p. 33.
"And if any refuse to observe and fulfill the aforesaid orders he shall incur a penalty of 6s. 8d. to the use of the community of the town of Beverley . . . all the penalties aforesaid when incurred shall be exacted by the stewards of the brotherhood . . . and levied by distress or by the common sergeant." *Ibid.*, p. 74.
21 By 1492 the gild was exacting tribute from townsmen who frequented fairs and markets in order to buy cloth to sell in Beverley. *Hist. MSS. Comm. Report, Beverley,* 1900, p. 80.
22 A borough ordinance of that year decreed that "evere Burges of the towne of Beverley be free to bye or sell hys owne gudes so that he kepe no oppyn shopp in retayling. Nor no man by any maner of merchandyse for redy money to sell itt again in retaylyng bot it sal be presented by the Alderman of Merchaunts to the XII Governors for the yere beying." *Ibid.*, p. 49. In 1494 the Beverley merchants' and mercers' company elected two searchers to test all weights and measures used by its brethren. By 1582 the searchers were to be "substantial, honest and credible men of the said science" who should search the weights and measures of all who used the trades of merchants or mercers or any part thereof. Moreover the ordinances drawn up in that year ordered every person "setting up or occupying the trade, viz.,

founded," registered their statutes "with the consent of" the twelve governors of the borough. To all appearances the drapers of Beverley had prospered sufficiently to warrant them in setting up their own gild.[23]

Often again, the records of some borough show that a merchant gild existed in one form at one time which at another had completely changed its personnel. Materials furnished by the gild history of Bristol offer valuable evidence that the pure traders of that city were very differently organised at different periods; but although the relationship which existed between these gilds, established at different times, was doubtless very intimate, it is impossible to determine how close it really was. We know, however, that in 1370 about one hundred and forty of the most worthy men of the city, besides "plusours aultres merchauntz et drapers," met together and formed an organisation.[24] They drew up a set of ordinances regulating, among other things, the sale of cloth, and they agreed upon the policy which should thereafter govern the townspeople in the purchase of various articles coming into the town.[25] We cannot say how long the drapers remained loyal to this gild of merchants. It is now evident that the condition of the Bristol gilds in the seventeenth century was quite different from that in 1370, for in 1647 there was an associated gild of mercers and linendrapers on the one hand and a separate gild of woollendrapers on the other, both existing in the city at the same time.[26] Between 1370 and 1647, the dates of the record of these two gilds respectively, Bristol documents testify to the existence of another fellowship of merchants, which, although it did not by 1467 include all the local merchants, yet had authority to compel them when summoned to attend at their hall, and fixed the price to be charged for various kinds of wares.[27] In addition to this fraternity, a fel-

in buying, selling and retailing of wares and merchandise of what kind soever they be, to the value of £10 to come to the Warden and bind himself to observe the ordinances and pay 10s. to be divided between Town and Occupation." *Ibid.*, pp. 82–83.

[23] *Beverley Town Documents*, p. 99 (Selden Soc. Pub.). Records under date of 1662 refer to a Preston "Companie" of Drapers which may doubtless be interpreted to mean that local drapers had deserted the local merchant company to erect one of their own. Hardwick, *Preston*, p. 285.

[24] *Little Red Book*, vol. ii, p. 51. Among these worthy men was included William Canynge, who twenty years later became the mayor of Bristol.

[25] Articles such as gorse, straw, coal and hay were to be purchased only at the place assigned therefor. "And if any go against this ordinance he shall pay to the commonalty for each load 4d."

[26] *Trans. Bristol and Gloucestershire Archaeol. Soc.*, vol. xxvi, pt. ii, p. 288 et seq.

[27] According to a summons which this gild issued in that year, "all merchaunts of Bristowe" were to "be redie to come and appeare before the saide maister and felaweschipp att suche tymes reasonable as they ben warned to the common plaace to theym assigned and ordeyned for the good expedicon of the saide Rewle and Ordenaunce of and uppon the saide fower marchandices (meat oyle, woll oyle, yren and waxe) or eny of theym" under penalty of paying one pound of wax to the master and fellowship "atte evy defaulte

lowship of merchants, separate and distinct from all the craft
companies, was organized in 1500,[28] and half a century later the
Merchant Adventurers of Bristol secured incorporation upon their
"lamentable representation" to Edward VI that "divers Artificers
and men of manuell arte inhabitinge the same Citty haveinge alsoe
occupacions to gett theire liveinge (whoe were never apprentice or
brought upp to or in the recourse or trade of the arte of the
marchants aforesaide, nor haveinge anie good knowledge in the
same arte) Doe commonly exercise, use and occupie the saide recourse or trade of marchandize to and from the partes beyond the
seas in strange shippes or vessels." In order to prevent this, it
was ordered that thereafter no artificer or any other person should
traffic in merchandise, either in domestic or foreign ports, unless
he were admitted into the society.

One wonders what the connexion was between these four companies all embracing local merchants and mercers; whether the
seventeenth-century company was a new organisation [29] or merely
a continuation of the fourteenth-century gild of small merchants
whose members, excluded from the Merchant Adventurers' gild,[30]

that they ben callyd if that they bee in towne." Latimer, *History of the
Merchant Venturers of Bristol*, p. 17.
    [28] *Ibid.*, p. 42. In all probability the fellowship of merchants recorded in
1500 became the chartered Merchant Adventurers of a half-century later. In
that year the mayor and his associates passed an ordinance for the "Wele not
oonly of the said marchaunts adventurers but also of all other burgesses of
the said Toun" which decreed that "fromhensfurth no marchaunt nor other
Burgeis . . . shall cary or do to be caryed ne send or do to be sent or delyred
to any pson or psones dwellyng oute of the said Toun and Franchise of
Bristowe any wyne wax woode yron or other marchaundise onlesse that all
the same marchaundise be frste playnly and wtoute any fraude coloure or
male engyne solde by the said Burgeis to hym or theym to whom they so
shuld be caryed or sent or to his or theire Servauntes or attorneys." *Ibid.*,
p. 27.
    [29] *Trans. Bristol and Gloucester. Archaeol. Soc.*, vol. xxvi, pt. ii, p. 288.
Mr. Latimer, who published the account of this company of mercers and
linendrapers, says that it was not really established by the civic body until
1647. At that time the company was devoting its energies towards carrying
out three main objects which its members had greatly at heart. These were
the suppression of interloping tradesmen who set up drapery shops in the
city; the prosecution of Londoners who brought down goods to the great
Bristol fairs and offered their wares to the public a few days before or after
the eight statutory days which they could not be debarred from enjoying;
and the rigorous extirpation of hucksters and petty chapmen. *Ibid.*, 288–292.
    [30] It is curious to read how in 1571 the Bristol Adventurers sought to
justify their right to incorporation on the lines specified in their charter.
They naïvely complained that a "merchant cannot be a retailer for want of
skill and acquaintance of customers, which requires an apprenticeship to
bring him to it, neither can he have a fit place to dwell in, for all the houses
that stand in the place of retail are already in the hands of retailers." No
retailer, they go on to say, has at any time built any shipping and one poor
merchant has sustained more loss in the service of the Prince than all the
retailers in Bristol. Yet the rich retailers, namely the grocers, mercers,
haberdashers, soapmakers, vintners and their kind "adventuring themselves
must needs undo all the poorer sort who do not adventure and eat out the

were forced by alliance with the linendrapers to form a company of their own. Some such inference may be drawn, inasmuch as the mercers and linendrapers of the seventeenth century are emphatically styled "shop-keepers," while the Merchant Adventurers in forming their fellowship pointed to their interest in commerce "beyond the seas." Some members of this local mercers' company may also have belonged to the Merchant Adventurers; indeed they may have been instrumental in founding the organisation, a circumstance which would not necessarily have hindered local retailers later from starting a society of their own.[31] Membership in the company established by the Chester Adventurers was opened to local mercers in Elizabeth's time;[32] yet in 1604, fully forty-three years before the rise of the Bristol fellowship, the mercers of Chester in company with local ironmongers begged the king to "vouchsaffe vnto theyme" letters patent whereby they might be incorporated into a society, because as they declared, as well diverse citizens as strangers, "not being first admitted into the sayd Com-

meer merchants who have but those to whom they may make their vent." Latimer, *Hist. of the Merchant Adventurers*, p. 54. In 1612 the society received the city's sanction to an ordinance forbidding non-members from using the trade of a Merchant Adventurer and members from trading other than as Adventurers. Six years later, in 1618, the Merchant Adventurers made a pretence of compromising with the retailers or artificers, whom they apparently classed together, by inserting in their by-laws the provision that "Noe Retailer or artificer whilest they remaine Retailers or Artificers shalbee receyved or admitted into the Freedome of this Societie for anie fine whatsoever without approbacion and allowance of a special Courte houlden for that purpose." *Ibid.*, p. 74.

[31] Whatever may have been the reason for its rise, by 1656 the company's right to control the retail trade of Bristol was upheld by the municipal authorities. In that year they issued a warning to non-members forbidding them to sell mercery or drapery under penalty of being amerced five pounds. By 1663, mercers evidently predominated in the organisation, there being eighteen mercers to a dozen linen-drapers. *Trans. Bristol & Gloucester. Archaeol. Soc.*, vol. xxvi, pt. ii, p. 288.

[32] No person who exercised a manual occupation or who sold by retail could at first gain admittance to the Chester company of Merchant Adventurers, much to the chagrin of the tradesmen thus debarred. The mercers in particular seem seriously to have objected to this restriction, for in 1559, within six years of the grant of Queen Mary's charter to the Chester Adventurers, a marginal note attached to a transcript of Elisabeth's charter conferred upon them in that year, declares that the "mersers" were "to be free." *Harleian MS*. 2054, f. 46. This concession may temporarily have pacified the mercers of Chester, although in 1604 we found the men of that occupation associated in a gild with the ironmongers. *Ibid.*, f. 56. But the retailers of other trades, more especially those interested in exporting calf skins, continued to resent their exclusion from trafficking in foreign lands. They finally appealed to the privy council for redress, and went so far as to ask that the Merchant Adventurers' charter might be annulled. The controversy was settled in 1589, when both sides seemingly gained some advantage from the decision of the arbitrators. This accorded to the Adventurers or "Meere" merchants, as they were called, permission to "make choise of eny other trade (beinge not a manuall crafte) as draper, vintner, mercer, iremonger, and such like," and to all "retaylors" liberty to use "the trade of marchandise together with there retaylinge:" Morris, *Chester*, pp. 464-67.

pany," attempted to use their trades to the great damage and hindrance of the freemen.[33]

It would seem that in the seventeenth century economic conditions in Chester and Bristol were such as to warrant local mercers in founding gilds apart from those maintained by local adventurers, when in communities like York and Newcastle-upon-Tyne one organisation was made to do duty for general mercantile purposes. Tracing the development of the mercantile gild in York, one finds that the gild or "fraternity of the Blessed Mary," founded in 1357 [34] by a dozen and one local merchants under a "licencia" emanating from the king, by 1420 had become the "Gyld of the holy Trynytes." The "Free Brethren of Mercers and Merchants" as the members of this "Gyld" were designated, established their headquarters in "Fossegate," [35] a region which later became noted as the site of Trinity Hall, the meeting place of the merchant adventurers of York. This was the merchant adventurers' company incorporated by Queen Elizabeth in 1581, to include all persons who used the art of merchants or mercery within the city and suburbs,[36] although later its membership evidently comprised not only merchants and mercers,[37] but grocers, apothecaries and ironmongers as well.[38]   In Newcastle-upon-Tyne, however, a com-

[33] *Harleian MSS., British Museum,* 1996. The mercers of Chester seem not to figure in local annals until 1525, by which time they had become extensive dealers in caps. Morris, *Chester,* p. 435.

[34] Sellers, *The York Mercers and Merchant Adventurers, Surtees Soc. Publications,* 1918, vol. 129, p. 3. A year before a piece of land in Fossgate had been conveyed to three citizens and merchants, two of whom were mercers. These two mercers—one of whom was the John Freeboys who served as the gild's first master—in conjunction with thirteen other citizens obtained the licence to found the gild. Among the thirteen there were two hosiers, a draper, a potter, a "litister," a spicer, a "verrour" and a tanner. Listed in the gild's "Compotus" for 1366—after an existence of nine years—we find a "coco" or two, a "bower," two "Scheremen," a "cissor," a "pictor," a plasterer and an "Iremangher." Manifestly the mercers of York like their Shrewsbury brethren, admitted to membership at least in the beginning, the handicrafts of their city. *Ibid.,* pp. 16–26.

[35] Sellers, *The Merchant Adventurers of York (Handbook for the British Association Meeting Held at York,* 1906), edited by Mr. George Auder, p. 213.

[36] Gross, *Gild Merchant,* vol. ii, p. 282.

[37] Miss Sellers claims that the York company of Merchant Adventurers was a specialised branch of the local mercers' company. Its membership, she says, was not limited to one particular body of traders, but embraced the prominent members of all the chief trades as distinguished from the handicrafts of York. Miss Sellers also maintains that so many of the local mercers availed themselves of the extension of privilege afforded by the passing of the act of 12 Henry VII. c. 6 (which granted to every Englishman on the payment of a fine of ten marks sterling liberty to trade to any place within the jurisdiction of the Merchant Adventurers of England), that within a few years a court of Merchant Adventurers was grafted on to the mercers' company; and as all the more important members of the older organisation were connected with foreign trade, the name of what was originally only a section of the society was gradually applied to the whole fellowship. *Handbook,* etc., pp. 213–15.

[38] At Exeter, too, a company of Merchant Adventurers chartered in the

pany of adventurers, incorporated by King Edward VI for the purpose of controlling the entire trade that centred in the city,[39] seems from all accounts, to have grown out of the union of three gild groups, the mercers, drapers and merchants of corn or "boothmen," as the latter group was usually designated.[40] In the twentieth year of the reign of King Edward IV, this united company, or "Felleship" of merchants as the record has it, had issued a set of ordinances avowedly "for thair allers well and profet," and by 1506 was buying wool and wool-fels, grown in districts adjoining the city and shipping them to foreign parts. Moreover, long after this company had lost its exclusive rights in adventuring, it still retained control over the entire trade of the city.[41] So far as we can determine at this late date, the connexion between the London

second year of the reign of Queen Elizabeth was given control of the trade in "merceries" as well as in all sorts of "marchandies" and "marchand wares," proof evidently that at that epoch Exeter supported only one organisation for general mercantile purposes. Further corroboration of this fact is found in the authorisation given the company's officials to "make serche and serches among all the trafiquors and users of the mysterie or arte of marchandizes . . . of wayghts, measures and other things incident or respecting the said mysterie and to make inquisicion, vewe and examincion and of takinge and haveinge, correcting and reformynge defaulcte in the same and of ponysshinge and abolysshinge the defaulcte." Cotton, *Merchant Adventurers of Exeter*, pp. 6–8. Available records of Exeter make no mention of an early gild of mercers, so that it is not possible to trace the evolution of this local company of merchant adventurers.

[39] *The Merchant Adventurers of Newcastle-upon-Tyne, Surtees Soc. Pub.*, vol. 93, p. 280.

[40] As late as 1659 the brethren of this society were designated "as well Drapers as Mercers and Boothmen." *Ibid.*, p. 76.

[41] *Ibid.*, pp. 1, 24. In 1564 we learn that the "comodyte of lead haithe in tyme paste ben a cheyff traide and levinge to the bretherynge of this Felloshype," which in 1695 considered "Tradeing in and cutting of silks, callicoes, musslings" as "intrenching" upon its privileges. Ten years later the company tried to keep non-members from selling not only groceries but broad cloth, silk, buttons and mercers' wares of other sorts. *Ibid.*, pp. 42, 239, 248. Not all the merchant companies who engaged in adventuring were chartered merchant adventurers. For instance, in 1499 "in the Gilde Hall of Kyngeston uppon Hull," the mayor and aldermen of the borough set their seal to a set of ordinances which were drawn up in that year "for the liberte and Freedom of the Merchaunts Inhabitaunts" who, according to their own allegation, had no other science "cunnyng ne crafft wherwith to get their lyvyng bot oonly by the way and the meanes of bying and sellyng and by grete aventour." Moreover it was to a society of merchants inhabiting the town of Kingston-upon-Hull that Queen Elizabeth conceded a charter, three quarters of a century later. Again, at Dublin in 1438, when "Henri the fyfte" was king, a merchant gild was given charge of that city's commercial affairs, which seem to have been concerned largely with the sale of iron, salt, coal and wine. Besides these four commodities, all manner of merchandise that came into the city, "as well merceri as groceri and halberdashe," hides and leather, seem to have been handled by this company which was incorporated by Queen Elizabeth in 1557, and empowered to buy and sell all kinds of merchandise "in grosso siue retallia." *Corporation Records, City of Dublin, Egerton MS., B. M.*, 1765, ff. 1–10. Also *Records of the Dublin Gild of Merchants, Royal Soc. of Antiquaries of Ireland, 5th ser.*, vol. 10, pp. 49–50.

mercers [42] and the Merchant Adventurers of England must likewise have been very intimate.[43]

The Shrewsbury mercers' society has an additional interest because from the beginning it seems to have included in its membership local goldsmiths [44] as well as ironmongers, two important
callings in early medieval trading society which in London and in
various other English towns of standing were able to maintain
their own gilds. It is evident, however, that in the early fifteenth
century Shrewsbury did not possess goldsmiths or ironmongers [45]

[42] The very first royal charter granted, in 1394, to the London mercers
favours the idea that they were at that time engaged in foreign merchandise.
It tells how the mercers had called the attention of the king to the poverty
and destitution to which many men of the mystery of mercery in the city had
been reduced "by mischance at sea or by other casual misfortunes," as a consequence of which they had little or nothing to live upon but the "alms of
other Christians pitying and assisting them in the way of charity," *London
and Middlesex Archaeol. Soc. Trans.,* vol. iv, p. 134; see also *Mercers'
Charters and Ordinances,* p. 3. This company evidently included merchants
and shop-keepers, because ordinances which it issued in 1410 provided that
once a year the wardens were to examine the weights and measures of members and fine those who used any which proved defective. *Parl. Papers,*
1884, pt. ii, p. 4. Moreover, in 1573, at least one member was known to be
both a "mercer and a merchant," while in 1642, not alone "shopkeepers of the
mercerie" but a group of "silkmen" also had special privileges conferred upon
them by the company. *Ibid.,* p. 3.

[43] The relationship between the London mercers and the Merchant Adventurers of England is not clearly established, although by 1474 it was so close
as to give the wardens of the mercery power to punish those who contravened
certain ordinances which were adopted at a court of the Adventurers' Company held in that year. Nine years later, because the governor of the Adventurers had spoken disparagingly of the wardens of the mercers he was
obliged to humble himself to the point of asking pardon on his knees, in
accordance with the sentence imposed upon him by the general court of the
mercery for the offense. *Parliamentary Papers,* 1884, pt. ii, p. 5. Moreover
down to about 1526, minutes of the meetings of the Merchant Adventurers
and of the London mercers seem to have been kept in the same book, and
until the fire in 1666, the Mercers' Hall was the London headquarters of the
Adventurers. Gross, *Gild Merchant,* vol. i, p. 149.

[44] A gild of goldsmiths was among the so-called "adulterine" gilds recorded in the twenty-sixth year of King Henry II. *The Great Roll of the
Pipe,* vol. xxix, p. 153. By 1327 the goldsmiths of London were incorporated
by the king. Herbert, *Twelve Great Livery Cos.,* vol. ii, p. 289. At Norwich,
too, local goldsmiths seem to have preserved a separate gild. This ranked
in 1622 sixth among the twelve big companies organised in that year in the
city. *Reliquary;* n. s., vol. iv, p. 208. Also *Records of Norwich,* vol. ii, p. 383.
On the other hand the goldsmiths of Newcastle-upon-Tyne were not able to
establish their own society until 1716, having been previous to that date members of an amalgamated company which included also local plumbers, glaziers,
pewterers and plumbers. *Archaeologia Aeliana,* vol. xv, iii, pp. 397–405.
The goldsmiths of Exeter seem not to have been incorporated until 1700.
Devonshire Association for Advancement of Science, vol. 44, ser. iii, vol. 4,
p. 439.
In communities like Hereford and Carlisle local goldsmiths are found
incorporated with different groups of metal craftsmen. *Hist. MSS. Commis.
Report, Hereford,* p. 319. *Municipal Records of Carlisle,* p. 134, while at
Salisbury by 1612, local goldsmiths were numbered among the members of the
merchant gild. Hoars, *Wiltshire,* vol. vi, p. 340.

[45] The ironmongers of London organised as early as 1310, took rank later

influential enough to establish their own gilds, and they accordingly joined with the general merchants and mercers in forming a society.

From the foregoing account of the amalgamations of traders established at Bristol and Shrewsbury, we can now readily picture to ourselves something of the way in which these societies grew up in most of the English boroughs. If we may judge from the evidence furnished by the Bristol record of the organisation formed by the merchants, mercers and drapers of that borough in 1370, which antedates the account of the Shrewsbury mercers' gild by something more than fifty years, there can be little doubt that when the Shrewsbury gild merchant lost out,[46] the merchant dealers, who

as one of the twelve great livery companies. At York, too, by 1342 a dozen master ironmongers had established a gild of their own. *Memorandum Book*, pt. i, p. xxxvii. In 1571 a Chester "Companye" of ironmongers paid "weeklye" a "subscription of monye" towards the "Makinge of the Haven," although thirty-five years later the ironmongers seem to have joined with local mercers in forming "one Bodie corporate." *Harleian MSS., B. M.* 2104; 1996. no. 42. An extant document appraising the stock of a London ironmonger in 1356, shows that in addition to such articles as battle-axes, hatchets, hammers, gauntlets, braces and other weapons of defense, there were all sorts of cooking utensils, such as pots, pans, plates and pitchers, as well as bedding, carpets, tapestry, hangings, cushions and bench covers. Noble, *Hist. of the London Ironmongers Co.*, p. 6. In 1578 the business of a Nottingham ironmonger was defined as "a craft, mystery or manual occupation . . . of small-made wares, to-wit of nails, horseshoes, slips, spade-shoes, hatchets," etc. *Nottingham Records*, vol. iv, p. 53.

[46] Extant documents of the fourteenth century testify to the end of the gild merchant's commercial activity in many communities. For instance, if the gild merchant had not ceased to control Bristol's trade and industry, there would scarcely have been need in 1370 for one hundred and forty of the most worthy men besides various other merchants and drapers to form a society for the purpose of determining the policy which should govern the city in the purchase and sale of different articles consumed within its precincts. The determination of such matters had originally fallen to the gild merchant. Then too, the fact that by 1318 the gild merchant rolls of Shrewsbury record only a list of names of men with their callings, may be taken as evidence that the gild merchant of Shrewsbury no longer controlled that borough's commercial affairs. It is true that there is no evidence of the activity of the Shrewsbury mercer's society prior to 1424; yet in all probability that organisation had been founded at an earlier date. It will be recalled that by 1380 the gild merchant of Leicester had become merely a mechanism for enrolling the names of those who desired to become burgesses. By 1328 the gild merchant of Preston had apparently come to a parting of its old ways. In that year the "Maire, balifes and burges withall the comonaltie be hole assent and consent" declared it to be lawful for them and their "heyres and successors to sett a Gyld Marchant at every xx yere end or ever if they have nede to conferme chayrters or other distres that longis" to their franchise. Abram, *Memorials of the Preston Guilds*, p. 2. A meeting definitely set for only once in twenty years would not dispose of the business bound to crop up in the course of a month to say nothing of a year in a borough such as Preston. Just how soon after 1328 or even before that date, local retail dealers of Preston got together and formed an association does not appear. Unfortunately not until 1628 is there evidence that a group made up of local mercers, drapers and others of their sort had taken control of the borough's commercial interests. However, Mr. Dendy (*Merchant Adventurers of Newcastle-upon-Tyne, Surtees Soc. Pub.*, vol. 93, p. xxv.) maintains that the

must have been prominent members of that body, wishing to carry on worthily the traditions of the gild merchant,[47] sought to embody some of them in an organisation of their own. In this way the various mercantile trades in Shrewsbury and the other provincial towns could still preserve the dignity of their several callings, hold their own against the numerous gilds set up by the different handicrafts and keep their power and influence in civic life.[48] As time went on new industries developed and old ones declined, so that while the men concerned in forwarding a rising industry were establishing new gilds,[49] those who still kept their interest in one

"feloship of marchaunts" recorded in Newcastle in 1480 was still the gild merchant of the town. The fact that as early as 1342 three of the twelve mysteries then founded in Newcastle were manned by men representing three distinct trades seems to refute such a contention. Besides, Beverley records dating from the early fifteenth century distinguish between a merchant gild of St. John, which, in all probability was the old gild merchant, to the aldermen and stewards of which rent (firma) was then being paid for the use of the Gild Hall (*Beverley Town Documents, Selden Society Publications,* xliii), and the merchants' and mercer's gild sometimes called the Trinity Guild (*Historical MSS. Commiss. Report,* Beverley, 1900, pp. 5, 159). The earliest evidence of the rise of this latter gild under date of 1446 has already been discussed. *Supra,* p. 28. Moreover, contemporary merchants and mercers of Dublin and of York in their turn christened their gild Holy Trinity. Nor is there anywhere to be found traces of a local mercantile gild working side by side with a gild merchant to regulate local commercial operations. It is true that the "Guild Merchant" figures in local records of the seventeenth and even the eighteenth centuries but only to designate a town assembly or a "Common Hall" where freemen were taken in, or certain community business was disposed of. For instance, at Totnes in 1663, a certain number of shillings and pence were acknowledged to have been "Received off sutche" as have been taken into the "Company of Gwilde Marchants comenly called freemen." *Devonshire Association for the Advancement of Science,* vol. xii, p. 323. Again, as late as 1791, Guildford's mayor commanded the sergeants-at-mace to notify borough magistrates and bailiffs as well that a Guild Merchant or Common Hall was to be held at the Council Chamber at four o'clock in the afternoon of a certain day for the purpose of discusing ways and means by which to raise a sum of money sufficient to discharge debts which had been incurred by the corporation in various building enterprises. *Surrey, Archaeological Collection,* vol. ix, p. 329.

[47] Miss Sellers (*Handbook for the British Association Meeting,* 1906, p. 213) found no evidence of any connexion between the mercers and the old gild merchant of York, because the latter organisation had probably disappeared long before the mercers' gild was contemplated. As we have seen, by 1272, reference to the gild merchant of York had vanished from civic records even as a vehicle for enrolling the names of newly made freemen. From that year onward through succeeding centuries, lists of men who "intraverunt Libertatem Civitatis" were registered annually in "Freemen's Rolls," sponsored by the mayor who held office for the year. *The Freemen of York, Surtees Society Publications,* vol. 96, pp. 86–213. See *supra,* p. vi.

[48] According to rule No. 1, as outlined in the ordinances drawn up by the Beverley mercers in 1582, "there shall be one fraternity . . . as in time past without memory of man hath been used . . . as there hath been and is of other brotherhoods within this town." *Historical MSS. Commiss. Report,* Beverley, p. 82.

[49] The occupation of "Lynen-Drapers" was not made a "whole and full occupation of itselfe, distincte and separate from other Occupations" within the "cittye" of Chester until the sixth year of the reign of King Edward VI. *Harleian MS. No. 1996,* f. 546.

of the waning industries were doubtless compelled gradually to renounce their own organisations. Their interests by that time being largely those of the shopkeeper they would inevitably join the general trading company. This hypothesis may account for the gradual incorporation with the Shrewsbury mercers of the pewterers, cardmakers, founders and cappers.[50]

[50] On the other hand, one wonders whether the pewterers or founders who joined this Shrewsbury gild in the early fifteenth century never had or contemplated a society of their own. Indeed, the insight which we gain in 1424 into the varied membership of this company leads us to question seriously the relationship which existed between the general mercantile fraternity and the craftsmen in a medieval town. Until particular groups of craftsmen could gather together enough men to form a gild on their own account they may have joined the society of mercers because they had to belong to some organisation if they wished legitimately to carry on their calling within an urban community. The draper who joined the Shrewsbury mercantile gild in 1424 did so presumably because there was then no gild of drapers to join, an explanation which may account for the presence of the many other handicraftsmen in the fraternity at this stage in its career. Why else, should entrance into a merchant company bind a man to the "pewterers crafte only" to the "goldsmiths only" or to "cappers only." Besides, it was undoubtedly to the advantage of handicraftsmen to join the general mercantile organisation which evidently could levy tribute from those who ventured on their own account to trade beyond the confines allotted to them. Toward the end of the fifteenth century according to an order issued by the gild of merchants of Kingston-upon-Hull, "every man of crafft within this town" was to remove from his "howse, shoppe or wyndowe" any kind of ware or merchandise "openly shewed other than which to hys crafftt apperteyneth" in order to make sale thereof, and "nevyr effter to shew it ne non other unto tyme that he haff made fyne . . . uppon payn of xxs. as offten as he thereoff shalbe convicted." Lambert, *Two Thousand Years of Gild Life*, p. 158. Moreover local mercantile bodies enforced orders of the sort as is evident from the earliest entries extant in the Minute Books of the merchants of Newcastle-upon-Tyne. These record the "Fynes taken by the Feloship of Marchaunts of crafftes-men for occupying the occupacin of marchaunts withouten licens of the said marchaunts." *Merchant Adventurers of Newcastle-upon-Tyne, Surtees Soc. Pub.*, vol. 93, p. 81. The records of Beverley furnish good ground for the belief that these associations of merchants often exacted tribute from handicraftsmen even though they belonged to some other gild. Thus one of the bylaws of the company of merchants and mercers recorded in that borough in 1582 orders that any one, whether he happened to be a "brother" of another trade or not, who should exercise any part of the science of a mercer "to the value of 6l. 13s. 4d." a year should pay an annual contribution of 5s. to the merchants' and mercers' company. *Hist. MSS. Comm. Rep. Beverley*, p. 83. It is noteworthy too, that certain merchant companies which up to the sixteenth century had opened their membership to handicraftsmen, began to make their admission increasingly difficult and in some instances even impossible thereafter. For example, in the sixth year of the reign of King Edward VI, the merchant gild of Dublin finding itself "sore oppressed and hindered" by the admission of "tayllors, bowchers, shomakers and men of occupacon" who by their occupations could "gett and win there living honestly according there voccacon," established for a law that thereafter no person whatsoever should be admitted into the gild under a "fyne of XL pounds starling unless he wineth the same by byrthe, maryage or prenteshipe." A little later an additional payment of "double quarterage forever" was demanded from men of "occupation." *Egerton MS. 1765*, ff. 16, 20. Not until Exeter craftsmen "doo desiste and leave the exercise, occupacon and use of his handycrafte and mysterie" could they gain admittance into the city's Merchant Adventurers'

Particular stress, however, ought to be laid on the fact that, with few if any exceptions, one of these federated mercantile societies existed among the gilds of practically every town of any size or standing throughout the kingdom. This aspect of the subject has heretofore failed to receive the emphasis due to it. Professor Gross, for example, in discussing these companies of local merchants claims that they were not very numerous and that their organisations differed very much in different places. We have found, however, that these companies were exceedingly numerous and that their organisations differed in no essential particulars. Upon a closer study of the point of Dr. Gross's argument, it appears that he had for some reason been led to draw a distinction between mercers' companies and "companies of merchants." As far as we can judge, however, the only difference between the two kinds of organisation is that the so-called companies of merchants, which appear to be associations of ordinary local traders, included a group of merchants apart from the mercers, while the mercers' companies did not apparently include a separate set of merchants. Dr. Gross discusses somewhat in detail, as typical English examples of merchant companies, the organisations found at Carlisle and Alnwick. But the records of the Carlisle company show that its members consisted not only of the merchants, but also of mercers, drapers, grocers and apothecaries—in fact, of all the traders in the city who were not actual handicraftsmen. In the course of his argument Dr. Gross himself acknowledges that the enactments of the Alnwick company, the members of which are not designated, prove that they were general shopkeepers who dealt mainly in mercury and grocery wares. Why Dr. Gross makes the distinction between ordinary mercers' companies and companies of both merchants and mercers is not clear, especially as he defines the word merchant, in accordance with accepted usage in the fifteenth and the greater part of the sixteenth century, as applying preeminently to all who made a business of buying for resale.[51] This

society, chartered by Queen Elizabeth. Cotton, *Merchant Adventurers of Exeter*, p. 6. Of course, it was to the interest of merchant companies which wished to identify themselves with "grete aventour" to repudiate their connexion with local handicraftsmen.

[51] *Gild Merchant*, vol. i, pp. 125-32, 155. The very first roll of the Gild Merchant of Leicester, under date of 1196, mentions the "mercator" as distinct from the mercer of the period but fails to tell the difference between the two species. Bateson, *Leicester Records*, vol. i, p. 12. Later, however, the Eastland Company of York not only drew a distinction between the mercer and the merchant of that epoch, only admitting the latter, but in their ordinances took care to define the merchant as "such an one as hath of some good contynuance not lesse than three yeres traded at home and abroade beyond the seas merchantlike." Sellers, The Merchant Adventurers of York, *Handbook for the Brit. Assoc. Meeting*, p. 215. Nor was the relation which existed between the two species close enough evidently to warrant the authorities everywhere in incorporating them in one and the same company. For example, when the borough of Norwich distributed all her trades and handicrafts into twelve corporations, the mercers were given a place at the

definition would include retailers as well as wholesale dealers, but not handicraftsmen. It is true that many of these mercantile fraternities do not mention a group of merchants as distinct from the mercers, but the inclusion or exclusion of the merchants seems to make no difference in the aim or ambitions of the body.

Professor George Unwin likewise maintains that these amalgamations of traders were not a general feature of industrial organisation in the English boroughs. On the contrary, he holds that the tendency of the trading occupations to draw together within the limits of a single association, so as to make a sharp distinction between traders and craftsmen, was only a passing phase in the history of the larger commercial centres, and that only in one or two smaller towns did this form of organisation survive as an arrested development.[52] Yet we have had abundant proof that the traders in the majority of the boroughs combined thus with the view of protecting their commercial interests. Professor Unwin, too, sees a difference in the part played by these companies of mercers and merchants in various localities. He argues that the amalgamations headed by the mercers which remained wealthy and influential bodies in such towns as Chester, Shrewsbury, Gloucester, Salisbury and Durham, possessed no exclusive right to regulate trade, and were often confronted by other combinations more recently formed and sometimes even more powerful. He refers here to the gilds of drapers or clothiers which, according to his view, by the middle of the sixteenth century "took the leading part in the local organisation of trade."[53] We have found, however, the gen-

head of the first and the "Marchants" of the second. *Records of Norwich,* vol. ii, p. 383. On the other hand, the first of the dozen companies recorded at Kendal in 1578 included among its different groups the local merchants, and the second, local mercers. *Hist. MSS. Commis. Rep.* x, app. iv, p. 312.

[52] *Industrial Organization in the Sixteenth and Seventeenth Centuries,* p. 78. It is a matter of record that in most of the larger boroughs as in the smaller, the ordinary traders drew together into single associations not only for the purpose of making the distinction between them and local craftsmen, but of maintaining it until the end of gild domination. Professor Unwin endeavours to show that the antagonism of interests which developed between the English trades and handicrafts was due to a conflict between commercial and industrial capital, a theme which he discusses at some length. *Ibid.,* pp. 70–102.

[53] The distinction which Mr. Unwin draws between the companies of merchants and those of drapers is that the leading motive of the merchant companies was to exclude the craftsmen, while the drapers' organisations aimed rather at controlling them. There is little evidence, however, which permits us to infer that the companies differed in any such respect. It is questionable whether the drapers' organisations included craftsmen in their membership list to a greater extent than did those of the mercers and merchants. Indeed the Shrewsbury mercers were admitting handicraftsmen into their gild at a time when local drapers secured recognition from King Edward IV for a gild which for a "long tyme passed" they asserted they "hadde by gonnen of themselfs." *Trans. Shropshire Archaeol. & Nat. Hist. Soc., 3rd ser.,* vol. v, *Miscellanea,* iii, p. iv, pub. 1905. And when "varyance and dyscorde" broke out in 1515 between the drapers and shearmen over the latters' "byinge, sellinge and shearing of Welshe cloth," the differences were adjusted by

eral trading societies taking the leading part in the regulation of the local trade. It is true that there is a difference in the constituent elements of the merchant companies which were organised in different towns. For instance, in Carlisle, Preston, and Lichfield, the merchant fraternities included the drapers among their members, whereas in Chester, Shrewsbury, Gloucester, and the other boroughs enumerated by him, they did not, inasmuch as the drapers had gilds of their own. But the mere fact that the drapers maintained gilds apart from the ordinary merchants cannot be taken as proof that they, rather than the merchants, took the leading part in the regulation of all the local trade. Indeed, it is unlikely that the drapers ever took the leading part in the regulation of any trade other than that of cloth; and even if they did, it by no means alters the fact that gilds of ordinary local dealers, whether they included a group of merchants apart from the mercers or not had a place in almost all the boroughs and corporate towns.

If conditions in Beverley and Shrewsbury can be considered typical of those which prevailed in the other English boroughs, the relations existing between the drapers and the other dealers seem to have been far more harmonious where drapers retained their membership in the general mercantile society. The merchants of Beverley evidently refused to acknowledge the right of the drapers to monopolise the local trade in cloth. The merchants continued to handle that commodity and in 1572 forced the drapers,[54] in defence of their trade interests, to draw up a special ordinance, forbidding the "marchantes" under penalty of paying a certain fine, to "occupie within the town of Beverley buyinge and sellinge of any wollen clothe belonging to the Drapers crafte." Fully a century after the incorporation of the drapers of Shrewsbury they were waging war upon the mercers for presuming to deal in cloth, a commodity over which the drapers claimed to have sole control.

local "Counsaillours and Comyssoners" who decided that such shearmen as had bought Welsh cloth should be "Brethren of the seide crafte of drapers paying therefore as other forrens do." In this instance, however, it was rather as merchants who bought cloth than as handicraftsmen engaged in its manufacture that these Shrewsbury shearmen were admitted to membership in the drapers' gild. See The *Earliest Book of the Drapers' Company of Shrewsbury, Trans. Shropshire Archaeol. & Nat. Hist. Soc.*, 4th ser., vol. iii, p. 145, for the account of this controversy. True in 1566 the Shrewsbury drapers seem to have kept more than six hundred shearmen employed in dressing cloth before it was sent to the London market (8 Elisabeth, c. 7), but whether the shearmen thus employed belonged to the drapers' gild is a question. There was a gild of shearmen recorded in the borough as early as 1514. *Trans. Shropshire Archaeol. & Nat. Hist. Soc.*, vol. xi, p. 154. "Orders of the Corporation of Shrewsbury." Furthermore at a time when the drapers' gilds of Devizes and Kingston-upon-Thames held together different groups of the textile handicrafts, the gilds of mercers in their turn included also various other handicraft groups. On the whole it would seem that any control which the drapers exercised over local craftsmen was exerted altogether independently of their gild relations.

[54] *Beverley Town Documents (Selden Soc. Public.)*, p. 108.

And the judicial powers of both central and local executives were taxed severely in their efforts to determine the validity of the claims of these two groups of tradesmen to dominate the local cloth trade.[55] Again, at Chester after the linen-drapers had established a gild of their own, they came into conflict with city mercers for invading what those men claimed as their special territory. And from the trouble which the Chester municipality had to settle the points in dispute between her mercers and linen-drapers, we can well appreciate the wisdom of the policy of Bristol in encouraging within her borders the amalgamation of the men using those two trades. In many other communities we meet with accounts of friction between the mercers and some one or other group of traders. Indeed the mercers seem to have made themselves exceedingly unpopular with their neighbours by trading in any wares which brought them in a profit. In addition to many things sold at retail by small scales, such as spices and drugs, merceries seem to have included in the beginning haberdashery, silk,[56] various kinds of wearing apparel and cloth as well. Later they appear as extensive dealers in commodities like boots, gloves, caps, pins, and other articles.[57] Thus in the ordinary conduct of their daily business, mercers were naturally rivals of most of the other merchants, and they seem to have encroached at will upon their special rights, even in defiance of charters guaranteeing a monopoly to particular

[55] The mercers claimed the right both by custom and practice to carry on the trade in cloth. But a committee of the privy council appointed to consider the points at issue between the drapers and the mercers decided in favour of the drapers, on the ground that, as they said, "the trade of draperie by reason of the variety of clothes requires men of experience and that the mercers accordingly ought not to meddle." Mr. Unwin gives an account of this quarrel between the drapers and mercers of Shrewsbury based on evidence which he has obtained from the privy council registers. *Industrial Organisation*, p. 98. The drapers had a good deal of justification for the stand they took in the controversy. Their rights over the cloth trade had been early acknowledged. For instance, in the act of 1363 parliament had ordered drapers to "buy and purvey their sorts of cloth according to a stated price so that so great plenty of such cloths be made and set to sale in every city, borough, and merchant town and elsewhere within the Realm." 37 Edward I, 111, c. 15.

[56] *Harleian MSS., B. M.*, 2054, ff. 37–47. Seventeenth-century mercers of Chester evidently claimed the exclusive right to handle silk, a claim which the municipality approved in forbidding the linen-drapers to sell or even to "utter" for sale any silk or stuff having silk in it. *Ibid.*, ff. 66–72. By 1561 the London mercers held the retail dealers of other companies, more especially the grocers, guilty of handling silk goods, at a time when they sold not alone silk but "velvetts, sattens and damaskes" as well. Herbert, *Twelve Great Livery Cos.*, vol. i, p. 237.

How little regard local mercers showed for the rights of the handicrafts in whose wares they dealt, will be apparent in the study dealing with the conflict between the trades and handicrafts.

[57] A sixteenth-century mercers' bill still preserved in the Hereford archives shows the variety of articles in which such a tradesman dealt. The items enumerated include bombast, black thread, silk garters, "blew stockinges," leather "poyntes," English ribbon, silver fringe, and a "boton for the scarf." *Hereford Customs*, p. 144.

trades. It is little wonder that in these circumstances, municipal authorities encouraged the consolidation of local dealers.

In the seventeenth century when so many strangers were entering the towns the merchant gilds themselves adopted a common policy in order to retain control over the local trade. We have already noted how both Lichfield and Preston incorporated their mercantile companies expressly to prevent non-freemen from setting up in business or even from hawking their wares within the limits of the town.[58] Hawking was especially obnoxious to the medieval trader[59] and one of the most highly prized privileges of the mercers' societies, as we have seen in the case of the Nottingham gild in the fifteenth century, was that of regulating the sale of their wares by hawkers.[60] The Lichfield mercers' ordinances of 1623 specifically ordained that "no Milliner, Pedler, or Pettie Chapman or any other person whatsoever which doth not now dwell and inhabitt within the said Cittie (except he hath served seaven yeares apprentishipp dulie to some of this Com-

---

[58] See above, pp. 24–6. From Leicester in 1540 a petition was addressed to the chancellor of the duchy, calling his attention to the suffering entailed upon townsmen by the admission in the past of foreigners to a share in the retail trade in victuals, and asking him to obtain letters patent authorising them to exclude strangers thereafter from all retail trade. Half a century later the trouble again arose, and again the borough tried to restrain "artisantes and tradesmen of the countrie from retaylinge of their wares in Leicester except they will come and dwell in Leicester and become free burgesses thereof." In 1599 Elizabeth's charter to the townsmen contained a clause denying the right to any but freemen to use any trade or buy or sell other than in gross, except only in fair time, unless he were specially licensed by the mayor. *Records of the Borough,* vol. iii, pp. 43–44, 301.

[59] As early as 1398 we find the towns taking steps to stop traders from disposing of their wares in this fashion. In that year the court and community of Beverley ordered that no pedlar, "alien or denizen," should "thenceforth wander within the liberty for the purpose of selling or buying" goods, but that they should have "stalls in the Lord's open market at the time of selling their chattels and not elsewhere, under pain of imprisonment, and the loss of 6s. 8d. as often as any of them should be caught." *Hist. MSS. Comm. Beverley,* 1900, p. 70. In 1772 the Doncaster corporation preferred a petition to the county members begging them to use their influence in parliament to stop the licensing of hawkers and pedlars. *Records,* vol. iv, p. 243.

[60] According to an ordinance of the merchant gild of Kingston-upon-Hull registered in 1499, whoever "goth in the town abowte fro howse to howse in hawking with his merchandise shall forfeit and lose iii s. iiii d. as offten as he so shalbe founden and therwith taken." Lambert, *Two Thous. Years of Gild Life,* p. 159. In 1504 the London mercers issued an ordinance forbidding any person under their "obeisance" to sell or "deliver to any person any mercery ware which he knoweth to be an hawker a bearer about and a seller of the same within the Franchises of the City nor send nor envoy into the country to no chapman nor other to sell without it be first bought sold, bespoken, or sent for, and so accorded of the price without fraud or 'malengine' nor none other manner colour by which the Fellowship or secrets of the same in any wise may be hurt or discovered upon pain to pay to the Box . . . 5L." *Charters and Ordinances,* p. 67. In 1678 the Newcastle mercantile gild had little sympathy with "sojourners and such as had noe habitations in the towne." *The Merchant Adventurers of Newcastle-upon-Tyne, Surtees Soc. Pub.,* vol. 93, p. 223.

pany within this Cittie) shall not at any tyme herafter keepe any shopp booth or stall within this Cittie, but onelie in tyme of Faires," without the consent of the company.[61] Perpetual vigilance was needed to prevent non-residents from securing a share in the town's trade. In 1732 the Derby company of mercers [62] was still so determined to stop "those persons and others" who "have of late and do frequently expose goods to sail to the prejudice" of its members, that it promised to "indemnify whoever of the company shall be at any expence in prosecuting any such person or persons so offending." [63] Doubtless in many instances the more complex traders' associations originated in consequence of the influx of aliens in such constantly increasing numbers that the townsmen in a body had to join together in order to protect their interests. Circumstances called for decided action; hence the formation of the collective gilds of merchants.

We may conclude then, that these associated mercantile fraternities rose upon the dissolution of the gild merchant, the town traders as a body naturally succeeding to the mercantile rights which they had enjoyed in the palmy days of that organisation. Whereas at Shrewsbury the goldsmiths and ironmongers had become prominent members of the general mercantile fraternity established in that borough by 1424, at which date men engaged in various other occupations were also admitted, as early as 1370 the Bristol merchants, mercers, drapers, and other dealers found it to their advantage to form a union. Although we cannot say how long the men of Bristol kept up this organisation, or how many other merchant traders, such as the grocers, haberdashers, and their kindred, may gradually have followed their example and joined the general trading society, we have ample evidence that the traders in many other boroughs gradually combined. We can well understand why they did so. The number of simple mercers, or grocers, or haberdashers, or even drapers, would not be very great in an average town, and only by rallying to each other's support could merchants make a showing respectable enough to entitle them to a position of consequence among the other gilds.[64] We have every

---

[61] *Trans. Royal Hist. Soc.*, n. s., vol. vii, p. 121.

[62] *Derbyshire Arch. and Nat. Hist. Soc. Journ*, vol. xv, p. 143.

[63] Sometimes too, permission was conferred upon special gilds to protect themselves from this sort of competition. During the first quarter of the seventeenth century the London ironmongers were "at all times needful" to have the help of the Lord Maior or any officers "belonging to him" in the "apprehension of hawkers of wares of their trade in a hawking manner contrary to the custom" of the city "to seize all such deceitful wares and apprehend the bodies of such hawkers to be brought before the Lord Maior and disposed of as he shall see fit." Nicholl, *Hist. of The Ironmongers' Co.*, p. 197. In 1717 the drapers of St. Albans were given "power and liberty to prosecute all such pedlars and chapmen who sell in the Borough linen cloth, muslin, and such other goods belonging to the drapers' trade." *Corporation Records*, p. 108.

[64] Among the fifty members enrolled in the mercers' company of Derby in 1676, there were sixteen mercers, eight apothecaries, four grocers, twelve

reason to believe, for instance, that in the late sixteenth century the merchant company at Alnwick did not boast a membership of more than sixteen.[65] But however limited the number of gildsmen associated in these societies may have been, they never showed any great reluctance in assuming the responsibilities which devolved upon them. On the contrary, not content with their legitimate commercial privileges, they did not scruple, as we shall see, to deal in wares over which the various handicraftsmen claimed to have the monopoly, in spite of their vigorous protest. And when, in the course of time, the townsmen in the less considerable communities began to realise that they must work together if they hoped longer to protect the town's trade from the invasion of alien merchants and itinerant artisans, both traders and handicraftsmen forgot their personal jealousies and joined together in forming one great body corporate. By so doing they could still dominate the local economic situation.

In attempting to account for the amalgamations in which the haberdashers figured apart from the general trading societies, we are at the outset at a great disadvantage, since, apart from the evidence furnished by the records of the London company, we have very little material upon which to base any definite conclusions. The London haberdashers are usually spoken of as an offshoot of the mercers, who had taken over the latter's small-ware business.[66] For a long time they remained isolated, though the grocers had much earlier shown them the advantages of consolidation. However, in the seventeenth year of the reign of King Henry VII, the haberdashers formed an alliance with the hatters and cappers or "hurers" as they were then designated, two crafts which not long before appear to have combined their forces. The three groups of tradesmen secured a royal charter incorporating them under the style of the Fraternity of Merchant Haberdashers in the City of London.[67] The haberdashers at this epoch seem to have been chiefly engaged in the sale of hats, caps and head gear generally,[68]

ironmongers, and single representatives of most of the other trades. *Derby-shire Archaeol. & Nat. Hist. Soc. Journ.,* vol. xv, p. 137. In 1702 there were only twenty-three names enrolled in the membership list of the Bristol mercers' company. *Bristol & Gloucestershire Archaeol. Soc. Trans.,* vol. 26, pt. ii, p. 288.

[65] Tate, *History of Alnwick,* vol. ii, p. 321.

[66] We get an interesting glimpse into the different kinds of ware offered for sale in 1376 by haberdashers from an extant record of a London shop. They were extremely miscellaneous, including apparently every kind of fancy article then known, not only of wearing apparel, such as fancy laces, beads, painted cloth, girdles, various sorts of caps and coats, but also purses, spurs, and iron chains as well. There were also different kinds of writing utensils, such as ink horns, pen cases, quires of paper, and skins of parchment; and other articles made of wood, such as boxes, whistles, and gaming tables. There was even a fly cage, which could be hung up as an ornament. Riley, *Memorials of London,* p. 422.

[67] Brewer, *Letters & Papers of King Henry VIII,* no. 1317.

[68] In King Henry VIII's days, individual haberdashers of London were

so that it was natural for them to attach to themselves the hatters [69] and the cappers.[70] But by 1517, within fifteen years of their incorporation, the haberdashers were denounced as the "riche men" who were "reson" upon the "distruction of the pore people." They were held accountable for the miserable condition to which many of the London artificers had been reduced. A contemporary writer, who designates the haberdashers as "a sorte" who "beganne to occupie to bye and selle alle soche handycraft wares," says that until they appeared upon the scene "pore handycraft peple, which that wer wont to kepe shoppes and servaunts and hadd labour and levying by makyng pyns, poynts, girdells, glovis, and all such other thyngs necessary for comon peple, hadd thereof sale and profits daily." [71] But the haberdashers did not rest content even with interfering with the "pore handycraft peple"; in the early sixteenth century, when felt hats began to be extensively made in England, they endeavoured to control that industry as well. In doing this, however, they came into conflict with the feltmakers, a strong body of artisans, whose business was that of making felt hats, and who resisted the encroachment of the merchant haberdashers upon their special field of industry. The feltmakers were at a decided disadvantage, not only because, as they said, they had no "government of themselves as other companies have," but also because they were denied any effectual representation in the haberdashers' company. As merchant traders the haberdashers' chief interest lay in forwarding the distributing branch of the hat business, while the working feltmakers naturally looked after the manufacturing part of it.[72] The relations between the two groups grew more and more

being licenced to import French, Milanese and other caps, and "Brugges" hats as well. *Ibid.*, no. 5239.

[69] In order to insure to the public properly made hats, city haberdashers and hatters proposed that three or four men chosen from their ranks be authorised to make diligent search for "false" hats, and to submit any they should so find to the judgment of the mayor and his associates at the Guildhall. Riley, *op. cit.*, p. 90. In the early fifteenth century the haberdashers and the hatters were evidently on much better terms with one another than with city cappers as appears from a complaint voiced to the mayor by officials of the first-named groups, that the officers of the cappers had seized "longe cappes" belonging to a haberdasher, an action which they said was unwarranted because the right of search touching false "cappes, hures or hattes" belonged of old to men of the mystery of hatters and haberdashers as well as of cappers. *Letter Book*, I, p. 176.

[70] That the haberdashers elsewhere concerned themselves with the sale of hats and caps is evident from an order issued by the mercers' and drapers' company of Reading—which included local haberdashers—to the effect that no haberdasher "except he be a freeman" might sell hats or caps by retail within the borough. Walford, *Gilds*, p. 90.

[71] *A Treatise concerninge the Staple and the Commodities of this Realme*, in Pauli's *Drei Volkswirthschaftliche Denkschriften*, p. 39.

[72] This is well illustrated by what occurred when, as a compromise, the haberdashers and feltmakers were given joint authority to search all foreign wools. The feltmakers soon complained that the haberdashers "have not used" the search "because the chiefest and most part of the merchants that bringeth in and the ingrossers of the said wools are haberdashers." Unwin, *Industrial Organization*, pp. 131–5.

strained, inasmuch as the haberdashers, in spite of the feltmakers' protests, persisted in asserting their rights. The feltmakers at last made formal application to the crown for a charter which should confer upon them alone full authority to regulate their own craft.[73]

So far as we can judge from the scanty particulars which the smaller towns have left us of the associations which the haberdashers formed with the local hatters, cappers, and feltmakers, the local authorities seem not to have had quite the same difficulty to contend with. They adopted from the start a safer means of preserving harmony among these various occupations by associating them apparently on a more equal footing. The union of haberdashers, cappers, and feltmakers at Exeter, and that of haberdashers and feltmakers at Bristol, seemed to have been formed with some such end in view.[74] In this way the commercial privileges of both trade and craft were doubtless more equally balanced and their separate economic interests better protected. At Andover, in the early seventeenth century, the haberdashers had the distinction of giving their name to the all-inclusive mercantile fraternity, one of the three gild organisations then sanctioned within the borough precincts. In establishing the haberdashers' company the authorities naturally had to group many different trades with the general merchants, and, of course, in such a conglomeration of trades there could no longer be any insistence upon careful gild regulation. Indeed, from the meagre record which the haberdashers have left—and they seem to have been alone among the three companies in giving any account of the local conditions which led the townsmen to institute these trade corporations—we infer that all that the town and trades still hoped for was to keep up some show of gild existence, as their ancestors had done long before in

---

[73] Not quite seven years after they had become "a trade and company of themselves" the feltmakers still had cause to complain of being "kept under by the haberdashers ingrossing the Commodeyte of woolls brought in merely for their trade of hatmaking and for noe other use, and by that means haveing both the meanes of the feltmakers trade (for woolls) and the meanes of their maintenance (for bueying their wares being made) all in their power, by which the feltmakers . . . doe fynd 'themselves much wronged and by meanes of yt and their daily threates did feare the overthrowe of their trade." Unwin, *Ibid.,* p. 240.

[74] The members of the Bristol company of haberdashers and feltmakers seem to have agreed as to the way in which they should conduct the affairs of their company. For example, in 1611 they permitted foreigners to sell hats and caps in the city on one day in the week after the wares had been approved by the company and upon the payment of a toll of threepence a dozen for hats and one penny for caps. Latimer, *Annals of Bristol in the seventeenth century,* p. 26. In 1568 the records of Chester account for a company of skinners and haberdashers paying its assessment towards the construction of the quay and a little over a century later for one of skinners and feltmakers, the later company being concerned lest its members countenance the binding of their apprentices to the haberdashers' trade. *Journal Chester & North Wales Archaeological & Historic Society,* n. s., vol. 21, pp. 126, 113. At York, in 1591 the cappers, it seems, were "joyned to the hatters, haberdashers and feltmakers." *Memorandum Book,* ii, p. 283.

the days of Henry III; for he, they claimed, had originally granted to the townsmen the privilege of having a "guild of merchants." [75]

Thus, all that we can truly say about these haberdashers' associations is that they included the hatters, cappers, and, outside of London, in most instances, as may be gathered from Bristol, Exeter, and Kendal, the feltmakers as well. These amalgamations seem to have been formed largely to advance the common business interests of their members, which centred chiefly in the sale of hats and caps. And from the discord which arose between the London haberdashers and the feltmakers we can easily comprehend the advantages which the provincial cities and towns secured for themselves by encouraging these two occupations to combine their forces.

The associations entered into by the drapers and tailors form a second group which may be considered in connexion with the merchant companies. So close was the relation which these two trades bore to each other that civic officials were often much exercised to keep them distinct. Thus at one time the mayor of London went the length of disfranchising a citizen "for using drapery he being a tailor." [76] But it was practically impossible to separate the two trades. Both the drapers and the tailors had been accustomed to sell cloth by retail, and to judge from acts of parliament they continued to do so through succeeding centuries. [77] It was especially fitting that the drapers and tailors should yield to the general impulse towards amalgamation, and so secure for themselves the advantages attaching to the system. Even though the two trades in London did not unite their gilds, they demonstrated the closeness of their business interests by working together to further them on more than one occasion. [78] If the companies of

[75] See the preamble of the "Ordinances of the Guild of Merchants in Andever in the County of Southampton, which Guild is divided into three several Fellowships whereof these are only of the Fellowship of Haberdashers," reciting how King Henry III had incorporated the men of Andover, otherwise called the approved men of Andover, by letters patent, and by the same letters had granted to them, among other things, "a guild of merchants." *Wiltshire Archaeol. and Nat. Hist. Soc. Mag.*, vol. xxi, p. 306.

[76] Herbert, *Twelve Great Livery Companies*, vol. i, p. 30, note.

[77] The statute 5 and 6 Edward VI, c. 6, speaks of the "Draper, Merchaunt-taylor, Clothworker, or other person whiche shall retayle anye of the Clothes . . . aforesaid." In 4 Henry VII, c. 8, we read of the "Drapers & Taylours and other in the Citee of London and other places wythin this Reame that usen to sell wollen clothe at retail by the yerdys, sellen a yerde of cloth at excessive price." As early as 1347 the Bristol tailors were complaining that others who used their craft sold and bought new cloth. Therefore in claiming in Charles II's time the right to engage in the trade in cloth they were fully confirmed in their rights by ancient usage. See Fox and Taylor, *Merchant Taylors of Bristol*, p. 87.

[78] In Edward IV's day the officers of the London drapers and merchant taylors exercised joint powers of search over all the cloth which was brought to the fairs of St. Bartholomew and Southwark, cloth being the great commodity sold at both these fairs. Herbert, *Twelve Great Livery Companies*, vol. i, p. 427. The united efforts of these two companies are said to have kept the local shearmen from securing royal incorporation until the sixteenth century. *Report of the Livery Companies Comm.*, 1884, pt. ii, p. 674.

the city thus acknowledged their interdependence, it is not surprising that the provincial gilds went a step further and made their unions permanent. Even York found it expedient to combine the two trades,[79] and as late as the fourteenth year of the reign of King Charles II the united company of drapers and tailors was exhibiting considerable activity in trying to maintain its standard of workmanship in the sphere allotted to it.[80]

That it was to the manifest interest of the community to have the drapers and tailors working in harmony is demonstrated by the Chester records.[81] There in Elizabeth's reign the drapers and hosiers were allowed to unite,[82] while the tailors kept to their own gild. This arrangement was not altogether successful. Eventually the tailors delivered to the authorities "the Quenes Majesties wryt of monition" which had authorised them "to suppresse and put downe all those drapers who use and trade their occupacion." Thereupon the authorities sent for the stewards of the drapers and "enjoyned them and all others of their occupacion" at no time thereafter to "exercise, use, nor occupy in cutting nor sowinge of any garment or other thing which merely doth or ought to belonge or appertaigne to the occupacion of tailors aforesaid," proceeding with the clause, "untill the said drapers have duly and orderly proved that it is and shalbe lafull for them so to doe." It is not stated whether the drapers took up the challenge or meekly submitted. Elsewhere the drapers were certainly not subdued.[83] In Reading, as we have

---

[79] The York drapers and taylors asked for a royal charter in that year, because, as they said, being not incorporated, they were not able to make and put in execution any by-laws for the well ordering of their respective trades and for the punishment of those of their number who daily committed offences against the company. *Addit. MS. B. M.,* f. 8935.

[80] They engaged, "if the wares be adjudged base and unserviceable so that any penalty be due to the King or the master, wardens, and assistants, to deliver one moiety to the King's Receiver-general for use of his Majesty and half to be kept by the Company." *Municip. Corp. Comm. Rep., 1835,* p. 1765.

[81] Morris, *Chester,* p. 436. The tailors in their turn occasionally headed a small association with some craft other than the drapers. The company of tailors and hosiers formed in 1580 in Winchester asked for incorporation because, as they said, "there were those who come into the city, take houses, set up the mysteries . . . at divers quick times of work and against high feasts while others again carried on their labours in closets, inns, alehouses, and other secret places within the city." All of these, they go on to explain, "do depart from this said city afterwards . . . to the great hindrance and utter undoing of tailors and hosiers." Bailey, *Transcripts,* p. 36.

[82] By 1570 a company composed of "Marchant Drapers" and hosiers evidently held it to be prejudicial to its interests when non-members sold "woollen Cloathes." *Harleian MS.* no. 1996.

[83] That the business of drapers, taylors and hosiers overlapped considerably is illustrated in the case of Beverley. There one of the ordinances drawn up by the company of merchants and mercers in 1492, which at that date still included the drapers, expressly required that every member of the drapers' craft dwelling in the town should "be free to fit, sew, and make hose in his shop and to have a boy or apprentice to keep his shop without payment of any contribution to the tailors' craft." Beverley, *Town Documents,* p. 75. The Beverley drapers and tailors, to all appearances, never adopted amal-

seen, they were influential enough to give their name in company with the mercers to the large trading corporation established in the late sixteenth century as the chief of the five local companies; but they took good care at the same time to protect their immediate commercial rights by inserting in the company's by-laws the provision that neither the mercers nor the tailors should retail cloth or women's hose.[84] Rye also upheld the monopoly of her company of drapers and tailors by confirming their ordinance that "none should occupy the mystery or occupation either of woollen-draper or tailor within the said town other than such as had either been apprenticed with one of the said company, or being freeborn, should first make agreement with the said company."[85] The drapers and tailors at Northampton[86] also found it to their mutual advantage to unite, as we learn, "as well for the expelling owte of Forrayners, as for the good government of their said companyes and the common weall of her Majesties loving subjects." Before long, however, they had to make their "humble requeste for the renewing" of "their seide constitutions and orders," on the ground that these were "nowe frustrated and voyde"; and it was promised that their constitutions should be "of force and so contynued as other constitutions within the same town."

It was not everywhere that consolidation worked smoothly. At

gamation as a means of settling their trade differences. As a consequence, in 1494 the twelve governors of the town were called upon to decide as to the merits of the claims of these two groups of traders to use cloth in their daily work. The drapers seem to have profited most materially by the town's intervention at that date, by securing permission to exact a fine of 2s. 4d. from every tailor "who should buy and sell cloth by retail . . . beyond four marks a year." The drapers were also to be free to make gaiters, women's boots, and "le soles" without being called upon to contribute to the tailors' gild, although if "they should make any other clothes" they were to pay 2s. a year. *Rep. Hist. MSS. Comm., Beverley*, p. 105.

[84] Walford, *Gilds*, p. 90.

[85] *Hist. MSS. Comm. Rep.*, xiii, app. iv, p. 59. In 1574 the Warwick gild of drapers and tailors besought "Mr. Bailiff" and the principal burgesses "please to reforme their book of the said occupacions especially in·making the somes of composicion of straungers greater, which was graunted together with other reformacions and addicions." One of these "other reformacions" provided that "no forrener whether he dwell in the towne or out of the towne which before this tyme or at this present is not admytted as one of the company of drapers or taylors of this borough although he have bene admyttid to sett upp . . . within this borough or suburbs until he have agreid and compoundid with the maister and wardens of the said arts or misteryes upon payne of forfeit for eury day so dooing 10 shillings." *Black Book*, pp. 117-20.

[86] *Borough Records*, vol. ii, p. 295. In 1588 we find the Windsor corporation adopting measures to restrain foreigners from practising these two trades within the town. In that year it declared that certain "Taylors and Drapers" should have "agreement under the Towne seale" that "no forrainer of that occupation shall be admitted into the freedom of the Towne hereafter without their consents, they paying yearely to the Maiors owne use ten shillings." Tighe and Davis, *Annals of Windsor*, vol. i, p. 652. In 1541 the tailors and drapers of Sandwich together agreed to rebuild Newgate. Boys, *Sandwich*, p. 685.

Oxford,[87] for instance, in 1569 the city council permitted the tailors and woollen-drapers to form an alliance; yet within a few years it had to admonish them "that upon all controversyes happeninge in or aboute the occupations or corporacion of taylors and drapers, eyther betwene the Cittie and them or emongst themselves," which should come to their knowledge, they should be "wholly therein at the order and ponishment of the maior and his successors." Even this warning did not have the desired effect, for on 9 September, 1572, the gild of tailors and drapers was summarily dissolved; the drapers incorporated their interests with the mercers, leaving the tailors to shift for themselves.[88] On the other hand, impending dissolution was sometimes averted. In 1601 the Tewkesbury drapers, tailors, and dyers, after having held together for years in one gild, had a disagreement which threatened to break it up for ever. Thereupon the corporation encouraged them to reunite, and ordered that henceforth "they should be reputed and allowed to be one companie," to be known as "the fellowshipp of drapers, dyers, and taylors of the burrough of Tewkesburie." [89] Very often the domineering drapers and tailors lost their distinct identity entirely, and had to be content with a more or less subordinate position in one of the miscellaneous combinations of trades which were formed in many of the smaller towns. The Devizes company of drapers and tailors, which in 1565 was still one of the more important of the local gilds, ceased to be independent in 1614; for at that time the local magnates apparently deemed three organisations sufficient. Possibly they gratified the drapers by permitting them to give their name to the large society which they then headed.[90]

In uniting with the tailors, or for that matter, with the hosiers, the drapers were but making a virtue of what must in many cases have become a necessity in view of the close identification of the business interests of these occupations. The evil results of the antagonistic attitude assumed by the Chester tailors towards the

---

[87] Turner, *Records of Oxford*, p. 333.

[88] The following June the mercers and drapers had their "booke" properly "engrossed and sealed," after having provided "for the suffycyent auctorytye of the Mayor for the time beinge to order and reforme all complaynts and contencyons;" to the steward they paid "a resonable fee for the same." This late bringing together of the mercers and drapers seems to have been a return to the earlier arrangement, when those two trades had naturally drifted into the same gild. Turner, op. cit., p. 348.

[89] Bennett, *History of Tewkesbury*, p. 199. In 1654, because the tailors belonging to the "companie of Drap's and tailors" of Pontefract "doe exact excessive rates," the borough authorities determined the rates thereafter to be paid master tailors, their journeymen and apprentices. *Booke of Entries*, p. 19. In 1668 the Ripon authorities granted a set of ordinances to the company of drapers, dyers, apothecaries, and barber surgeons, "to the intent that the said company . . . as they have heretofore of ancient time been shall be henceforth altogether one company and brotherhood:" *Millenary Record*, p. 49.

[90] *Wiltshire Archaeol. and Nat. Hist. Soc. Mag.*, vol. iv, pp. 160–62.

drapers proved how advantageous it was to a community to let them amalgamate, if for no other reason than to put an end to trade rivalry. The situation which prevailed in Rye and Northampton illustrates the need of concerted action in order successfully to keep struggling outsiders from securing any share in the local trade. On the other hand, the Oxford records testify that neither the prospect of doing away altogether with commercial rivalry, nor of preventing aliens from trading in the town, were strong enough inducements to influence these two groups of cloth dealers to settle their commercial feuds by sacrificing their independent organisations. In smaller boroughs, such as Devizes, the drapers and tailors, in common with the rest of their fellow-townsmen, relinquished their gild independence only when all the trades had to unite in forming a limited number of gild groups in order to keep up some semblance of gild existence.

III

THE CAUSES OF THE AMALGAMATION OF THE HANDICRAFTS

In the industrial world there were any number of kindred handicrafts which trenched so closely upon one another's sphere that it became practically impossible for the most zealous advocates of a division of labour to keep them separate. Throughout the latter part of the fourteenth century the London authorities attempted to confine different crafts to their own work. For instance, in 1371, they bound the "reputable men of the trade of bowyers" and "of the trade of fletchers" to see that "for the profit and advantage of all the commonalty . . . no man of the one trade shall meddle with the other trade in any part."[1] We do not know how long these mediaeval bow and arrow-makers succeeded in isolating their respective callings. But the existence of a sixteenth-century record of an amalgamated gild comprising both bowyers and fletchers proves that, by that time, they had found it expedient to join gild forces. Bowyers and fletchers of other communities probably came to terms at an earlier date. By 1428 a combined gild of Beverley bowyers and fletchers was exacting tribute from non-members who concerned themselves with the making of new bows, clubs, arrows and other articles, which, in the judgment of the gild "properly belonged to the aforesaid crafts."[2] By 1475 the bowyers and fletchers of Chester[3] seem to have supported a joint gild and there were doubtless similar associations in the more important cities and boroughs of the land.[4]

Sooner or later in almost every sphere of industry kindred crafts entered into association following years of effort directed toward keeping separate the individual interests of each. In this connexion the history of the union entered into by the London armourers and braziers is interesting and illuminating as an expla-

[1] Riley, *Memorials of London,* p. 348. During the reign of Queen Elizabeth these bowyers and arrow-makers dissolved their corporation and established separate gilds. This procedure was so unorthodox as to be beyond the comprehension of their contemporary chronicler, who, for his part could see "small reason" for "sundering bows from arrows." He concluded, however, that "since they had divided themselves into two several companies" the fault was "on their own heads," and so he "leaves them," as he claims he "found" them. Stow, *Survey of London,* vol. ii, p. 217. Also Herbert, *Twelve Great Livery Companies,* vol. i, p. 175.
[2] *Historical MSS. Commis. Report, Beverley,* p. 98.
[3] Morris, *Chester,* p. 572.
[4] Drake, *Eboracum,* vol. i, p. 322.

nation for the creation of similar bodies elsewhere. By the early fifteenth century the armourers, who were occupied in making armour and various other kinds of weapons, had become a well-defined gild group endowed with the corporate privileges usual to the period. In process of time, however, the armourers found their business gradually slipping from them and in consequence they were obliged to extend their sphere of operations to copper and brass work generally. In doing this they invaded the special province of city braziers, a separate body of gildsmen who about 1479 seem also to have attained to corporate rank. After an inevitable period of conflict, apparently of longer duration than any yet considered, the armourers and braziers agreed to combine their forces. This combination seems to have been effected largely through the efforts of the armourers who petitioned good Queen Anne for a charter on behalf of themselves and of other workers in copper and brass in the city, giving as their reason that of late years many of their members who had employed themselves in making vessels and wares of copper and brass wrought with the hammer, had come to be called "braziers" and for want of more ample powers of search had been committing great fraud in the making of the ware.[5] Even at that late date, the fusion of the two handicrafts still formed the most satisfactory method of putting an end to the rivalry which seemed inevitable between craftsmen who competed for the same business. Combination enabled both sets of workmen to subscribe to a common policy which should govern them alike in the conduct of each department, of their industry.

The time came when brewers could not be deterred from baking even though they had never been apprenticed to that calling "nor so laufully servid . . . as they thereby maie justlie challenge to use the said occupation of bakeinge to the utter ympoverishment" of the bakers [6] and consequently they were encouraged to join forces with the bakers for the common good.[7] The bakers and brewers of Boston were licensed in 1569 "to be a commonaltie

---

[5] *Report Munic. Corporat. Commis.,* 1837, vol. 25, pp. 110–111.

[6] Some boroughs went so far as to make the baking of white bread and of black two distinct crafts. Thus, in 1393, Canterbury required the bakers of white bread to swear under pain of a severe penalty to bake no black bread and the bakers of black bread to bake no white. *Archaeologia,* vol. 31, p. 205. In the days of the Tudors the city of London prohibited bakers of white bread and of brown from uniting their corporate forces. In fact at that time the authorities had nullified letters patent which the bakers of white bread had secured from the Lords of the Council sanctioning their union with bakers of brown bread, on the ground that by ancient orders of the city, bakers of both varieties of bread had been two distinct occupations. And to enable them to be kept apart, the authorities besought the Council to allow them to deal with such matters in future as they had in the past. *Index to the Remembrancia,* p. 91.

[7] The bakers of Rye brought this accusation against local brewers who, they said, "oughte by the lawes of this realme not to be bakers also." *Hist. MSS. Com., Rye,* p. 47.

of themselves for their maintenance and good order," which may be taken as testimony to the fact that neither object had been attained when each group was arrayed against the other.[8] Not that amalgamation necessarily kept local bakers and brewers on friendly terms. The bakers and brewers of Newcastle-upon-Tyne had been associated in a common gild at least from the time of Queen Elizabeth, and yet in 1661 their meetings were disturbed because one brother struck another with his fist or any other weapon he had at hand.[9] There was apt to be trouble in a town, too, when the victuallers or alehouse-keepers made a business of baking or brewing contrary to the custom prevalent in the Kingdom which looked to those crafts to buy their bread and beer from the common bakers and brewers. As late as the reign of King Charles II, the borough of Marlborough endeavoured to revive this custom which it seems "consequent upon the late troubles" several local victuallers had had the temerity to disregard by offering for sale bread and beer of their own making.[10] In fact as early as the seventh year of the reign of King Richard II, the borough of Northampton passed an ordinance prohibiting innkeepers from baking bread of any sort to sell in inns under penalty of paying a fine of twenty shillings as often as they should contravene the ordinance.[11] During Tudor times because "divers' franchised mens' wifes . . . called Tipplers" were baking white bread to sell "against ancient statutes and ordinances of the Common Baker . . . to the utter destruction of the occupations," the York bakers besought the city council "to make full order and direction for the maintenance of the sayd occupations." [12] Innkeepers and ale-sellers of Chester of this period begged in future to be protected from such "vexations" as they had been subjected to in the past when the brewers [13] sold ale and beer which they had also brewed.[14] The problem of

---

[8] Thompson, *History of Boston*, p. 159. The two callings were probably united at Leicester in 1591, because the man who became the mayor of the borough in that year was known to be a "baker and a common brewer." Nichols, *History of the County of Leicester*, vol. i, pt. ii, p. 406.

[9] Brand, *History of Newcastle-upon-Tyne*, vol. ii, pp. 316–7.

[10] Waylen, *History of Marlborough*, p. 330. At Stratford-upon-Avon in 1595 an order was issued warning local innholders and others of their sort to "fatche" their ale and beer from the "comen ale bruers upon peyne that everie one that shall do contrarye to this order shall be utterly suppressed and put downe." *Council-Book*, p. 90. At Evesham in 1614, by an order which emanated from the mayor's court, victuallers and alehouse-keepers were not to brew beer or ale but were to "have the same of the common brewers assigned" for the purpose. Gibbs, *History of Aylesbury*, p. 123.

[11] *Liber Custumarum*, p. 56.

[12] *Archaeological Review*, vol. i, p. 133.

[13] *Harleian MSS., B. M.*, no. 1996, f. 34.

[14] At Kingston-upon-Hull, brewers, bakers and innholders alike concerned themselves to keep members of one group from interfering with the business of the others. Thus in the days of Queen Mary, persons "having and occupying other good and sufficient trades to lyve appone . . . beynge not expert in exhercysing" the occupation of "Berbruying" were to refrain from using it. "Inholder or alehousekeeper or other inhabitants" were not to bake "any

isolating the victualling crafts seems to have been further complicated by the fact that town officials themselves handled foodstuffs. For instance, in 1531, aldermen of Oxford were guilty of using not one but often two or even more of the victualling crafts.[15] The practice grew so flagrant, finally, as to force the town council to forbid townsmen under any consideration to "usse II occupations of vytlelyng crafts, that ys to say a baker and a brewer, a bocher and a brewer, a brewer and a innholder, a brewer and a fyshemonger, nither baker and fyshemonger, nor noe dobyll vytlelyng craftes, but to leve one of the same vytlelyng craftes" or forfeit the surety which each alderman had to pay into the town treasury when he entered upon his duties.

The carpenters and joiners of many communities found it to their interest to amalgamate.[16] Thus, in 1579, by-laws which constituted the two groups in Newcastle-upon-Tyne a "body corporate of themselves," specified the work which the joiners alone should undertake as well as those which the two crafts might use in common.[17] By 1692 the carpenters and joiners' gild of Worcester contrived to secure for its members upon equally advantageous terms, the timber which they required for their business.[18] In

kinde of bread to sell againe" unless they were free of the company of "bakeres." Bakers in their turn, were neither to "keep any Inn or Hostry or take in any Horses into their Houses or precincts thereof," nor to "harbour or lodge any Guests of whom they shall take money for their victuals." Lambert, *Two Thousand Years of Gild Life*, pp. 303–6. The frequency with which the borough of Shrewsbury threatened to admit into the liberties, dealers from adjoining country districts unless local bakers, brewers and butchers conformed to the community's rules regulating these occupations, shows that the local victualling crafts were extremely belligerent. *Shrop. Archaeol. & Nat. Hist. Soc. Trans.*, vol. xi, pp. 172, 209.

[15] Turner, *Selections from the Records*, p. 107.

[16] The state at an early date declared itself opposed to the amalgamation of builders. During the reign of King Edward III alliances and "covins" between masons and carpenters were forbidden. As late as 1517 the daubers and masons of Coventry were denied the right to combine. Harris, *Life in an Old English Town*, p. 279.

[17] *Archaeologia Aeliana*, 3rd series, vol. 5, p. 170. Joiners were to work at the "sealing of houses within"; to make "dorments and windows . . . drawn tables of frame-work . . . buffet-stools . . . forms . . . cupboards . . . pressers . . . chairs and scones of frame-work . . . casements" and to engage in all other kinds of work usually delegated to joiners. The two handicrafts had in common various undertakings, such as the making of "buttries," of "chists for corpses," and other chests not "pinned with wood." They could together remove beds, cupboards and draw-tables, as well as construct doors and windows and other articles of a like nature.

[18] Smith, *English Gilds*, p. 208. A civic ordinance issued in that year decreed that "if any freeman of the said company shall buy any parcell of Timber or Boards that come to the city . . . to be sold . . . fitt for the said crafts or either of them, that then it shall be lawfull for every one of them "to have a Share therein, not exceeding one third part thereof, upon request and paying ready money for the same after the rate of the said timber and boards were bought." Any member who should refuse to share or divide such timber or boards "contrary to the intent of this Article shall forfeit for every such refusall twenty shillings."

1714, a Boston company protected the interests of its members by forbidding strangers to ply either craft within borough precincts.[19] The joiners of London, however, preferred seemingly to throw in their gild lot with city carvers, an arrangement which may have redounded to the benefit of joiners and carvers, but entailed considerable trouble upon the city when the interests of joiners and carpenters clashed.[20] However, that joiners could sometimes work more advantageously with carvers than with carpenters seems evident from the history of the relations which developed between these handicrafts in Chester. In that city, sometime during the early years of Queen Elizabeth, the joiners and carvers, who had the transporting to Ireland and other lands beyond the seas, frames, cupboards, chests, trestles and other articles which they manufactured, found it expedient to amalgamate their gild interests [21] not only with local carpenters or wrights as they were then called, but with sawyers and slaters as well. Union with these three groups of handicrafts failed, apparently, to give the joiners and carvers free enough play for their energies and in 1576 they concluded to withdraw from it. Accordingly, they appeared one day before the city assembly charging "certain persons of other occupations" with intermeddling with their business and asked that the union they had formed with the wrights, sawyers and slaters be dissolved and in its place, they be given a charter which would enable them jointly to control the city's timber business. The joiners and carvers offered the city a certain sum for this privilege and in addition promised to supply timber to citizens more cheaply thereafter. About twenty years earlier, the joiners and carvers had been expressly forbidden to buy any timber except that which they needed "for their own occupying." However, the inducement the craftsmen offered the city assembly at this time probably helped their cause, for before another three years had passed that body was lending the weight of its authority toward upholding the right of the joiners and carvers to monopolise the sale of timber in Chester.[22] A combine which limited its membership to joiners and

---

[19] Thompson, *Boston*, p. 159.

[20] The wrangles of the London carpenters and joiners enlivened considerably the city's seventeenth-century gild annals. Jupp, *History of the Carpenters' Company*, pp. 265, 304–5. In fact, the only time during that period when the two groups appear to have been on friendly terms was when they worked together to prevent the incorporation of local sawyers. *Ibid.*, p. 307. In 1606 we find the joiners' gild of Bristol fining carpenters who presumed to do joiners' work. Latimer, *17th Century Annals*, p. 25. The carpenters and joiners of Kingston-upon-Hull contrived to maintain separate organisations but each group took care to designate the territory beyond which the other should not presume to step. Smith, *English Gilds*, pp. 257–9.

[21] Morris, *Chester*, pp. 403, 405. These joiners and carvers had prospered exceedingly in their undertakings, having it is said "greatly enriched themselves" although "the citizens were therein unserved."

[22] It was to the advantage of the joiners and carvers to gather up timber as they came across it on their journeying. Otherwise outsiders might have secured the raw material they needed and charged them an exorbitant price for it.

carvers doubtless served better to protect a monopoly in the developing than one open to groups interested in other handicrafts.

Then, too, not alone the peace but the welfare of the towns often called for the amalgamation of rival handicrafts as the history of the marshals and smiths of York seems to prove. In the early fifteenth century, these two handicrafts supported separate gilds, although it seems they "were many days and years in variance and either crafte troubled the other and yearly took and held distress of the other, so that many years mayor and the chamber was hugely vexed with them." The trouble began apparently when the "smyths" asked the marshals who occupied the smiths' craft and "had thereof the most part of their living" to help pay towards the support of their pageant. This the marshals refused to do, saying that certain smiths in their turn "wrought and sold diverse things pertinent to the marshals" craft and for that reason they ought to pay to the marshals "pageant silver." [23] Eventually the craftsmen settled the difficulty by combining their mysteries and so contributed jointly toward the support of the celebration of the Corpus Christi festival, one of the most important civic duties then devolving upon the gilds. Here seems to be an important justification for the early amalgamation of the English crafts. The Corpus Christi celebration was a civic undertaking and the crafts were obliged to share between them the burden of its support. If the single gilds could not or would not voluntarily do so they were forced by the municipalities to affiliate and meet the obligation between them. Thereafter the York marshals and smiths had an equal interest in upholding the rules and regulations governing their common gild. In the beginning the trend of the times had been towards effecting a rigid division of labour, and marshals and smiths along with other crafts had probably erected separate gilds. But it is evident that the most rigid gild supervision could not prevent marshals from doing smith's work and vice versa. Even London found it difficult to keep these handicrafts distinct, the local farriers in 1356 vehemently denouncing "those who kept forges in the city and intermeddled with the works of farriery by reason whereof many horses had been lost to the great damage of the people." [24] In continuing to insist upon the separation of local marshals and smiths, the authorities of York apparently only stored up trouble for the city. As they soon discovered it was more profitable to all parties concerned to encourage the two factions to identify their gild interests.

It seems to have been equally advantageous for the mediaeval communities to have the barber surgeons merge their gild interests. At York, in 1486, we find the members of those two professions pledging themselves "to be trusty and true unto the King . . . to this City . . . and also to the Science of Barbers and

[23] *The Antiquary,* vol. ii, p. 105.
[24] Riley, *Memorials of London,* p. 292.

Chirurgions within the same." In addition they entered into an agreement not only to keep all the customs which had been in vogue in the practice of their professions, but to obey the laws drawn up by the associated gild, to guard its secrets and respect its councils. Individual gildsmen pledged themselves never to intrude into the presence of a brother while he was attending a patient who had been wounded, unless he were especially requested to do so. The barbers were neither to "powle, trim or shave" a brother's customer, until "such time as the said brother be fully contented and paid." [25] Furthermore, not content merely to specify the duties which individual members might perform, the gild concerned itself to prevent itinerant vendors of drugs from disposing of their wares within city limits. Two years later the surgeons and barbers of Canterbury wanted "to have gode rules and orders . . . wherby they myght increace and floryshe in welth and pspite as other cyteis and townys doth yn whome soche gode rules and orders ar executyd." [26] In the later years of Queen Elizabeth, the barber-surgeons of Windsor agreed to pay annually to the city a specified sum of money provided that, without their consent, no foreigner were admitted to the freedom of the borough.[27] The ordinances of the barber-surgeons of Norwich, who, according to their records, had established their company "anciently and time whereof the memory of man hath not been to the contrary" had become obsolete by 1648 "for want of use" or defective "for want of well penning and framing"; whereupon a new set of by-laws [28]

---

[25] The *Antiquary*, vol. vi, pp. 154–5. The York barber-surgeons are said to have maintained a gild in common before 1413. *Memorandum Book*, i, p. 207. In 1493 the "searchers" of the company were authorised to "serche" strangers who came into the city and exercised any "poynt of surgerie."

[26] Civic, *Canterbury*, no. xix. One of the company's rules forbade any "man of the said crafte" to take a customer "by the quart tyll the tyme he know how his old barbor be paid."

[27] Tighe and Davis, *History of Windsor*, vol. i, p. 652.

[28] *Antiquary*, vol. 36, p. 274. The barber-surgeons of Bristol who, in 1670, claimed to be one of the "ancientest" corporations in the city, tried to protect the interests of the surgeons by forbidding one surgeon to take another's patient from him without his consent. Latimer, *17th Century Annals*, pp. 357, 239. Membership in these barber-surgeon companies was not always confined to the men who practised these two callings. A "Register Boke" of the Chester "barbur Surgeons waxe and Tallow chaunlors" records the "Election daye" for the "choyce of new officers" in 1606. *Archaeol. & Historic Soc. Proc. of City of Chester and North Wales, n. s.,* vol. 18, p. 103. In 1664 a Shrewsbury company of barber-surgeons, wax and tallow chandlers elected local apothecaries to membership, in order that the members might "establish good order, tranquillity and com'on wealth." *Shropshire Archaeol. & Natural Hist. Soc. Trans.,* vol. v, p. 269. By that time in Oxford the profession of surgery had risen to a point where an alliance with the "makers, dressers and sellers of perewiggs, borders, artificiall Heade or haar and all other the like Employe which are notoriously known to belong to the Trade, mistery or occupacon of a Barber" was a thing to be deprecated. *Old Order Book, f. 7. Oxford Barbers' Company, MS.* Bodleian Library. In 1714 the barber-surgeons and peruke-makers of Kingston-upon-Hull agreed to "be, remain, and continue one society . . . as tending to the good of the

was issued for the "better ordering and regulating" of the company. Fortunately we need not depend upon the memory of the Londoners to learn something of the way in which the barber-surgeons of their city built up their association. Their records tell that in order to achieve "good and due order, exercise and knowledge . . . as well in speculation as in practise" in the science of surgery, an achievement which had proved to be impossible while the men engaged in these professions continued "severid a sundrie and not joyned," they were allowed to unite by the grace of King Henry VIII [29] and to enjoy jointly the privileges conceded to the barbers by King Edward IV. To these privileges which apparently included the exercise of the art of surgery "as well respecting wounds, bruises, hurts and other infirmities" as the "letting" of blood and the drawing of the teeth of the city's "liegemen," was added, in 1481 the supervision of the work of the surgeons, who, it seems had no "manner of corporation," although they were said to be a "Company." This arrangement, however, proved unsatisfactory in the working, and so, shortly afterwards for "the increase of the credit of the profession," the metropolitan barbers and surgeons met together and agreed upon a common set of rules which were thereafter to be binding upon the members of both mysteries.[30] However, in order to insure independent action, each group reserved the right to elect its own warden who was to superintend the practice of the members of the group which he represented. However satisfactory this plan may have proved at the time of its adoption, by 1540 the barbers and surgeons decided to do away with reservations of the sort and join in forming one corporation.

It seems to have mattered little whether these unions included bowyers and fletchers, armourers and braziers, bakers and brewers, carpenters and joiners or carvers, marshals and smiths or barber-surgeons, since like those entered into by the drapers and 'taylors,' they were formed to put an end to rivalry and keep the peace. Of course none of these craftsmen recognised at once the advantages to be gained by union. In many cases it took years of strife and the expenditure of considerable energy directed toward confining their members to the duties peculiar to their own craft, before they were induced to amalgamate.

That rival craftsmen were averse to amalgamating their gild interests is not surprising in the light of English gild history. It is, however, surprising to find town executives sanctioning the amal-

Weale," and for the better government, order, rule and direction of the three callings now resident and dwelling" within the borough. Lambert, *Two Thousand Years of Gild Life*, p. 357. In 1746 the Kinsdale peruke-makers seem to have taken the initiative in founding a society, for in that year they asked the borough to be made a company by charter and "that the Surgeons and Apothecaries be included with them if they desire it." *Council-Book*, lxxix.

[29] 32 King Henry VIII, c. 42.
[30] *Annals of the Barber-Surgeons*, pp. 27, 51, 55-6.

gamation of the crafts in view of the legislative act of 1363 which called for their separation. To be sure, within a year after the passage of this act, parliament weakened to the extent of recalling the part of it which had aimed at limiting the merchants in their commercial ventures, but left on the statute-book the clause which restricted the handicrafts to their chosen field; [31] and a little over a quarter of a century later, extended the policy of isolating the crafts to include tanning and shoemaking. In this way tanners and shoemakers were made to realise that the state was determined to hold them accountable for their trespasses one upon the others' territory.[32] The powers in authority had not always favoured the separation of these two branches of the leather industry. Indeed, long before the passage of the act of 1363 when local governors tried to restrict cordwainers to the making of boots and shoes, the king himself deliberately conceded to the cordwainers of certain localities the right to practise also the art of tanning. This right was conceded to the cordwainers of Shrewsbury in 1323, in answer to the petition they had forwarded to the king, in which they recounted the persecution to which they had been subjected by the bailiffs of their borough, who, in order to prevent the cordwainers from tanning, had ruthlessly seized such of their goods as they found "in their houses of tanning and at this time hinder them so that they cannot use the said mistery." The cordwainers begged the king to let them keep on tanning on the ground that from time immemorial they had done so "equally with the tanners." [33] The king was evidently impressed with the justice of the cordwainers' plea, for he allowed them a special license, authorising them thereafter to "tan skins at their pleasure." [34]

The cordwainers of Shrewsbury were not the only men of their craft to win this royal concession. In fact, at about the date of the passage of the act which forbade artisans to use any except their chosen craft, the cordwainers of Bristol,[35] in their turn, secured the king's licence authorising them also to tan skins.[36] However,

---

[31] *Supra,* pp. 1–2, 20.

[32] 13 Richard II, c. 12.

[33] The cordwainers told the king that "from time out of mind" they had been accustomed to "tan skins at their pleasure without disturbance ever before just as the tanners of the town," and they begged him to issue a writ under his great seal endowing them with the authority necessary to enable them to "use their mystery of tanning." They asked, too, that their goods "now lately seized may be delivered to them." *Shropshire Archaeol. & Nat. Hist. Soc. Trans., 2nd series,* vol. vi, pp. 285–89.

[34] To the bailiffs of Shrewsbury the king sent an order directing them to permit the cordwainers to tan skins at their pleasure as heretofore.

[35] "Quod sutores de Bristoll . . . possint uti mistera tannariae." *Patent rolls 37 Edward III,* pt. i, no. 45. *Public Record Office.*

[36] *Little Red Book,* vol. i, p. 54. The warden of the tanners' gild bound himself by a similar oath to restrain men who tanned from making boots and shoes. In 1388, the provost of the city of Dublin was instructed "to deal justly with all corporations not suffering another to exercise the trade contrary to the corporation of which he is free, unless it be for his own particular use for the present." Warburton, *History of Dublin,* vol. i, p. 175.

the tanners of Bristol evidently proved a foe sufficiently formidable to make local cordwainers think better of their ambition to be tanners, for within a few years their warden pledged himself to see that cordwainers did not meddle with the tanners' occupation. Whether the Shrewsbury tanners persisted in their efforts to keep cordwainers from tanning does not appear, but in 1362 and again in 1387, local cordwainers evidently deemed it expedient to have the central authorities confirm their right to tan.[37] At this time the community of Beverley was determined to keep her cordwainers from tanning also, and to this end proposed to fine each cordwainer forty shillings as often as one was found "blameworthy."[38] A curious divergence of sentiment between a local sovereign and his subjects as to the wisdom of isolating tanners' and shoemakers' callings is witnessed to by a document from the city of Chester. It seems that about 1362 city tanners were petitioning their earl, the Black Prince, for a charter forbidding cordwainers to meddle with their craft on the plea that other tanners throughout the country were protected from such interference. They secured the charter at the time, but eight years later it was revoked on the ground that the separation of the two crafts was not to the interest of the city.[39] In its place tanners, shoemakers and skinners were given a charter for the joint exercise of the three crafts. It seems somewhat inconsistent for the Black Prince to have compelled these three handicrafts to associate at a time when the government had already legislated to keep all the crafts in separate gilds.[40] However, perhaps the act of 1390 lent weight to the claim of the Chester tanners, for before another twenty years had passed they had evidently succeeded in organising a gild of their own.

The state, at all events, has left us in no doubt as to its motive in keeping these two callings distinct. Shoemakers and cordwainers had been in the habit not only of selling leather which they had "falsely" tanned but also of making boots and shoes of this defectively tanned leather and selling them "as dear as they will to the great deceit of the poor commons." In the interest of fair play for all concerned, the craftsmen in future were required by

---

[37] *Shrop. Archaeol. & Nat. Hist. Soc. Trans.*, vol. vi, p. 285. "Quod cordewannarii Salop possint tanniare et aliae libertates."

[38] *Hist. MSS. Com. Rep., Beverley*, 1900, p. 90. The community likewise ordered the tanners under pain of paying the same penalty to refrain from exercising the shoemakers' art.

[39] It is doubtful whether tanners of other communities were, at this time, organised in separate gilds. At any rate there is no record that establishes the fact. Before 1416, the year in which the York tanners set up their own gild, they had belonged to an association which included the glovers and parchment makers. *Memorandum Book*, vol. i, p. 81.

[40] Morris, *Chester*, pp. 410–44. The Prince seems to have let the county officials decide whether the tanners should have the charter they asked for. The officials were directed to "make inquest . . . touching the matter and if it should be found reasonable and to the profit of the people of Chester" they were "to make out a charter" to the tanners.

law to change their tactics and exercise only one branch of the trade. The state expected, doubtless, to secure a better product by holding men responsible for one part of a process. It was, however, not easy for men to mend their ways all at once even at the stern command of the state. This the state well understood, since it continued to insist that such of its subjects as were employed in cutting leather should not use two or more branches of the business.[41] Within a short time both the tanners and shoemakers issued gild regulations to that effect in order, doubtless, to insure to the public, boots and shoes made of properly tanned leather.[42]

Nevertheless in the face of state, municipal and gild determination to keep separate not only the tanners' and shoemakers' callings but that of the curriers as well, consolidated gilds composed of these crafts are frequently met with in local records. With the exception of the evidence which Chester provides to show that in 1370 her authorities considered it to the interest of the borough to have the tanners, shoemakers and even skinners amalgamate, there is no early material at hand furnishing the slightest clue to the rise of these unions. When records of the consolidation of these leather crafts later appear, the act of union must of course be considered as already accomplished. Thus, in 1481, records of Exeter tell of the renewal of the charter which had constituted local cordwainers and curriers one society, under the common seal of the city.[43] In 1555, we learn from the records of Boston that, on the twenty-sixth day of October, the cordwainers and curriers were incor-

---

[41] I Henry VII, c. v., forbade tanners to curry or curriers to tan, while 19 Henry VII, c. xix, enjoined curriers and cordwainers from meddling with one another's calling. The chief function of the currier was to prepare leather for the use of cordwainers. It was inevitable that the interests of these two handicrafts should on many occasions have clashed. In 1427 we find the cordwainers of Beverley exacting tribute from local curriers "to the repairs of the castle and the use of their gild." *Hist. MSS. Com. Report, Beverley*, p. 90.

[42] So altruistic were the Bristol tanners in 1415 that they supplicated most humbly the "very honoured and wise" city officials for new articles in the interest of the common people, who, they said, were being deceived and forced into purchasing boots and shoes made of leather which was "disloyally" tanned and curried. *Little Red Book*, vol. II, p. 110. In 1563 the Hull cordwainers entered into a covenant with the mayor and burgesses in which they promised "yat none of yat felloweshippe shall occupie ye crafte or misterye of a tanner or curryer nor permytt or suffer any tanner or curryour to use or occupie ye mysterye of a cordwainer." Lambert, *op. cit.*, 321. As late as 1734 the officers of the court leet of Manchester were obliged to "inquire of tanners that have used the occupation of a cordwainer or a currier or that hath put any leather to sale." *Court Leet Records*, vol. vii, p. 34. See also *Quarter Sessions Records*, vol. ix, The North Riding Record Society, p. 6. *Presentments*, 1691.

[43] Izacke, *Exeter*. p. 91. These two groups of handicrafts appear to have been amalgamated as early as 1387. *Ibid.*, p. 63. By 1518 a gild comprising shoemakers, curriers and cobblers at Canterbury concerned itself to see that masters employed no more journeymen "beyng aliants" than "jornymen beyng englisshemen." Civis, *Canterbury*, Supplement to Minutes, no. xx.

porated and endowed with the right to appoint two wardens who were to search throughout the company once a month at least, or oftener if required, with a view to exposing any unlawful wares or leather.[44] However, scarcely more satisfactory as an explanation of the reasons for organisation are the memorials which the Lichfield corvisors and curriers have left of their "auncyente societe and brotherhood" under date of 1625. It is true that they bewail the fact that their crafts are mightily decayed for lack of good rules and because many strangers who have never served a proper apprenticeship have "hither repayred and sett upp both or one of the said Trades by meanes whereof the said Trades are much hindred and ympoverished." [45] The members fail, however, to tell why in the first place they felt the need of amalgamating. Their failure to reveal their innermost secrets to the public forces it to draw its own conclusions. It can readily be seen that even at that late date the united efforts of the Lichfield cordwainers and curriers had not kept strangers from trading in the town. If the leather men had originally formed their union with a view to preventing aliens from competing with them for any share of the local trade, their efforts had manifestly proved unavailing. In all likelihood the desire to exclude aliens was a cause which operated later to draw kindred handicrafts together and these unions of tanners or curriers and cordwainers had originally been formed for some reason more directly affecting the men's economic ventures. By opening the membership of their gilds to shoemakers, curriers who dressed their leather or tanners who sold them that commodity tanned, could more easily prevail upon shoemakers to stop their complaints about the quality of the leather offered them by their associates, and so prevent the public from placing the blame for leather which was illegally tanned or curried.[46] Unless

[44] Thompson, *Boston,* p. 158.

[45] *Lancashire & Cheshire Antiq. Soc. Trans.,* vol. x, p. 12. At Ripon in 1614 "it was resolved that Cordyners and Curryers should be from thenceforth of one Company and Brotherhood." *Millenary Record,* p. 49. Half a century later the mayor and his associates ordered the officers of this company to summon their members in order that between them they might consider "what new rules or orders may be necessary for the better regulation" of their affairs. *Ibid.,* p. 65.

By 1632 if not earlier, to the cordwainers of Morpeth had been annexed local curriers also. *An account of the Customs of the Court Leet & Court Baron of Morpeth, Archaeologia Aeliana,* vol. xv, iii, n.s., p. 52.

[46] In 1395 and again in 1396 the tanners of Nottingham were accused of selling leather not well tanned. *Records of the Borough,* vol. i, pp. 269, 317. As late as 1576 the Earl of Bath endorsed as reasonable and true, a petition directed by the Devonshire shoemakers to the Council in which they deplored the quality of the leather at that time sold by tanners. *Lansdowne MS. B. M.* 22. One of the ordinances drawn up in 1564 by the shoemakers of Kingston-upon-Hull directed the officers of the company to be on their guard lest "curriours . . . doe cuire any lether but suche as before ys well and perfytly tanned and woorke and currie the same perfilelie, sufficientlie and substancyallie in all pointes and respectes according to the statutes thereof provyded." Lambert, *Two Thousand Years of Gild Life,* p. 317. In 1604 the London

shoemakers had some special motive for keeping quiet they were apt to condemn leather [47] which failed to measure up to the required standard especially since they were held responsible for the quality of the boots and shoes they sold.[48] On the other hand, shoemakers may well have had reasons of their own for affiliating with tanners and curriers. Since shoemakers were forbidden by law to tan or curry the leather which they used in their work as many had long been accustomed to do, it was the next best thing for them to join forces with tanners or curriers and arrange matters so that, if they felt inclined, they might ignore altogether the laws restricting them to the business of making shoes.[49] That

shoemakers refused to pay the fines which they were assessed "for faulty leather." They claimed that the fines ought not to be paid by them but by the curriers. *State Papers Domestic, James I,* vol. vii, no. 88.

[47] In 1378 the officers of the London cordwainers made short work of a city tanner who tried to work off on the trade falsely tanned leather. On the occasion in question, they brought him up before the city authorities on the charge of exposing for sale forty-seven tanned hides which were denounced as "raw, false and forfeitable." The tanner, however, claimed the right as a freeman of London to buy and sell all merchandise as he might please, but the jury of leather workers which he demanded to try his case and which, in addition to the cordwainers, included tanners, saddlers, pouchmakers, girdlers, bottle-makers and curriers, decided that the hides in question were not serviceable and should be forfeited. See *Calendar of Letter Books, H,* p. 93, or Riley, *Memorials of London,* pp. 420–1 for the account of this incident. To Professor Unwin the tension which marked the relations between tanners and shoemakers at this stage, appears as a revelation of the change which, to use his words, "undermined the gild or handicraft system by separating the trading function and the handicraft function from each other." *Industrial Organization,* p. 19. In proof of his contention, Professor Unwin cites the controversy just referred to, which raged between the London cordwainers and the tanners, over the quality of the tanned hides which the latter placed on the market. Just how this particular quarrel proves the theory of the separation of the trading function and ˊthat of the handicraft is far from clear. Cordwainers and men engaged in other branches of the leather business might be expected to refuse to buy poorly tanned leather and punish the offender in order to keep him from repeating the offence. But this scarcely proves that tanning was more distinctly a trading occupation than was shoemaking or any other department of the leather industry represented on this jury. Tanners, it is true, sold leather, but they bought bark and hides, while cordwainers bought leather and sold boots and shoes. In 1645 the tanners of Alnwick appointed four of their number to be "buyers" of such bargains of "woode and barke" as should that year be bought within the borough. Tate, *History of Alnwick,* vol. ii, p. 338. Undoubtedly the act of 1390 called for a division of labor, but the division was drawn between two distinct branches of the leather business. And rather than being undermined by separating the functions of traders and handicraftsmen, it would seem as if the gild or handicraft system came into being expressly to keep them apart.

[48] As early as 1362 officials of Lancaster prohibited local shoemakers from selling shoes made of leather which was insufficiently tanned and curried. Simpson, *History of Lancaster,* p. 117.

[49] The determination as to what constituted reliably tanned leather seems to have rested with cordwainers and curriers alike in some places. In York, officers of both companies searched and sealed all sorts of tanned leather before it could be offered for sale. Drake, *Eboracum,* vol. i, p. 308. Indeed they took a special oath, pledging themselves to "well and truly serve Mr. Mayor . . . in the office of searching and sealing of leather," to make true

it was practically impossible for two groups of handicrafts who were governed by the same gild laws, to prevent their respective members from using one another's occupations, seems evident from the anxiety displayed by the tanners of Chester in 1362 to procure a charter to protect their business from the cordwainers with whom they were associated. The fact that crafts amalgamated shows that they were more concerned to unite than to separate their economic interests.[50] Furthermore, in amalgamating, tanners, curriers and shoemakers could more easily keep in touch with each other's affairs, and at the same time guard all branches of their work from the interference of outsiders. Not that these craftsmen needed necessarily to associate in order to effect their purpose.[51] The London curriers and cordwainers contrived to safeguard their interests on several occasions without combining in one gild. However, such combinations could be at best merely sporadic in their nature while amalgamation offered more permanent advantages. For example, the consolidated gildsmen could better make agreements of an enduring nature, and thus united, could more successfully disguise or cover up altogether transactions to which suspicion might attach. In many of the smaller towns the leather business never probably assumed proportions sufficient to support an able body of tanners whose sole concern it was to sell "tanned leather unwrought."[52] In such places tanners in all probability drifted into union with local shoemakers or curriers much as a matter of course. It would seem as if the interests of the three crafts at Ludlow had been sufficiently close to warrant town authorities in incorporating them in one society.[53] Later, one ques-

search and view four times in the year at least, of and for all boots and shoes, buskins and other wares and things made of tanned leather in all houses and places within the precincts and liberties of this Corporation and make thereon a true certificate or presentment of every default they should find in the making or unsufficiency of the said wares," etc.

[50] In 1581 the London authorities insisted that the bakers of white bread and of brown be kept apart so as to prevent the inconveniences which would arise if the "white bakers" were permitted to bake brown bread and vice versa. *Index to Remembrancia*, p. 91.

[51] By combining in some sort of scheme with local butchers, the tanners of Coventry contrived to buy hides "in gret sale" against the orders of city executives. *Leet Book*, pt. iii, p. 585. In 1590 the London curriers induced city cordwainers to leave to them the dressing of all leather bought in "Leadenhall Southwarke markett and three miles compasse" of their city; the two groups of craftsmen between them agreed upon the price to be paid for the work. *Lansdowne MS.* lxiii. Quoted also in *Economic Journal*, vol. x, p. 409. Professor Unwin states that in 1616 after much litigation the London cordwainers and curriers came to an agreement to ignore the statutes relating to the leather industries. *Industrial Organization*, p. 22, note. So, too, in 1623, at the bidding of the cutlers and ironmongers, city authorities were induced to issue a bylaw which bade strangers bring cutlery and other wares made of iron to Leadenhall to be examined as "heretofore." Noble, *History of the Ironmongers' Company*, p. 23.

[52] This seems to have been a privilege reserved exclusively for tanners. *Hist. MSS. Com. Rep.*, iii, app. p. 5.

[53] *Parl. Papers*, vol. 26, p. 2803.

tions whether in amalgamating tanners, curriers and cordwainers tacitly confessed that they were no longer concerned in restricting their men to their own callings. By that time, the competition of aliens had become so menacing as to impel local leather men to forget their personal differences and to combine their forces, in order at all hazards to keep local business in their own hands. It is a matter of record that towards the end of the sixteenth century Winchester persuaded her shoemakers and cobblers to settle the difficulties which they had to contend against, by associating themselves "for that divers and sundry persons by colour of freedom of the said city have lately set up and do use the trades, sciences, mysteries of the shoemakers and cobblers." [54] By asserting, in 1625, that strangers repaired to their city and set up at will one or both of the crafts represented in their organization, the Lichfield company of curriers and corvisors notified the persons concerned that they were still in control of both occupations; and they proceeded to exert it by forbidding non-members under any consideration to practise the mysteries within local precincts.

That amalgamation offered skinners and glovers also certain advantages seems proved by the joint unions established by those two handicrafts in many provincial towns. The glovers and skinners of Exeter upon their incorporation in 1462, tried to prevent gild members from handling foreign-made goods, a policy which they pursued just as persistently a century later.[55] A company in Warwick composed of similar crafts made every effort to hinder non-members from buying "any maner of shepes skyns" in the local market to which all skins had to be brought for sale. Indeed, they went so far as to order all skins so bought to be forfeited, "one moytie" of the forfeit "to be to the use of the chamber of the borough and the other to be given him "that shall take the same skynnes." [56] In 1610 the skinners' and glovers' company of Doncaster was still holding itself responsible for the quality of work

---

[54] Bailey, *Transcripts from the Archives of Winchester*, pp. 33–36. In some localities town and gild authorities went even further and did their best to draw more rigidly the lines between the crafts, frequently admonishing shoemakers and cobblers not to work at each other's craft. "If any one has to do with old shoes he shall not meddle with new shoes among the old," say the articles of the London cordwainers drawn up in 1375, "in deceit of the people and to the scandal of the trade." Riley, *Memorials of London*, p. 392. In 1562 the Lincoln cordwainers directed their energies toward seeing that "no cobler shall use or occupy the craft of cordwainer in making shoon of new leather or of any horse skin or other unlawful leather in deceit of the common people." *Hist. MSS. Commis. Rep.* xiv, app. viii, p. 53. In 1609 they were still contesting the right of local cobblers to make new shoes. *Gough MSS., Collections for a History of Lincoln,* f. 228., *Bodleian Library.* Because the shoemakers of Reading persisted in mending and repairing old snoes against the ancient orders of the borough which forbade the practice, in 1662 they were warned not to repeat the offence. *Reliquary,* n. s., vol. iv, p. 147.

[55] *Western Antiquary,* vol. iv, p. 187.

[56] *Black Book,* p. 66.

turned out by its members.[57] According to Shrewsbury records, in 1727, local skinners and glovers had drawn together so as to resist the encroachment of mercers and other "that Intrud. of the Company."[58] In all probability, the Alnwick company had the same difficulty to contend with.[59] The glovers were doubtless dependent either upon local skinners or mercers [60] for the material they needed. If, by amalgamating with glovers, skinners could get glovers to buy skins from them rather than from mercers or from other outsiders who had them for sale, assuredly they were aiding their cause while glovers would doubtless secure their material upon better terms than they would otherwise have been able to do, and at the same time be sure of a fairly adequate supply.[61] Perhaps it was also to the advantage of the glovers and skinners to combine in order to apportion between their members the exact share of the trade each group might monopolise, and thus avoid the friction which might arise from the indiscriminate exercise of the two occupations. In 1588 the glovers of Kingston-upon-Hull appear to have maintained an independent gild existence and yet enjoyed the privilege of buying leather "to th' end to sell the same againe," an arrangement which local skinners must have

[57] *Records,* vol. iv, p. 21. The members were warned that whoever should "hierafter take any lether to dresse or worke and shall spoyle the same the party agreeved shall complaine him to the wardens . . . and satisfaction shall be made to the party greeved by the said offender at the discretion of the said wardens."

[58] *Shrop. Archaeol. & Nat. Hist. Soc. Trans.,* vol. x, p. 71.

[59] Tate, *Hist. of Alnwick,* vol. ii, p. 324. In 1609 the merchants' company was sending searchers "for shepe skynnes and goate skynnes to goe into the countrye upon charges of the fellowship."

[60] Mercers sometimes retaliated by forbidding the members of their gild to buy skins of glovers. "No man fre of this Felyshipe shall bye skynnes of any glover, nor of any other man bying the same skynnes of a glover nor no other man . . . knowing the same skynnes to be bought of a glover," say the ordinances of the Newcastle gild of merchants issued in 1554. *The Merchant Adventurers of Newcastle. Surtees Soc. Pub.,* vol. 93, p. 48.

[61] We find most of the towns taking steps at this time to keep within their boundaries a goodly supply of skins for the use of the glovers. An extract frm the Chippenham Minute Book, dated 1597, orders all butchers "bringeinge fleshe to sell in yhe market" to "bringe with them also the hyde and fells of all such ware." Goldney, *Records of Chippenham, Wilts.,* p. 7. See also *Black Book of Warwick,* p. 22; *Coventry Leet Book,* pt. iii, p. 795, and Johnson, *Customs of Hereford,* p. 127. Almost a century later the Court Leet of Leominster issued an order much to the same effect. Townsend, *Leominster,* p. 310. In 1594 the glovers of Leicester were anxious to exclude glovers of neighboring market towns from the retail trade in Leicester, largely it appears because they came to buy fells. The Leicester glovers succeeded in getting the town council—who apparently recognised the necessity of keeping plenty of leather in the town to provide materials for the glovers' industry—to protect local glovers by issuing an edict that every tanner "bringinge in to be solde in oure markett half as muche tanned leyther theire to bee solde in the Leyther Hall as he shall buye rowghe hides theire, and the fellmounger bringinge in halfe suche quantitye of wooll to our Wooll Hall weekelye, theire to be solde as they buye in oure markittes, shall have libertie to buye of ourr freemen butchers sloughter ware in the open markitt vpon the sayturdaye markitt onlie." Bateson, *Records,* vol. iii, p. 406.

resented.[62] By associating with the skinners of their respective vicinities, the glovers of Shrewsbury, Warwick and Doncaster were spared the necessity of preventing local skinners from purchasing skins destined for the glove trade, as we find the glovers of Bristol attempting at one time to do.[63] Amalgamation offered handicraftsmen the opportunity to arrange such matters quietly among themselves, an opportunity of which, sooner or later skinners and glovers of various communities availed themselves. It is true that in so doing they sometimes kept separate books, with the intent doubtless to retain some control over their individual interests.[64]

In the fifteenth century necessity rather than choice seems to have driven various handicrafts in different parts of the kingdom into joining gild forces. For example, in 1439 because there were only two freemen left in Oxford who used the weavers' craft, the fullers were invited to join the weavers' gild. The two weavers who remained, however, evidently preserved a sufficiently independent spirit to insist upon electing a weaver to serve as one warden, who, in conjunction with one chosen by the fullers should "equally and in turn have the ruling of the said misteries within the said borough and its suburbs for one whole year." [65] These Oxford weavers, whose predecessors had been among the first of the English crafts influential enough to secure a gild, must have been in sore straits to renounce it at this date. Indeed by the time of King Edward I, they had become so reduced in numbers and so decayed in fortune that that monarch, in order to relieve their distress, had reduced the amount of the contribution they had annually made to his Exchequer.[66] Apparently, in spite of this concession, the decay of the weavers proceeded apace until, in 1439, the few still faithful to the city were obliged to admit local fullers to membership in their gild so as to save it from utter extinction. In the case of these Oxford weavers, amalgamation seems clearly proof of the decay of local gild power and prestige.[67] Moreover, the reluctance manifested by many kindred handicrafts and the compromises they often tried out before consenting to consolidate their interests, leads to the inference that the movement was in reality against early craft traditions all of which made

[62] Lambert, *Two Thousand Years of Gild Life,* p. 219.

[63] Latimer, *18th Century Annals,* p. 21.

[64] This state of affairs existed among the skinners and glovers of New-castle-upon-Tyne, who joined forces apparently only in 1703. Brand, *History of Newcastle-upon-Tyne,* vol. ii, p. 315.

[65] *Calendar of Patent Rolls,* vol. iii, pt. i, p. 347. 1907. Weaving was no longer being done within Oxford. Materials, it seems, were collected in the city but woven outside the limits of five leagues. In this way the weavers avoided contributing to the king's farm of forty-two shillings a year, which was payable under letters patent issued in the third year of King Edward I.

[66] Madox, *Exchequer,* vol. i, p. 338. See Kramer, *English Craft Gilds and the Government,* pp. 32–33.

[67] By 1505 the number of drapers and tailors in York are said to have dwindled so that those left in the city joined gild forces. Johnson, *History of the Worshipful Company of Drapers,* vol. ii, p. 173.

for the independent management and control of individual handicrafts. When men realised that their own gilds had lost ground they joined forces with some other group with whose interests theirs were sufficiently close to enable them together to make the most of the authority they could still exert. After all, sharing gild privileges with one's fellows was better than having no share at all in any gild. Then, too, in the city of Norwich during this same epoch "scarstes of peple" had "drawen and ioyned into one" various groups of "smale mysteris" which before seem not to have been "had in dewe correccion and rewle." So to the city's "smythes crafte" was added the "bladsmythes locksmythes and lorymers." [68] Again, because the "peyntours, stenours and goldbetours" of York lacked that "governance as well of searchers as of ordinances" which was held to be as necessary and profitable to the people at large as to the artificers concerned, articles incorporating the three groups a common society were duly registered in the Council Chamber.[69] At Canterbury, local crafts had for some reason ceased to take part in the Corpus Christi play "to the great hurte and decay of the seide city." Whereupon the authorities commanded that "from hensforth every craft . . . being not corporate for their non sufficience of their crafts, be associate, incorporate and adjoyning to some other crafts moste nedynge support, yf they will not labour to be corporate within themselfe." [70] Elsewhere, too, the necessity of providing for the Corpus Christi celebration seems to have brought certain crafts to join gild forces. In 1475, the Chester bowyers and fletchers quarrelled with city coopers over the respective part each craft should take in performing the particular Corpus Christi play that had been allotted them in that year.[71] The quarrel assumed such proportions as to call for the intervention of the mayor, who evidently succeeded in bringing the coopers to terms with their adversaries; for later an amalgamated gild comprising bowyers, fletchers and coopers had taken its place among the permanent gilds of Chester. Evidently the consolidation for civic purposes proved the foundation for unions which were maintained later for the transaction of general gild business.

Moreover, the prevalence of fifteenth-century combinations comprising closely related craftsmen, tends to prove that no matter what may have been the cause of their creation, municipalities of the epoch had given up the attempt wholly to keep them apart.

[68] *Records of Norwich,* vol. ii, p. 280.
[69] *York Memorandum Book,* p. 164.
[70] *Hist. MSS. Comm. Rep.* ix, pp. 173-5.
[71] Morris, *Chester,* p. 572.
After the Reformation "instead of setting forthe the pageannttes on the day and feast of Corpus Xpi" the various gilds of Hereford paid "an annuity or certen sum of money to the use and behoffe of the cytey such as the same crafts shall agree to give for those grauntes of corporacions hereafter delivered under the common seale of the cytey." Johnson, *Hereford Customs,* p. 119.

Indeed, from the situation which prevailed in Coventry, in the metal industries, in 1435, it seems clear that townsmen had become reconciled to the amalgamation of two crafts even though they still looked askance at that of four. In that year the smiths, brakemen, girdlers and cardwire-drawers of the borough had entered into some sort of an alliance by which they succeeded in acquiring control over their joint crafts and as a result were passing off upon the public poorly tempered iron. The community was considerably stirred up about the affair, and before long induced the mayor to send round to the worthy men of the leet to see what could be done to stop the practice. The concensus of opinion seems to have favoured splitting up the combination into groups of two handicrafts instead of four. The smiths were the greatest malefactors, having, it was claimed, wrought and sold "myche disseyvabul wire." The townsmen, therefore, conceived the idea of separating the smiths and brakemen from the girdlers and cardwire-drawers in order to make the two last-named crafts, who had to buy their wire from the smiths, more particular as to the quality of the material they purchased. They proceeded on the principle, that, if the cardwire-drawer were once or twice "disseyved withe ontrewe wire he wolde be warre and then wold he sey vnto the smythier that he bought that wire of: Sir, I hadde of you late badde wire . . . amend your honde or in feith I will no more bye of you. And then the smythier lest he lost his customers wold make true goode; and then . . . the craft shuld amend and the kinges peapull not disseyved withe the ontrewe goode." [72] There is no record to show that this plan was ever really adopted in Coventry. But the incident is instructive in proving that, at least for consumers, the harmonious working together of the crafts had its drawbacks. As Coventry learned to its cost, it prevented the authorities from placing responsibility for defective workmanship.

In spite of the opportunities open to consolidated craftsmen to deceive the public, we sometimes find them pleading for incorporation for the express purpose of ensuring to it honest work. Thus, as early as 1403, the cutlers "fferours, smyths and lockyers" of Bristol petitioned the city authorities for permission to set up a common gild and to have their ordinances enrolled in the "yeldhalle," because many of their number not sufficiently "ylerned in the seyd craftes" work falsely by "default of surveying and goode rewle," to the "grete deceyte and harme of the people and all so wel grete desclaunder of the seyd goode folke of the craftes aforseyde." [73] The fact that these handicrafts laid the blame for poor workmanship upon lack of adequate supervision and "goode rewle," seems to indicate that the men concerned had never had gilds of their own to attain those ends.[74] If that were so, it is the more

---

[72] *Leet Book,* pt. i, p. 181. The Mayor's Register for 1430 accounts for a "Wiredrawers Companie." *Ibid.,* p. 131.

[73] *Little Red Book,* vol. ii, p. 181.

[74] By 1347 the Bristol fullers had ordinances newly made before the

interesting to notice them now asking to be allowed separate masters, presumably to supervise the work turned out by the members of the group which each represented in the corporation. In making this, as it were, a condition of their amalgamating, the crafts immediately concerned appear to be registering a protest against a movement that was, in reality, contrary to the principles that had led the English handicrafts to withdraw from the gild merchant and erect gilds of their own, in order that they might manage their own affairs unhampered by outsiders. Of course, with four distinct craft masters, one at the head of each of the four groups in the combination, these metalmen might reasonably hope to protect their individual interests, even though they were compelled to associate in a common gild. Handicrafts who amalgamated in other communities seem to have had much the same end in view. For example, in drawing up ordinances in 1536, the goldsmiths, plumbers, pewterers, glaziers and painters of Newcastle-upon-Tyne stipulated that their crafts should be under the guidance of four wardens, one each for the goldsmiths, plumbers and pewterers and one for the glaziers and painters jointly, and each warden was to see that none followed a craft other than the one to which he had been apprenticed.[75] Handicrafts, who upon amalgamating, did not safeguard their individual interests in some such fashion, were sometimes forced later to do so. In 1626 because of "much debate and controversie . . . betwixt the cutlers and girdlers" of Chester (groups which, in conjunction with certain others, had about 1490 joined in forming a society) "about intermedlinge with one anothers trade and profession," it was decided that the cutlers were not thereafter to sell "anie manner of Girdles, belts or hangers," or the girdlers "anie Blades or knyfes or other commodity whatever" which belonged to the cutlers' craft.[76] However, when the London pinners and wire-workers affiliated with city girdlers in 1451, "inasmuch as they would not otherwise be able to maintain the charges" of the city, each group insisted upon governing its members in accordance with laws of its enacting, but both agreed to submit to the general oversight of the girdlers' officials.[77] Mani-

authorities and by 1364 the shoemakers, tailors and weavers had followed their example. *Ibid.*, pp. 2, 7, 10, 41, 59.

[75] *Archaeologia Aeliana*, vol. xv, pt. iii, pp. 398–9.

[76] Simpson, *City Gilds of Chester, Journal Architect., Archaeol. & Historic Soc. for County & City of Chester & N. Wales*, n. s., vol. xx, pp. 5, 16. Indeed already in 1580 because "variance and controversie grewe" between the smiths and cutlers included in this group, of which the cutlers seem to have been the instigators, the company forbade "anie" cutler either to "mende or dresse anie gunne" or any other "thinge" belonging to the blacksmiths' trade, but held it lawful for them to sell them "beinge brought to theire shopp." *Ibid.*, p. 15.

[77] Smythe, *History of the Girdlers' Company*, p. 47. By the beginning of the eighteenth century a distinction had been drawn between the coach-wheelers and the cart-wheelers who were associated as the wheelwrights' and an order insisted that if the master and one warden were chosen from the coach-wheelers, the other warden must be a cart-wheeler and vice versa. Scott, *History of the Wheelwrights' Company*, p. 22.

festly civic burdens fell as heavily upon handicraftsmen in the metropolis as upon those who dwelt in smaller communities. The union formed by these three groups proved sufficiently satisfactory to warrant them in besieging Queen Elizabeth for a charter in 1567. This incorporated "the Master and Wardens or Keepers of the Art or Mystery of Girdlers of London" with permission to have, "without molestation or interruption, the liberties and franchises touching their arts and mysteries heretofore possessed." One wonders, incidentally, whether the girdler who in 1558 left a bequest to this company "so long as the said Company of Girdelers shall remain still girdelers and be not transported to any other Company," would have reconciled himself to this association.[78] Would he have resented it or have consoled himself with the prominent position ceded the girdlers in the fraternity? However, the incident is suggestive as showing that individual members did not view favourably the general tendency to amalgamate. Even at this time to some craftsmen, corporate independence was still worth striving for.

Like the pinners, certain leather crafts in London were obliged during the fifteenth century to renounce their separate gilds and help swell the ranks of some other organization. Fortunately the surviving records of the London leathersellers' company give us a real insight into the way one such association was gradually built up. They may also furnish a clue to the occasion of the rise of similar societies elsewhere. It seems that, by 1372, a body of men calling themselves leather-sellers had been organised for the purpose as they alleged of "selling, sorting, whiting and staking" leather, pursuits evidently followed to such good purpose that by King Henry VI's day they were said to have branched out almost entirely as wholesale leather dealers.[79] During this same period, the white-tawyers, who were mainly engaged in preparing white leather with alum, salt and various other ingredients for the trade, had also been enjoying a gild of their own. By 1479, however, having "so few persons in number that they have no choice to make any wardens to rule" their craft, the white-tawyers asked permission to join the leathersellers' company; whereupon we are told "they brought in their Book and thereupon took their clothing" with that company.[80] Meanwhile, the leathersellers had succeeded in securing the sole supervision not only over all the leather goods

---

[78] Sharpe, *Calendar of Wills,* vol. ii, p. 671. As it proved this particular girdler might have had full confidence in the ability of his fellows to safeguard their particular interests. In the combination they had entered into with city girdlers the pinners seem to have been the chief sufferers, as appears from the petition they forwarded to the king in 1637, wherein they begged to be separated from the girdlers and incorporated separately, because the officials of the corporation, in addition to neglecting to enforce the laws governing the two crafts had taken advantage of their power to convert its revenues to other uses. Smythe, *op. cit.,* p. 48.

[79] Hazlitt, *Livery Companies,* p. 148.

[80] Black, *Hist. of the Leathersellers,* p. 38.

manufactured in London but also over the raw material which was brought to the market there to be sold.[81] But to judge by the complaints brought against them in 1451 by the glovers, the leathersellers, not content with the powers they then enjoyed, had begun to "usen, make and sellen gloves" and other "necessaries" rightfully belonging to the glovers' craft. The leathersellers, however, tried to justify their incursion into the glove trade on the ground that glovers on their side had been turning out "pointes, tawed lether" and other articles properly belonging only to the leathersellers' business.[82] Be that as it may, prompted, apparently, by the desire to restore something like "unite and good accord" between their men and to prevent further encroachment upon one another's territory, the leathersellers and the glovers agreed to let each company choose two wardens who should together search "well and trewly and present unto the mayor or the chamberlains" of their city "all the defautes touchyng or concernying in eny wise" the wares made by their respective members. The glovers, however, soon realised the hopelessness of attempting alone to compete with their powerful adversaries. In their extremity they turned for support to the pursers, another group of leather men whose business had also suffered from the aggressions of the leathersellers, and, in 1498, as they confessed because of decay "both in number of persons and substance of goods," the glovers and the pursers got leave to form a company together.[83] A few years' experience, however, sufficed to convince both handicrafts that their union had not materially helped their cause. Accordingly, in 1502, they dissolved their alliance of a few years' standing and, apparently, as a last resort together joined the leathersellers' company.[84] By the absorption of the pouchmakers [85] fifteen years later, the leathersellers' company had a membership which included besides the leathersellers, city whittawyers, glovers, pursers and pouchmakers.

In all probability the same forces which led these metropolitan leather crafts to renounce their single gilds and join the leathersellers' company, were tending also to draw together gildsmen

---

[81] *Ibid.*, p. 24.

[82] *Ibid.*, p. 30. In 1476 the leathersellers attempted to fulfill their part of this contract by effecting an arrangement "for searches to be made for forfeitable wares so that the leathersellers should not conflict with the Pursers and the Glovers." *Ibid.*, p. 37.

[83] Black, *History of the Leathersellers' Company*, p. 42.

[84] By joining their two "several bodies or Fellowship" to the leathersellers' combination, the glovers and pursers expected apparently to achieve a perfect union and so continue from henceforth. *Ibid.*, p. 124.

[85] The pouchmakers begged to be "freely" translated or "transmuted into the said name of Lethersellers without any exaction of fine to be made, asked or levied in this behalf, like as other pore Felishippis, in such manner transmuted have done." *Ibid.*, p. 47. Fully two centuries earlier, the leathersellers and the pouchmakers had worked together to forward the interests of both handicraft groups. Riley, *Memorials*, p. 364. In entering into formal alliance at this stage the two crafts may have closed an interesting chapter in their history.

working in the leather occupations in the less important industrial centres. If London's glovers, pursers, whittawyers and pouchmakers could no longer support single gilds, there was little chance for similar crafts to do so in places like Lincoln, Worcester, Tewkesbury, Boston, Bristol, Canterbury or Salisbury. The fact that they were obliged to consolidate indicates clearly the decay of these separate gilds of handicrafts. The economic situation had changed considerably since the time when separate craft gilds could hope adequately to regulate each branch of an industry. Gilds had lost so much of their power and authority that they could evidently no longer count upon the loyalty of their own members. In London, the leathersellers and glovers alike trespassed at will upon one another's special rights.[86] Moreover, if gildsmen themselves mani

---

[86] The relations which developed between the London leathersellers and the glovers who had joined their company did not prove altogether happy. Indeed, by the beginning of the seventeenth century the glovers were evidently dissatisfied not only with the state of their trade, but also with the position which had been assigned them in the leathersellers' company. If the glovers' version of the controversy can be credited, the leathersellers had induced them to join their ranks on their promise that the glovers "should ever be esteemed of their body." Yet the glovers alleged that "having once translated them from the local circuit of their jurisdiction" the leathersellers had in process of time "wormed them out of their freedom allowing none of the breede and posteritie of those workemen to be free to whom they made so large a promise there not being at this day a leather-dresser free of the Leathersellers Company." Quoted from Unwin, *Industrial Organization*, p. 128. Accordingly, the glovers began negotiations for a charter to incorporate them alone, apart from the leathersellers, and with untiring energy persisted a full twenty-six years until, in 1638, they succeeded in establishing an independent corporation. The glovers seem to have had an experience similar to that of the pinners who sacrificed their independence in associating themselves with the girdlers, and in order to regain it, had to secede from the girdlers' organisation. The glovers appear to have joined the leathersellers' company at a time when their fortunes were at a low ebb and they had no recourse left except to follow the example of other crafts similarly placed and seek membership in some other reputable gild. But there is little to show that the glovers or any other craft, for that matter, ever renounced its own organisation from choice or retained membership in a combination after it was prosperous enough to support a separate organisation. In many cases, even in amalgamating, individual handicrafts insisted upon electing their own officers in order to retain independent control over their own affairs. The London glovers may not at first have been in a position to demand representation in the leathersellers' company, or else they neglected to take the necessary steps to secure it, with the result that they were ignored in the government of the company with which they had allied themselves. The glovers did not even reap the advantage of securing leather from their allies on reasonable terms. In petitioning for their charter, they informed the king that the decay of their business was due not alone to the fraudulent dressing of leather which made it practically impossible for them to distinguish good leather from bad, but to the "great oppression" of certain leathersellers who first "engrossed" all sorts of leather and then sold them to glovers at extraordinary rates. *State Papers Domestic,* vol. cccxxvi, *Charles I,* 1636.
     Professor Unwin takes a different view of the situation in these cases. He claims that "because in the sixteenth century the industrial world had outgrown its medieval framework that new classes were arising which had no recognised status and that it was the policy of the monarchy to take them

fested so little ésprit de corps they could scarcely expect outsiders to cultivate a great regard for any. In many instances, therefore, the men engaged in the leather industries were probably compelled to join forces to enable them to keep up some show of gild existence. Even so they were engaged in a constant struggle to hold anything like their own. Thus, in 1570, a fellowship of glovers and white leather tawyers of Boston issued an order which forbade strangers from selling gloves or "whit-leather wares on the market-day," to the injury of local glovers.[87] In the later sixteenth and seventeenth centuries, all the leather companies were bending their energies toward protecting their monopoly against alien intruders. In 1633, companies of glovers, fellmongers and whittawyers of established standing in Wigan, Preston, Lancaster, Liverpool, Manchester and various other big towns, petitioned the government to protect their interests against outsiders who were making persistent efforts to usurp a share of their industry.[88] In 1648, a Bristol company of whittawyers, glovers and pointmakers imposed fines and forfeitures for breaches of their laws, thereby causing considerable trouble and even some shedding of blood, until city officials stopped the practice by ordering all penalties for similar offences to be recovered thereafter through actions brought in the mayor's court.[89] Frequently, too, glovers who, at one time were able to maintain a gild in common with local skinners, had finally to enlarge their organisations sufficiently to admit men working in other leather occupations. We have already noted how, in 1563, the Lincoln glovers and skinners admitted girdlers, pinners, pointers, scriveners and parchment-makers into their organisation, and gilds of these artisans which had earlier existed in Durham, Kendal, Morpeth and in many other places were being likewise converted into larger corporations. Even the Shrewsbury glovers and skin-

under its protection." *Op. cit.*, p. 136. Therefore the glovers for example, broke from the leathersellers' domination and organised a company of their own. One might say, however, that when craftsmen found that the framework of the industrial organisation into which they had been drawn failed to meet their needs, they freed themselves from its bonds and erected on their own account organisations better suited to their purposes. There was nothing especially original in the policy of the crown, in encouraging ambitious craftsmen of the seventeenth century to establish independent organisations. From the time of King Henry I the English monarchs accorded men the privilege of having gilds just as soon as they could pay the price demanded for them.

As we shall see, in combining with various merchant traders to organise the clothworkers' company, the London shearmen and fullers contrived to achieve a basis for a union which enabled them to work together until almost the middle of the eighteenth century. *Municipal Corporation Commission Report*, 1837, vol. 25, p. 61.

[87] Thompson, *History of Boston*, p. 159.

[88] *Transactions, Lancashire & Cheshire Archaeological Society*, vol. x, p. 6.

[89] Latimer, *Annals of Bristol in the 17th Century*, p. 217. The city authorities were then rather philanthropically inclined, and ordered any proceeds which should flow into city coffers from the collection of the fines to be applied to works of charity.

ners had finally to give up their joint union and permit the point-makers, pursers, fellmongers, leathersellers and parchment-makers to enter the ranks. If the leather crafts in these well-known communities, were forced to renounce their corporate independence, it is not difficult to account for the complex leather corporations which in Reading, Ipswich, Dorchester, Maidstone, Abingdon and Andover were formed by the union of all the men engaged in the manufacture of leather goods. It is interesting to note, that, in order to insure the success of the leather company organised at Reading,[90] in the later sixteenth century, by merging local tanners, leathersellers, shoemakers, curriers, glovers, saddlers, jerkin-makers, collar-makers and cobblers, the authorities there apportioned the entrance fees according to what they thought the various members could afford to pay. These ranged from four pounds which were assessed upon the tanners to five shillings charged against the collar-makers.[91] Local authorities were evidently taking considerable pains to keep the gilds of leather crafts in existence.

[90] Professor Unwin considers the combinations of leather crafts found in Reading and Lincoln examples of what he terms a modified form of trading organisation which "served as a focus to bring together very diverse elements." He says that "besides members of the original trading occupations, such as the mercers and the haberdashers, there were found included in this type of organisation the prosperous craftsman who had become a shopkeeper, the member of the decayed craft who was employed in repairing or supplementing foreign commodities, and the small master of the rising domestic industry." *Industrial Organization*, note, p. 38. The facts, however, seem scarcely to justify such a view. Mercers, haberdashers or men engaged in other trading occupations are not found in the organisations established by the leathersellers. On the contrary, mercers and dealers in ordinary merchandise not only in Reading and Lincoln but elsewhere, formed their own combinations and the leather men formed theirs, the one for the most part irrespective of the other. This was the case even in a borough like Andover, when of the three trade organisations which were constituted within its precincts one was given over to the leathersellers; the members eligible to membership therein were tanners, saddlers, glovers, shoemakers, curriers, collarmakers, butchers, chandlers, dyers, upholsterers, besides pewterers and braziers. *Wilts. Archaeol. & Nat. Hist. Soc., Trans.*, vol. xxi, p. 306. Indeed, only in the very smallest towns where the trades and handicrafts were forced to join in forming one or even two comprehensive groups are the leathersellers found in the membership list of the mercantile gild. As a rule the leathersellers threw in their gild lot with craftsmen who worked with leather. Perhaps the fact that these amalgamated companies of leathersellers recruited their membership from handicraftsmen, such as in the words of the London organisation "made, drest and sold wares of tanners' leather," accounts for their not joining with local traders in forming common societies. It seems strange that Mr. Unwin did not perceive how universal the organisations of pure traders became in the English boroughs. His assertion that, in the few communities in which such organisations survived, they represented only a passing phase in the history of the gilds seems incompatible with his theory of the conflict which existed between commercial and industrial capital. *Opus cit.*, p. 98. The exponent of such a theory might be expected to have seen how very marked a feature of industrial organisation the mercantile fraternities became, and how almost everywhere ordinary traders organised themselves apart from local craftsmen in order better to dominate the purely commercial interests of their particular boroughs.

[91] Professor Unwin also claims that the difference in the amount of the

By the sixteenth century large combines of metal crafts seem to have become the order of the day in most boroughs. For instance, a company at Lincoln, which then comprised smiths, iron-mongers, armourers, spurriers, cutlers, horse-marshals and wire-drawers, was established in 1563, according to their testimony, "for the maintenance of good and cunning workmanship and the extir-pation of uncunning deceivers of the common people." [92] The proper authorities, it seems, confirmed the gild's ordinances because they still considered gildsmen the best judges of the different pro-cesses which pertained to these mysteries and therefore wanted them to train skilled workmen to carry them on in their city. In this way Lincoln still declared her faith in the efficacy of gild control. The Gloucester metalmen likewise sought confirmation of their union in 1607, following the gift to the city authorities of a charter authorising them to reduce into some company all the mysteries which before had not been under any uniform order or organisa-tion. The document explains that the particular persons who exercised the crafts of goldsmiths, pewterers, brasiers, copper-smiths, wire-drawers, cardmakers, pinmakers and plumbers were having much "chevisaunce and dealing among themselves" and "for want of composition between the persons exercising them they are much decayed." Wherefore the town council willingly conceded that the twenty-one metalmen who appeared before them and such others as should afterwards serve a proper apprenticeship with any one of these charter members should "be taken and reputed" to be Gloucester's only company of metalmen.[93] The gild's officers were endowed with the customary authority to correct and punish

entrance fee assessed the members shows the greater variety of classes which were found in this species of society compared with those established by the ordinary traders. Yet the entrance fee charged members of Reading's mer-cers' and drapers' company which included local traders only, also varied con-siderably, since the mercers and drapers were assessed twice as much as were the haberdashers. Differences of some sort evidently existed among the trading occupations of Reading as well as among her leather crafts. One need not necessarily regard the girdlers and collar-makers in the Reading leathersellers' company as craftsmen employed by local traders just because they were taxed less than were other members of the company. Saddlers and cobblers, who were also members, were assessed only one-fourth as much as tanners and one-third as much as shoemakers. Yet a local saddler was pre-sumably as much a trader as was a shoemaker. Professor Unwin's argument in this case is to be found on pp. 83–84 of his *Industrial Organization*.

[92] *Hist. MSS. Comm. Rep.* xiv, app. viii, p. 57.

[93] *Hist. MSS. Comm. Rep.* xii, app. ix, p. 427. Professor Unwin regards this company as an expression, as he terms it, of "the ascendency of trading capital over industrial capital," although he qualifies the statement because the company included in its membership the wire-drawers and the pinmakers. Their inclusion, he says, was probably due to the opposite influence (presum-ably the ascendency of industrial capital over trading capital) since within a few years of the date of the amalgamation, Gloucester had become an impor-tant seat of the pin manufacture. *Industrial Organization*, p. 38, note, 2. The fact that Profesor Unwin needs to qualify his explanation necessarily detracts from its worth as a reason for the association of these various groups of handicrafts.

the practices which they should find deceptive. Ostensibly the consolidation was destined to serve a two-fold purpose in the community; in addition to protecting the consumers from fraudulent products, the craftsmen themselves were to be preserved from utter extinction. In Gloucester, also, industrial organisation was still the one hope of the industrial leaders, albeit they recognised that the organizations inaugurated for the purpose could no longer afford to be too exclusive in their membership.

A company composed of somewhat similar crafts founded at Hereford in 1554, included the goldsmiths, blacksmiths, cutlers, plumbers, glaziers, braziers, pewterers and cardmakers. The company at that time was passing through some kind of crisis, sufficiently grave apparently to warrant its members in appealing to the Council of the Marches for redress against the mayor of their city who, they said, had refused to hand over the company's charter and certain "stock" which he had in some way been manipulating. For this misdemeanor the Council admonished him to "administer justice in the matter accordingly not failing hereof as ye will answer at your peril." [94] Manifestly different members of the company had been quarrelling among themselves. The blacksmiths, it seems, were very much provoked because, after they had admitted the other crafts to membership in their gild, the members as a whole failed to elect a blacksmith to serve as one of the gild wardens, a state of affairs unprecedented in the annals of the blacksmiths' history. And smarting under the insult thereby offered them, the blacksmiths seceded in a body from the fraternity and founded a gild of their own. The members of this Hereford corporation were so busy quarrelling among themselves that they have neglected to account for the appearance of their association in the gild firmament.[95] The omission must therefore be supplied

---

[94] *Hist. MSS. Comm. Rep.* xiii, app. iv, pp. 319–326.

[95] Professor Unwin finds in this amalgamated metal company further proof of the domination by traders of the handicrafts. He arrives at this conclusion because of the presence in it of the blacksmith who, he claims, remained more of a craftsman and possessed less trading capital than the other members of the group. This conception of the status of blacksmiths of that epoch scarcely tallies with one gained from a contemporary record which describes them as engaged in the "making of nails, locks, spurs, bridle-bits, buckles, stirrups and arrow-heads, and in the slitting, stringing and ingrossing" of iron. *Historical MSS. Commis. Report,* iii, p. 11. This description of the function of the blacksmiths of one community of the period, makes one hesitate to conclude that the blacksmith of Hereford was less a trader than was any of his allies, the cutlers, plumbers, glaziers, pewterers, cardmakers, or even the goldsmiths in the Hereford combine. Whatever may have been the amount of trading capital possessed by these blacksmiths of Hereford, they evidently possessed sufficient independence of spirit to withdraw from a company which failed to accord them treatment commensurate with their rank in the community. And they not only withdrew themselves from the organization but probably influenced local cutlers to desert four years later and to join with them in forming a common society. All things considered, therefore, the blacksmith of Hereford should be accorded his full share of dignity among contemporary craftsmen. Indeed, the blacksmiths of

as best it can. There seems to be no reason to suppose that the Hereford metal workers combined their forces for motives different from those actuating other craftsmen of their day and generation. And one point at least stands out clearly from the record. The Hereford blacksmiths were still imbued with a sense of the importance of their calling to the community and, what is more to the purpose, they succeeded in making their arguments convincing enough to get them what they wanted, high-handed though their method of procedure appears to have been. Obviously it was no easy task to reconcile within one organisation the conflicting interests of the many different craftsmen who gained admittance into it; their sense of independence seemed bound to crop out on all occasions.[96]

At this stage large unions seem to have become the rule among the building crafts, the Exeter carpenters, masons, joiners, glaziers and painters frankly confessing in 1586 that they wanted a gild "albeit few in number and slender in welth" they were yet "desirous to be partakers of so many good benefits whereby they myght become and bee the more profitable members of the commonwealth."[97] Suffice it to say that they got their charter. Twenty years before, in Lincoln, a gild with a membership twice as large as that of the Exeter organisation, secured municipal approval for reasons similar to those which had gained local metal workers their corporation, to enable the craftsmen to provide "for the mainte-

Doncaster seem to have been sufficiently influential to give their name, in conjunction with the lorimers, to an association which at the time included whitesmiths, cutlers, hardwaremen, sword-slippers, pewters and braziers. *Records*, vol. iv, p. 206. As late as 1690 the blacksmiths of London claimed that clockmaking was "but a branch of ye art of smithery" and for that reason they were entitled to control the members of their organisation who had branched out as clockmakers. Overall, *History of the Worshipful Company of Clockmakers*, p. 118. Professor Unwin dwells considerably upon the fact that these gild groups were formed in the interest of the shopkeeping class. That is almost a foregone conclusion, since master craftsmen had naturally to dispose of the commodity they manufactured and like the traders had to have a "hows" for their "exibicion." In the later years of Queen Elizabeth the horners of London bestirred themselves to see that the freemen of their company "being workemen traders and shoppkeepers for themselves" received a due share of the rough "hornes" gathered up by their officers. Rosedale, *The Horners' Company, Proceedings of the Society of Antiquaries*, 1909, p. 7. Among the wheelwrights of the same city, as late as 1683, every member had to be a "shopp-keeper for himselfe" before he could have an apprentice "bound unto him." Scott, *History of the Wheelwrights' Company*, p. 58.

[96] Despite the difficulty inherent in any attempt to harmonise the different factions in these large federations, in 1715, the hammermen of Ludlow still worked to increase the membership of their society. In fact the company is said to have owed its large membership to the pertinacity with which its officials prosecuted hammermen who refused to join the ranks. To all appearances, men who wished to work at the metal crafts in the borough of Ludlow were practically forced to join the organisation. *Shropshire Archaeol. & Natural History Soc. Trans.*, vol. xi, pp. 291-314.

[97] *Devonshire Assoc. for Advancement of Science*, vol. v, p. 120.

nance of good and cunning workmenship and the extirpation of uncunning deceivers of the people." [98] At this time, in Dublin, carpenters, masons and "heliers" or slaters, who, it appears, had affiliated in order "to inquire into all extortions and defects" committed by persons who practised the arts represented in their company, busied themselves in bringing to book "all that do intrude on the occupations contrary" to their "composition." [99]

Reference has already been made to a combine including the wrights, sawyers, slaters, joiners and carvers which is on record during the early years of the reign of Queen Elizabeth as one of the Chester gilds, but which lost the joiners and carvers when, in 1576, those two crafts established a gild by themselves. The wrights, sawyers and slaters, however, in their turn, merged their interests, being affiliated "under the seale of this cittie freely in respect to their former service." [100] In other communities, also, the men who worked with wood associated themselves apart from the other building crafts. For example, in 1664, at Pontefract, in order that they might meet the "charges whereunto the company be yearely putt in the said Towne," the wrights, bowyers, coopers, "patewners," turners, sawyers and "sewers," being as they said "poore men" drew up a set of ordinances for their joint "governance" and relief. And the better to effect these ends, the association levied a tax which such members as presumed to sell "tubbs, kitts," dishes or other articles made of wood were annually to pay.[101] At Beverley, in 1416, the fletchers, joiners and turners became co-brethren and "partners" with the "Bowers" in a gild in which they were to share equally in "all costs and ordinances, pertaining thereto.[102] From having to conform to the rules which governed the Newcastle coopers' industry, turners and pulley-makers who settled in the city seem later to have attained to membership in the coopers' gild.[103] Again, communities which maintained single gilds of carpenters, joiners and coopers and others of their kind, frequently established an amalgamated gild composed of the other building crafts. At the end of the sixteenth century in Kingston-upon-Hull, the bricklayers, tilers, wallers, plasterers and pavers were, it appears, incorporated "upon the desire and sute of the saide artificers and to the intent that the saide severall artes or trades may the

---

[98] *Hist. MSS. Com. Rep.* xiv, app. viii, p. 60.

[99] *Journ. Roy. Soc. of Antiq. of Ireland,* vol. 35, pt. iv, pp. 321–30.

[100] Morris, *Chester,* pp. 453. 403–05. In this form this company seems to have endured to the end. *Parl. Papers,* vol. xxvi, p. 2634.

[101] *The Book of Entries,* p. 372.

[102] *Historical MSS. Com. Rep., Beverley,* p. 97.

[103] Walford, *Gilds,* p. 150. Later these three handicrafts tried to get local rope-makers to join their association. But the rope-makers preferred to establish a gild by themselves, in order as they said, to be free from molestation from the other three crafts. The rope-makers accused their adversaries of imposing upon the public by charging excessive prices for their wares. *Ibid.,* p. 206. At Lancaster, however, by 1688, the rope-makers and coopers seem to have been associated with local carpenters and joiners. Simpson, *History of Lancaster,* p. 275.

better flourishe within the towne." The "Book of Orders" drawn up within a year of the company's incorporation shows that its ordinances were made "for the utilitie and good government of the occupations being incorporated into brotherhoode by composition in writing from the right worshipfull the maior, aldermen and burgesses of the said towne." One article in this "composicon" makes it obligatory upon the "breickmaker" who made "any breicke or tyle within this towne or countye to sell herein Hull" to have them duly "vewed by the . . . searcheres and if the same be not good and sufficient it shalbe seized and forfaited by theim." In addition, the company urged upon its members the necessity of seeing that lime should be honestly burnt "in the townes Kilne." [104] Details such as these are especially interesting in an account of an amalgamated builders' gild if only to test the theory advanced by certain writers who find a difference between the organisations established by the building handicrafts and those founded by the other occupations which flourished under the gild system. For instance, Professor Unwin states that in general under the system, the master craftsman who produces work on materials of his own and sells it direct to the consumer is the predominant figure, whereas the master in the building trades is either a kind of entrepreneur or else he is merely a privileged journeyman.[105] Yet in addition to the usual regulations which were deemed essential to the government of contemporary gilds, the builders of Hull undertook to oversee the manufacture of bricks. This fact would seem to indicate that, like their fellows in the other occupations, master builders assumed responsibility for the quality of the product they placed upon the market. There were, it is true, functions which were peculiar to the building business, but these also master builders undertook to regulate. Thus, as a final boon for the gift of incorporation, the company in Kingston-upon-Hull pledged itself to assign

[104] Lambert, *Two Thousand Years of Gild Life*, pp. 273–5. In order to have a reliable place in which to burn the products of neighbouring quarries, the corporation supplied a kiln and fixed the rates which the townsmen had to pay for its use.

[105] Professor Unwin makes this claim in connection with the large company composed of ten different building crafts which was incorporated in Lincoln and with that established by the wrights, sawyers and slaters in Chester. *Industrial Organization*, p. 67. Yet, we have already observed that the Lincoln builders secured their charter for the reasons which gained the metal crafts theirs—because the local governors still thought master craftsmen the best judges of skilled workmanship and this they were anxious to secure for their city. The Chester wrights, slaters and sawyers have been considered in connection with the joiners and carvers, crafts with which in early Elizabethan days they maintained a common gild. *Supra*, p. 56. That local joiners and carvers held the three first-named groups in sufficient esteem to establish a joint union proves, perhaps, that they were more than mere journeymen, however privileged their position may have been. And when the organisation split in two later in the century, the wrights, sawyers and slaters contrived to support a society between them, and ruled it so autocratically as to provoke from city authorities the threat to dissolve their "corporacon" unless they changed their tactics. Morris, *Chester*, p. 436.

to "everie inhabitant . . . upon II daies warning or request . . .
given at the dwelling house of the warden or his deputy . . . at
soche time and times hereafter as the saide workmen can not
easilie be gotten . . . sufficient workmen to do any worke according to the lawes and statutes of this land . . . and to teache or
procure to be taught their servauntes and apprentices as well to
pave as other partes of their traide, which shalbe likewise coven-
aunted by theim in the indentures of apprenticeshipp." Master
builders evidently realised that bricks and tiles too, for that matter,
had to be laid as well as made and they regulated the exercise of
both functions in their gild by-laws.[106]   At Coventry, prior to 1454,
the tile-makers had annually to come before the mayor and pledge
themselves neither to sell nor to place semi-tiles.[107]   To seventeenth-
century brick-makers of London was entrusted the supervision of
the making of bricks for their city.[108]   Taken all in all, therefore,
it would seem that the men engaged in the building crafts like their
brethren in the other occupations established large gild groups and
for precisely similar reasons.   Indeed, after the passage of the
act which made it possible for "any freemason, rough mason, carpenter, bricklayer, plasterer . . . borne in this realme or made
denison to work in any of the seide crafts in anye cittie, borough
or town corporate albeit the said person or persons" neither "in-
habit or dwell . . . nor be free of the same," master builders were
practically compelled to join their forces in order to keep alien
builders from gaining a foothold in their respective communities.[109]
Apparently only by so doing could the builders of Hull hope to
flourish, a hope which was doubtless shared by the municipality in
sanctioning their organisation.   Besides, if seventeenth-century
traders confessed to uniting their gild forces expressly to keep
aliens out of their respective boroughs when the state sympathised
sufficiently with their policy of exclusion to enact laws authorising
them to enforce it,[110] it is scarcely surprising to find the different

[106] On the whole, whether these craftsmen be regarded as manufacturers
of bricks, tiles or of different articles made of wood, or even as contracting
employers who, upon demand, supplied both men and materials, they seem to
have been always master craftsmen bound by the rules of the game.   Mr.
Unwin's interpretation of their rôle appears insufficiently to emphasise the
fact that membership in the gilds was open only to masters who had served
a proper apprenticeship.

[107] *Leet Book*, pt. ii, p. 279.

[108] Cunningham, *Development of English Industry and Commerce*, vol. i,
p. 305.   In 1652 officials of the Tilers' and Bricklayers' Company of London
petitioned for additional power to enable them to reform certain abuses which
had crept into the making of tiles.   Inderwick, *Interregnum*, p. 85.

[109] 2 & 3 Edward VI, c. 15.   Mr. Hibbert claims that gilds of workmen in
the building crafts had been seriously affected, if not destroyed by the
passage of this act.   *Influence & Develop. of Eng. Gilds*, p. 133.   The act,
however, was repealed the following year.   3 & 4 Edward VI, c. 20.

[110] In 1628 the Preston mercers' company petitioned the town council for
incorporation on the ground that alien traders had failed to obey not only the
act of 1 & 2 Philip & Mary c. 7, which had forbidden countrymen to sell "by
retaile" various sorts of merchandise "except it bee in open Faires" but the

building handicraftsmen forming associations, when the state deliberately authorised outsiders to practise their callings in any urban community they saw fit, despite the opposition of gilds of local builders. Fortunately for the organised builders, they could, apparently, still count upon the sympathy and cooperation of local executives.

By later Tudor times in practically all the boroughs amalgamated clothing corporations, more or less comprehensive in their make-up had received official sanction. Indeed, the monopoly which Oxford had conferred upon local weavers and fullers in the fifteenth century was confirmed to them in 1571.[111] By 1565 a Durham company comprising clothworkers and walkers counted among its privileges that of supervising the cloth which came into the borough from the surrounding country and of seizing that which was "deceitfully wrought." [112] From Warwick, in 1572, comes a "declaracion of the constitucions and orders agreid upon . . . as well by the company and felowshippe of Walkers and Dyers . . . as consentyd unto by the Bailief and principall Burgesses of the same Borough" by the said crafts to be "fulfilled and kept." [113] In 1585 the assembly of Northampton granted a new constitution to local fullers and shearmen at their asking, for the better conduct of their occupations and for the "lawful using of their fellow townsmen and neighbours in the country who had woollen cloth to be wrought." [114] Five years later Queen Elizabeth conceded a charter to her "well beloved" weavers, walkers and clothiers of Worcester, because their affairs "through default of good and provident government, oversight and correction" were "insufficiently done" to the prejudice of her "lieges and subjects." [115] In 1591, at Ipswich, in order "to avoid the great increase of foreainers" and the better to regulate their work and govern their apprentices, the clothiers, clothworkers, weavers, shearmen and dyers were encour-

Elizabethan statute of apprentices which had required that craftsmen should serve an apprenticeship of seven years preliminary to mastership in any trade. *Supra*, p. 25.

[111] Turner, *Records of Oxford*, p. 341.

[112] Fretton, *Memorials of Coventry*, p. 20.

[113] *Black Book*, p. 71.

[114] *Borough Records*, vol. ii, p. 288. Fullers and shearmen elsewhere had probably merged their interests, because in 1555 the fullers of Bristol were offering to "be as one craft" with local shearmen as they said "it is in all places in this realme." Fox and Taylor, *Bristol Weavers*, p. 98.

[115] Green, *History & Antiquities of Worcester*, vol. ii, append. lxxi. Before amalgamating their interests, these weavers and fullers had evidently supported separate gilds. For in the fourteenth year of the reign of King Henry VIII, an ordinance issued by the gild of weavers bade each member walk hand in hand with the "Walkers" when they proceeded to the cathedral for services. Moreover, each gild contributed liberally to defray the cost of the reception which was accorded Queen Elizabeth in 1575, upon the occasion of her visit to the city, when she is reported to have said that "she liked as well" the citizens there as "any people in all her progresses." *The Clothiers' Company of Worcester*, Reports and Papers, *Assoc. Architectural Societies*, vol. xv, pp. 334-5.

aged to establish a joint union.[116]   This union gains an added interest from the fact that fifteen years before its formation, all the trades and handicrafts of Ipswich were grouped together into four heterogeneous combinations, the only ones which were then allowed in the borough. Seemingly the older miscellaneous combinations of crafts failed to provide for the best interests of Ipswich's clothing industry and consequently the crafts concerned in its development were reunited under one gild management. In the reign of King James I an Exeter gild composed of weavers, fullers and shearmen secured a new charter which conferred added authority upon its members.[117]   The minutes of the Common Council of Nottingham, under date of November 22, 1630, record, how on that day, "the companie of the Dyers and Clothworkers" moved it for a "confirmacion of theire ordinances and the same beinge redd," the council signified its approval of the "same ordynances, so that the same occupacion from tyme to tyme yearly, att or before the Chamberlaynes accompte, doe paye to the vse of the corporacion in regard to theire assistance and allowance thereof the some of xls. togeather with such other profitts as shall yearely arise or growe to the benefitt of the corporacion by reason of the penalties or forfeytures mencioned in the saied ordynances." [118]   The clothing crafts of Nottingham probably made it well worth the city's while to support their consolidation. Because the Doncaster weavers, walkers and shearmen had neglected to enforce their corporate rules to the loss of the "occupiers of those trades," in 1655 the gildsmen promised in future to do good work or give proper redress to the "partie offended." [119]   In 1682 a Coventry fellowship which included "taylors" and clothworkers took measures to prevent its members from employing "a forrenyer" who was "no freeman of this City." [120]   Six years later the "Taylors" of the "Burrough" of Newbury who, in the reign of Queen Elizabeth, had been "incorporated into and amongst the clothiers" were ordered to continue so "for the tyme to come" because that arrangement was "most convenient" for all the parties concerned.[121]

The existence of consolidated clothing corporations is thus fully established, although available records fail to give us a real insight into their internal economy. It is evident, however, that, in addition to the handicraft groups, many seem to have included a body

[116] Wodderspoon, *Memorials of Ipswich*, p. 198. How long this company protected Ipswich's clothing industry does not appear, but by 1619 a corporation composed of "Taylors and Clothworkers" was condemned for making "profitt off their illworkmanshipp." *Lansdowne MSS., B. M.*, 162, f. 195.

[117] *Trans. Devonshire Assoc. for Advancement of Science*, vol. v, p. 137. In 1616 the records of Lichfield certify to the existence of a company of dyers, weavers and clothworkers. Harwood, *Lichfield*, p. 570.

[118] *Records of the Borough*, vol. v, p. 147.

[119] *Borough Records*, vol. ii, p. 288.

[120] *Book of the Taylors and Clothworkers' Company*, MS. *Muniment Room, Gildhall, Coventry*, England.

[121] *History of Newbury*, p. 306.

of clothiers or tailors who dealt in cloth and for that reason looked after the mercantile interests in the organisation, leaving the manufacturing end of it to the different sets of craftsmen. Extant records of the London clothworkers' company which was founded in that city in the sixteenth century seem to prove this to have been true of their organisation. According to these records, in the nineteenth year of the reign of King Henry VIII, "for the good of the handy Trade" the freemen of the art or mystery of "Shermen as of the art or mystery of fullers" were incorporated as "one entire art . . . by the name of clothworkers only." [122] In pursuance of the rights conferred upon the company by its charter, the master, wardens and fellowship "willing" it seems and "desiring to have amonge theym good ordre, rule and governaunce" devised such statutes as they considered necessary for their "conservacion." Unfortunately almost the first decade of the companies' activities are unaccounted for, since its earliest extant records date from 1536.[123] These reveal a membership which comprised various groups of merchants who traded by wholesale as well as by retail, and in conjunction with two handicraft groups —the shearmen and fullers—worked together to forward the local cloth industry. However, even at this early date things were not running to the handicraft liking, for the more conservative among them objected to the methods pursued by the mercantile class. It was, for instance, to the interest of the handicraft not to have cloth exported unfinished; yet by 1540, the mercantile members were exporting it so in direct violation of a law which forbade their exportation in that state. By 1568, the handicraft were further aggrieved because the merchants "doo in their own ware houses privilie packe up their clothes." As one way of stopping further irregularities of this sort, the handicraft proposed that certain of their number whom they might appoint, be given the "view of all the merchaunts' clothes hereafter to be wrought" within the company, and the seeing to it that no member should "folde, tak or press or to delyver to the owner any merchaunts' cloths" before it had been "viewed" by two of the "said psons so appoynted."[124] The merchants, however, failed to approve of this proposal for reform; whereupon the handicraft appealed to the Privy Council and urged that body to find a way to adjust the points in dispute between them and the merchants. But the merchants would have none of this second way out of the company's difficulties. On the contrary, they declared that, in appealing to the Privy Council,[125] the handicraft had "very scaunderously touched

---

[122] *Ordinances of the Clothworkers' Company*, p. 21. Also Herbert, *Twelve Great Livery Companies*, vol. ii, p. 654.

[123] We are indebted to Professor Unwin for publishing extracts from the Clothworkers' records. *Industrial Organization*, Appendix, pp. 228–234 et passim.

[124] *Industrial Organization*, p. 45.

[125] *Ibid.*, p. 122.

and complayned of this companie as touching their rulers and superiors." This claim of the merchants to superiority over the handicraft failed naturally to allay handicraft dissatisfaction with their associates. They considered the merchants far from "skylfull yn the handicrafte" [126] and too preoccupied with their own interests [127] to take into account those of the handicrafts. But for that matter, neither one of the handicraft groups in the organisation showed any especial concern for the interests of the other. The shearmen, in particular, took advantage of the fullers when the opportunity presented itself, as is evident from what occurred in 1567, in which year six of the fullers appeared before the court of the company "yn the name of the whole" and asked that "none of the sheremen shulde from hensforthe make price with the merchaunts for the rowyng of clothes." [128] They insisted that they should "be called to make their owne prices and receyve their owne money for their wokemanshipp." On the whole, however, despite occasional clashes such as these, the society seems to have kept its various groups working fairly well together to the forwarding of the city's clothing industry. Undoubtedly both the shearmen and fullers had jeopardised their independence in associating themselves with men who frankly pronounced themselves the rulers and superiors of the handicraft members; yet in the long run the advantages the latter gained from the alliance probably reconciled them to its disadvantages. First of all, the clothworkers' company scored an immediate triumph in securing a place among the twelve great livery companies, many of whom boasted a more ancient lineage. Having become one of these elect companies, the cloth workers had no longer to fear that such of its members as were ambitious to hold office would desert its ranks and join the drapers or merchant taylors.[129] The clothworkers could claim a station as exalted as that held by both the purely mercantile groups. Then, too, what was more advantageous to them from an economic standpoint, the shearmen and fullers were, probably for the first time in

[126] An item dated 1559 tells that because "this yere the fower wardens of the yomanry be merchaunts and not skylfull yn the handicrafte" eight assistants were appointed "to execute their authority concerning the handycrafte." *Ibid.*, p. 114.

[127] Included in the organisation were also "diverse" members "which occupye cottonyng," who asked "ayde of the house towards a sewte which they have before my lorde mayor and Aldermen concerning that no freman shoulde putt any cloth to cottonyng to any foreyn but onely to fremen." *Ibid.*, p. 228. Householders, too, were included who "occupied buying and selling of fustians and silk," but in a way which provoked from city officials a warning to sell better pennyworths thereafter. *Ibid.*, p. 113. By 1639 the company's membership had been extended to include mercers, silkmen, grocers and hosiers. *Ibid.*, p. 234.

[128] Unwin, *Industrial Organization*, p. 231.

[129] The shearmen had suffered this indignity in 1515, when, much to their disgust, a member who had been elected an alderman had himself translated to the drapers, as being more ancient and one of the twelve great livery companies. Herbert, *Twelve Great Livery Cos.*, vol. ii, p. 647, note.

their history in a position to hold something like their own against the drapers and merchant taylors who together had dominated the mercantile end of the cloth business and handicapped the handicraft groups in more ways than one.[130] Indeed, the opposition of the merchant groups seems to have kept the shearmen from securing incorporation until 1507. It may be that the merchants' persecution had driven the shearmen to renounce their gild independence and to associate themselves with city fullers and such merchants as were willing to join with them in forming a common union. However, no matter what the reason for the rise of the clothworkers' company, its position was assured and its handicraft members able to secure a considerable amount of protection and an even greater freedom of trade than they sometimes found either desirable or profitable.

The success which followed the incorporation of the London shearmen and fullers may have led clothing craftsmen of other communities to follow their lead and combine their forces. In all probability the men engaged in making cloth had always suffered from the competition of local drapers whose interest in the sale of that commodity inevitably impelled them to confine the different clothing handicrafts to their immediate branch of clothmaking. The drapers of London made their purpose clear to city dyers, "listers" and fullers in 1364, when they bade these craftsmen keep to their own mysteries and in no way meddle with the making, buying or selling of any sort of cloth or drapery.[131] It is clear that at that early date the drapers regarded theirs as a business apart from that of the clothing crafts.[132] It was probably only because the gilds of drapers played a different rôle from that assigned to the clothing crafts that they were allowed to exist side by side in the same community. Professor Unwin, however, sees little difference in the part played by the single gilds which were established by the drapers, and the larger groups organised in common by the different clothworking crafts.[133] To his way of thinking, both

---

[130] In the exercise of the joint powers of search over all the cloth brought to the fairs of St. Bartholomew and Southwark which the London drapers and merchant taylors had enjoyed since the days of King Edward IV, these merchant groups had had many opportunities to harass the clothing crafts. Besides in 1479, assurance had been given the two merchant companies that "no charter of incorporation should be given to the Sheermen." *Parl. Papers, London Livery Cos. Commission*, 1884, pt. ii, vol. xxxix, p. 674. The fullers of the city, however, were incorporated in 1480.

[131] *Letter Book G*, p. 167. Also Herbert, *Twelve Great Livery Cos.*, vol. i, p. 480.

[132] In attempting to restrain clothworkers from "buying cloth and selling the same again" in 1634, the London drapers still claimed that the dressing of cloth was "the subject matter" of the clothworkers' "trade" while the selling of them was the business of drapers. The clothworkers, however, had a different view of what constituted their "trade." In their turn they insisted that they got their living by buying rough, undressed, country-dressed cloth, perfecting their dressing and then selling them. *State Papers Domestic*, 1634-5, nos. 39, 104, 278.

[133] *Industrial Organization*, p. 97.

species of gild represent the rise to predominance of organised industrial capital and he contrasts these gilds with those established by trading capital, which was represented by the companies of merchants and mercers. For instance, he regards the gilds of drapers of Shrewsbury and the amalgamated clothiers' companies which are found in Worcester and Ipswich as the same type of organisation. Yet we have found the drapers' company of Shrewsbury supported by merchants who were bent primarily upon selling cloth, while the clothing companies of Worcester and Ipswich included various groups of clothing crafts who were chiefly concerned with the different processes of the manufacture of cloth. Moreover, Professor Unwin admits that in securing their charter in 1364, the drapers of London proposed to exclude the clothing crafts from competing with them as traders. If that had been the aim of drapers, in the nature of things, they would scarcely have opened their gilds to the handicrafts. Besides, in boroughs of consequence, drapers and the different clothing crafts are rarely found members of the same gild group; this fact doubtless proves that the gulf that separated them in the beginning remained for the most part insurmountable to the end.[134] Even in the smaller communities the drapers and the clothing crafts are scarcely ever found members of one of the stated number of gild associations into which in later Elizabethan days the local trades and handicrafts were being merged. The membership of the clothiers' and clothworkers' company in Reading was limited to men who made cloth, while the drapers in their turn joined forces with the mercers and other traders of the town.[135] It is true that when, in 1614, the borough of Devizes reduced her gild groups to three, the drapers headed one in company with the various clothing crafts. In this connection, however, it is interesting to note, that the drapers tried to restrict the handicraft groups to selling woollen cloth "of their own making."[136] In this instance, the mercers' company, in its turn, included in addition to different groups of traders, various handicrafts also.

Despite the advantages which accrued to the clothing crafts who associated, they did not always prosper in that state. A union of serge-makers, serge-weavers and wool-combers which was sanctioned in 1609 at Southampton, endured only a decade, when it was dissolved with the consent of the parties concerned. For some reason the organisation had failed to thrive upon the privileges

[134] Later in the *"Gilds and Companies of London,"* p. 87, Professor Unwin states that the clothing crafts, the weavers, dyers, fullers and shearmen, tended to fall into groups which were headed by drapers.

[135] The one exception to this rule which has come to light, is the Dorchester clothiers' company recorded in 1630 as one of the five associations then fostered by the authorities. Included in this company were the clothiers, woollen drapers, haberdashers of hats, weavers, dyers, tailors, hosiers, feltmakers, clothworkers, and "borellers." Hutchins, *Dorset*, vol. ii, p. 338.

[136] *Wiltshire Archaeol. & Nat. Hist. Soc. Mag.*, vol. iv, pp. 160–2.

which had been conceded to it.[137] A corporation composed of shearmen and dyers which flourished in Gloucester about 1575 seems to have become quite decayed by 1634.[138] At Bury St. Edmunds a gild limited to a number of clothiers, clothworkers, woollen weavers and tailors was incorporated by the borough in 1609, unbeknownst, it is said, to the other clothing groups. When the craftsmen who had been excluded from membership learned of the new corporations' existence they asked the borough to suppress it on the ground of its having been instituted by a few persons against the wishes of the majority. The whole project they claimed was a scheme concocted to extort money.[139] By 1730, in Leeds, the clothing manufacture had declined owing, it appears, to the failure of local clothworkers to enforce their corporate authority. Whereupon the city authorities summoned forty of the most "sufficient and honest clothiers of the Borough" to a meeting which was called for the purpose of discussing ways and means to keep the corporation going.[140]

Whether or not these amalgamated clothing corporations prospered, they were established primarily to enable their members to strengthen their hold over the cloth industry under their jurisdiction. Manifestly neither towns nor gilds relished losing control over the industry that for centuries had produced a goodly part of the national wealth. Possibly for this reason the clothworkers were encouraged to combine their forces in order that they might control the cloth business left in the towns.[141]

[137] Davies, *History of Southampton*, p. 275.
[138] Fosbrooke, *History of Gloucester*, p. 404.
[139] *Hist. MSS. Comm. Rep.* xiv, App. viii, p. 141.
[140] Wardell, *History of Leeds*, p. 70. By 1626 the manufacture of woollen cloth in Leeds seems to have reached a point where it needed corporate protection; for according to a provision contained in the charter which in that year was conceded to the authorities, the borough was "to have all reasonable gilds" for the better government of the inhabitants and especially of those who manufactured woollen cloth.
[141] From the days of Richard II, the cloth industry had been migrating from the towns into the rural districts throughout the west and north. An act passed by the parliament of Edward IV (4 Edward IV, c. 1) gives an interesting picture of its progress in those directions. The towns had never succeeded in keeping the making of cloth entirely in the hands of local gildsmen. With the rise of craft gilds, individual clothiers were evidently manufacturing cloth in certain of the boroughs and corporate towns. Indeed in the early days of King Edward I, Reading had become noted for its cloth, and boasted among its inhabitants a rich clothier named Thomas Cole. Coates, *History of Reading*, p. 456. When King Edward III decreed that wool should be worked up into cloth within the kingdom and that all who would, should make cloth wheresoever they might wish, he encouraged individuals to embark upon the cloth industry. No wonder, therefore, that in 1339, Thomas Blanket and certain other Bristol weavers protested to the king when local authorities levied a tax upon their plant and otherwise "troubled and aggrieved" them and their workmen, because they were making cloth within the city. Latimer, *History of the Merchant Venturers of Bristol*, p. 10. Later the story of "Jacke of Newbarie" with his hundred looms (*Journ. Brit. Archaeol. Assoc.* n. s., vol. ii, p. 261), and of Stump the clothier who set up

In places where all the trades and handicrafts merged their gild interests, large federations of victualling crafts took their place along with the rest. Indeed, theirs was a place of sufficient importance to their community to warrant the authorities in setting apart one organisation for them to maintain.[142] This accounts for a company like the victuallers' and innholders' of Reading, one of five which was sanctioned in the borough of that day. Its membership included local vintners, bakers, brewers, butchers, fishmongers, chandlers,[143] malt-makers, salters, flax-drapers and woodmongers. Again the membership of two of the four companies which were established in St. Albans in the later sixteenth century was likewise confined to these craftsmen. And when, in the reign of King Charles II the number of local gilds was reduced from four to two, the victuallers were influential enough to head one of them.[144] Likewise, in Gravesend the victuallers' company formed one of the two organisations which were organised in 1573, for the purpose of providing for the better government "of so great a multitude" as the borough then supported.[145] And when communities like Wallingford and Faversham could maintain only one organisation for their trades and handicrafts, purveyors of foodstuffs in company with other townsmen, lost their separate identity and found a place in the one great trade organisation which was

his industry in the monastery at Malmsbury (Leland, *Itinerary,* vol. ii, p. 53) testify to the growth of the cloth manufacture in borough precincts in defiance of local gilds.

[142] It seems that local innkeepers, victuallers and ale-house keepers were taxed to entertain any strangers of note who visited the mediaeval boroughs. In 1587 at Shrewsbury, under penalty of being discharged by "Mr. Bailiffs of victualling hereafter," members of the above-named groups were ordered to provide the funds needed to entertain the "Counsell of the Marches." *Shropshire Archaeological & Natural History Soc. Trans.,* vol. xi, p. 160. And when in 1728 "the several guilds and innkeepers" withdrew the contributions they had been accustomed to make towards entertaining the Judges, the corporation of Shrewsbury concluded to "expend no money on that account" thereafter. *Ibid.,* p. 207.

[143] An Act drafted in 1620 which proposed to exempt the tallow-chandlers' company of London "out of the statutes against regrators, forestallers and ingrossers, by their proper nomination of Tallow chandlers," may serve to explain why chandlers associated themselves with the victualling crafts. It seems that by classing themselves under "the general name of victuallers," chandlers had contrived to escape paying the fines imposed by the laws which condemned such practices. But, having, of late, been "much molested by informers," the tallow-chandlers probably considered it prudent to protect themselves thereafter by having confirmed to them as tallow-chandlers, the right to enjoy the privileges conceded to the victualling crafts. See *Hist. MSS. Commis. Rep.* iii, *App.* p. 19, for a copy of this act.

[144] *St. Albans, Charters,* p. 7.

[145] The proportion of victuallers in this multitude which according to the record resolved itself into fifty inhabitants, was twenty-six, to twenty-four members ascribed to the mercers' company, the second organisation sanctioned in the town, at that time. Five of the twelve jurats elected to serve the town at the same time prove to have been victuallers. Cruden, *History, of Gravesend,* p. 197.

then maintained in order to guard the gild business still remaining to local gildsmen.

We have thus far accounted for the rise of combinations of crafts which represent in the main either the mercantile, or the leather, metal, building, clothing and victualling crafts. However, not all the associations of which we have evidence fall naturally into one of these six divisions. Now and again the records disclose handicraft combinations which can scarcely be justified by the fact that they used similar materials. For example, in the last decade of the sixteenth century, in Kingston-upon-Hull, local musicians, stationers, book-binders and basket-makers in company with five groups of metalmen and the glaziers and painters, applied to the local authorities for permission "to be but one entire company and not severall companies to the intente that the said artes, occupacions and misteries may better flourish within the towne." At the time of the company's creation, two supervisers, a smith and a pewterer were appointed to enforce the rules and regulations which were deemed essential to its government. The company seems to have directed its energies toward keeping non-members from opening a shop or from selling or even offering for sale within borough limits, except on market days, commodities handled by gild members.[146] Evidently borough and gild authorities were impelled to stretch a point and encourage the consolidation of unrelated handicrafts in order to preserve local business for Hull's own people. Again, oddly enough, at Chester, in 1649, a society which was composed of the painters, glaziers, embroiderers and stationers applied to the mayor and council for help in restraining non-freemen from practicing the embroiderers' art.[147] From Dublin comes evidence to account for the bond which in the seventeenth century linked together wholly unrelated crafts. According to charges preferred in 1627 by the Irish "commons," barber-surgeons, glovers and fishmongers, handicrafts who were "far beyond many of the other city corporations" in wealth and numbers, were wont to join one or two other corporations of recognised standing, albeit the latter "had little need of them." In this way wealthy tradesmen escaped contributing their share when a "cess" was imposed or a loan raised, to the despair of the "weaker sort" of corporations, who in consequence, were obliged to pay more than their share of

---

[146] Lambert, *Two Thousand Years of Gild Life*, p. 262.

[147] *Hist. MSS. Comm. Rep.* viii, p. 385. In 1602, in the same city a linen-drapers' and bricklayers' company was incorporated, when, according to tradition, a bricklayer, who was mayor of Chester took to wife a lady who was a linen-draper. *The Bricklayers' Company of Chester, Journal Chester and N. Wales Archaeol. & Historic Soc.*, n. s., vol. xxii, p. 55. By the end of the seventeenth century, however, differences seem to have arisen between members of the two bodies which the linen-drapers brought to the attention of the mayor. That official, after hearing the matter in dispute between the contestants, decided that the "Lynen-drapers and the Bricklayers should be separated as one Company, the latter being troublesome and unserviceable to the former."

the charges levied upon the gilds for civic purposes. As one way
of apportioning those charges more equitably, the weaker corporations urged the assembly either to have the wealthy craftsmen join
one of the corporations which really needed their support or else
"attend their own charter." Apparently, acting upon the urging,
the assembly commissioned city officials to summon the offending
barber-surgeons and their associates and instructed them to ascertain the facts in the case. If they found the crafts in question
illegally joined to another organisation they were to certify the
finding to the board of aldermen, who, by the authority vested in
them might annex the men "to such companies as most stood in
need of their assistance." [148] Manifestly this was an instance where
craftsmen deemed themselves justified in using any means to attain
their corporate ends. In the same "cittie of Dublin a certain small
and inconsiderable number of wett Glouvers" [149] hit upon the
scheme of confederating with and taking into their "pretended
society," as their opposers termed it, weavers, tailors, gardeners
and various other handicrafts for no reason except "to make their
companies to seem more numerous." The glovers and their con-
federates hoped thereby to obtain a hearing to the petition they
were forwarding to the Lords Justices of Ireland, asking them to
use their influence toward securing the enforcement of certain
measures which had been passed with the object of preventing various sorts of skins from being exported from Ireland. The craftsmen begged that this be done in order that their business "long at a
standstill," might be revived and made to prosper.[150] In Ireland,
evidently at this time, desperate cases required desperate remedies.

Professor Unwin advances a theory to account for the rise of
miscellaneous craft combinations which may add enough to our
discussion to warrant consideration in this connexion. He regards
a fourteenth-century clash between the London saddlers on the
one side and on the other, joiners, painters and lorimers, three
groups of handicrafts who, in their day were employed in different
branches of saddle-making, as evidence that a species of amalgamated gild in which "one of the members of a group acquired an
ascendancy over the others," prevailed universally among the English crafts.[151] In this particular case, the three so-called auxiliary
crafts took sides against the saddlers and accused them of trying
to hinder the three crafts in question from "selling any manner of
merchandise pertaining to their trades to any tradesman except the
saddlers." The saddlers, in their turn, charged the other three

---

[148] *Journ. Royal Society of Antiquaries of Ireland,* vol. 33, pt. iii, 5th
series, p. 229.
[149] *State Papers Domestic, Charles II,* 1669, no. 27.
[150] In order to retrieve the losses which they had sustained in the great
fire of 1666, the London grocers enlarged their company by admitting local
druggists and tobacconists. *Parl. Papers,* 1884, pt. v, p. 399.
[151] Unwin, *Industrial Organization,* pp. 22–23. Also Riley, *Memorials,* pp.
156–162.

groups with entering into a compact to strike work in common and even to close their stalls in the event that any of their craftsmen had further trouble with the saddlers. The saddlers also complained that "the painters and joiners do set every point of their trade at a fixed price . . . by reason whereof they are making themselves kings of the land." Professor Unwin claims that the moral to be drawn from this dispute between the four handicrafts, was the necessity for unity and that amalgamations "of this nature" became subsequently a common feature of industrial organisation. Although evidence of the amalgamation of kindred crafts for the purpose of settling commercial feuds has been abundant, little of it serves to prove that crafts which represent such varied industries as saddlers, joiners, painters and lorimers, commonly adopted such a policy. Apparently they did not in London, where, from all accounts, both the saddlers and the lorimers maintained separate gilds to the end.[152] And when the joiners of that city renounced their gild independence, they amalgamated, not with city saddlers, but with the carvers,[153] while the painters, in their turn, joined with stainers in forming a common society.[154] Combination seemingly never appealed to the four metropolitan handicraft groups and therefore could scarcely be said to form a precedent for their union elsewhere. Furthermore, there is no evidence of a sufficient number of combines entered into in other localities by craftsmen who represented such diverse occupations, to justify their being regarded as examples of a type which prevailed universally. The handicrafts with whom the saddlers amalgamated, worked either with leather or with metal. For example, at Morpeth, in the reign of Henry VIII, the saddlers joined with local smiths and armourers to form a common gild as they explain, "for voyddyng of grugges." [155] This was a praiseworthy sentiment, one which probably commended itself to Morpeth authorities, who had doubtless suffered from the failure of these craftsmen to work harmoniously together when they were organised separately. The relations which existed between the saddlers and armourers of various communities seem to have been very close. For example, in Boston, in 1581, we find that the saddlers entered into an agreement with the smiths, armourers, "ferrors," braziers and cutlers "to have a corporation of themselves," although seventeen years later the saddlers and armourers withdrew from the corporation.[156] In Chester, however, the saddlers associated themselves with local curriers and in Stratford-on-Avon with the shoemakers, while in Lichfield they established a gild in company with the glovers and whittawyers.[157] In smaller communities like Reading and Devizes, the saddlers

[152] Sherwell, *Historical Account of Guild of Saddlers*, p. 142 et. seq.
[153] Hazlitt, *The Great Livery Cos.*, pp. 560–573.
[154] *Municipal Corporations Commis. Report*, 1837, vol. 25, p. 201.
[155] Hodgson, *History of Morpeth*, p. 66.
[156] Thompson, *History of Boston*, p. 159.
[157] Harwood, *History of Lichfield*, p. 569.

sought membership in the large companies which were headed by the leathersellers. Manifestly neither the saddlers nor any of the craftsmen who worked with leather followed any one rule in amalgamating. Taking industrial organisation as it appears among the leather crafts in different sections of the country, we find, for example, in London one consolidated leathersellers' company, while the other leather crafts, the saddlers, skinners, tanners, curriers and cordwainers persisted in separate gild state. In Chester, where already in the middle of the fourteenth century the tanners, shoemakers and skinners were united in one organisation, we later find the tanners and shoemakers maintaining themselves in solitary state, while the skinners joined forces with the feltmakers, the glovers with the fellmongers and white tawyers, and the saddlers with the curriers. Again, in addition to the skinners' and glovers' combination which was registered in Newcastle-upon-Tyne, the tanners, saddlers, cordwainers and cobblers established single gilds, while the curriers combined their forces with the feltmakers and the armourers. And combinations varied just as much in other places in these as in other industries. It can conscientiously be said that there were amalgamations of tanners or curriers, shoemakers and cordwainers, and of skinners and glovers, which were established so far as we can judge, to safeguard the business interests of their members; for instance, to enable shoemakers, cordwainers and glovers to get their material upon better terms than they otherwise might and to insure to the tanners and skinners on their part a ready market for their wares within their city. By putting an end to their rivalry and working together in peace and amity, both parties could battle for their rights and keep enterprising outsiders out of the towns. The more comprehensive leather companies rose even in the metropolis only when certain of the minor crafts could no longer support individual unions.

Of a different type were the extremely heterogeneous associations which, in early Stuart days, were formed by combining the handicrafts as well as the trades in one general aggregation; such for instance, as we have noticed at Wallingford in Berkshire and at Faversham in Kent. The town council of Faversham, in drawing up the ordinance incorporating their mercers' society, dwelt on the great good which had hitherto been attained by distributing the crafts among several companies. They averred that by committing the various crafts to the care of "men of gravity best experienced" in the mysteries, the "particular grievance and deceits" which were practised in every trade or craft could best be "examined, reformed, and ordered."[158] But though the town may at one time have approved of organising the crafts in separate gilds, it perceived that the power of the gilds was considerably limited in the seventeenth century, and accordingly resolved to protect the trades and crafts in their local monopoly, insisting that thereafter

---

[158] *Kent Archaeol. Soc. Trans.*, vol. ix, p. lxviii.

"no one might sell or utter any other ware or stuff but such as belonged to his trade." Although the idea of maintaining the local trades and handicrafts in individual unions was given up, it was still considered necessary to maintain some form of industrial organisation.[159]

However, not all the smaller towns disposed of their separate gild groups so summarily by forcing all their traders and handicrafts to unite in forming one great corporation. It may be worth while, therefore, to notice the various stages through which the complex associations passed before they finally culminated in these large federations. The first evidence which we have of the tendency to draw together the trades and crafts into large gild groups appears from the records of Reading.[160] About the middle of the sixteenth century the merchants and artisans of the town were distributed into five groups, one of which, the mercers' and drapers' company, comprised the mercers, drapers, potuaries, haberdashers, chapmen, tailors and cloth-drawers. Thus here the various trades and crafts were classified in groups with a due regard to their natural economic relations. Most of the other boroughs, however, which gradually followed the same policy and incorporated great federations of labour, were not equally happy in their method of grouping. We find, for instance, that in 1576 Ipswich was supporting four large companies, each of which included the most varied trades and handicrafts. Thus in the mercers' gild were the mariners, shipwrights, bookbinders, printers, fishmongers, swordsetters, cooks, fletchers, physicians, hatters, cappers, and merchants.[161] In the smaller communities, when the trade grouping called for yet fewer organisations, they naturally became more heterogeneous in character. The three companies organised at Devizes in 1614, which are known as the drapers, the mercers, and the leathersellers, are interesting examples of this type of organisation.[162] In the mercers' gild were grouped together the grocers, linendrapers, haberdashers, vintners, innholders, bakers, brewers, apothecaries, barbers, surgeons, chandlers, painters, braziers, and glaziers. On the other hand, at Abingdon the grocers and not the mercers, drapers, or haberdashers, gave their name to the gild, which included all the ordinary merchant traders as well as such of the handicrafts as the local officials agreed should be "sorted and severed to make upp the Company of Grocers" and be called "the Company of Grocers and their Fellowes."[163] In these in-

---

[159] This Faversham company seems to have served the purpose which had called it into being. In 1835 it was still preserving its corporate existence and exerting some influence in civic affairs. *Munic. Corporation Comm. Report,* 1835, p. 967.

[160] Walford, *Gilds,* p. 90.

[161] Wodderspoon, *Memorials of Ipswich,* p. 174.

[162] *Wilt., Archaeol. Soc. Trans.,* vol. iv, p. 162.

[163] The mayor, bailiffs, and the rest of the common council, were led to take this step in 1669, as they said "for the better service to be had of all the Freemen of the said Borough and for the better, exact and more civill gov-

stances, as at St. Albans, Kingston-upon-Thames, and other towns, where but two great companies survived, it became as impossible to apportion the crafts according to any natural classification as it had been at Faversham and Wallingford. The forces which had driven men in the fourteenth century to organise individual unions for the purpose of developing specific commercial and industrial occupations were no longer operative. An historian of Ipswich,[164] referring in particular to the miscellaneous combination of trades which the mercers' and the drapers' companies held together in that borough, quaintly says that the mysteries of each could not be worthy of preservation when "coks and fletchers" mingled with "merchaunts and prynters," or "caskett makers and surgeons" with "carryers and innholders." Obviously the gildsmen were making a last despairing fight for existence.

ernment of the same, and the comonalty thereof." The company, one of three then organised, comprised grocers, mercers, woollen-drapers, linendrapers, haberdashers of hats, feltmakers, dyers, hosiers, apothecaries, "maultres," ironmongers, spurriers, "scholemasters," scriveners, barbers, upholsterers, clothworkers and shearmen. Just about a century earlier the town had made an effort to put into practice this idea of grouping all the trades and crafts into "severall companyes." In 1559 it was ordered that "the inhabytantes of this Borowghe shalbe Divided into Severall Compaynes for the better utylytie and good order of their selfes and theyre famylyes," but the council reserved to themselves the right "to Devide so manye Mysteryes or facultyes into every compayne as theye shall thinke good." *Selections from the Records,* pp. 159, 123.

    [164] Wodderspoon, *Memorials of Ipswich,* p. 174.

IV

CONCLUSION—THE SIGNIFICANCE OF THE AMALGAMATION MOVEMENT

Having in the foregoing pages reviewed the conditions which led to the rise and fostered the development of amalgamation among the trades and handicrafts, we have now to ask what was the significance of the movement in the evolution of the gild system. It has been seen that the London merchants, the pepperers, canvas dealers and spicers were the first of the gilds to join their forces and that their members prospered greatly and acquired the name of grocers. The other merchants, however, with the exception of the haberdashers, apparently never followed their example, but preferred to keep to their own gilds. Even the haberdashers waited a century and a half before forming an alliance with the hatters and cappers. However, in the provincial cities and the more important boroughs, immediately upon the break-up of the gild merchant various groups of merchants seem to have drawn together into one organisation. In 1370, the Bristol merchants, mercers, drapers and other dealers together formed a common gild for the purpose of regulating their own and the city's commercial affairs. Scarcely a half century later, the Shrewsbury mercers, goldsmiths, and ironmongers are found in a joint association, which, strange to say, was at the same time welcoming recruits from many other occupations. By forming this gild the Shrewsbury merchants seem to have secured for themselves as a body the mercantile privileges which they had all enjoyed in the days when the old gild merchant held sway. Furthermore, that outside London, and perhaps in a few other places, the merchants were ready to welcome a joint association to enable them to look after their trading interests may be inferred from the fact that by the middle of the sixteenth century, if not indeed much earlier, amalgamated trading gilds were the rule in the English commercial communities, and there continued an active force. It is not unreasonable, therefore, to regard all these associations as a direct outgrowth of the gild merchant, which not long before had been guarding the commercial interests of the burgesses. We can readily comprehend how amalgamated companies, which sought to confine their membership to men engaged only in mercantile pursuits, had many advantages which would recommend themselves more and more to the medieval traders, the mercers, grocers, apothecaries, haberdashers, and the rest, as the struggle to maintain separate gilds became increasingly severe.

Occasionally, as we have noticed, the haberdashers did not combine with the rest of the general merchants, but endeavoured to head a fraternity on their own account. In these instances the haberdashers formed associations in conjunction with the hatters, cappers, and later with the feltmakers, trades with which the haberdashers were naturally kin. In London the haberdashers combined with at least two of these trades, the hatters and the cappers, and their joint society flourished exceedingly upon the privileges they had acquired, their members thereby gaining greater prestige and power; but they did not show a like favour to the feltmakers. Other places however, particularly Bristol, Exeter, and Kendal, incorporated their haberdashers with the feltmakers, as well as with the hatters and cappers; thus the gildsmen all together shared the fortunes or misfortunes attendant upon their commercial ventures. In those amalgamations which the drapers sometimes preferred to form apart from the general traders the tailors appear most often to have been included as joint partners. It was a suitable arrangement, since both the drapers and the tailors claimed the right of dealing in cloth. The associations formed by these two occupations served doubtless to put a stop to rivalry and to keep the peace.

Sooner or later not only the peace but the well-being of the boroughs forced their officials to divert the efforts which they had directed toward the isolation of kindred handicrafts to their amalgamation. In consequence, we have the associations of bowyers and fletchers, armourers and braziers, bakers and brewers, carpenters and joiners or carvers, marshals and smiths and the rest, which, from the late fourteenth or early fifteenth centuries gradually superseded the single gilds first established by the different occupations. By encouraging rival handicrafts to merge their gild interests, the authorities prevailed upon them to fulfill their civic obligations and play their part in the community's economic life.

Still other handicrafts, notably the weavers of Oxford, were forced into association with a kindred group from lack of numbers to support a gild of their own. However, in associating with local fullers, the few weavers left in Oxford were sufficiently imbued with early gild traditions which made for equality and independence, to insist upon electing a warden of their own so as to ensure their control of the weaving industry left in the city. Evidence that elsewhere, in amalgamating, various handicrafts attempted to safeguard their individual interests, appears from the surviving records of their unions. When the cutlers, farriers, smiths and lockyers of Bristol became one company in 1403, each craft elected a warden from its own group to look after its special interests; the Newcastle goldsmiths and their associates, the plumbers, glaziers and pewterers did likewise, in 1536. However, when the feltmakers of that city amalgamated with the curriers and armourers, each craft took the precaution specifically to warn its members not to meddle with the others' callings. The whittawyers, pointmakers and glovers of Bristol went even further when, in 1605, their gild authorities invoked the aid of city officials to restrain pointmakers from making gloves and glovers, points. Again, a special ordinance issued by the stitchmen's gild of Ludlow, warned tailors and skinners, two of the different groups included in the corporation, that neither might with impunity trespass upon the territory over which the other held sway. In this way the handicraftsmen registered their protest against the movement. Their opposition is not surprising in view of the fact that, in amalgamating, they were doing violence to the ideals which had led them in the first place to establish single gilds. If, as appears from the history of the Chester tanners, handicrafts sought separate incorporation in order to regulate their individual affairs free from outside interference, they could not consistently take to the idea of associating even with the most closely related craftsmen. Members of the same association could scarcely be kept in ignorance of general gild plans or excluded from gild councils. The fact that so many crafts in the more important towns never amalgamated, but guarded their gild independence to the last, leads to the inference that among the handicrafts at least, the movement toward amalgamation was in reality proof of the decline of early craft ideals. The handicrafts which were unable alone to protect and develop their individual interests joined some group with relations sufficiently close to make a joint union feasible. In associating with the glovers of their particular borough, the skinners doubtless made and in return gained certain concessions which redounded to the profit of each group, while union strengthened the powers of both to repel alien competitors from usurping a share of local trade.

In the more or less heterogeneous associations which the authorities in the less important towns established by merging in one great body various handicrafts and various trades we see in effect the end of any attempt longer to isolate local occupations. In those communities the problem of excluding aliens was so absorbing as to overshadow all others. Indeed, the influx of strangers probably acted as a spur to link together handicrafts which might otherwise have continued indefinitely to compete with one another. From the late sixteenth century onward, evidence prevails of the willingness of rival craftsmen to combine in order to debar from the towns strangers who made or endeavoured to dispose of their wares. By that time the danger that threatened local trade and industry from the invasion of foreigners became more and more formidable in the small towns until even the merchants were forced to raise the barriers maintained for centuries between them and the handicrafts, and to join with the latter in forming common societies. Accordingly there arose the large bodies embracing different trades and handicrafts until in the great seventeenth-century aggregations which were established in Faversham and Wallingford the whole process of gild grouping reached its culminating point. The plan of association could scarcely have been carried further.

We may conclude, then, that the amalgamation of the English mercantile crafts may be deemed a natural step in the evolution of the gild system, by means of which upon the break-up of the gild merchant, various groups of tradesmen entered into association in order that they might together protect and develop their joint commercial interests.[1] Among the industrial crafts, however, the movement appears to have been a sign of the decay of the early ideals which had led them in the first place to establish separate gilds. The earliest craft gilds on record in an English borough were formed by single groups of handicrafts, not by associations of two or more. In the beginning the more important handicrafts had set up individual organisations for the purpose of safeguarding their individual interests. As division of labour progressed, however, gilds multiplied so rapidly in practically every branch of industry in most localities, that it was found impossible to keep kindred groups confined to their particular sphere and consequently they were allowed to amalgamate. And although for the most part, only the crafts who used similar materials seem at first to have joined forces, gradually from either necessity or expediency, the handicrafts, least in demand and therefore in numbers, allied themselves with such other artisan groups as conditions in their particular district warranted. Finally, in the smallest towns, craftsmen of all sorts had no recourse except to accept membership in one of the few comprehensive gild groups which were then being formed as the one species of organisation possible of maintenance within local precincts. In sacrificing thus their corporate independence the handicrafts at least had departed far from early gild traditions.

[1] Local merchants who were probably more influential in the government of the gild merchant, if not indeed largely in control of that organisation, might have been content to keep it going indefinitely. The handicrafts, however, subjected doubtless, for the most part to the rule of the merchants, would naturally feel the need of closer unions, where, as men directly concerned in developing a particular industry, they could make regulations which they deemed essential without fear of outside interference. In Leicester, artisan weavers and fullers, not merchants were first discovered meeting together and formulating ordinances for the regulation of their own industries free from the gild merchant's domination. In Bristol, weavers, tailors, tanners and shoemakers set up their own organisations long before 1370, the year in which the merchants formed their union. In York, the process of gild development was similar, except that the mercers in that city founded their gild a dozen years earlier than the Bristol merchants. The ordinary traders in both cities had, probably, to combine their forces in order to hold their own against the numerous bands of organised craftsmen which were already in the economic field. Besides, there was no law which forbade the amalgamation of the merchants. For the clause in the act of 1363 which had aimed to limit the merchants to one branch of trade, had been repealed the year following its enactment.

THE CONFLICT BETWEEN THE ENGLISH TRADES AND HANDICRAFTS

The foregoing study has doubtless shown that the conflict between kindred trades and handicrafts often proved to be such as to force them into association although the sentiment of the times favoured their separation. This being so, it may be interesting to attempt next to get at the cause of the conflict which proved the source of so much local disturbance throughout the period of gild domination. The first evidence of friction comes from Shrewsbury, in 1323 due to the war waged by the tanners upon local cordwainers for presuming to tan skins in addition to their regular business of making boots and shoes. This resulted in the seizure of such of the cordwainers' goods as were found in their "houses of tanning." Resenting this interference with their liberty, the cordwainers laid the matter before the king and on their plea that from time immemorial they, "just as the tanners," had tanned skins, secured a license authorising them to continue the work.[1] The king's interference in their behalf at this time evidently proved sufficiently effective to warrant the cordwainers in having the king again confirm their right to tan, in 1362. Then followed the passage of the act of 1363 which deprived merchants and handicraftsmen alike of the right to follow more than one calling.[2] Despite this act, indeed within the year of its enactment, the cordwainers of Bristol won from the king a license similar to that accorded their Shrewsbury brethren years before, authorising them to tan skins also. By empowering the cordwainers of Bristol and Shrewsbury to practise

---

[1] *Supra,* p. 60.

[2] By that time, too, trouble was brewing between different groups of London merchants. For example, the fishmongers, drapers and vintners in turn petitioned for incorporation on the ground that freemen of other mysteries were meddling with their respective trades. Not that members of either three groups showed any special regard for the trading rights of the others. Scarcely two weeks after the London fishmongers had received the letters patent which empowered them to control the city's fish business, the mayor was told to summon all the men of the mystery of fishmongers who were of the liberty of the Halmote and inquire on oath as to those fishmongers who had meddled in another trade, contrary to the statute made in the last parliament. *Letter Book G,* p. 168. Apparently the fishmongers could not maintain the monopoly after they had secured it. For, in 1382, they complained of the "many enemies of the common weal" who, "from one day to another do compass how that they may undo the good and profitable ordinances which have been made in the city as to the buying and selling of fish." Riley, *Memorials of London,* p. 469.

simultaneously two occupations the king deliberately encouraged them to disobey the act which had been passed with the view of isolating trades and handicrafts.   Obviously the Shrewsbury tanners clashed with local shoemakers for persisting in tanning, merely because they had always done so, ignoring the fact that local tanners had been given control of their calling.   Moreover, in insisting upon their right to tan, the cordwainers undoubtedly claimed a right denied to tanners when the latter attempted to add shoemaking to their own business.[3]   The government apparently soon realised the impossibility of isolating these two occupations as long as it licensed tanning by cordwainers.   Accordingly the measure enacted by the parliament of King Richard II stipulating that tanning and shoemaking should thereafter be two distinct occupations, "notwithstanding any charter or patent made to the contrary," expressly declared it to be the will of the king that any such charter then in existence should be, "utterly annulled and holden for none."[4]

This account of the clash between tanners and shoemakers over the latters' right to tan is peculiarly significant for our discussion in that it brings out clearly the cause of the disturbance then agitating English economic society.   We have, as it were, been following division of labour in the making between the crafts of tanning and shoemaking, a division which under the gild system, could scarcely have been effected peaceably either between these two handicrafts or any other two.   In all probability the cordwainers of Shrewsbury and Bristol who tanned their own leather as a matter of course established gilds long before the art of tanning had developed sufficiently to justify its being separated from the other branches of the leather business.[5]   Once in control of

---

[3] In 1364 the tanners of Beverley were forbidden to exercise the art of a shoemaker together with the art of a tanner under pain of paying to the community a fine of forty shillings for each offense. *Hist. MSS. Com. Rep. Beverley*, p. 90.   That during the reigns of Queen Elizabeth and King James I tanners were not averse to making shoes is evident from the provisions in 5 Elizabeth c. 8, and 1 James I, c. 22, prohibiting the practice.   In the fourteenth century, however, shoemakers and cordwainers probably trespassed upon tanners' rights oftener than tanners did upon shoemakers', since the act of 13 Richard II, c. 12, prefers charges against shoemakers and cordwainers only.   It forbids tanners in future to use the craft of shoemaking but does not accuse them of having done so in the past.

[4] 13 King Richard II, c. 12.

[5] The cordwainers of Oxford had obtained recognition for their gild as early as the reign of King Henry I, long before the records disclose the existence of a tanners' organisation either in Oxford or in any other English borough.   At Rouen the cordwainers had their right to have a gild recognised by Henry I, but the tanners seem not to have been similarly favoured until the reign of Henry II.   Chéruel, *Rouen pendant l'Epoque Communale,* vol. i, pp. 34–5, note.   In England the earliest record of a gild of tanners thus far noted bears date of 1288.   In that year the tanners of Norwich were fined for having a gild.   Hudson, *Leet Jurisdiction in Norwich, Selden Society Publications*, vol. v, pp. 13, 39, 43.   Tanners seem to have been attracted to York in the days of King Edward I, twelve of the sixteen freemen

their calling, tanners aimed to restrict shoemakers to their own branch of the business, an aim which was easier conceived than executed. The shoemakers of Shrewsbury and Bristol kept on tanning much as though local tanners were not in the running, going the length of defying local officials who intervened in behalf of the tanners. In all probability until tanners enlisted the sympathy and cooperation of local officials they had little or no chance to isolate their calling.[6] Moreover, that the problem of keeping separate the business of tanners and shoemakers continued to vex the economic world in spite of the specific ruling of King Richard II seems evident from the measures passed by his successors, defining the respective relations of these two groups of leather crafts.

In practically every trade and industry, established gild groups are found whose refusal to confine themselves to their immediate business and to permit others the exercise of special branches made for trouble in their immediate vicinity. For example, when gilds of drapers were put in control of the local cloth trade[7] they found themselves confronted, not alone by the mercantile groups, the merchants, mercers and tailors, who at one time or another had handled cloth, but also by the textile handicrafts, the weavers,

registered in 1277 being tanners. *The Freemen of York, Surtees Soc. Publications,* vol. 96, p. 3. Not until 1416, however is there evidence that the tanners had established a gild of their own. *Memorandum Book,* ii, pp. 162–3. At Newcastle-upon-Tyne, by 1342, there seems to have been a gild "detannatoribus" as well as "de allutariis." Brand, *History of Newcastle-upon-Tyne,* vol. ii, p. 154. It is interesting to note, in this connection, that in 1378, the borough of Liverpool had use for one tanner to four bootmakers. Muir, *History of Liverpool,* p. 45.

[6] This seems evident from the difficulty experienced by the Chester tanners in separating their gild interests from those of local shoemakers. It has been seen that Chester's governor went so far as to revoke a charter previously given to city tanners forbidding the cordwainers to meddle with their craft on the ground that the separation of the crafts was not to the interest of Chester. Not until the second decade of the fourteenth century is there evidence that the tanners had secured control of their own craft, *Supra,* p. 60.

[7] According to Professor Unwin "the separation of the draper from the other trading occupations" occurred in the middle of the sixteenth century. It is a matter of record, however, that in 1460, "Edward the fourthe Kyng of England and of ffraunce and lord of Irlond consideryng how that his true sujetts and liegemen Drapers of the towne of Shrovesbury in honoure of the blessed Trynyte long tyme passed hadde by gonnen of them selfe a Gilde which for asmyche as hit was not lawfully founded by liklyode hit myght not endure. Of his specyall grace for that the said Gilde for evermor shulde stande and endure he hath takyn uppon his p'sone" to grant them a charter with "many grete pr'rogatifs and sp'ial grauntes." *Shropshire Archaeol. & Nat. Hist. Soc. Trans. 3rd series,* vol. v, *Miscellanea,* iii. In 1492 the Beverley drapers established themselves as a group separate and distinct from local merchants and mercers. Moreover in bidding drapers "buy and purvey their Sorts according to the same price, so that so great plenty of such cloths be made and set to sale in every city, borough and merchant town and elsewhere within the realm," (37 Edward III, c. xv), parliament seems to have testified to the definiteness of the drapers' sphere of trade. At any rate, the drapers of London evidently considered theirs a business by itself, because the following year they had themselves incorporated in order to safeguard it.

fullers, dyers and shearmen, who from the beginning had probably dealt more or less extensively in that commodity. From the earliest times local merchants and mercers sold cloth in the different boroughs [8] and they apparently continued to sell it in spite of the opposition of the drapers.

Fully a century and a half after the incorporation of the Shrewsbury drapers, local mercers still claimed the right by both custom and practice to deal in cloth. Moreover they kept on exercising "draperie" even after 1619, the year in which the Privy Council decided that this commodity belonged rightfully to local drapers, with the result that two years later this body revoked their earlier decision, and on the ground of inexpediency, took from the drapers the monopoly of Shrewsbury's cloth trade.[9] It is true that in 1492 the drapers of Beverley withdrew from the union they had formed with local merchants and mercers and set up their own gild, as it would seem for the purpose of monopolising the local trade in cloth, but they failed to make the merchants respect their monopoly. The latter continued to handle cloth on their own account, apparently regardless of the ordinances which the drapers issued from time to time forbidding the merchants "to occupie within the town of Beverley buying and selling of any wollen clothe belonging to the Drapers crafte." [10]   At Reading too, as in many other well-known communities, not alone mercers but also tailors defied local drapers by selling cloth. Like merchants and mercers, tailors had been accustomed to sell cloth by retail and they never willingly relinquished the custom. With a reputation for being great importers in the time of King Edward III,[11] by 1487 the merchant "Taylors" of London had parliament confirm their right to sell "wollen clothe at retail by the yerdys." [12]   In all probability by that time many members of the company bought and sold more cloth than they made up into garments. In 1575 the tailors of the borough of Kendal were accorded liberty by the municipality to

---

[8] According to the drapers of London, by 1364 scarcely a shop could be found in that city in which drapery of some sort was not offered for sale. See Letters Patent issued to the company in that year published in Johnson, *History of the Worshipful Company of Drapers*, vol. i, p. 204. At about that time, city fullers were evidently selling or exposing for sale in their "houses" as "elsewhere" cloth other than their "own," a practice which had been forbidden by the city fathers under penalty of forfeiting the value of the cloth. *Letter Book G*, p. 159. In Bristol, too, by 1370, the merchants, mercers and drapers had formed an association in order to regulate the sale of cloth along with other commodities. *Little Red Book*, vol. ii, p. 51. In Ripon, according to evidence furnished by the roll of the poll-tax imposed in 1370, merchants and mercers as well as drapers traded in cloth. *Millenary Record*, p. 13. As late as 1745, the mercers of Sandwich considered the selling of "Broad" cloth and other woollen cloth an important branch of their business. *Addit. Mss. no. 27462*, fol. 132, B. M.

[9] Unwin, *Industrial Organization*, p. 99.

[10] *Selden Society Publications, Beverley Town Documents*, p. 108.

[11] Herbert, *Twelve Great Livery Cos.*, vol. ii, p. 391.

[12] 4 Henry VII, c. 8.

use the science of a woollen draper.[13]   As late as 1640 the tailors of Bristol maintained their right "at their will and pleasure" not alone "to buy as hath beene anciently used and accustomed all kinds of cloaths and kersies and all manner of cloth lynnen and woollen and freely sell the same againe . . . as well as to make the same" into garments "to their most profitt and comoditie without trouble or molestation to any one."[14]   Tailors naturally "came to the knowledge and skill of all sorts of cloath" and when the opportunity presented itself made use of it.   They did this not only in places "wanting one that dealt in cloath"[15] but in towns like Beverley, where two years after the drapers had severed gild relations with local merchants and mercers, a "certain great altercation and matter of discord" which they had with the tailors was decided by the municipality in favour of the drapers, to whom thereafter every tailor "who should buy and sell cloth by retail . . . beyond four marks a year" had to pay tribute.[16]   In 1503 we find the drapers and "taylors" of the metropolis referring their differences to the mayor and aldermen for adjudication.[17]   In communities like York, Rye, Warwick and Northampton, local tailors trespassed so openly upon the drapers' business that it was found expedient to let them amalgamate.   Probably in this way the above-named boroughs contrived to avert continued friction in the conduct of the local cloth trade.

Drapers even in the more important trade centres could well reconcile it with their pride to settle their commercial feuds with ordinary merchants, mercers or even tailors, by amalgamating their interests, since as traders they occupied much the same rank in the gild firmament.   The case was different when it came to weavers, fullers, dyers and shearmen.   From the draper's point of view, the men using those occupations were merely artificers, with no legitimate rights to purchase or sell cloth generally.   Needless to say drapers failed to impress handicraftsmen with this viewpoint of their mission.   To the London weavers, fullers and dyers, who by

[13] *Hist. MS. Com. Report,* vol. x, iv, p. 312.
[14] Fox and Taylor, *Merchant Taylors of Bristol,* p. 85.
[15] A man who had served an apprenticeship to a tailor opened up a draper's shop at Framlingham, which at that time seems not to have had one of the sort.   His success at the business, however, is said to have aroused the jealousy of certain townsmen who "out of malice" had him indicted at the "Sessions" for using a "manual occupation" to which he had not been bound "seaven yeares," which was a breach of the act 5 Elizabeth c. 4.   *Extract from Privy Council Register,* dated 1669, quoted in Unwin, *Industrial Organization,* p. 252, Appendix A.   Because a tailor who kept a shop at Newcastle-upon-Tyne in 1738 had branched out by selling cloth and other drapery goods, he was obliged to release his apprentice whom he had kept "employed in attending and taking care of the shop," instead of instructing him in the "business of a Taylor."   *Merchant Adventurers of Newcastle-upon-Tyne, Surtess Soc. Pub.,* vol. 93, p. xlv.
[16] *Report Historical MSS. Commission, Beverley,* p. 105.
[17] Johnson, *History of the Worshipful Company of Drapers,* vol. i, pp. 232–3.

1364 had not only become makers of cloth, but forestalled other cloth and sold it at their own discretion, the incorporation of city drapers probably worked considerable hardship. We have no means' of judging the extent to which London drapers of that epoch kept local clothing craftsmen from engaging in drapery. To be sure, towards the end of the century men of the mystery of drapers contrived to have one weaver disfranchised for occupying drapery or the selling of cloth.[18] Only three centuries later, in 1634, they had evidently not succeeded in convincing city clothworkers that they had no right to sell cloth which they had bought and dressed.[19] Elsewhere too, in spite of the opposition of local drapers, the men engaged in the different processes of making cloth continued to deal in that commodity. By 1415 according to the drapers of Coventry, local dyers had become "great makers of cloth," having taken for the purpose the very "flower of the wool."[20] In 1490 Bristol weavers were evidently "sending over the sea" drapery called "Brodemede."[21] By 1515, too, there was "varyance and dyscorde" between the drapers and shearmen of Shrewsbury because of the latter's buying, selling and "shearinge of Welshe cloth."[22] Scarcely half a century later the fullers and dyers of Beverley dealt so extensively in cloth that they called forth a prohibition from local drapers against their further buying "of wollen clothe or clothes to thintent to sell the same againe by hollsaille or retaile by yerde or otherwyse, under paine . . . to forfett xxs. th' one half thereof to the Comonynaltie and th' other half to th'-expences of the said occupacion of Drapers."[23] In 1615 the "Tuckers" of Youghal were selling not only their own "frizes" but other "clothe" to freemen.[24] Oddly enough, the parliament of King Edward VI evidently took it for granted that clothworkers throughout the country should "retayle" cloth.[25] The textile handicrafts seem to have acted on the principle that they had as much right to sell cloth as the drapers had to make it. In bidding London weavers, fullers and dyers to refrain from buying and selling cloth,

[18] *Letter Book H*, p. 260.
[19] These clothworkers maintained that they got their living for the most part of the year by buying rough, undressed or country-dressed cloth and selling it after it was perfected and dressed. If they were restrained from doing this thereafter, they said, all the advantage would accrue to the drapers who neither paid custom to the king nor increased the stock of the kingdom and whose proper trade it was to buy and sell by retail. The drapers, for their part, however, denied the facts in the case as stated by the clothworkers. They claimed that they had always bought and sold cloth by wholesale and retail, and on that ground claimed the right to the selling of that commodity. The clothworkers, the drapers said, should have the dressing of cloth, since that in their opinion "is the subject matter" of the clothworkers' "trade." *State Papers Domestic*, vol. 278, no. 104.
[20] *Coventry Leet Book*, xxxii. Also *Rotuli Parliamentorum*, vol. iv, p. 75.
[21] *Little Red Book*, vol. ii, p. 123.
[22] *Trans. Shropshire Archaeol. & Nat. Hist. Society, 4th series*, vol. iii.
[23] *Selden Soc. Pub., Beverley Town Documents*, p. 105.
[24] *Council Book*, p. 35.
[25] 5 & 6 Edward VI, c. 6.

fourteenth-century drapers frankly reserved to themselves certain rights in the making as well as in the selling of that commodity, thereby serving unmistakablè notice of their intention of trespassing upon handicraft rights.   It was probably with some such end in view that this "feleship" of drapers secured from King Edward IV a patent assuring it that city shearmen should have neither a "Corporacion" nor "any correccion of the Drapers or Taylors." [26] Moreover, in 1619, the Shrewsbury drapers contended that the greatest part of their business consisted in the "bying of clothes at Oswestry rawe and undressed and in the working and dressing sometimes dyeing them." [27]   Not content with the monopoly of the cloth trade awarded them in 1492 by city fathers, the drapers of Beverley wrested from local tailors the right to make in addition "certain clothes" such as gaiters, women's boots and "le soles." [28] At Coventry, in 1533 the "assemble" gave a local draper liberty to occupy the craft of "wadd-settyng." [29]   Elsewhere drapers did not wait for permission to engage in some one or other of the clothing handicrafts.   At Warwick, in 1588, it was shown that a local draper "dooth coten and dresse his welch cloth and fryse in his owne shoppe contrary to the statute." [30]

However, retail drapers probably met their match when merchant adventurers appeared upon the scene proclaiming their right to adventure cloth as one exercised "tyme out of mynde." [31]   Local drapers did not apparently loom large in the eyes of the bigger merchants, even though many had once belonged to their order.[32] Seventeenth-century adventurers of Newcastle-upon-Tyne refused to acknowledge the existence of a gild established early in the previous century by drapers ot their city, on the ground that they were "noe company" but merely "a sort of people who traded in the making of capps." [33]   One wonders whether the adventurers of

[26] Johnson, *History of the Worshipful Company of Drapers*, vol. ii, p. 235.
[27] Unwin, *Industrial Organization*, p. 99.
[28] *Historical MSS. Commission Rep., Beverley*, p. 105.
[29] *Leet Book*, p. 714.
[30] *The Book of John Fisher*, p. 155.
[31] *Surtees Society Public.*, vol. 101, p. 10.   The adventurers of Newcastle-upon-Tyne made this allegation in 1559.
[32] At least seven of the men to whom the charter of the Merchant Adventurers of England was granted in 1564 were influential drapers.   Johnson, *History of the Worshipful Company of Drapers*, vol. ii, p. 180.
[33] Brand, *History of Newcastle-upon-Tyne*, vol. ii, p. 313.   By 1657, however, the adventurers appointed three of their brethren "to treat with the Drapers of this towne, to see if they can happily compose the difference betwixt them and the drapers of this company."   And when "the difference betwixt the Merchant Drapers," members of the Adventurers' company and the "now drapers of this towne" was judged to be a "buisiness" more "fitt to be heard before a Common Councill then in this court," certain members of the fellowship were ordered to attend the common council in order that "an end and period to that difference may be had."   *Surtees Society Publications*, vol. 93, pp. 189, 191, et seq.   The majority of the city's retail drapers probably belonged to this discredited drapers' company. Because of the two hundred and fourteen members ascribed to the Adventurers in 1668, fourteen only were listed as "Merchant Drapers." *Ibid.*, Preface, p. ix.

Chester did not include drapers among the retailers when they tried to keep them as well as the artificers from joining their society. We know that the "retaylors" were exceedingly chagrined at being excluded from trafficking in foreign lands and did not rest until they had had the adventurers' charter modified so that they could share in the advantages of foreign trade.[34] Nor were adventurers of other communities allowed to enjoy their corporate privileges unopposed. Charging the "Maior and certain other Inhabitants within" their city with having obtained at the hands of their "Sovereign Lady" letters patent incorporating them a society of Merchant Adventurers "upon certen pretenses, suggestions . . . by them rather of a covetous and gready desier of luker invented and imagined,"[35] the different handicrafts of Exeter in company with other freemen of the city, prayed the Queen to appoint a commission to inquire into and report upon the validity of their charges. At the end of the inquiry, which took about two years to conduct, a compromise seems to have been effected between the contestants, the company agreeing to open its membership to "everie Taylor or other Artificer minding to use the trade of Merchant" on the payment of a reasonable fine. In the event, however, that such artificer could not or would not "be free' of the company, he was "not to be prohibited of such his trade so that he will give a reasonable contribution by the year for a knowledge."[36] Nor did the adventurers of Bristol have smoother sailing than the Exeter adventurers.[37] Not quite two decades after they had received their

[34] Morris, *Chester*, pp. 464–67.
[35] Cotton, *Some Account of the Ancient Guilds of the City of Exeter, Devenshire Association for Advancement of Science,* etc., vol. v, pp. 123–4. In their answer to the commission the merchants blamed those "busy seditious and noysome cuttynge tailors" for fomenting the disturbance. They claimed "that the other parties mentioned had nothing to do with it." In addition the merchants accused the "taylores" and other "theire accomplyces" of having "skaunderously" and untruely interpreted the merchants' "graunt" from the Queen as being a "breache" of the liberties. *Hist. MSS. Comm. Rep. Exeter,* pp. 379–80.
[36] It appears that certain of the older merchants of Exeter feared that the adventurers would not be able to maintain their monopoly and waited, it is said, ten years before joining the society. For a number of years after it had been incorporated, the court of the company seems to have been occupied chiefly with settling controversies between members, and in inflicting penalties for offenses committed against the by-laws. Cotton, *The Merchant Adventurers of Exeter,* p. 25.
[37] The city corporation appealed to Lord Burghley, declaring that the act was injurious to the trade of the city. It is said that a bill to that effect which was read a first time at the fifth sitting of the House of Commons, passed through all its stages in both houses, in spite of vigourous resistance and finally received the king's assent. However, no copy of the act which thus restored freedom of trade to the Bristol merchants is to be found in the city records. *Bristol in the 16th Century, Newspaper Clippings* gathered by Latimer. Brit. Mus., no. viii. See Latimer, *Merchant Venturers of Bristol,* p. 53, for a summary of the Case. It is interesting to read how in 1571, the Bristol Adventurers sought to justify their right to incorporation on the lines specified in their charter. They naively complained that "a merchant cannot

charter, other traders in Bristol prevailed upon the city council to join with them in an effort to have repealed the parliamentary measure which had conferred the monopoly upon the Bristol adventurers. At Leeds, too, a certain set of adventurers incurred the enmity of other merchants for setting up "amongst the clothiers," and at little or practically no charges to themselves, buying merchandise much as they pleased.[38] The adventurers also met with opposition from such merchants as had been accustomed to adventure on their own account long before the advent of the adventurers. Thus, in the reign of King Edward VI, the mercers of York pursued their trade to Flanders apparently as part of their regular routine, although at that time they complained that "contrary to the ancient customes of olde tymes," they were not fairly dealt with by the merchant adventurers there.[39] In many places, despite the adventurers, local dealers and handicraftsmen alike, apparently, took to adventuring.[40] In 1593, a certain feltmaker was indicted by the adventurers of Exeter for "bringing home from Brittaine five or syxe yards of whitware not being free of this Companie."[41] Sometimes, too, the grocers of London in company with local salters, vintners and other dealers, turned Spanish merchants on their own account.[42] After disposing of as much goods in England as was possible, at least one linen draper is known to have sent the rest of his stock over into Spain "seeking rather vent than profit."[43] By 1661 the Merchant Taylors of London openly traded not only as Spanish, French and Turkey merchants, but as Merchant Adventurers of England as well.[44] Moreover, although so ready to keep local merchants and artificers alike from trespassing upon their own domain, the adventurers seem to have trespassed indiscriminately upon that of all the others. Apparently, not for nothing did the foremost of the adventuring companies warn its members neither to sell nor even to cause "to bee sold for him by retayle," nor to keep "open shoppe or shew-house upon pain

be a retailer for want of skill and acquaintance of customers, which requires an apprenticeship to bring him to it, neither can he have a fit place to dwell in, for all the houses that stand in the place of retail are already in the hands of retailers." *Ibid.*, p. 54. Although these adventurers did not at the time open up "Marchandize" to retailers, in 1618 they made a pretence of compromising with them and with artificers, whom they apparently classed together, by inserting in their by-laws the provision that "Noe Retailer or artificer whilest they remaine Retailers or Artificers shalbee receyved or admitted into the Freedome of this Societie for anie fine whatsoever without approbacion and allowance of a special Courte houlden for that purpose." *Ibid.*, p. 74.

[38] Lambert, *Two Thousand Years of Gild Life*, p. 170.

[39] Sellers, *Merchant Adventurers of York, Handbook*, p. 220.

[40] The fullers of Bristol attributed the miserable condition in which they found themselves, in 1568, to the decay of the city and the port, and as the result of so many persons engaging in maritime trade. Fox and Taylor, *Weavers of Bristol*, p. 68.

[41] Cotton, *Merchant Adventurers of Exeter*, Appendix, p. 161.

[42] Unwin, *Industrial Organization*, p. 174.

[43] *Ibid.*

[44] Herbert, *Twelve Great Livery Companies*, vol. ii, p. 421.

of three skore poundes sterling";[45] and in 1599 "ppore clothwork-ers" of London were charging "marchaunts adventurers" of Eng-land with sinister and hard dealings,[46] whereas seventeenth-century wardens of the yeomanry of the London clothworkers brought a "Suite in Court of King's Bench at Westminster . . . upon VIII Elizabeth" against the Merchant Adventurers whom they charac-terised as "being stronge" both "in purse and frendes."[47] How-ever, the Bristol adventurers were incorporated upon a lamentable representation that "divers Artificers and men of manuell arte . . . haveing alsoe occupacions to gett theire liveinge . . . Doe com-monly exercuse, use and occupie . . . trade of marchandize to and from the partes beyond the seas," but they had no scruples against using artificers' occupations. "No man must medell with merchauntes craft" charged the Bristol fullers in the days of good Queen Bess, and yet "they will entarmedell with other mens, for they have taken upon them to fold and tache cloth by whiche meanes also the poore crafte of towckars is impayned of theyr lyvyng."[48] And these same adventurers used the clothiers of the countryside so "unhonestly" that the latter threatened to sell their cloth at London or various other places and "beare theyr losses" rather than have any further dealings with city "marchantes." If they had had their way, merchant adventurers would have debarred from the trade of "merchaundize," country merchants too,[49] as well those who dwelt in villages as in "uplandish townes." For that matter, the different adventuring groups showed little regard for the rights of rival groups of adventurers. For instance, in 1669, the adventurers of Newcastle-upon-Tyne aired their grievances against the "Marchants Adventurers" of England for dealing "very unkindly" with them, to give the actions of the "Marchants Adven-turers," as they added, "noe worse tearme."[50] During this same

[45] Gross, *Gild Merchant*, vol. i, p. 155.

[46] *Lansdowne MSS., B. M.*, No. 154.

[47] Unwin, *op. cit.*, p. 233, Appen. A.

[48] Fox and Taylor, *Bristol Weavers*, p. 93.

[49] In 1580 the "Marchauntes of Totnes" wrote to their "verie loving freundes," the "marchaunte adventurers of the Cittie of Exeter" to ascertain their views as to the feasibility of "joyning with other Cities for the exhibit-ing of a bill at this present parliament" which had been drawn up for the purpose of admitting to the trade of "Marchaundize onlie suche as dwell in cities or towns corporate." Cotton, *Merchant Adventurers of Exeter*, Append. p. 129.

[50] *Merchant Adventurers of Newcastle-upon-Tyne*, Surtees Soc., vol. 101, p. 137. At this time the question arose as to whether the merchant adven-turers of Bristol, Exeter and Newcastle should free themselves "from the bondage off the Marchants Adventurers of England." It seems that in 1637 the merchant adventurers of London "beinge of greater wealth and power" than the Newcastle company tried to exact from them "at their owne pleas-ures" a "greater Imposition" than the Newcastle company had been paying them. *Ibid.*, p. 18. By 1678 the Newcastle company of Adventurers had not only to take into serious consideration "that great affaire of defending theire privileges against the infringers thereof," especially the "Hambrough Com-pany" (as the Merchant Adventurers of England was commonly called) but against the "Muscovia" company as well. *Surtees Soc. Pub.*, vol. 93, p. 222.

year by order of the king's council the committee for trade gave
a hearing to "Ye Merchants of ye Citty of Bristol and likewise to
ye Company of Merchants Adventurers and to ye Turkey Company
in order to ye composing ye differences between them in point of
trade." [51] In time too, merchant adventurers had to reckon with
competitors such as the Eastlanders, a corporation endowed by
Queen Elizabeth in the twenty-first year of her reign, with exclusive rights to control the export trade in the Baltic. In the beginning this Eastland company apparently meditated keeping out "any
marchaunte free of any other companye or societie tradinge marchaundyze beyond the Seas," but thought better of this, apparently, and in the end admitted into their organisation merchants
and adventurers of other communities.[52] These Eastland merchants exported such varied commodities that they too, soon clashed
with other groups of traders. In fact they so seriously menaced
the trade in skins as to force the skinners of London to take
measures to have the Eastlanders excluded from that branch of
trade.[53]

In truth, whether local merchants traded in a big or small way,
abroad or at home, they had always to be on their guard lest outsiders infringe upon their liberties. Local mercers in their turn
seem to have suffered considerably from outside competition. By
1341, for instance, mercers of London were seizing silk kerchiefs,
Aylesham thread and linen cloth which men of Norfolk exposed
for sale within their city.[54] In 1363 mercers of the same city had
several freemen disfranchised for that "being free of the haberdashers they occupied merceries,"/[55] whereas by 1561 they held
retail dealers of certain other companies, more especially the grocers
"guilty" of handling silk goods.[56] It has already been shown how
hard put the mercers of both Shrewsbury and Beverley were to
maintain their hold over the local trade of woollen cloth in the face
of competing woollen drapers. Despite the diversity of their business the mercers of Beverley represented it to be a "science" the
principles of which others must of necessity know enough to respect,
or pay the penalty attaching to ignorance or disobedience. In the
early seventeenth century, the mercers of Chester warred not only
with local linen-drapers [57] for intermeddling with mercery, but

[51] *State Papers Domestic, 1669*, No. 44, p. 267.
[52] *Eastland Company of York, Camden Soc. Pub.*, Appen., p. 147. According to a provision of their charter neither they nor their successors should "in
any wyse admytt into their fellowshipp any marchaunte free of any other
companye or societie tradinge marchaundyze beyonde the Seas or any Arty-
ficer or handy craftsman or any Retayler."
[53] *Camden Soc. Pub., Eastland Co. of York*, Introd., lii–iii.
[54] Unwin, *Gilds and Companies of London*, p. 90.
[55] Herbert, *Twelve Great Livery Cos.*, vol. i, p. 30. Note.
[56] *Ibid.*, p. 237.
[57] *Harleian MSS., B. M.*, No. 2054, ff. 37–47. By 1634 Chester linen-
drapers could evidently trade in all sorts of cloth, in buckram, in stitching
silks in all colours, in needles, thimbles and various other articles of a like
nature. *Ibid.*, f. 68.

went so far as to disfranchise a local embroiderer for intruding upon their trade "before to him forbidden." [58] In 1675 the mercers of Derby prosecuted a "taylor" for taking up the trade of a mercer and keeping "open shop there." [59] In 1698 the Bristol mercers "paid the Mayors' officers and constables" a considerable sum "for keeping down the Londoners windows." [60] Not that mercers themselves ever apparently relinquished their rights over a commodity which they had once enjoyed, for they did not. Mercers who sold "London waires and Stamford waires" in Kingston-upon-Hull in 1598, contrived to "sell any waires within their howse belonging to the occupacion of a glover" without paying the fines levied by the local glovers' company upon non-members who presumed to sell articles included in their category, within the environs of the city. [61] In the seventeenth century Gloucester mercers forced local metal-men to insert in their by-laws a provision reserving to mercers the right to buy and sell pins as they had been wont to do. [62] Moreover, although exceedingly zealous in protecting their own rights, mercers for their part showed little regard for the rights of handicrafts in whose wares they dealt. Indeed, almost everywhere at some time in their history, mercers had to be warned not to trespass upon the special rights of some one of the handicrafts. Even in the fifteenth century the Lincoln authorities forbade the mercers to sell boots, to the end, doubtless, that local cordwainers might be upheld in their monopoly. [63] By 1517 the mercers of Newcastle-upon-Tyne were not supposed even to exhibit in their shop windows any "manner of thyng that belonges the occupacion of sadelers." [64] Again, because the Chester mercers had been underselling the cappers, in 1520, they were prohibited from selling caps any longer except at a stated price. [65] In 1635 the London mercers were accused by the goldsmiths of buying and selling "deceitful goldsmiths' wares, especially in the Old and New Exchanges." [66] In 1727 suit was entered by the Shrewsbury company of glovers and skinners against mercers "that Intrud. of their company." [67] In some places the mercers were made to realise that handicraftsmen had certain rights which even they were obliged sometimes to respect.

So, too, at the time that London haberdashers were calling merchant "taylors" to account for making hats and caps, they in their turn were overstepping the limits of their legitimate gild rights

[58] *Harleian MSS.*, no. 2104, ff. 44–7.
[59] *Additional MS., B. M.* 6694, f. 96. "After much time and money spent" the recalcitrant mercer submitted himself to the Derby mercers. Whereupon they "admitted him to follow the trade of a mercer."
[60] *Bristol & Gloucestershire Archaeol. Soc. Trans.*, vol. xxv, pt. ii, p. 290.
[61] Lambert, *Two Thousand Years of Gild Life*, p. 219.
[62] *Hist. MSS. Comm. Rep. xii*, app. ix, p. 430.
[63] *Hist. MSS. Comm. Rep. xiv*, app. viii, p. 21.
[64] *Surtees Soc. Pub.*, vol. 93, p. 56.
[65] Morris, *Chester*, p. 435.
[66] *Journ. Brit. Archaeol. Assoc.*, n. s., vol. lx, pt. i, p. 48.
[67] *Trans. Shropshire Archaeol. & Nat. Hist. Soc.*, vol. x, p. 7.

by attempting to dominate the feltmakers' industry.[68] As vendors of hats, caps and small wares generally, the haberdashers were merely traders; they were therefore naturally related to the mercers, grocers and a few others of their sort—such, in the words of a contemporary writer, "as doe sell wares growinge beyond the seas," who "doe fetche oute oure treasure of the same"; whereas the feltmakers belong to a third class of those who, "we must cherishe well" because they alone "by theire misteries and faculties doe bringe in anie treasour." [69] As makers of felt hats, the feltmakers' interests were bound up with the development of one of the more important of the home industries. Consequently the interests of the two classes of craftsmen could never be wholly reconciled, and conflict, if not open hostility, was bound to result. The blame for the dispute must be thrown upon the haberdashers, who were utterly disregarding the accepted rules of the time. The act of 1363 had emphasised the gulf which custom had placed between traders and handicraftsmen; yet the haberdashers in attempting to dominate the feltmakers' industry, deliberately transgressed this act, not to mention the traditions in the matter. After persistent effort the feltmakers finally succeeded in breaking from the haberdashers' control by securing an organisation of their own.

Grocers, too, apparently got into trouble by taking more than the law allowed. By 1363 the grocers of London had aroused the animosity of other dealers for "engrossing" different sorts of merchandise.[70] Licensed often to sell not only grocery wares but apothecary wares, dyeing stuffs and whatever was sold by the hundred weight and gallon measure,[71] grocers were apt to conflict

---

[68] According to the feltmakers, the haberdashers never had any power by "Act of Parliament" to govern the feltmakers otherwise than to search and view their ware, neither "can they by their charter pretend to any right to govern them, the word feltmaker being not so much as mentioned in their charter." *The Case of the Feltmakers Truely Stated*, 1650. Quoted from Unwin, *Industrial Organization*, p. 242. And, although, in 1650, there were "aboute fortie Master Feltmakers free of the Haberdashers' Company, that, according to the feltmakers, gave the haberdashers no right "to challenge the Government of all the feltmakers any more than they could challenge jurisdiction on all the goldsmiths, drapers, etc., because some drapers and goldsmiths are free of their Company." *Ibid.*, pp. 244–5.

In 1566–7 the account-book of the merchant taylors shows the expenditure of a certain sum for drawing up a "Bill" exhibited to the "Mayor and aldermen" denouncing the "unlawful doings and proceedings of the Haberdashers in the making of an Act or Order amongst themselves that they nor none of them should buy any hats or caps out of their own Company nor set any awork in the same faculty but of their own Company upon a certain pain to their own private gain, contrary to the laws of the realm and godly orders and customs of this city." Clode, *Early History of the Merchant Taylors' Guild*, p. 203.

[69] Lamond, *Discourse of the Common Weal*, pp. 91–92.

[70] By that time the London grocers had affronted city fishmongers by dealing in fish.

[71] This evidently constituted the business of the grocers of Kendal in 1635. *Historical MSS. Commission Report*, vol. iv, app. x, p. 317.

with local apothecaries,[72] distillers, perfumers, confectioners,[73] chandlers,[74] and others of their kind. Later in adding starch [75] to their stock of merchandise, grocers clashed with starch-makers. With so many different trades concentrated in their hands there was considerable ground for the prejudice which existed against permitting grocers to be also general merchants or haberdashers.[76] Only it seems to have become practically impossible to maintain barriers between trades which overlapped so closely. Evidently by 1345 the city of London had given up trying to keep separate gildsmen who handled different grocery wares and permitted them instead to combine their interests. It is true that eighteen years

---

[72] In 1623 certain grocers of London coveted handling "Conserve of Barbary, Conserve of Roses, a certain preparation of ginger and various other drugs," which were at that time within the schedule of the apothecaries. Barrett, *History of the Apothecaries,* p. 20. On the other hand, at Shrewsbury in Elizabethan days, the two trades seem to have become identical, because in the second year of her reign, the local mercers' gild admitted certain freemen "to exercise the onlye science of Poticarye and Grocerye." *Shropshire Archaeol. and Natural History Society Trans.,* vol. viii, p. 314.

   In 1395 the apothecaries of Nottingham dealt in spices. *Records of the Borough,* vol. i, p. 279.

[73] By the sixteenth century, grocers were handling figs, almonds, raisins, Corinths, commonly called currants (Strype, *Stow's Survey of London,* vol. ii, p. 262), so that there were inevitable clashes with confectioners who sold similar articles. Thus, in 1713, a confectioner of Newcastle was indicted by the local merchant company for selling figs, a commodity which they claimed pertained to the grocer's trade. The interloper, however, defiantly answered, that, if he could make a profit he would not only sell figs, but sugars, also, and that after the figs he had were sold, he would "order to London for twenty barrels more." *Merchant Adventurers of Newcastle-upon-Tyne, Surtees Soc. Pub.,* vol. 93, xlii.

[74] In King Edward IV's day, "chaundelers" of Colchester handled salt, "otmele" and "cande." *Red Paper Book of Colchester,* p. 19. During that same period the tallow "chaundlers" of Coventry sold not alone "otemele and sope" but other "diuerse chaffers" as well. *Leet Book,* pt. ii, p. 400. By 1583, the chandlers of London counted soap, vinegar, butter, hops and oil among the commodities over which they exercised jurisdiction. *Lansdowne MS., B. M.* 38. The chandlers' occupation seems to have been coveted by many of the so-called "vitaler" trades. At Coventry, for instance, in the early years of the sixteenth century, bakers, butchers, and fishmongers had to be restrained from making "candell" other than "for their own howses" and from putting them to sale. *Leet Book,* pt. iii, p. 632.

[75] Starch seems to have been first sold by the London grocers in the days of Queen Elizabeth. Strype, *Op. cit.,* vol. ii, p. 263. In many communities, salters, too, seem to have had a gild existence apart from grocers. The seventeenth-century salters of London, who by that time were noted as one of the twelve great livery companies, certified to their brethren at Preston that traffic in flax and hemp formed "two principall comodities that doe belong" to their trade, which, they said "was one of ancient standing." Abram, *Memorials of the Preston Guilds,* p. 42.

[76] According to the records of the "Cinque Ports" in 1658, a French merchant living in Rye pleaded guilty to the indictment of exercising the misteries of a haberdasher and a grocer. Inderwick, *Interregnum,* p. 68. About a quarter of a century later, in Alnwick, local merchants indicted a certain inhabitant for trading both as a mercer and a grocer. Tate, *History of Alnwick,* vol. ii, pp. 325–6.

later, the practice of these dealers had become sufficiently obnoxious to provoke an act of parliament designed to curb their monopolistic practices, but nothing was done to dissolve the grocers' union. On the contrary, within a year as much of the act as had restricted the merchants was repealed and liberty given them to trade openly in all sorts of merchandise. Merchants who handled special commodities in the city, the drapers, vintners and fishmongers, apparently feared that their interests were jeopardised by such a liberal free trade policy, for they lost no time in having themselves incorporated with special powers to control their individual business.[77] In the provincial boroughs and corporate towns ordinary merchant dealers contrived to protect their interests by amalgamating, succeeding as time went on in bringing rival factions into their union. Only, while these mercantile associations managed for the most part to keep the peace between their own members, there were points at which contact with rival groups in other spheres made for trouble in their immediate vicinity. Thus, in 1715, the master of the barber-surgeons of Dublin was accorded a special vote of thanks commending his great zeal in defending their rights against the encroaching of members of the local merchants' company.[78] Three years later on behalf of such of their members as were apothecaries, the merchants of Newcastle-upon-Tyne appointed a committee which they endowed with authority to keep local surgeons from selling such goods as were supposed to belong exclusively to the apothecaries.[79] Again, in 1726, this mercantile company was itself brought to book for arbitrarily seizing from the city's organised bakers and brewers certain stocks of grain which the latter had purchased from an agency other than that of the merchants.[80]

And so the "merrie" war went on. There was never any telling what interests would clash or where trouble would break out. We have found merchant adventurers accusing not alone rival adventurers but other merchants wholesale as well as retail of not playing fair to their "undoing."[81] Retailers in their turn charged rival

[77] It seems to have been the policy of these different groups of London merchants to ignore the repeal of that part of the act of 1363 which had restricted them in their commercial operations. For instance, in the letters patent obtained by the vintners in 1427, from King Henry VI, the act is quoted to read "yt no merchant Englis ne use mercery, nether merchandises by him nor by non other by no manere of compaignie bot oone alloon the which he wil chose by fore the Fest of Candelmas last passed." etc. *Harleian MSS., B. M. 2054*, ff. 37–47.
[78] *Journal Royal Soc. of Antiquaries*, 5th ser., vol. 33, pt. iii, p. 233.
[79] *Harleian MSS.* 1996, f. 46.
[80] *Surtees Soc. Pub.*, vol. 93, p. 252.
[81] Stow's description of the retailer of his day as the "Handmaid to merchandising, dispensing by piecemeal that which the merchant bringeth in (*Survey of London*, Strype's edition, vol. ii, p. 677) draws a distinction between the two species of traders which practice evidently failed to uphold. Then, as indeed much earlier, the London executives were confronted with the difficulty of keeping wholesale dealers from retailing wares and vice versa. It seems that up to the later fourteenth century, by a "declaration" of

wholesale dealers with promiscuous and illegal trading besides denouncing as unlawful the "doings" of other dealers, at a time when they themselves took liberties with the trading rights of others.[82]

Handicraftsmen, in their turn, if the records can be credited, denounced merchant adventurers for impugning them of their living, and ordinary merchants for "unhonest" usage when they themselves trespassed upon the rights of rival handicraftsmen as though there were no reckoning in store.[1] Thus, when fourteenth-century officials in provincial boroughs exerted their authority to prevent cordwainers from tanning,[2] their London brethren intervened to

the wishes of the "Commons," every freeman of London might buy and sell by wholesale both within and without the city, any kind of merchandise that yielded a profit, but he could keep a shop and sell by retail only such goods as belonged to his own mystery. By the end of the century, however, this rule was not being adhered to, with the result that, to the dismay of city officials, men were not supporting the craft to which they rightfully belonged. *Letter Book G*, p. 179. If, as it appears, even the wardens of the grocers of the city were adventuring over the seas by 1348 (Herbert, *London Livery Companies*, vol. i, p. 306), it is not to be wondered at that seventeenth-century gildsmen of all sorts and conditions were selling diverse commodities "some by wholesale and some by retail." Strype, *op. cit.*, vol. ii, p. 262. Indeed, according to the charter conceded to the London merchant "taylors" in the nineteenth year of King Henry VII, "at least the sounder part" of the members of the company "had immemorially exercised merchandise in all parts of the globe and enjoyed the buying and selling of all wares and merchandises whatsoever, particularly woollen cloths as well wholesale as retail throughout England and more especially in the city of London." Herbert, *op. cit.*, vol. ii, p. 414. Prior to 1592, the horners of the same city seem to have been transporting "hornes." *Proceedings of Society of Antiquaries* of London, 1909, pp. 9–10. In 1636 "great deceate in the making of bad and slight nails of all sorts being for the most part of the worst iron, of lesse waight, strength and goodnes, then in former tyme" was charged to "wholesaile men who employ poor smiths to make the said nailes deceitfully in waight and substance." Noble, *Hist. of the Ironmongers' Company*, p. 226.

[82] As late as 1704 we find the mercantile gild of Dublin denouncing wholesale men who "keep a retail trade of such goods as they import," (*Egerton MSS. B. M.*, 1765, f. 59) when, according to the terms of the charter, conferred upon this Dublin gild by Queen Elizabeth, they were authorised to sell in gross or in retail all sorts of merchandise with the exception of food stuffs. *Proceedings of the Society of Antiq.*, 5th ser., vol. 10, p. 50. Indeed, by 1622, clashes between the wholesalers and retailers engaged in the clothing trade seem to have become so general, that one of the questions which the commissioners appointed in that year to inquire into its decline, were to take into consideration was, whether merchants should be retailers as well. *Rymer's Foedera*, xvii, p. 414. In Cork, by 1694, scarcely three years after local "Wholesale and Retayling merchants" had established a joint society, it had become so difficult to keep the two classes of traders apart, that it was "put to the vote whether all goods sold in shops shall be accounted retailing or not." *Council-Book*, pp. 217–18, 241.

[1] Archdeacon Cunningham believed that the act of 1363 was intended to prevent artisans from encroaching upon the business of merchants. *Growth of English Industry and Commerce*, vol. i, p. 383. According to fourteenth-century records, however, artisans seem to have encroached upon the business of rival artisans rather than upon that of merchants. Artisans apparently, did not take to trading until a later epoch.

[2] *Supra*, p. 60.

keep bowyers from being fletchers,[3] cobblers from working with new leather,[4] dyers and weavers from making cloth [5] and smiths from keeping forges in their city, and so from intermeddling with the work of farriery which according to the farriers, the smiths did not know how to bring to a good end.[6] Moreover, through succeeding centuries shoemakers, apparently regardless of consequences, continued not alone to tan [7] but to dress leather as well,[8] whereas cobblers never desisted altogether from making new shoes.[9] In addition to tanning [10] and "whitawing" [11] leather, curriers were often guilty of dyeing and selling that commodity to shoemakers.[12] Nor were tanners content merely to tan for the market. They, too, frequently defied the authorities by making shoes [13] or buying skins destined for glovers.[14] Glovers in their turn bought and sold

[3] It is interesting to learn of the efforts that were made by the London bowyers and fletchers in 1371 to separate their respective callings in accordance with the demands of the act of 1363. In that year, two representatives from each of the two occupations appeared one day at a meeting held by the mayor and aldermen and promised on behalf of their respective gilds that no man of the one craft should be allowed to meddle with that of the other in any point. But, in order that this promise might be fulfilled, since the men of each craft were accustomed to keep apprentices working in them both, they asked that the men be allowed sufficient time to finish such articles as they had begun, and decide as to which of the two crafts they might elect to adopt and thenceforth follow. They also asked that the craftsmen be allowed to offer for sale such bows and arrows as they had in stock. Riley, *Memorials of London*, pp. 348–9.

[4] By 1393 those having to do with old shoes would meddle with new shoes "among the old" to the disgust of city cordwainers. *Ibid.*, p. 392. And they apparently kept on meddling for fifteen years later, the city authorities were called upon to devise a way to keep the two callings apart. It appears that cordwainers would have restricted the cobblers' "pecyng" to a part of a quarter of a shoe, while the cobblers wanted it to include a whole "quarter." The mayor of the city evidently agreed with the cobblers, for he gave judgment in favor of their being allowed thenceforth to apply a whole "quarter." *Letter Book I*, pp. 73, 96.

[5] *Liber Albus*, bk. iv, p. 279.

[6] Riley, *op. cit.*, p. 292, also *Letter Book G*, p. 170.

[7] Lambert, *Two Thousand Years of Gild Life*, p. 315. In 1474 the "cordeners" of Coventry were forbidden to "cory no lethir within hym" under penalty of paying a fine of "vis. and viii.d." *Leet Book*, pt. ii, p. 401.

[8] At Sudbury, in Suffolk, in 1568, all the shoemakers were "amerced for that they offend for dressing lether in their own houses." *Calendar of the Muniments of the Borough*, printed in *Proceedings of the Suffolk Institute of Archaeol. and Nat. History*, 1909, vol. xiii, pt. 3, p. 277.

[9] In 1562 the cobblers of Lincoln were forbidden to use the craft of cordwainers "in making shoon of new leather or of any horse skin or other unlawful leather." *Hist. MSS. Com. Rep., Lincoln*, p. 53. Also *Gough MS. Collections for History of Lincoln*, fol. 229, Bodleian Library.

[10] 5 Elizabeth c. 2, made it a misdemeanour for curriers to tan.

[11] At Warwick in 1568, curriers were amerced for "whitawing of leather contrary to the statute." *The Book of John Fisher*, p. 15.

[12] Dalton, *The Country Justice*, p. 145.

[13] At late as 1734 in Manchester the jury was instructed to "inquire of Tanners that have used the occupation of a Cordwainer or a currier that hath put any leather to sale." *Court Leet Records*, vii, p. 34.

[14] In 1564 the tanners of Lincoln were forbidden under penalty to buy any

leather [15] and even made points to the hindrance of pointmakers. Pointmakers retaliated by making gloves.[16] Spurriers bought tanned leather and after dressing made "sayle" of it again despite the law which declared that the "dressing of leather doth not convert it into mayd wares."[17] Weavers would be fullers.[18] Fullers and shearmen alike wove cloth [19] and at least "needy dyers took up the occupation of both shearmen and fullers."[20] Dwellers in "Hamletts, throps and villages" not only took into their hands "dyverse and sondre fermes and become fermers, graziers and husbandmen"[21] but also "doo exercise, use and occupie the mysteries of cloth-makyng, wevyng, fullyng and sheryng." Cutlers made wares pertaining to the arts of the goldsmiths [22] as well as to those of the blacksmiths.[23] Carpenters worked at joinery [24] and joiners

sheep skins. *Gough MSS.*, Bodleian, *Collections for History of Lincoln*, fol. 232. In the eighteenth century, at Bristol, skinners were restrained from buying skins used by whitawers and glovers. Latimer, *Annals of Bristol in the 18th Century*, p. 21. In Warwick only members of the company of glovers, poyntmakers and skinners could deal in sheep skins. *Black Book*, p. 66. At Coventry, in 1474, tanners could "tanne no Shepys leddur, Derus leddur, Gettys leddur, horse ledur nor houndes leddur." *Leet Book*, pt. ii, p. 400.

[15] Lambert, *Two Thousand Years of Gild Life*, p. 219.

[16] Latimer, *Annals of Bristol in 17th Century*, p. 26.

[17] In 1659 a spurrier of Coventry was denounced for such an offense and "cast in dammage foreteen pounds." *MS. Records, Corporation of Coventry.*

[18] At Colchester, sometime during the reign of King Henry VIII, in order "to eschowe the grete hyndring and losse the whiche now late befallen to divers persones which have used to make cloth for this Towne in defaute of wefers that have woven Cloth, which wevers anone after have fulled that same cloth in her own howsys," the "Bayles and the councell" declared it a misdemeanour, punishable by payment of a fine, for any "maner of man, fro this day forward" to "holde the crafts of wevyng and of fullyng togedr." *Red Paper Book of Colchester*, p. 24.

[19] In 1586, at Warwick in the "tyme of the Sxt Bailwick of Rychard ffisher," it was ordered that "if any person being a weaver and using to weave have any fulling myle, Or if any Tucher or fuller or shereman have used to weave and doth keepe any weaving lomes" their names and defaults should be presented. *The Book of John Fisher*, p. 147.

[20] *Hist. MSS. Com. Rep. Lincoln* xiv, app. viii, p. 55.

[21] 25 Henry VIII, c. 18.

[22] Fourteenth-century goldsmiths in London claimed the right to supervise cutlers' work and exercised it in 1386 so far as to "search" their ordinances. Prideaux, *Memorials of the Goldsmiths' Co.* vol. 1, p. 14. Such a high-handed method of procedure naturally made for trouble between the two groups not only in the fourteenth century but in the sixteenth. In 1576, we find the cutlers asserting they had of old "occupied their works" of gold and silver as the change of time and fashion demanded, although they acknowledged that, the goldsmiths, subject to the oversight of city officials, had the assay of gold and silver work made by the cutlers. Herbert, *Twelve Great Livery Cos.*, vol. i, p. 104. In 1661 the goldsmiths seized diverse wares "wrought and made of silver" which had been put on sale by certain cutlers of Fleet Street. Prideaux, *Memorials*, vol. ii, p. 144.

[23] In 1583 the cutlers of Chester were forbidden to make blacksmiths' wares. Unwin, *Industrial Organization*, note 12, p. 83.

[24] Latimer, *Annals of Bristol in the 17th Century*, p. 25.

at carpentry [25] and neither craft apparently hesitated to furnish customers with locks, bolts, or hinges when the opportunity presented itself.[26] Bricklayers meddled with carpenters' work.[27] Plumbers became tilers;[28] and masons, slaters, tilers and plumbers alike worked at bricklaying or plastering ad libidum.[29]. "Plaisterers" for their part took to painting and colouring apparently whether or not local painters had "power to restrain them by virtue of any corporation."[30] Bakers brewed and brewers baked.[31] Victuallers and innholders indiscriminately baked[32] and brewed[33] both beer

[25] Jupp, *History of the London Carpenters' Co.*, p. 304, Append. E.

[26] Latimer, *op. cit.*, p. 26. In 1607 joiners or carpenters who contracted to supply locks or other ironmongery in Bristol did so under forfeit of forty shillings to local smiths and cutlers.

[27] In 1631 the bricklayers of London entered into an agreement with city carpenters whereby no member of one craft was to intermeddle with the others. Each company appointed representatives "to settle such order or course for the meddling with their owne trades, the Carpenters with their trade and the Bricklayers with their trade as to the Court of Aldren shalbe thought fitt and most convenient." Jupp, *op. cit.*, p. 275.

[28] In 1530 the Coventry Leet ruled that "no persone of this Cite occupieng or vsyng the Misterie and Craft of plummers shall fromehensfurth vse the Craft of a Tyler ner no Tyler to vse the Craft of a plummer upon peyn to forfett for euery defaut contrarie to this present acte vis. viiid." *Coventry Leet Book*, pt. iii, p. 702.

[29] In 1660 the wallers and bricklayers of Newcastle-upon-Tyne begged the city corporation to protect them from further molestation by the masons or slaters. Walford, *Gilds*, p. 205. In 1557 the carpenters of Dublin were not above doing mason's work. *Journ. Royal Soc. of Antiquaries of Ireland*, vol. 35, pt. iv, 1905, p. 329. In 1607 the carpenters of London were warned not to "intromitt or meddle . . . with any bargaine of the occupacions of Plumary, Masons, Dawbinge, Tilinge or any other occupacion except yt he vppon his owne proper houses and vpon his owne Dwellinge house." Jupp, *op. cit.*, p. 147.

[30] Strype, *Stow's Survey of London*, vol. ii, p. 301. The "Plaisterers" of London apparently objected to having the painters "engross" colouring as well as painting in the city. *Lansdowne MS.* 106, f. 5, also *Titus MS.*, iv, f. 36.

[31] *Hist. MSS. Com. Rep., Rye*, Rep. xiii, app. iv, p. 47.

[32] In 1586 a Warwick jury amerced a "comon victualler" for baking "white bread in his owne house" and retailing the same. *The Book of John Fisher*, p. 150. Again, an ordinance drawn up by the Kinsale gild of bakers about the middle of the seventeenth century and ratified by the borough corporation, forbade innholders, taverners, victuallers or hucksters to sell anywhere within the borough "for moneys" within their inns, taverns, or shops, any bread other than that bought from "the common bakers of the towne." *Council Book of Kinsale*, p. 33. As early as 1383 the innkeepers of Northampton were prohibited from selling in their inns bread of their own making. *Liber Custumarum*, p. 56. See also *Hist. MSS. Com. Rep. Beverley*, p. 87.

[33] At Abingdon in 1579, the authorities forbade innkeepers or alehousekeepers to "brue" in their houses "any Beere or Ale to be sold, offerid or drunke there, either by "the pinte, potte, quarte, pottell or gallon potte under the payne to lose for every potte so sould xs." *Selections from the Records*, p. 126. A somewhat similar order issued at Stratford-on-Avon in 1595, bade innholders, victuallers, typlers and alehouse-keepers "to fatche there ale and bere from the comen ale bruers upon peyne that everie one that shall doe contrarye to this order shall be utterly suppressed and put downe and shall not afterwards be suffered to vse or occupye any more victulinge within thys borowghe." Halliwell, *Stratford Council-Book*, p. 90.

and ale and a ta pinch neither glovers, shearmen or even husband-men were averse "audaciously to exercise for gaine the arts and mis-teries of innholders and cookes." [34] Vintners openly sold both beer and victuals of their own "dressing"; yet protested when "Macha-nack cowpers" took up the vintners' business.[35] Not content with dealing in wool, tanned hides, skins, tallow and candles,[36] butchers in certain communities even undertook to cook viands for those who would purchase them.[37]

Artificers were not content always to remain artificers. At Kingston-upon-Hull by 1499, tailors, shoemakers and other crafts-men "presumptiously" took it upon themselves "to by and sell as merchaunts and in their howses, shopps and wyndowes openly showed much ware." [38] In 1515 at Newcastle-upon-Tyne there was a "great groche" between city merchants and craftsmen because the latter were using the "occupacion of merchaunts and buthemen." [39] A century later at Youghal persons "professing mechanical trades and mysteries" dealt daily "in trade, in buying and selling wool, flax, and other like commodities." [40] In 1648, smiths, goldsmiths, tailors, weavers and coopers of Dublin set up wine taverns, cellars, shops and stalls wherein they bought and sold merchandise of all sorts.[41] A decade later at Gateshead there were persons who kept open shop and exercised "without Leaue or Lycence" several of "ye occupacions, misteryes and facultyes" which properly belonged only to members of the merchants' company.[42] Then too, urban

---

[34] *Harleian MSS.*, 1996, f. 25. In 1514 upon the complaint of the "In-holders" of Coventry that local bakers were "kepyng ynnes," the Leet or-dained that the bakers were thereafter to "kep no hostryes according to the olde rule of the citee." *Leet Book,* pt. iii, p. 637.

[35] Milbourn, *The Vintners' Company,* p. 4.

[36] Townsend, *Hist. of Leominster,* p. 310. Also *The Black Book of War-wick,* p. 22. At Lymington in Hampshire, in 1615, butchers sold "tallowe, accordinge" to the quantities of their flesh. *Old Times Revisited in the Borough and Parish of Lymington, Hants,* p. 52. In the days of King James I, butchers were also tanning skins, a practice which was forbidden by 1 James I, c. 22.

[37] An ordinance issued in 1606 at Bristol forbade local butchers to do this either in their own houses or elsewhere. Latimer, *Annals of Bristol in 17th Century,* p. 25. In 1467 we find the city of Worcester prohibiting the butchers from plying the trade of a cook. Smith, *English Gilds,* p. 405. At one time or another, apparently, men engaged in any trade or industry considered themselves justified in handling food stuffs. Indeed, it is said to have been the fashion for thirteenth-century mercers and merchants to keep taverns. Redstone, *St. Edmunds' Bury and Town Rental for 1295, Proceedings of Suffolk Institute of Archaeology and Natural History,* vol. xiii, pt. ii, p. 201. By the time of King Edward VI victuallers had taken so to meddling with one another's business, that parliament interfered by forbidding their doing so in the future or performing and finishing what another had begun. 2 & 3 Edward VI, c. 15.

[38] Lambert, *Two Thousand Years of Gild Life,* p. 158.

[39] *Archaeologia Aeliana,* 3rd series, vol. vii, pp. 77–87.

[40] *Council Book,* p. 7.

[41] *Egerton MSS., B. M.,* 1765, f. 40.

[42] *Records of the Company,* Edited by Mr. Edwin Dodds, 1907, p. 9.

authorities often had difficulty to restrain "artisantes and tradesmen of the countrie" from "retaylinge of their wares" within city precincts.[43] Merchants could not always continue to be merchants. Because of "Misadventure of Pyrates or Shipwrack on the Seas" or of mishaps of other sorts, seventeenth-century merchants were sometimes forced to "leave that course and betake themselves to some handicraft . . . proportionate to that means which they have left."[44] But whatever the reason it seems evident that by the sixteenth century, traders and craftsmen alike indiscriminately practised such callings as they deemed convenient or profitable, until the revolt against the existing order assumed such proportions as to force the authorities to intervene in the interest of industrial peace and prosperity. Thus, in particular, at Chester in the eyes of those best fitted to know, "the first bringing of things to head and order when before every man sould what liked him best in all sorts of wares" occurred in the reign of good Queen Elizabeth when the authorities issued an order forbidding "any arts, mystery, syence, occupation or crafts" to use, practise, sell, exchange or "other wyese intermeddle with any other arte or occupacion," than "shalbe appoynted, limityd and assigned by the committee appointed for the purpose."[45] In 1635 the authorities of Kendal outlined for the various groups of tradesmen the particular kind of wares each group alone might handle.[46]

However, trouble was not confined to members of rival gilds, but broke out at times between men who belonged to the same gild group. As early as 1377, in London, we find the poor "commons" of the mystery of goldsmiths denouncing the richer members of the company for making them promise to treble the price of all wares which they should thereafter sell to mercers, cutlers, jewellers and others of their class. And those who refused, they said "are imprisoned and in peril of death by grievous menace till they seal the bond as their poor companions have done before."[47] In 1650 the less prosperous feltmakers of the same city had cause to complain that their company "looke not at all at the preservation of their poore members but at the upholding of their better sort."[48] In 1633 city pinners, wireworkers and girdlers were aggrieved because merchant members having become "Governors" of their association, neglected to enforce certain ordinances which had been

---

[43] Bateson, *Records of the Borough of Leicester,* vol. iii, p. 301.
[44] Cunningham, *Growth of English Industry & Commerce,* vol. i, p. 345.
[45] Morris, *Chester,* p. 404.
[46] For instance, woollen drapers were to sell all sorts of woollen cloth, including hats and bands, while mercers and haberdashers of small wares were to be accounted as one business. Grocers, for their part, were authorised to deal in grocery wares, apothecary wares, dyeing stuffs, and such commodities as were sold by the hundred-weight and gallon measure. Linen cloth, however, was to be used in common until certain individuals undertook to ply that trade. *Historical MSS. Comm. Rep.* x, app. iv, p. 317.
[47] Quoted from Unwin, *Gilds & Companies of London,* p. 78.
[48] Unwin, *Industrial Organization,* p. 197.

promulgated for the regulation of the handicraft element, and in addition "by their greatness assuming power over the artisans," they have converted their revenues to other uses." [49] Clashes were not uncommon between the different handicraft groups which were united in one and the same organisation. Scarcely fifteen years after the London fullers and shearmen joined in forming the cloth-workers' company, representatives of the fullers complained to the court of the company that the shearmen were making "price with the merchants for the rowyng of clothes." The fullers felt qualified to "make their owne prices and receyve their owne money for their wokemanshipp." [50]   So, too, in 1739, certain barbers and perukemakers of Bristol begged the city council to protect them against such "diverse impositions and grievances" as their surgical brethren had been inflicting upon them. [51]

This friction was not always the result of commercial differences. [52] Controversies sometimes "happened" between crafts as to which should have "preheminence" in marching in the "Mayor's watch upon midsomer-Eve," [53] or as to the side on which they should walk in the procession "with thaire lights on Corpus Day." [54]

Thus, as far as one can judge, there was practically no limit to the friction likely to declare itself between different trades and handicrafts, in spite of laws insisting upon their separation or of charters guaranteeing a monopoly to particular groups. In fact, English industrial society seems never to have been free from fric-

[49] Smythe, *History of the Girdlers' Company*, p. 48.

[50] Unwin, *op. cit.*, p. 231 .

[51] Latimer, *Annals of Bristol in the 18th Century*, p. 219. The officials of the company addressed a counter-petition to the council, expressing their surprise that certain "uneasie" members should have presumed so to importune it "with unfounded discontents."

[52] Gildsmen evidently called one another to account for employing non-gildsmen. In 1495 wardens of the London carpenters collected a fine of 13s. 4d. from the goldsmiths for employing a foreigner. Prideaux, *Memorials of the London Goldsmiths' Company*, vol. i, p. 37. As a result of a quarrel which raged between the butchers and fishmongers of London in the thirty-fifth year of the reign of King Edward III over the use of "le stockes," the mayor of the city confirmed an agreement entered into between the two groups in the previous reign, under which the fishmongers were to sell fish there on fish-days and the butchers meat on meat-days. *Letter Book G*, p. 127.

[53] Izache, *Exeter*, p. 84. For the "appeasing" of this controversy it was decided that both companies should march together, "one of either company hand in hand." And a dispute which arose between the skinners and merchant taylors of London as to which group should take precedence over the other in civic processions, necessitating the arbitration of city officials, brought forth the edict that city skinners might precede the merchant taylors one year and the merchant taylors, the skinners, the next year. Wadmore, *History of the Skinners' Company*, p. 5.

[54] Morris, *Chester*, p. 349. During this same time we find the cordwainers of York preferring to pay the penalty for the "nown-beryng of their torches the morn after Corpus Xpi day" rather than "with their 14 torches to go on the weavers' left hand." Davies, *History of York*, appen. p. 250–52. In 1444 the mayor of Coventry had the weavers and "Coruesers" come before him because of "Varyans betwen" them and ordered "bothe the said craftis . . . to kep the peace." Coventry *Leet Book*, pt. i, p. 203.

tion from the time when artisans first established gilds of their own to control their various occupations. Indeed, on the one hand, Professor Brentano ascribes the origin of the earliest English craft gilds to the hostility which local merchants felt towards artisans and manifested by expelling them from the gild merchant,[55] while on the other hand, Professor Gross's dismissal as exceptional and therefore of little moment the only evidence of a struggle between merchants and artisans which he took into account, has apparently given certain of his readers the impression that, in his opinion, a struggle never occurred between the two classes of medieval craftsmen.[56] Mr, Dendy, the editor of the records of the Merchant Adventurers of Newcastle-upon-Tyne, apparently draws this inference and takes exception to it. He found unmistakable evidence of a struggle between merchants and handicraftsmen at Newcastle from 1342 down to 1730, for at this latter date, city merchants still attempted to enforce their trading monopoly.[57] Mr. Dendy, however, in this instance, seems to be taking exception to an assertion which Professor Gross neither made nor in all probability intended to make.[58] Professor Gross denied, in effect, the existence of proof of a struggle during the fourteenth, fifteenth, or indeed any other century, between the gild merchant and the different craft gilds, not between merchants and craftsmen organised in separate gilds, as they appear on record in Newcastle-upon-Tyne by 1342. This misconception of the relations which existed in medieval England between trades and handicrafts alike, arises probably from the failure of students to differentiate between the early gild merchant [59] and the associated merchant gilds which, apparently from the fourteenth century onward, were established in common by different groups of local merchants in most industrial centres. It has already been shown how, after the handicrafts, perhaps group by group, broke away from the gild merchant's domination, and established gilds of their own, the ordinary traders in their neighbourhood were forced likewise to organise so as effectually to protect their immediate commercial interests. In the provincial boroughs these interests were identical and could easily be served in one and the same organisation. So that, while a local gild merchant ceased to regulate the economic affairs of the handicrafts, its successor, a gild of merchants, soon arose to restrain them from engaging at will in mercantile enterprises. It was the enforcement of restraints of this nature that made for trouble between the trades and handicrafts.

Professor George Unwin, for his part, undoubtedly recognised the existence of an antagonism of interest between the trades and

---

[55] Smith, *English Gilds*, p. cxv.

[56] *Gild Merchant*, vol. i, p. 117.

[57] *Surtees Society Public.*, vol. 93, p. xxix.

[58] Professor Gross was careful to point out the fact of his being concerned only with the relation of craftsmen and their associations to the gild merchant. *Op. cit.*, p. 107.

[59] Supra, pp. vi, 22, note 3.

crafts, and interpreted it as a conflict between commercial and industrial capital.[60] Professor Unwin's argument, however, seems not to take into account the fact that commercial companies warred openly with one another as well as with industrial companies when their interests conflicted, and that industrial companies, in turn, clashed not only with rival industrial groups but with commercial bodies. Professor Unwin cites, as one case in point, the conflict which raged throughout the late sixteenth century and the first half of the seventeenth, between merchant haberdashers and artisan feltmakers in London when the former attempted to control the city's felt-making industry. This is all very well as far as it goes. But the feltmakers had scarcely carried out their "designe" of "cutting themselves from" the haberdashers when they set about opposing, evidently, as strenuously as the haberdashers, the efforts made by the city's beaver-makers to monopolise the making of beaver hats.[61] Granting, therefore, that the struggle between the haberdashers and the feltmakers was a struggle between commercial and industrial capital, the clash between the feltmakers and the beaver-makers grew out of the rivalry between two industrial groups, each one of which seemed bent upon gaining control over the same industry. So, when the linen-drapers of Chester sought to enforce the monopoly which they had acquired, they had to meet the resistance not alone of city mercers, but of local silk weavers as well.[62] Thus Professor Unwin's theory seems to take a rather limited view of the conflict which, at one time or another, embroiled practically all the different forces in economic society. That which Professor Unwin regards as a conflict between commercial and industrial capital, seems rather to be such a conflict as was bound to arise in a system which attempted to effect a rigid division between organised trades and handicrafts. The beginnings of the trouble date probably as far back as the days of the Angevin kings in towns like Oxford, Beverley, Marlborough and Winchester, which controlled trade and industry through a gild merchant and consequently looked askance at the separate gilds then being established by local weavers and fullers under royal protection. By the late twelfth century or the early thirteenth, those communities were scarcely prepared to countenance the separation of special economic interests and consequently took such steps as they could to prevent it. Later, in the thirteenth century, a certain number of artisans who belonged to the gild merchant at Leicester were discovered conspiring together to regulate their own business; yet there too the gild merchant was quick to detect and to thwart the conspiracy.[63] The gild merchant's opposition may for a time have delayed the withdrawal of the Leicester craftsmen into separate gilds, but separation was inevitable in the end.

---

[60] *Industrial Organization*, pp. 70–72.
[61] *Ibid.*, p. 244.
[62] *Harleian MS., B. M.*, 2054 ff. 37–47.
[63] See Kramer, *The English Craft Gilds & the Government*, pp. 17–27.

A spirit as hostile as that manifested by the gild merchant of Leicester towards rising craft gilds of the fourteenth century,[64] seems to have been displayed toward new organisations throughout the seventeenth, by corporations determined to keep control of their own interests. Thus, the feltmakers of London persisted in refusing to meet the conditions which city beaver-makers saw fit to impose upon them in the making of beaver hats; whereupon King Charles I intervened and marked out feltmaking and beaver-making as two distinct occupations neither one of which was ever again to encroach upon the other.[65] Again, failing in their attempt to prevent city apothecaries from severing gild relations with their company, seventeenth-century grocers of London sought to have set aside as illegal, because secured without their consent, the letters patent which gave the apothecaries the right apart from the grocers to appropriate to themselves the local trade in drugs and the distillation and sale of different sorts of water.[66] Scarcely had the city apothecaries justified their right to a corporate existence separate and distinct from the grocers before they, in their turn, initiated a campaign against city distillers for presuming to establish an independent society. In this instance, the apothecaries claimed that they alone had the right to distil within a circuit of seven miles about the city of London. Their threats to suppress the distillers' organisation proved ineffectual and the latter retained control of their cherished sphere of industry.[67] In 1629 at Chester about three hundred inn-keepers and victuallers were up in arms against local brewers for having procured a charter restraining any except members of their "companie" from brewing beer and ale to sell in the city.[68] Again, in 1690, more than half a century after the London clockmakers had been royally incorporated, they were

[64] In insisting in the act of 1363 that two of every craft be chosen to see that none use a craft other than that chosen, the English parliament of the period publicly proclaimed the wish to effect a systematic division of labour under gild control. Moreover, as late as 1657 the corporation of Kinsale apparently favored the continuation of the same policy, when, in that year, it announced that nothing was more conducive to the well-ordering of that borough than "to subdivide the body politic into several companies and to see that the members of each applied themselves to their particular branch of industry without meddling with that of the others." *Council Book*, p. 34.

[65] Unwin, *Industrial Organization*, pp. 145–6.

[66] Barrett, *History of the Society of Apothecaries*, p. 23. See also *Index to Remembrancia*, p. 96.

[67] Barrett, *History of the Society of Apothecaries*, p. 7. The apothecaries had their "doubts touching the Reformacon of abuses committed by the makers and distillers of hott waters and the makers of emplastors and conserves." They claimed the sole right under their charter of distilling within the city, and for seven miles around. The distillers, however, disputed the apothecaries' claim and insisted that the apothecaries' rights applied merely to medicinal distillation. Meanwhile the grocers took advantage of this division in the ranks of their competitors to petition the House of Commons to revoke the patent which had incorporated the apothecaries apart from the grocers and endowed them with the privilege of selling drugs and distilling waters. Barrett, *op. cit.*, p. 8. Also *Index to Remembrancia*, p. 96.

[68] *Harleian MS., B. M.*, 2104, f. 62.

opposed by city blacksmiths "in their present designe" to force all clockmakers to join the blacksmiths' company. Even at that late date the blacksmiths hoped still to control such members as had branched out as clockmakers on the ground that the clockmaker really needed the peculiar workmanship of "ye smith" to enable him to finish a clock, whereas the smith "can entirely do of himself because the whole is but a branch of ye art of smithery . . . having been always so accompted." [69] Although unable often to prevent some rival group from withdrawing from their control, established corporations appear frequently to have succeeded in hampering its movements, sometimes, indeed, in having its powers modified. Occasionally indeed a corporation of the period contrived to prevent the incorporation of a rival group. Because the carpenters and joiners of London and others of their kind considered the "saweing of timber" a part of their "severall trades" and "soe necessary a part thereof that without it their trades cannot be well" or "handsomely" performed, they kept city sawyers from securing independent control of their own industry.[70] The carpenters had experienced the disadvantage of suffering the incorporation of a group with interests closely allied to their own. Their failure in the previous century to prevent the separation of joinery from carpentry cost them years of controversy with city joiners as to where the rights of carpenters began and those of joiners ended, and vice versa.[71] The handicrafts were not perceptibly nearer an adjustment of the controverted points at the end of the century than they had been at the beginning. But then, in considering the carpenters' side of the controversy outlined in 1672, when the two groups were still at daggers'-drawn, one can readily understand why it never could be settled to the satisfaction of both sides.[72] The carpenters took the stand that when a craft which had once been a recognised branch of another, as was joynery to the carpenters' trade made of themselves a voluntary "separacon" from that craft and their "eleccon" to be a separate craft, they thereby "by their owne act" restrained themselves to that "occupacon" and so lost their privilege wholly as to the craft from which they separated themselves. "Yett by their act the other craft are not nor cannot in reason be barred from their inherent right and privilege

[69] Overall, *History of the Worshipful Company of Clockmakers,* p. 118. In the beginning the clockmakers evidently thought of incorporating themselves with city blacksmiths, but the negotiations which were entered into to bring about their union came to nought, although individual clockmakers continued to join the blacksmiths' company. *Ibid.,* p. 3.

[70] Jupp, *History of the Carpenters' Company,* p. 307, Appen. F. The sawyers' opponents contended that the incorporation of "theis sort of laborers wilbe drawn into an evill president" for others of their kind.

[71] In Elizabeth's days the joiners had united with city carvers in forming an association. *Supra,* p. 56.

[72] The earliest record of a clash between these carpenters and joiners is dated 1621, in which year the carpenters appointed a committee to meet a committee of the joiners "to treat with them about differences of works in the same Companies." Jupp, *op. cit.,* p. 265.

of using both occupacons" if "in truth and law" they were really to be "accompted severall trades and occupacons."[73] The carpenters evidently still had their doubts upon the subject. And, in having certain joiners of the period committed to prison for intermeddling with the trade of "carpentry," they must be credited with the courage of their convictions, fail as they might to convince their opponents of the justice of their contention.[74] Not unnaturally the joiners could not understand why a rule should not work both ways.[75] Whether unreasonable or not, the stand taken by the carpenters of London toward city joiners in the seventeenth century, differed little from that taken by gildsmen of standing not only of that century but of the fourteenth, when the cordwainers of Shrewsbury refused to stop tanning at the demand of local tanners. Seventeenth-century haberdashers opposed the incorporation of the feltmakers, and feltmakers in their turn that of beaver-makers. Grocers denied to apothecaries the right to an independent corporate existence and apothecaries took much the same stand towards the distillers. Blacksmiths would have kept clockmakers dependent upon them for whatever gild privileges they coveted and clockmakers, for their part, would have done the same to spectacle-makers. While fighting strenuously for their own independence, carpenters and joiners acted as a unit in denying an equal right to city sawyers. In truth, gilds neither of the fourteenth-century nor of the seventeenth were particularly keen about deputing to others the very least of their powers as division of labor developed.[76] On the contrary, throughout the centuries, different gild groups continued to assert their right to control various departments of their industries even though such claims were manifestly inconsistent with the progress which had been made in the division of employment. For example, in 1555, the city of Bristol supported a gild of shearmen whose origin dated back at least a century and a half; yet local fullers still declared that their work included the "burlyng, rewyng, tolnyng, volding, taching, yewnying" as well as the "sheer-

---

[73] *Ibid.*, pp. 304–5.

[74] Jupp, *History of the Carpenters' Company*, p. 265.

[75] At the time that the London feltmakers denied the right of the haberdashers to control the making of felt hats in their city, they took a fairer view of the rights of both sides in a controversy of this sort. Wishing to live themselves they were willing to let their opponents live also. They considered that the exercise of the power given them by their charter "cannot hinder the haberdashers from the exercise of the power given by theirs, but if both have a power which they may execute" for the prevention of fraud and abuse in their respective trades, they "could wish that the haberdashers would cease to hinder" them and "with diligence pursue the worke to which they pretend they are impowered." The *Case of the Feltmakers Truely Stated*, 1650, quoted from Unwin, *Industrial Organization*, p. 245.

[76] As late as 1815 the clockmakers protested when a spectacle-maker took up his freedom with the spectacle-makers' company rather than with the clockmakers', on the ground that the proceeding was an infringement of the rights of the clockmakers' company. Overall, *History of the Clockmakers' Company*, p. 137.

ing" of cloth.[77] With an association comprising bowyers, fletchers, coopers, turners, carvers, joiners and other wood-workers, the governors of Beverley of this period conceded to every carpenter "being brother with the carpenters" liberty to "occupy carving, embowinge, rabitting, jonynge and seelinge" without having to account to the "Bowers."[78] In 1613, at the time when the joiners of London refused to stop carpentering, they sought leave to search and supervise the making of coaches, trunks, gunstocks and flasks as being within the "compass" of their "skill and judgment."[79] Again, it is difficult to reconcile Queen Elizabeth conceding to the saddlers of London the right to oversee and correct the making of saddles, bridles, bits, reins, stirrups, girdles, harness and various other articles of the sort in 1558, when, for centuries, city lorimers and girdlers had had the control of their respective handicrafts.[80] Such a duplication of powers was bound sooner or later to bring the last-named crafts into conflict with the saddlers. Saddlers and lorimers had, in fact, clashed as early as 1320 over a set of ordinances issued by the lorimers and considered an infringement of the saddlers' liberties.[81] Moreover, a suit which the saddlers instituted at the time to test the legality of the ordinances in question, was decided in their favour; the offending ordinances being subsequently burned in "Westchepe."[82] Again, claiming that the right to confiscate girdles of inferior workmanship which had been conceded to the girdlers in 1356, interfered with their own interests, the saddlers succeeded in having the king stay the execution of the order by which that privilege had already been conferred upon city girdlers, pending the decision of the controversy by parliament.[83]

One group often condemned another for using practically the same sort of tactics which it employed. For instance, London saddlers who sought to prevent joiners, painters and lorimers from selling "any manner of merchandise" pertaining to their crafts to any except saddlers, openly accused all three crafts of "making themselves kings of the land" by setting "every part of their trade at a fixed price."[84] Incorporated in the twenty-second year of the reign of King Richard II for the purpose, apparently of using

[77] Fox and Taylor, *History of the Bristol Weavers*, p. 70.

[78] *Hist. MSS. Com. Rep., Beverley*, p. 99. The twelve "governors" of Beverley were obliged to make this concession to the carpenters, in order to induce them to withdraw the suit which they had instituted against the bowyers in London.

[79] *Index to the Remembrancia*, p. 95.

[80] Sherwell, *History of the Saddlers' Company*, p. 52. In the fourteenth century, the London saddlers enjoyed the right to search any "house, shop or chamber" within the franchise of the city wherever any saddles or harness were to be found. *Letter Book G*, p. 143.

[81] Sherwell, *op. cit.*, p. 23. It seems that the saddlers resented having destroyed as "unlawful" girdles which they had in the making. *Letter Book G*, p. 67.

[82] Sherwell, *History of the Saddlers' Company*, p. 9.

[83] *Ibid.*, p. 23.

[84] Riley, *Memorials of London*, p. 157.

"as well whiting, paring, poling, cutting and pointing of leather as well as the selling of leather and wares thereof made," city leather-sellers two centuries later opposed the incorporation of glovers on the ground that such a corporation "would turn to a plain monopoly and to a confederacy."[85] A tradesman of Chester who accounted himself at once an ironmonger, a vintner, a mercer and a "retaylor of manye commodities" considered it a misdemeanour for a local "retaylinge draper" to usurp the name of merchant.[86] Equally inconsistent in theory and practice appear gildsmen who, after enjoying centuries of monopoly themselves in their chosen fields, yet sought to have rendered null and void the patents which were, from time to time, granted to different monopolists. Thus, under date of 1594, the records of the London leathersellers frankly reveal that company's efforts to have revoked as "vexatious" the monopoly of searching and sealing leather accorded Sir Edward Darcie by Queen Elizabeth.[87] During this same time, the horners of the metropolis made known their objections to the "Lycence"[88] which had been issued to certain merchants on the ground that it "restreyned members of their company" from "their former traffic to theire undoynge in general." Again, in 1599, London grocers who first sold starch "were fain to make complaint to the Lord Treasurer" against letters patent conferring upon Sir John Packington the exclusive right to make and sell starch.[89] Likewise, in 1640, the London ironmongers' company appointed six of their number to "hearken and enquire of Mr. Attorney or some of his followers what is done by the Lords of the Councell concerning John Brown's patent for the making and selling of all sorts of cast iron waire wh'ch is prejudiciall to this Compã and the Comonwealth, to the ende that a peticion may be preferred to the Lords of the Councell in the Comp^es behalf for redresse therein, if it shalbe found convenient."[90]

At this point one naturally wonders whether newly organised companies really expected established corporations to take seriously their claim to monopolise specific branches of their calling. After all the rights of the newcomers could have been enforced only at the expense of those of the older claimants.[91] If Chester's brewers,

[85] Black, *History of the Worshipful Company of Leathersellers*, p. 102. Also *State Papers Domestic*, vol. ccclxxxvi, No. 90.
[86] Noble, *History of the London Ironmongers' Company*, p. 27.
[87] Black, *op. cit.*, p. 50.
[88] *Proceedings of the Society of Antiquaries of London*, 1909, p. 10.
[89] Strype, *Stow's Survey of London*, vol. ii, p. 263. See also *Index to Remembrancia*, p. 94. Grocers, too, kept on "using the trade of starch," regardless of the consequence of being summoned every month before the Privy Council for the infraction of the starch monopoly. Unwin, *Gilds & Companies of London*, p. 299.
[90] Noble, *History of Ironmongers' Company*, p. 231.
[91] That the privileges allowed a new corporation might conflict with those already enjoyed by an established group was a possibility which suggested itself to the powers in command. Before King Charles I conceded to the London clockmakers the charter they coveted, he consulted the "Lord Maior,"

for instance, had carried out such provisions of their charter as gave them the monopoly of brewing beer and ale, ruin might indeed have overtaken the three hundred or more innkeepers and victuallers who, according to their allegation "had used brewing tyme out of mynde." To listen to most crafts one might suppose that each had indeed exercised sole jurisdiction over the most extended field "from time immemorial" or "from the time the memory of man was not to the contrary" or from some equally mystical period. The allegation was probably true in the case of the handicrafts first in the field, the shoemakers, smiths,[92] carpenters,[93] weavers, fullers [94] and the like. Before division of labour delegated to special groups different branches of a craft, craftsmen had probably much as a matter of course exercised wide latitude in their respective spheres. Doubtless, from the start, the cordwainers of Shrewsbury tanned the leather they used in making boots and shoes; otherwise the king would scarcely have bidden them keep on, in the face of the opposition raised by the tanners. Organised, probably, before the shearmen, the fullers of Bristol used from the first the different processes of cloth-making which they claimed as their right two centuries later, and refused at that stage to yield to local shearmen. Division of labour was not introduced simultaneously in all branches of trade and industry, so that disturbance incidental to the creation of new groups inevitably menaced at one time or another a borough's industrial peace. For instance, the linen-drapers of Chester

---

the "Recorder" and certain "Aldermen of the Citie" of London as to whether the "grantinge" of a charter incorporating city clockmakers would "in noe sort be prejuditiall to any other Corporacons or Governments alreadie established." Overall, *History of the Clockmakers' Company*, p. 7.

[92] According to Archbishop Aelfrics' "Colloquium" written before 1051, eleventh-century smiths supplied the implements for every craft. Cunningham, *Growth of English Industry & Commerce*, vol. 1, p. 132. Later, the little smith of Nottingham did "the work that no man can." Wylie, *Old and New Nottingham*, p. 286. We have found seventeenth-century blacksmiths of London claiming that the whole art of making clocks was but a branch of "ye art of smithery."

[93] As late as 1672 the London carpenters averred that "as well the Joyners" as carvers, wheelers, cartwrights, boxmakers, instruments-makers as certain other crafts were formerly only "Limbes" and a "part of carpentry and Branches taken from them." Jupp, *op. cit.*, p. 304.

[94] The fullers of Winchester, like the weavers, were organised in gilds as early as 1131 (*Pipe Roll*, 31 Henry I, p. 37) and the fullers and weavers of Leicester seem to have led local handicrafts in the fight to free themselves from the gild merchant's domination, preparatory, presumably, to erecting gilds of their own. Kramer, *The English Craft Gilds and the Government*, pp. 23–4.

Ordinances "newly-made" by the fullers of Bristol, were sanctioned by city officials in 1347 and again later in that century and in the fifteenth; but we find no record of a shearmen's gild in either period. *Little Red Book*, vol. ii, pp. 7, 15, 75–6. In addition to their own share in the process of cloth making, the fullers must have sheared cloth also, because, later in their history, they tell how "thinking it not hurtful," they had vouchsafed the "sheermen" at their asking, the "sheering of both proof and merchants' work." Fox and Taylor, *History of the Bristol Weavers*, p. 98.

who were not made "a whole and full occupation of itselfe, distincte and separate from other occupations within the said Cittye" until the sixth year of the reign of King Edward VI, had, half a century later, to defend their right to that industry against the onslaught of local mercers.[95] The mercers had probably been the first group in Chester to handle linen-goods, and they were naturally loath to yield their place to later comers.[96]. Here, of course, lay the cause of the trouble. The severance of an occupation sought for by one group had of necessity to be imposed upon a competitor. When the chandlers of Coventry were put in control of candle-making in 1511, the butchers, bakers, fishmongers and the other crafts who had had the making of candles in common, were forbidden thereafter either to make or to "by eny candell to sell but only for their owne howses." [97] Here was evidently a distinction with a difference, the observance of which asked more of craft nature than it could perform. In 1480 the merchant gild of Newcastle-upon-Tyne "mayd" one act according to which no artificer was to "occupy no manner of merchantdis bod as myche as is necessary for hym for exibicion of his hows" and another, thirty-five years later, to the effect, that handicrafts use the "feate" of buying and selling "only for their family and households and not to be sold again." [98] Neither order evidently deterred local craftsmen from buying or selling on their own account, to judge by the disturbance the merchants raised over craft activity in either direction. The disturbance, in fact, reached such proportions as to cause the King to send a commission to investigate the points at issue between the two factions.[99] The smiths of Beverley, too, apparently, bought and sold iron neither altered nor wrought by them according to their "science," against a ruling of the merchants which forbade their engaging in enterprises of the sort.[100] It was of course simpler for merchants to issue such rules than to enforce them either peaceably or otherwise. Besides, the merchants could not materially have helped their own cause in disregarding laws governing their order so far as to buy materials from handicraftsmen when the purchase suited their convenience.[101]

Then, too, a sixteenth-century craftsman of Kingston-upon-Hull

[95] By 1634 the Chester linen-drapers were evidently trading in cloth of all sorts, in buckram and in stitching silks of all colours, as well as in needles, thimbles and other articles of their kind. *Harleian MSS. 2054*, f. 68.

[96] In 1504 in the city of London the power of choosing an official for the "meteing of Linen cloth" seems to have rested with the mercers' company. *Charters and Ordinances of London Mercers*, p. 78, No. 35.

[97] *Coventry Leet Book*, p. 632.

[98] *Surtees Society Publications*, vol. 93, p. xxviii.

[99] Mr. Dendy has published the Star Chamber Proceedings in this controversy in *Archaeologia Aeliana, 3rd series*, vol. vii, pp. 77–86.

[100] *Historical MSS. Commiss. Report, Beverley*, pp. 83–4.

[101] In 1554 the Merchant Adventurers of Newcastle-upon-Tyne forbade any man free of the fellowship either to buy skins of a glover or of any other man who had bought them of a glover or indeed from any one who knew the skins had been bought of a glover. *Surtees Society Public.*, vol. 93, p. 48.

might openly show wares in his "shoppe or wyndowe" other than those which "to hys crafftt apperteyneth" without breaking the rules on his own initiative.[102] That borough seemingly endowed her mercantile gild with authority as considerable as that bestowed upon others of the period, yet she saw fit to accord local glovers the right to buy leather "to th' end to sell the same again."[103] And while Hull joiners might with impunity "buye anie Rayles, sealinge boards or bedd tymber to sell againe," their Chester brethren were dealing in timber of various sorts.

There seems to have been no end to the allowing of concessions once the practice was begun, all to the confusion of the system and its inevitable ruin. When sixteenth-century retailers of Chester wrested from local adventurers the right to "use the trade of marchandize together with their retaylinge" they, in their turn, conceded to the adventurers the right to make "choice of eny other trade . . . as draper, vintner, mercer, iremonger and such like."[104] And because Shrewsbury shearmen "usyd nowe of late at dyuers tymes to bye clothe and dresse the same within theire howses to the great hyndraunce" of the drapers, therefore the drapers were from "hencefort" in their turn to "use and sett up in the craft of Sherman and to dresse cloth within their owne howses" until such time as a "full determinynacion be had betwene the said crafts concernyng the premises."[105] And in 1587 the drapers of London allowed one of their number to make his apprentices free of the clothworkers', with the understanding that "our Co. may occupy the clothworkers' trade according to the franchises of the City."[106] It was a bit late in the day for London drapers to appeal to city, "franchises" to justify their embarking upon an occupation other than their own, more especially as they had steadily ignored those franchises and continued to ignore them half a century later in denying to the clothworkers the right to use drapery when they claimed the right as freemen of London.[107]

The gilds could not boast of the consistency of their ruling in the enforcing of a division between the crafts. But then neither could the state or the boroughs for that matter.[108] Indeed in the city of London a year after the drapers and their fellows were

---

[102] Lambert, *Two Thousand Years of Gild Life*, p. 158.
[103] *Ibid.*, p. 245.
[104] Morris, *Chester*, pp. 464-67.
[105] *Shropshire Archaeol. & Nat. Hist. Soc. Trans.*, 4th ser., vol. iii, p. 139.
[106] Johnson, *History of the Worshipful Co. of Drapers*, vol. ii, p. 169.
[107] *State Papers Domestic*, vol. 278, No. 104.
[108] Boroughs might issue rules to this end but whether they enforced them was another matter. One can scarcely conceive of the town council of Hereford enforcing the order it issued in 1558 which informed local furriers that only so long as they made "furre gownes" as "good" as local tailors could they have "the doing thereof" (Johnson, *Customs of Hereford*, p. 127) ; or of Newcastle-upon-Tyne really confining her slaters and tylers to the use of only so much of the craft of bricklaying and plastering as was necessary to make, mend and plaster chimney-tops above the slates, in accordance with the order issued in 1691 to that effect by city officials. Walford, *Gilds*, p. 205.

given control of specific trades, the right of a man who gained his freedom in one mystery to pursue another was publicly proclaimed by city officials.[109] As it appears many availed themselves of the privilege and adopted different callings. For instance, a man who was admitted to the freedom of London in 1365 after serving his apprenticeship to a girdler, confessed about thirty-five years later to having worked since as an ironmonger.[110] After gaining his freedom in 1406 in the mystery of "Bruers" a London brewer in 1422 confessed to practising the mystery of "Talough chaundelers" and not that of "Bruers." [111] Later other boroughs authorised freemen to use an occupation other than the one they had adopted. Thus, in 1519 by order of the York officials "all enfranchised men who were free of one occupation were henceforth to be free of all." [112] Sooner or later burghal authorities seem to have countenanced greater freedom of trade within their boundaries than seemed justifiable, considering the authority conferred upon special groups ostensibly to prevent free trading. Thus at a time when the inhabitants of well-ordered communities were supposedly living by one occupation,[113] merchant adventurers were openly trading as mercers [114] or goldsmiths,[115] and mercers as cappers or chandlers.[116] Chandlers in turn were sometimes barber-surgeons,[117] and drapers, brewers,[118] while brewers were "pateners," [119] and butchers, licensed victuallers.[120] When the men of Oxford were supposedly practising one occupation, the innholders were allowed to be vintners as well.[121] In 1564 Northampton carpenters, joiners, curriers, cutlers and fullers [122] could exercise a craft other than their own

---

[109] *Letter Book G,* p. 203.
[110] *Ibid. H,* p. 446.
[111] *Ibid. I,* p. 237.
[112] Drake, *Eboracum,* vol. i, p. 212.
[113] A fifteenth-century defense of the system explains that the crafts were originally devised for the purpose of keeping one person from interfering with the work of another in order that each might earn a living. Emperor Sigismund is credited with expressing this sentiment in 1434. Quoted from Webb, *Local Government,* p. 397. Much the same view seems to have prevailed in England a century later, to judge from a paper written about that time discoursing about the Reformation of Many Abuses (see Cunningham, *Growth & Development of English Industry and Commerce,* vol. i, p. 559) and probably helped to provoke the Statute of Apprentices, a measure which virtually upheld a rigid division of labour since few persons would be apt to serve a long apprenticeship in more than one trade or industry.
[114] Brand, *History of Newcastle-upon-Tyne,* vol. ii, p. 235.
[115] Prideaux, *Memorials of the Goldsmiths of London,* vol. ii, p. 118.
[116] Hedges, *History of Wallingford,* vol. ii, p. 236.
[117] Sharp, *History of Hartlepool,* p. 73.
[118] *Historical MSS. Commission Rep.* ix, p. 174.
[119] *Ibid., Beverley,* p. 97.
[120] Ballard, *Chronicles of Woodstock,* p. 43.
[121] Turner, *Records of Oxford,* p. xix.
[122] Hartshorne, *Memorials of Northampton,* p. 92. According to an extract taken from the Chamberlain's Book of Minutes recorded in that year, persons who used any of the specified crafts were to be free of the liberties for xxs. if they used no other craft; but "if they do" they were to pay four pounds for the additional privilege.

provided they met the conditions imposed for the privilege of doing so. Of course, at some time in their history the boroughs were obliged to let freemen use a calling other than the one for which they had originally qualified. In 1620 conditions in the city of Dublin were such that certain builders had to take in hand work which others had begun. The men, it seems, were averse to meddling with the work; indeed houses were falling into ruin while they walked the streets "little regarding the damage" caused thereby. But the mayor of the city interfered by ordering the master of the company to which the offenders belonged to appoint others to finish the work "so left undone." [123] Again, about 1787, the slaters and tylers of Newcastle-upon-Tyne were forced to labour at the "Highways" and "at other Manual Works" when the weather did not permit their working at their own callings.[124] On the other hand, one seventeenth-century official is known to have "stirred the question" of enforcing a division between conflicting groups from a personal motive. Thus "under an order," [125] not apparently "putt in" actual practice until the "then present yeare," a Chester mayor "In the behalf of his own Sonne" notified the Privy Council of "Divers Riotts and Disorders" committed in that city because certain merchants ventured to exercise the trade of an ironmonger also. However, whatever the motive, division of labour could not be so effected as to satisfy each side involved in a controversy. The linen-drapers of Chester accused the city executive of discriminating against them when he sided with local mercers in a point concerning their respective trades about which the two groups differed.[126] Resenting the discrimination the linen-drapers threatened to appeal to the crown for a charter which would render them independent of the city. It does not appear that the linen-drapers enforced their threat, but independence secured even on royal terms rarely made for local peace, to judge from conditions prevailing elsewhere when a group obtained kingly sanction in furtherance of a pet project. A special set of privileges conferred by the crown upon one handicraft group was apt to conflict with a set previously bestowed by civic officials and for that reason prove a source of disturbance. Fifteenth-century records of the London vintners furnish one such an instance. Because the wine-drawers enjoyed certain privileges claimed as theirs by virtue of their charter, the vintners in 1445 prevailed upon the city's executives to have the lord treasurer intercede with the king to revoke, as contrary to the liberties of London, the letters patent he had accorded the wine-drawers.[127] And as late as 1743 the validity of a

---

[123] *Journal Royal Society of Antiquaries of Ireland,* vol. 35, pt. iv, p. 335.
[124] Bell, *Collections for a History of Newcastle-upon-Tyme, B. M.,* vol. i, f. 172.
[125] *Harleian MSS., B. M.,* 1996, f. 46.
[126] *Harleian MSS., B. M.,* 2054, ff. 37–47.
[127] *Transactions, London & Middlesex Archaeological Society,* vol. iii, p. 418.

crown charter given city brewers was contested by the Cork authorities on the ground that it impugned the city's chartered right to appoint its own industrial corporations.[128]

It would seem as if the best-laid plans for a well-ordered trade were bound to miscarry because a measure designed to help one group inevitably hindered another. Thus, sometime during the reign of King Edward IV, the patten-makers of London [129] told of the hurt they had suffered from the enforcement of an act which had "abridged them of the using of timber of asp" in making pattens and clogs, in order that the fletchers who used that sort of wood might sell their shafts at "easier prices."

No gild worthy of its name submitted to seeing a rival prosper at its expense. In seeking to restrain the three hundred or more innkeepers from brewing in Chester, the brewers reckoned without either their or the city's hosts, many of whom, averse to delegating that branch of their business to local brewers, contrived to secure from the city fathers "libertie" to brew beer and ale to sell to their guests if not to citizens at large.[130] And when the fullers of Bristol refused to concede the least of the "points that belong unto their crafte", when the latter questioned the fullers' right to the work they were doing, the fullers, interesting to relate, offered to be as "one craft" with the shearmen as "it was in all other places" in the realm.[131] This offer to join forces with shearmen was in keeping with established usage as the fullers were careful to point out. Only, union could not solve the problem of enforcing a division between two handicrafts which had not in the beginning and could not consistently with gild economy become "one." The union of fullers and shearmen, or of any other rival handicrafts, entered into for the purpose of insuring harmonious cooperation was only a form of compromise often conspicuous for its failure to fulfill the hopes entertained upon adoption.

Effort directed toward keeping the peace between rival groups did not always take the form of transferring a whole group to a rival fold. A truce to a clash which followed the pursuit by a member of one group of an occupation dominated by another, was sometimes called by translating the offender to the group whose territory he had invaded. Occasionally, too, a man's translation to a different gild was made conditional upon his retaining membership in the one with the first claim to his allegiance.[132] Whereas

---

[128] *Council Book*, p. 622.

[129] 4 Edward IV. These craftsmen also complained that turners, carpenters, wood-mongers and charcoal-makers were allowed to use this wood without restriction; and that although fletchers could use asp-timber to make their shafts, it was not at all suitable for patten-makers. Lambert, *History of the Worshipful Company of Patten-makers*, pp. 26–27.

[130] *Harleian MSS., B. M.* 2104, f. 74.

[131] Fox and Taylor, *History of the Bristol Weavers*, p. 98. Otherwise, said the fullers, rather than that the shearmen should have even one "fote more we wyll surrender up all and be as no Craft."

[132] Johnson, *History of the Worshipful Company of Drapers*, vol. ii, p. 167. At Beverley in 1498, at the command of the governors of the borough, a bar-

preserving membership in two organisations may have settled the particular problem it was meant to settle, the settlement was apt to carry with it possibilities of future conflict. For example, seventeenth-century clothworkers of London who gave over cloth-working to become "merely drapers," justified their change of occupation on the ground that being free of the Merchant Adventurers' Company they were privileged to buy and sell cloth by wholesale and retail.[133]   In the working, simultaneous membership [134] in different companies served to complicate the system and increased the difficulty of keeping apart gild groups concerned with different branches of an occupation, thereby serving to defeat the purpose the gild system had been instituted to further.[135]

Moreover, as the centuries progressed, the division of employment became so minute as to make it impossible of enforcement, whether peaceably or otherwise, by the best regulated of systems. Men content at one epoch to buy and sell old cloth could not at others be kept from handling new.[136]   It was merely a question of time when men who baked white bread would bake black bread too,[137] and those who baked bread of corn, bake it of barley as well.[138]   One can scarcely conceive of a system of espionage rigid enough to isolate a craft subdivided into "pye-bakers, pasty-bakers, Flaune-bakers, Otemele-bakers and Dyner-makers" as was the cook's craft at Beverley in 1485.[139]   A cutler of Dublin might upon entry into the gild of cutlers pledge himself in good faith to be either a "long cutler" or a "short cutler" but his pledge carried with it no guarantee of perpetual fulfilment.[140]   The horners of

ber "who newly" set up a shop within the precincts being "a brother of some other craft" was not to "be further charged" for that year. Beverley, *Town Documents, Selden Soc. Public.*, p. 113.

[133] *State Papers Domestic*, 1634–5, No. 106.

[134] In certain localities the authorities seem to have intervened to prevent simultaneous membership in different gilds. As early as 1518, according to a ruling issued by the Coventry Leet, any person dwelling within that borough having "a good occupacion to live by" who would leave it to "occupie with another occupacion" was "to agre with the seid occupacion that he wold be with-all." *Leet Book*, p. 655. And, in 1670, when the bricklayers and plasterers of Dublin were incorporated with power to control their occupations, all persons using them were to be discharged from all "obseruances heretofore enjoyed them by any other corporation" in the city. *Egerton MS., B. M.*, 1765, f. 203.

[135] At Shrewsbury the situation finally became so complicated that a local ironmonger was discovered paying tribute to the ironmongers, the smiths, and was being summoned to pay to a third company of tinmen. *Parl. Papers*, vol. 25, p. 2016.

[136] *Letter Book G*, p. 174.

[137] *On the Municipal Archives of the City of Canterbury. Archaeologia*, vol. 31, p. 205.

[138] Hutchins, *History of Dorchester*, vol. ii, p. 362. In 1414 Dorchester bakers were evidently baking bread of either sort.

[139] *Historical MSS. Comm. Rep., Beverley*, p. 103.

[140] Any one who joined the Dublin cutlers, painter-stainers and "staconers" company in 1676, with the intent to practise cutlery, was obliged to state whether he was a "long cutler or a short" one. *Egerton MS., B. M.*, 1765, *Dublin Corporation Records*, p. 158.

London could not forever deny to local comb-makers the right to press horns as well,[141] or the wheelwrights see that men who made coach wheels never made cart wheels, too.[142] To coopers [143] the temptation to pack herrings and salmon in hogsheads of their making, or brewers to make barrels to hold their beer and ale must frequently have proved irresistible.[144]

The point is that a system so evidently based upon the idea that trade and industry would remain stationary could not work peaceably when men branched out and used two handicrafts or kept two shops, regardless of whether in so doing, they trespassed upon the territory of their neighbours. Incorporating groups separately failed to prevent their trespassing no matter how closely the lines were drawn to effect the separation. The most closely drawn lines were bound to overlap at some point and so foment strife. Apparently "unite and good accord" could not be secured by allowing rival handicraft groups to appoint wardens of their own "to serche to giders well and trewly unto their power and present unto the Maior and Chamberleyn" of their city the "defautes touchyng or concernyng in any wise" the two occupations. The glovers and leathersellers of London tried this experiment in 1451 because "persones enfraunchised of the craft of Leathersellers usen, make and sellen gloves, cuffes, and all other necessaries and thinges belongyng to the occupacion and konnyng" of the craft of glovers, whereas "diverse persones enfraunchessed of the craft of Glovers usen, make and sellen pointes, tawed lether and all other necessaries and thinges belongyng to the occupacion and konnyng of the craft of Lethersellers." [145] But neither set of handicrafts succeeded in securing the end sought for, either at that time or later when the glovers threw in their gild-lot unreservedly with the leathersellers. The withdrawal of the glovers from the leathersellers' association followed years of strife and dissatisfaction with the part that had been assigned them in the combination. Moreover, amalgamation did not always prove more satisfactory to other crafts who adopted it as a way out of their difficulties. Scarcely a decade after the carpenters and joiners of Newcastle-upon-Tyne united their gild forces, there prevailed amongst their members not the "great quietness, profitt and comoditie" they had counted upon, but "great

---

[141] In the first year of the reign of William III, the London horners prosecuted a comb-maker for pressing horns, on the ground that that industry was a branch of their calling and his use of it was an infringement of the statute of 5 Elizabeth c. 4. Compton, *History of the Horners' Company*, p. 13.

[142] Scott, *A Short Account of the Wheelwrights' Company*, p. 22.

[143] Lambert, *Two Thousand Years of Gild Life*, p. 285.

[144] After learning that a seventeenth-century brewer had furnished the timber and workshop where a number of coopers were set to work making barrels, the authorities of the city of Salisbury issued an order forbidding brewers thereafter to use any part of the art of a cooper except so much as was necessary to rehoop or mend his vessels. Haskins, *The Ancient Trade Guilds & Companies of Salisbury*, p. 341.

[145] Black, *History of the Worshipful Company of Leathersellers*, p. 30.

debates, quarrellings, malice and strife, to the great perill of some of the parties and to the daily trouble of the magistrates of" the city.[146] The dissolution of the combination which followed apparently left the members of each group as free as they had been in the beginning to trouble the others. Even where amalgamation proved enduring, it was at best only a form of compromise, inconsistent with the principles of a system which was adopted and ordered primarily to enforce a rigid division of labour.[147]

Indeed, there was practically no way of eliminating friction in a system so evidently based upon the principle that handicraftsmen needed corporate protection to enable them to work with any degree of freedom.[148] The freer one group became to extend its sphere of industry the more extended the protection accorded it, the more restricted in consequence became the sphere allotted a less favoured group, to the confusion of the system and its inevitable overthrow. The end of gild conflict coincided with the end of the system of gild restraint.

In its broadest aspect, the course of the conflict between the English trades and handicrafts which has thus been traced from its inception in the economic scheme, appears, as it were, a conflict between the opposing economic principles of protection and free trade as they worked out in the economic life of medieval England. Each step forward in the direction of free trade naturally resulted in a step backward for protection and for the protected trades and handicrafts. Free trade triumphed with the repudiation of protection and of the trades and handicrafts organised in its service.

[146] *Archaeologia Aeliana*, 3rd ser., vol. v, p. 172. About 1493 in York at the desire, apparently, of local blacksmiths, it was decreed by the mayor and city council, that, for the "appeasing of diverse matters of variance, and after being often moved between the crafts concerned, the crafts of blacksmiths may be separated and discharged from" the bladesmiths "as well of serche makyng in everything pertenyng to tham as of paying tham pagaunt silver or any other dewties." Likewise any other ordinances made betwixt the said occupations were to be void and cancelled. *Memorandum Book*, ii, p. 249.

[147] According to the Metalmen of Gloucester, the "Want of composition" prevented them from controlling and regulating the various industries represented in their organisation. *Historical MSS. Commissions. Report xii, Gloucester*, app. ix, p. 427. Sixteenth-century feltmakers in London told of the disadvantages under which they laboured, not having any "government of themselves as other companies have." Unwin, *Industrial Organization*, p. 131.

[148] At Hartlepool by order of the "councel" made for the good government of the borough in 1673, traders or handicraftsmen who wished to ply their occupations within the liberties had, for their better preservation and encouragement, first to secure the liberty or consent of the "free trades" as the local gilds were designated in the records of Hartlepool. Sharp, *History of Hartlepool*, p. 72, note.

THE END OF THE ENGLISH CRAFT GILDS

I

LOSS BY THE GILDS OF THE POWER TO ENFORCE THEIR SYSTEM PARTICULARLY OF APPRENTICESHIP

The preceding studies have offered an account of the amalgamation of the English trades and handicrafts, and of the conflict which developed between them as they struggled with one another, often from their rise, for the right to gild existence. The account of the two movements appears for the most part one of conflict between local gildsmen, but their final acts reveal them quarrelling not with one another as much as with outsiders who were doing business on their own account against the rules of the established gilds. This seems particularly true of the eighteenth-century activity of the mercantile companies. For instance, in 1732 the Derby mercers prosecuted those who "expose Goods to sail" to the prejudice of their company.[1] At Carlisle, in 1741, the gild of merchants took similar action against a mercer and several grocers for setting up trades for which they had not qualified.[2] Five years later the mercers of Sandwich collected fines from persons who retailed wines contrary to their ordinances and for other "irregular trading."[3] In 1760 the haberdashers of Andover levied a certain sum upon the goods and chattels of a non-member who kept his shop open in defiance of the company.[4] In 1771 the mercantile gilds of Newcastle-upon-Tyne[5] and of Alnwick[6] still restrained non-members from exercising the business of a merchant within local precincts. In 1823 the mercers of Shrewsbury forced a recalcitrant merchant to pay their company tribute,[7] and even as late as 1835 the mercers' company of Faversham still imposed certain restrictions upon all persons who sought to trade within corporate limits.[8]

Like the merchant gilds, those maintained by the artisans directed their later efforts toward keeping outsiders from working in the precincts under their jurisdiction. Thus, in 1705 at Carlisle

---

[1] *Derbyshire Archaeol. & Nat. Hist. Soc. Journ.*, vol. xv, p. 143.
[2] *Municipal Records*, p. 116.
[3] *Additional MS.*, No. 27463. B. M., f. 144.
[4] Gross, *Gild Merchant*, vol. ii, p. 350.
[5] *Surtees Soc. Pub.*, vol. 93, p. 263.
[6] Tate, *History of Alnwick*, vol. ii, p. 327.
[7] Hibbert, *Influence & Development of English Gilds*, p. 134.
[8] *Kent Archaeol. Soc. Trans.*, vol. ix, p. lxviii.

the shoemakers were called upon to share in the expense incurred by their gild in prosecuting countrymen who made shoes in the borough without gild credentials.[9] About a decade later, the shoemakers of Boston shut up the shops of non-freemen found practising their mystery.[10] In 1737 the barber-surgeons of Shrewsbury expended considerable sums in prosecuting an intruder.[11] According to an entry dated 1743 in the records of the cordwainers of Ruthin, in Denbighshire, that company agreed to pay the charges of a suit brought to defend its ancient privileges against a determined invader.[12] In 1751 the wheelwrights of London prosecuted non-members for practising their industry.[13] In 1760 and again in 1806 the barbers of Oxford brought suit against non-apprenticed barbers who opened shops within the districts controlled by their company.[14] Contemporary gilds of Chester used various expedients to bring outsiders to their terms. For example, officers of the skinners' and feltmakers' company took away the tools of one found selling felt hats contrary to the rules,[15] while the threat of prosecution seems to have brought a defiant brewer into the ranks of Chester's brewers' gild in 1761.[16] In the first quarter of the nineteenth century, the merchant tailors and the amalgamated innholders, victuallers and cooks forced interlopers to join their respective companies.[17] Again, the hammermen of Ludlow brought sufficient pressure upon recalcitrant strangers to bring them into their fold; [18] and in 1826 the gold and silver wyre-drawers of London took action against non-members who contravened their by-laws.[19] These are but a few of the instances which might be cited.

[9] *Municipal Records of Carlisle*, p. 188. Moreover, as late as 1793 these Carlisle shoemakers entered into an agreement to prosecute non-members who should "presume to make any new shoes or boots" or even "to translate old ones." Quoted from Dunlop, *English Apprenticeship*, p. 117.

[10] Thompson, *History of Boston*, p. 159.

[11] *Shropshire Archaeol. & Nat. Hist. Soc. Trans.*, vol. v, p. 290.

[12] *Parl. Papers*, vol. 26, p. 2855. Twenty-one members are said to have subscribed different sums to defray the cost of this suit. And as late as 1825, an outsider gave up his business rather than yield to the company's demand that he join its ranks.

[13] Scott, *History of the Wheelwrights' Company*, p. 23. One man who had been committed to Newgate by this company in 1740, was anxious to get back to his work and accordingly notified the "Worthy Company" of his willingness to "make all suitable and just return" to it. He said that his long confinement and sickness in that "deplorable place" had given him a "true sense of his past faults to the company" which he had "wilfully and obstinately offended." *Ibid.*, p. 17.

[14] *Oxford Barbers*, MS., Bodleian Library, ff. 50, 88.

[15] *Journal Chester & North Wales Architectural, Archaeol. & Historic Soc.*, n. s., vol. 21, p. 105.

[16] *Parl. Papers*, vol. 26, p. 2633. In 1772 officials of the barber-surgeons, wax and tallow chandlers pledged themselves to proceed according to law against townsmen who used these occupations, but failed to join the company at the urging of the stewards. *Journal Chester & North Wales Architectural, Archaeol. & Historic Soc.*, n. s., vol. 18, p. 178.

[17] *Parl. Papers*, vol. 26, pp. 2636–37.

[18] *Shropshire Archaeol. & Nat. Hist. Soc. Trans.*, vol. xi, p. 321.

[19] Stewart, *History of Gold & Silver Wyre-Drawers' Co.*, p. 97.

Moreover, in standing upon their right to monopolise trade and industry in the last two centuries of their existence, the gilds seem, for the most part to have been upheld by burghal authority. In 1646 we find the tailors of Boston bringing suit in the name of the corporation against tailors who infringed gild rules and regulations.[20] Thirty years later the glovers, collar-makers and sieve-makers of Salisbury secured a "Letter of Attorney" empowering their company to sue for breaches of its orders.[21] Again by an act passed by the London common council in 1727 city butchers, and in 1754 plumbers were forced to purchase their freedoms in those respective companies.[22] In 1730 the corporation of Youghal declared it lawful for the gilds of clothiers and leathermen to prosecute "encroachers and to attach them by their bodies or goods until they make due satisfaction as shall be adjudged by the Magistrates."[23] In 1732 the amalgamated company comprising drapers, dyers, apothecaries and barber-surgeons of Ripon was authorised to begin a suit in the name of the borough against a non-freeman who presumed to use an occupation within the jurisdiction of the company.[24] During the same year the city of Cork appointed an attorney to help local barber-surgeons uphold their corporate rights against certain "refractory persons" who had preferred charges against the company.[25] As late as 1778 the common council of London endorsed an order issued by city leathersellers obliging non-free leathersellers to join the leathersellers' company.[26]

There are instances during this time where certain boroughs enforced on their own account the monopoly of local gilds. For example, at Wallingford, in 1705,[27] sergeants-at-mace shut down the shop windows of a goldsmith who refused to pay for the privilege of plying that trade in the borough, and a tailor was given ten days to gain the good will of local tailors or leave the borough. In 1772 Leominster prosecuted two men for using the craft of a "taylor" without being free of the "Taylors'" company.[28] And a full quarter of a century later Oswestry collected fines from certain foreigners for trading without being free of the company "wherein they intended to trade."[29] Most of the boroughs seemed determined to confine the exercise of local trade and industry to freemen,

[20] Thompson, *History of Boston*, p. 158.
[21] Hoare, *History of Wiltshire*, vol. vi, p. 475. Indeed, by 1664, a dozen years earlier, the wardens of the joiners had likewise been empowered to sue such individuals as they found breaking the rules. *Ibid.*, p. 455.
[22] Pulling, *Treatise of the Laws, Customs & Regulations*, pp. 77, 284.
[23] *Council Book*, p. 431.
[24] *Millinary Record*, p. 96. In this instance while the company was obliged first to give security to the corporation, the interloper had the alternative of taking up his freedom or leaving the borough.
[25] *Council Book*, p. 512. The freemen who "do assist" such persons were, in their turn, to be disfranchised.
[26] Black, *History of the Leathersellers' Company*, p. 128.
[27] Hedges, *History of Wallingford*, vol. ii, p. 237.
[28] Townsend, *History of Leominster*, p. 193.
[29] *Parl. Papers*, vol. 26, p. 2827.

—hence their zeal in punishing trespassers at this late date. In 1700, acting under its chartered rights, the city of Cork seized goods which non-freemen sold by retail, and disposed of them "to the use of the corporation." [30] A decade later at Nottingham, a by-law drawn up "for the restraining Forreigners Trading in this Town had by consent of this Hall the Common Seale affixt to itt in order to be presented to the Judge att the next Assizes for his allowance of the same." [31] "Att a Councill" held in 1712 at Liverpool, the town clerk was ordered to prosecute such persons as "inhabitt and keep shops within this towne and exercise trades . . . not being free in such manner as the Recorder shall advise and direct," the actions to be brought in the name of the "Mayor, Baylives and Burgesses of this burrough, at the charge of this Corporation." [32] In 1722 a weaver, designated as a foreigner and "no freeman" was fined ten shillings for working against "ye laws and privileges of this town of Hartlepool." [33] Six years later, Woodstock fined several persons for following the trade of a tailor without being free of the borough.[34] At a court of "burghmote" held in Maidstone on August 4, 1747, non-freemen were forbidden to ply any trade within the town "according to ancient usage." [35] In 1768 the corporation of Bedford agreed to indemnify the bailiffs for "taking distress" of those persons who have "no right given by law to exercise trades" within the borough.[36] In 1772 Preston [37] prosecuted merchant strangers for establishing themselves in the borough without possessing freemen's qualifications. As late as 1833, Chipping Norton collected damages from non-freemen who presumed to trade in the town,[38] and the following year the Minute book of Kingston-upon-Thames records the names of three men convicted and fined for trading "they not being freemen of the borough," [39]

By the middle of the eighteenth century, despite the effort expended, the power of boroughs and gilds to confine local trade and industry to free gildsmen seems to have broken down in most places of importance. Indeed, to judge by the evidence of local records, it had begun to give way by 1654, fully a century earlier, when boroughs and gilds worked together to keep strangers from using the trades and manufactures of the nation.[40] At this time, too, by order of the borough of Bedford, strangers were neither

---

[30] *Council Book*, p. 283. Five years earlier the common council of Abingdon forbade any "Forraigner" whatsoever to use any manner of trade within the borough until he should have paid the sum of fifty pounds for his freedom. *Records*, p. 182.
[31] *Records*, vol. vi, p. 49.
[32] Picton, *Liverpool*, p. 53.
[33] Sharp, *History of Hartlepool*, p. 77.
[34] Ballard, *Chronicles of Woodstock*, p. 29.
[35] James, *History of Maidstone*, p. 219.
[36] *Corporation Records*, p. 97.
[37] Hardwick, *History of Preston*, p. 286.
[38] Ballard, *History of Chipping Norton*, p. 18.
[39] *Geneaological Magazine*, vol. iii, p. 341.
[40] Prideaux, *Memorials of the London Goldsmiths' Co.*, vol. ii, p. 68.

to practise a craft nor sell their merchandise within the liberties.[41] In 1651, "Maister Maior" of Nottingham was authorised to "shutt upp forainers' shopp windowes yat trade in the Towne," the business to be managed and the charges borne by the borough.[42] At Kinsale, too, in 1687, the shopkeepers and "taylors" who failed to agree with the corporation for their freedoms were to have their shops summarily shut up,[43] and a gild of the standing of the Shrewsbury mercers was diverting considerable sums toward the suppressing of "Forrayners and Intruders."[44] Still others, notably the merchants of York, appealed to the "powers above" for help in strengthening their privileges against "stirring opposers"[45] while the wheelwrights of London applied to the crown for a charter, hoping thereby to keep aliens at bay.[46] The London goldsmiths, however, for centuries had enjoyed the authority supposedly inherent in a royal charter; yet in 1653 they confessed to being well-nigh ruined by the encroachment of aliens, who, they alleged, "work privately and are so numerous that they have taken upon themselves under the pretence of religion, a liberty of conscience to petition parliament for a toleration of free trade, to the general ruin of the freemen" of the city.[47] But whether or not established corporations were being ruined or late comers brought to beggary,[48] according to the barbers of Oxford, inconveniences and disorders which followed the exercise of townsmens' occupations by persons who "ought not so to do," continued to vex gildsmen in 1675, largely, "by reason of the late troubles in this Nation."[49] Manifestly civil war could not be waged without disarranging economic and consequently gild procedure. We learn from the weavers of London that foreigners who were admitted to fill vacancies in their

[41] *Corporation Records,* p. 76. From many of the small boroughs petitions were addressed to the Council of State calling attention to their declining trade and attributing it to the presence of numerous strangers within their borders. Inderwick, *Interregnum,* p. 93.

[42] *Records of the Borough,* vol. v, p. 257.

[43] *Council Book,* p. 177.

[44] In 1646 a certain "sessment" was levied upon the mercers for this purpose. *Shropshire Archaeol. & Nat. Hist. Soc. Trans.,* vol. viii, p. 407.

[45] In 1650 an alderman of York asked the merchants of Newcastle-upon-Tyne to join the York merchants in petitioning the "Councell of Trade" for support in their endeavor. *Surtees Society Pub.,* vol. 93, p. 164. A few years earlier we find the carpenters of London putting aside a certain sum to meet the expense of "goeing to apprehend ffrenchmen forreyne carpenters working in little Moore feilds." Jupp, *History of the Carpenters' Company,* p. 159.

[46] Scott, *History of the Wheelwrights' Company,* p. 11.

[47] Prideaux, *Memorials of the Goldsmiths' Company,* vol. ii, p. 46.

[48] According to the button-makers, this was their condition in 1637. *State Papers Domestic, Charles I,* ccclxxii, 75.

[49] *Rules and Orders of the Barbers' Company,* MS., Bodleian. No. 5. Contemporary tanners of Leicester who alleged that time out of mind they had had the selling of their wares within the borough, evidently prided themselves upon the fact that no "forraigner nor Stranger was admitted to expose to sale any of his goods or wares untill the usurped times . . . which abuse has often beene desired" by them and "others to be rectified." Stocks, *Records of the Borough of Leicester,* 1923.

ranks when their own members "engaged for the Parliament . . .
by degrees got all the trading." [50]   As a result many weavers were
forced to take up other callings in order to gain a living. So, by
the passage of an act to enable soldiers who had served in Cromwell's army to re-enter the business world, boroughs and gilds were
forced to lift the embargo they had placed upon the exercise of
trades and industries. Thus, during the Commonwealth civic ordinances forbidding non-freemen to carry on their crafts in Bristol
were suspended so that several old soldiers might engage in business in that city.[51]

It seems, however, that at the Restoration local authorities ignored this measure and forced soldiers to pay gild tribute for
trading privileges.[52]   For instance, at Sandwich in 1661, a man who
stated that he had had "his freedome graunted him by this towne
by vertue of an Act of Parliament entitled an Act for enabling
soldiers of this Armie now to be disbanded to exercise Trade," was
"desirous to be free" of the local gild of merchants and so paid
the required fee for his admittance, when warned to appear before
the company and meet the obligation.[53]   Moreover, burghal authorities apparently ignored measures passed by the parliaments of
King William III and his successors [54] which authorised not only
soldiers but mariners as well, "to set up and exercise without let
or molestation from any person whatsoever, such trades as they
were apt and able for, even though they had not for the space of
seven years served an apprenticeship to the trade." In 1725 several
soldiers were discovered keeping open shop in Kinsale to the disadvantage of the "poor inhabitants"; whereupon the authorities
forbade their continuing in business.[55]   However, it seems certain
from complaints which continued to emanate from gilds deprecating
the practice, that, despite the opposition local gilds could muster,

[50] Unwin, *Industrial Organization*, pp. 207–8, quoted from the *"Case of
the Commonalty of Weavers."*

[51] Latimer, *Merchant Venturers of Bristol*, p. 169.

[52] The son of a freeman of Bedford who set up in business in that borough found himself molested by several inhabitants for not having served an
apprenticeship even though he had "served as a Souldier." *Corporation
Records*, p. 76.

[53] Register of Minutes and Accounts of the Mercers' Co. of Sandwich,
Additional MS., B. M., No. 27462, f. 12. After having served his apprenticeship to the trade of a "Taylor at Bishopps Lideard," after a residence of seven
years, a man who had "beene since a souldier in the Parliaments service by
the space of 4 yeares," upon "cominge back to inhabite att" the same place
in order to exercise his said trade and "rentinge a howse there," found himself "disturbed by the inhabitants of the same pariche." The court of quarter
sessions to which he appealed in protest against the treatment accorded him
by the inhabitants, ruled that he "bee and stand settled at Bishopps Lideard
until the next general Sessions and from "thencefourth unless Bishopps
Lideard haveinge notice hereof shall then show good cause to the contrary."
Somerset Quarter Sessions Records, vol. 3, p. 153.

[54] 10 William III, c. 17. 12 Anne, c. 14. 22 George I, c. 44. 3 George III,
c. 8, sec. 19.

[55] *Council Book*, lxxv.

outsiders continued to encroach upon local trade. Indeed, the first quarter of the eighteenth century had scarcely passed before the records of the mercantile gild of Newcastle-upon-Tyne list fully one hundred and fourteen non-freemen who kept "open shop" and sold by "retaile" goods, which, according to the company, rightfully came under its exclusive jurisdiction.[56]

It is a wonder, considering the effort expended by borough and gilds to keep them out, that so many non-freemen managed to secure a footing in the business world of Newcastle-upon-Tyne. Elsewhere, however, in spite of gild opposition to outsiders, borough officials frequently invited them to come in. The policy of the gilds in restricting the number of labourers in any one field, inevitably resulted at times in a shortage of labour. This was a detriment to the boroughs, many of which, out of regard for their own interests, had to supply the deficiency as best they could. Such a predicament seems to have faced London in 1651, a year in which the city without prejudice "unto itself" could not be "sufficiently supplied by the free Sawiers thereof without the fforreine Sawiers."[57] The presence of foreign artisans imported to repair the damage occasioned by some sudden catastrophe inevitably menaced afterwards the rights of organised gildsmen. The status of the "Forein Workmen" who "assisted at the Rebuilding" of London after the havoc caused by the fire of 1666 was later secured by an act of parliament, which stipulated that those among them who had been therein employed should, for seven years thereafter, enjoy the same liberty in working at the building crafts as freemen, and that having so worked for seven years, they should for the rest of their lives enjoy the liberty of working as freemen.[58] When gildsmen took advantage of their power to raise arbitrarily the price of their labour the boroughs retaliated by bringing in outsiders to take their place. In 1673 the mayor of Hartlepool, in Durham, was empowered to invite foreign artisans to come into the liberties of the borough "when the freemen will not work at a reasonable rate."[59] Again, when Dover built a gaol in 1747, the common

---

[56] *Surtees Soc. Pub.* vol. 93, p. 253.

[57] The "ffre Sawiers" of London had to take account of this fact in that year when they "indited a fforreine sawier at the sessions at the Old Bayly, London, for working within the freedome of this Cittie." Jupp, *Hist. of Carpenters' Co.*, p. 160.

[58] Jupp, *History of the Carpenters' Company*, p. 311, Appendix 1. The city carpenters were decidedly against the governments' protecting artificers who used the carpenters' trade for, as they alleged "very small and inconsiderable fines" and who, in addition, "procured themselves to be made free of London . . . and refused to submit themselves to any government or bylaws" of the carpenters' company. All this they claimed was contrary to their charter in accordance with which "all artists exercising the trade within the city are required to be subject to and regulated by the constitution and ordinances of the said company." *Ibid.*, p. 312. It seems, too, that the urgent necessity of supplying timber to rebuild London after the fire of 1666, played some part in depriving the Eastland Company of their monopoly. *History of the Eastland Company, Camden Soc. Pub.*, vol. xlviii–ix.

[59] Sharp, *History of Hartlepool*, p. 73. Note.

council ordered such bricklayers to be employed "as will work cheapest whether they be freemen or not," [60] while, in 1700, in order to defeat a confederacy entered into by local workmen, Bristol ordered city officials to admit to the freedom without fee or formality any skilled workmen who could be got from London.[61] In 1730 the corporation of Shrewsbury threatened to admit country butchers to sell meat in the borough unless local butchers contrived to furnish the market with sufficient stores, and at the time ordered the admission of country bakers because local bakers refused to pay the fine they were accustomed to pay to the corporation for the favour they enjoyed.[62] Evidently borough support was not to be had merely for the asking.[63] On the contrary, it would seem as if most boroughs excluded aliens only so long as local craftsmen made it worth their while in one way or another. Thus an order issued in 1582 by the corporation of Windsor directing that "fforrainers" be "kept out upon market days . . . took no effect," it seems, because the "Mercers being required to contribute something to the Bailiffs for the loss of their stalls refused." [64] In fact the boroughs did not prevent the coming in of foreigners until they were fully supplied with efficient workmen,[65] and many deliberately imported artisans in order to establish new industries,[66] or to set their poor to work so that they should become "less chargeable to the Inhabitants." [67]

One might note too, that while the community of Winchester had no occasion to induce aliens to come in, it realised the desirability of making entrance easier for them in the future than it had been in the past. The officials charged with the government of the borough confessed in 1650 that the custom of assessing non-freemen annually, "according to their discretions" was arbitrary and likely to bring disaster to all concerned and accordingly they

[60] Quoted from Webb., *Local Government*, vol. i, p. 400.

[61] *Ibid.*, p. 399.

[62] *Shropshire Archaeol. & Nat. Hist. Soc. Trans.*, vol. ix, p. 209.

[63] On the contrary, in 1599, the corporation of Shrewsbury made it clear that country bakers would be kept from selling their bread in the borough only as long as local bakers paid annually the sum of "3li" to the use of the borough. *Ibid.*, vol. xi, p. 164. During this same epoch a certain yearly fine paid by the handicrafts of Windsor to the mayor of the borough seems to have been conditioned upon the fact that without their consent "no forreigner be admitted into the freedome of the Towne." Tighe & Davis, *Annals of Windsor*, vol. i, p. 652. In 1617 the butchers of Hereford pledged themselves to contribute ten pounds towards the renewing of the borough's charter provided that, when country butchers came to market, they were allowed to stay from eight o'clock until one. *Hist. MSS. Commis. Rep.* xiii, app. iv, p. 340.

[64] Tighe and Davis, *Annals of Winchester*, vol. i, p. 642.

[65] This was in accordance with the advice proffered in the *Discourse of the Common Weal*, published in 1549. See Cunningham, *Growth of English Industry & Commerce*, vol. i, p. 564. (1905.)

[66] In 1 & 2 Phil. & Mary an act was passed for the making of "Russelles Sattins, Sattens Reverses and Fustian of Naples in the Cittie of Norwiche and skilled craftsmen were imported from the continent for the purpose.

[67] *Nottingham Records*, vol. v, p. 419.

reduced to a sum not to exceed five pounds, the amount of the fee which might thereafter be charged non-freemen.[68] And in altering the constitution of their city in 1672, "for the better regulating of the corporation," Dublin provided for the admission to its freedom of merchant strangers and artificers, foreigners and "aliens" as well "protestants" as others, upon their paying the sum of twenty shillings.[69] Elsewhere during these days penalties for irregular trading were sometimes dispensed with altogether. During the Commonwealth the greater part of a fine levied upon an alien merchant who had traded at Rye without being properly qualified, was returned to him.[70] Boroughs still bent upon exacting the full penalty for irregular trading were obliged to resort to law to collect it. In 1713 by order of the council of Wallingford, legal proceedings were taken against certain ironmongers who refused to pay the price demanded for exercising that trade within the borough.[71] However, even before 1713, the authorities of Derby doubting the propriety of invoking the law against "any forainer . . . knowne to infringe the liberties of any of the trades united in the company" of local mercers, in accordance with a by-law issued to that effect in 1675 by the company, and endorsed by the authorities, bound it to save, keep harmless and at the same time indemnify them and their successors against any legal proceedings which might ensue from the execution of the by-law.[72] In 1704 the council of Woodstock, in its turn, agreed to "assist the freemen of this corporation that are inhabitants (so far as by law they may) to keep out all persons that are not free from following any trade . . . or manual occupation . . . the Tradesmen bearing the charge of any suit that may arise thereupon and that bye-laws be made accordingly." [73] Again, in 1713 the corporation of Wokingham, in Bershire, seems to have exacted from the inhabitants the promise to indemnify it against any suit which might follow the levying of tribute from outsiders who plied their trades within corporate limits.[74] Still other boroughs, uncertain as to the best course to pursue against alien intruders, consulted their counsel before taking action. At about this epoch, apparently in a quandary whether to proceed against an alien who had defied the municipality by opening up a shop before compounding for his freedom, "on custome or by-law or both," the borough of Kingston-upon-Thames sought legal advice as to "what proof is sufficient to maintaine the said custome or By-law." [75] And in 1760 the opinion of a certain Mr. Weller "touching the right of persons carrying on trades within the borough they

[68] Bailey, *Transcripts from the Archives of Winchester*, p. 59.
[69] Warburton, *Dublin*, vol. i, p. 217.
[70] Inderwick, *Interregnum*, p. 68.
[71] Hedges, *History of Wallingford*, vol. ii, p. 237.
[72] *Derbyshire Archaeol. & Nat. Hist. Soc. Journ*, vol. xv, p. 128.
[73] Ballard, *Chronicles of Woodstock*, p. 29.
[74] *Parl. Papers*, vol. 23, p. 2939.
[75] *Records Relating to Kingston-upon-Thames, Gough MS., Bodleian*, f. 19.

not being free thereof" was ordered to be gotten by the corporation of Sudbury in Suffolkshire.[76]   Eight years later when the borough of Abingdon had its recorder draw up a by-law obliging all persons who kept shops to take up their freedom, it took care to "advise with Mr. Recorder" as to its authority to enact such a by-law.[77]

The failing confidence of the boroughs in their power to restrict local trade and industry wholly to freemen, inevitably lessened the confidence of the gilds in their ability to do so. As a consequence, we find the gilds taking steps to protect themselves from the consequences likely to follow the suppression of intruders. For example, in 1676, the cordwainers and curriers of Lichfield agreed among themselves to indemnify the wardens of their company for "distraining for forfeitures" for breaches of its rules and regulations, whereas fourteen years later twenty-one members of the organisation offered to "share expenses in prosecuting and defending any suite concerning the company." [78]   At Oswestry in 1689, nineteen members of the local tanners' gild pledged themselves to defray the costs of a suit which was instituted to test the right of a "foreigner" to buy hides and skins in the borough "to the breaking and infringing of their liberties." [79]   Still other organisations followed the example of the boroughs and sought legal advice concerning the propriety of proceeding against outsiders. Thus, in 1787, the barber-surgeons of Shrewsbury ordered "Mr. Bold Olivers' opinion to be taken as to compelling apothecaries to become freemen." [80]   In the early years of the nineteenth century, the fourteen members, who apparently constituted the membership of the haberdashers' company of Andover, asked their counsel how far their ancient privileges justified them in compelling persons who used the occupations represented in their organisation to join its ranks.[81]   However, the solicitor consulted in 1768 by the drapers and taylors of York as to whether the power held by their company under their charter justified it in collecting damages from outsiders who practised their handicrafts, gave as his opinion that legally it did not. He considered a gild by-law which conferred an exclusive right to trade a restraint of trade and contrary to the natural rights of mankind.[82]   It does not appear that this particular

---

[76] *Calendar of Muniments of Borough of Sudbury, Proceedings of Suffolk Institute*, p. 301.

[77] *Records of Abingdon*, p. 207.

[78] *Lancashire & Cheshire Antiq. Soc. Trans.*, vol. x, p. 21.

[79] Price, *History of Oswestry*, p. 69.

[80] *Shropshire Archaeol. & Nat. Hist. Soc. Trans.*, vol. v, p. 290.

[81] Gross, *Gild Merchant*, vol. ii, p. 350.

[82] This particular counseller further advised that in his opinion the company could not maintain any action either upon the ground of the charter or the by-law; that if the city of York had an immemorial custom to exclude foreigners, the action should be brought upon it in the name of the corporation of the city and that if the city had any by-laws based upon such a custom, the action might be brought upon it. *Additional MS.*, No. 8935, Charter to the Tailors and Drapers 14 Car. II, with counsel's opinion in a case touching

organisation ever again put its rights to the test, but efforts made by other corporations to enforce powers of monopoly based only upon their by-laws seem to have proved their undoing. At Haverfordwest in Pembrokeshire, a certain shoemaker whose goods were "distrained" by local shoemakers for doing business before he had secured membership in their gild, retaliated by suing the wardens for "trespass," and won his suit, the jury sustaining him on the ground that the by-law which was enacted by the shoemakers during the reigns of Queen Elizabeth and King James I and founded on a custom to exclude foreigners from trading in the borough, was illegal.[83] This verdict is said to have put on end forever to the pretensions of the Haverfordwest shoemakers. An adverse decision rendered by the courts appears likewise to have brought about the dissolution of the cordwainers' gild of Nottingham in 1747.[84] A verdict against restraint of trade did not always bring to an end the organisation involved, yet was apt to cause disaster. This, the fate of the merchant company of Kingston-upon-Hull seems to prove. In 1664 certain members of a corporation known as "Ye Trinity House," objecting to the restrictions which the merchant company continued to impose upon local trading, appealed to "His Majestie's Counsell" to the end that the merchants' "charter and power therein expressed might cease" thereafter. Answering the appeal the "Counsell" thus invoked, directed that the "Societie's charter for the exclusion of all persons from the exercising of any merchandise by importation or exportacion other than of such as be free of this Company, and for the forfeiture and seizure of all goods so exported or imported, shall not for ye future be

their privileges. Moreover this seems to have been the opinion which prevailed at the time in regard to the matter. Two years earlier the merchant taylors of Bath won the suit they had instituted against a stranger for using their craft without being free of the city under a by-law drawn up by the city in the fourth year of the reign of King Charles I, according to which no foreigner who had not first been made free of Bath should at any time thereafter use the mystery of a taylor within the boundaries. *4 Burrows, 1952.* By 1831 the butchers of Newcastle seem to have had their doubts as to whether they could keep out any person who desired admittance "by any law to them unknown." However they resolved that if they were compelled to admit a newcomer who should refuse to pay the usual fee charged for admittance, "though he may attend the company's meetings and make apprentices free, he shall not on any pretence whatever be admitted to any share of the accumulated wealth of the company," because that had "entirely arisen from the fines imposed on its members incurred by a breach of its laws" and from "fees paid by apprentices on their enrollment on the company's books and on their being admitted to the freedom of the company." *Archaeol. Aeliana,* 3rd ser., vol. 14, p. 24.

[83] *Parl. Papers,* vol. 23, pp. 233–4.

[84] Wylie, *Old & New Nottingham,* p. 288. In 1784 an action was brought by the wardens of the Bridgnorth mercers at the Shrewsbury Assizes, against a man for using the trade of a grocer and haberdasher "not being free of the said company." The judge examined two of the defendant's witnesses and directed the jury to find a verdict for the defendant. They, "without hesitation" as the record has it, "found the same accordingly." Skeel, *Bridgnorth Company of Smiths, English Historical Review,* vol. xxxv, p. 248. 1920.

put in execution" against either the men who had issued the appeal or any of the other inhabitants of the borough. However, despite this order, in 1678, and again in 1690, the Hull company made so bold as to issue warrants authorising the seizure of goods of various persons "for their unfree trading." During the closing years of the century the company still sought to enforce its authority, though fain to confess that its "antient grandeur . . . is much of late decreased."[85] But despite its obstinate stand, the company's grandeur decreased so far as to leave it little or no use for its plate, since this, together with the company's books hitherto kept in their own "Hall," were removed to the Town Hall "for their better security in regard to the Governor's absence and that Courts there are very seldome kept." That they were ever again kept is problematical. At any rate history seems to have little more to say regarding this particular merchant company.[86]

Other companies of the sort seem to have come to a parting of their ways even before that date, for the merchant adventurers of Exeter had collapsed, it is said, during the parliamentary wars.[87] However, the organisation maintained by the Newcastle merchants kept control over local trade well into the eighteenth century until forced to yield to the pressure exerted against them by rival gildsmen as well as by individual outsiders. Like the merchants of Kingston-upon-Hull those of Newcastle found their right to monopolise local trade contested by a rival corporation. In their case it was the bakers and brewers who, in 1726, protested against the merchants seizing as forfeited, certain stocks of grain purchased from a source other than that of the merchants, on the ground that such a seizure was unreasonable and tended to a monopoly. Moreover, the bakers and brewers contrived to make good their protest in the Exchequer Court where it was given a hearing. Four years later, in spite of the assurance given the Newcastle merchants by their "Councell learned in the law," that their company might still defend its rights and privileges against trespassers, and that upon receiving this assurance, "Mr. Governor did move that the former committee might meet and report what person or persons they were of opinion ought to be sued att law for infringing upon the liberties and privileges of the merchants Company" nothing

[85] Lambert, *Two Thousand Years of Gild Life*, pp. 181–88.

[86] By 1647 the company was evidently forced to overlook and even to condone certain infractions of its earlier laws, because, according to an order recorded in that year, "noe breach of acts in the . . . oulde book shall have anie penaltyes paide until they be openly read in courte except such as are mentioned in this booke." Then, too, during this epoch, the penalties assessed for gild offenses were considerably mitigated, while the open and continued defiance of a prominent merchant of the borough "his badde answere" to the gild officials who tried to show him the error of his ways, all point to a weakening of the company's power and prestige in the community. Lambert, *op. cit.*, pp. 175, 179, 183. Interesting to relate, during this epoch the Attorney-general seems to have passed favorably upon its charter. *Ibid.*, p. 182.

[87] Cotton, *An Elizabethan Guild of the City of Exeter*, p. vii.

seems to have been done at the time to bring the guilty parties to book.[88] In fact the committee appointed four years earlier to consider the proper course to pursue with the hundred and more defiant non-freemen who kept shop and sold by retail goods which the company claimed the right to control, seems to have advocated a course calculated rather to soothe the vanity of its members and conciliate city officials than to fill the company's coffers or restore its waning prestige. "Knowing by experience" that "inditements" are both "tedious and expensive," this committee suggested that thereafter intruders be assessed a weekly sum to be used to aid the city's poor, in such a way as "Mr. Mayor" and the magistrates might deem "most proper." This course they hoped might influence the culprits to betake themselves to their respective trades and so enable the company to preserve unto itself and its successors its "antient" privileges entire and undisturbed. There is nothing to show that this concession to the city's interests rather than to the company's was ever really made. We know only that in different years of the century, committees appointed to bring to terms those who still infringed the company's rights met with a considerable degree of success. Even as late as 1786, seven of the twenty and one persons who were called to account for using the trades over which the company claimed jurisdiction, submitted to the conditions which it saw fit to impose. Only, the committee that was ordered to meet for the purpose of considering the proper course to pursue with such of the company's own "brethren" as had refused to pay their "fines of absence," their monthly pence and annual dues failed to bring in any report.[89] Evidently gild brethren were even less keen than outsiders about paying the gild further tribute, and the gild had, perforce, to abandon any such attempts to levy tribute either from members or non-members.[90] Again, the eighteenth century found the Dublin merchants, questioning the legality of the power under which they had been

[88] *The Merchant Adventurers of Newcastle-upon-Tyne, Surtees Soc. Publications,* vol. 93, p. 255. This company seems to have lost out when, by act of 1 William & Mary, c. 12, the Merchant Adventurers of England were deprived of their exclusive rights in foreign trade. *Ibid.,* p. lxiv.

[89] *Surtees Soc. Pub.,* vol. 93, pp. 267–68.

[90] According to Miss Sellers, the York adventurers continued to exist in the form of a Chamber of Commerce and as such remained a factor in the local trade of York. *Merchant Adventurers of York, Handbook,* etc., p. 227. The Bristol adventurers are heard of again in 1668, in which year their society was accorded a "confirmacon" of all charters, privileges and liberties formerly granted to or enjoyed by the "Master, Wardens and society of Merchant Adventurers within the Citty of Bristoll." *State Papers Domestic, Charles II,* vol. 23, p. 289. By 1803, the master, wardens and commonalty of the merchant "venturers" in company with the mayor, burgesses and commonalty of the city of Bristol and such other persons as subscribed the sum of one hundred pounds were incorporated by an act of parliament as the Bristol Dock Company. *Parliamentary Papers,* vol. 24, p. 1204. At Salisbury, in 1786, a commercial society was established to protect and promote the general trading interests in the city. Haskins, *The Ancient Trade Guilds and Companies of Salisbury,* p. 54.

monopolising local trade. In 1755 the "Recorder" of their city assured them that the right to seize as forfeited such merchandise as non-freemen exposed for sale within corporate limits was valid in law because their charter had the force and authority of an act of parliament; but the assurance failed to fill the company's depleted treasury.[91] Indeed two decades later the only "emolument" the company could count upon was that derived from the quarterage hitherto paid by non-freemen. "This of late," it appears, had "not been received at all." [92] In addition members lamented their failure to meet the civic obligations still devolving upon them, and viewed with concern the heavy debt, still due "former masters," and which, from present indications, they feared more likely to be increased than diminished. By 1783 the fines assessed upon non-freemen had not perceptibly diminished that debt, and as there seemed little likelihood of its ever being diminished from that source, the company at a meeting held on April 1, of that year, passed a resolution repealing the "By-law restraining to receive Quarteridge from non-freemen." [93] The repeal of this by-law marks the end of the Dublin merchants' efforts to handicap local trade.

By this time, too, the handicraft companies found themselves obliged to relax in one way or another the severity of their régime. For instance, the cutlers, painter-stainers and stationers of Dublin, realising in 1767 how repugnant certain of their by-laws were to the spirit as well as to the intention of the charter under which they had been drawn up a century earlier, adopted in their stead a new code, more consistent with the freedom, dignity and independence held to inhere by that time in corporate bodies.[94] By 1782, at Chester, local smiths, cutlers, plumbers and the various other groups associated with them practically abandoned further efforts to force into their ranks craftsmen who seemed unwilling to enter. According to an order issued in that year the company's stewards were directed to wait on half a dozen craftsmen "to have

[91] *Dublin Merchant Gild, Egerton MS.,* No. 1765, f. 67. The recorder held that the power conceded the merchants by their charter, to seize and convert to their use merchandise exposed for sale by non-free persons was legal because Queen Elizabeth had conferred the power by authority of Parliament, the chancellor and chief judges of the realm having decided in a former case that the words "by authority of Parliament" in a charter gave it the force of a parliamentary measure.

[92] *Ibid.,* f. 78. In 1773 the company could not find the funds necessary to defray the cost of attending the chief magistrate in perambulating the franchises of the city, as had been customary.

[93] *Ibid.,* f. 182.

[94] *Dublin Corporation Records, Egerton MS.,* No. 1765, B. M., ff. 167-9. The committee to whose consideration the former by-laws of this corporation were referred to, seems at this time to have gone over them point by point, noting in the margin opposite each item its possible usefulness or hindrance to the trade and the probability of enforcement by the company. Almost half a century later the by-laws under which the company had been operating were again repealed and in their stead was adopted a new set drafted by a committee appointed for the purpose on October 6, 1812. *Ibid.,* p. 199.

their respective answers to know if they or any of them will become Brothers of this Company." Only one of the six showed any intention of joining its ranks; whereupon it was ordered that no further application be made to those who had intimated that they would not become members.[95] In 1792, in order it seems to revive the manufacture of clothing which was being rapidly extinguished in Newbury, local weavers renounced their company's hold over the industry. In that year an advertisement appeared in a local newspaper telling all "whom it might concern" that the boroughs' organised weavers had agreed to disannul their corporate powers by giving liberty to strangers to come into the borough and manufacture silks, muslins, cottons, linens and worsteds free from interference of their company.[96] Just what vicissitudes this company suffered before thus giving up the struggle can of course only be conjectured. At least the merchant taylors of Bath, who at about the same time seem to have gone as far as to dissolve their corporation, did so after struggling in vain to keep it intact. Moreover, in the course of their struggle, the Bath taylors, on the one hand, so harassed certain non-gildsmen as to compel them to leave the city, and on the other, unduly favoured others whom they admitted to membership in their gild when they were not entitled to the privilege; in both cases they offended the civic authorities who had a special interest in preserving the status of freemen as well as non-freemen dwelling within the liberties.[97]

But, then, later-day corporations had for some time been offending borough authorities by admitting members "unbeknownst" to them. For example, at Evesham, during the reign of King Charles II several handicraft groups were censured for taking advantage of the confusion attendant upon the "licentiousness" of the late wars, to make outsiders free of their organisations, without so much as acquainting the mayor and common council with the fact. As a consequence it appears that "under the notion of this supposed freedom such strangers . . . refuse to be admitted and sworn freemen . . . to the undervaluing and contempt of the good government" of the borough.[98] In 1678 the goods of the cutlers,

---

[95] *Journ. Architectural, Archaeol. & Historic Soc. for County & City of Chester & N. Wales,* n. s., vol. 20, pp. 51–2.

[96] The Guild or Fellowship of the Clothworkers of Newbury, *Journal Brit. Archaeol. Assoc.,* n. s., vol. ii, p. 265. Among the butchers of Newcastle free trade with foreigners which was sanctioned for only one year in 1804 seems to have been adopted as a permanent policy in 1822. *Archaeol. Aeliana,* 3rd. ser., vol. 14, p. 14.

[97] Dunlop, *English Apprenticeship,* pp. 233–4.

[98] May, *History of Evesham,* p. 341. As early as 1505 the city of Chester deemed it expedient to issue an order requiring every "foriner" who had been admitted into an occupation to come into the franchise and he who was "able and of powre to be franchised." Morris, *Chester,* p. 385. According to the "vsuall custome" of a borough like Doncaster, a man was sworn a true townsman and made a freeman of the company which he elected to join, before the mayor; thus he became free of the borough and gild at the same time. Tomlinson, *Doncaster,* p. 329.

painter-stainers and "staconers" of Dublin were distrained by order of the city assembly because they had sworn men free of their society before they were sworn free of the city.[99] In 1684, the "taylors" of Abingdon were disfranchised and their charter "made void" for a time, for making free of their company men who had not been made free of the borough.[100] At Youghal, seven years later, because several corporate groups had admitted persons to the freedom of their trade without the consent of the mayor and "Bayliffs," "contrary to the covenant in their several charters . . . and in contempt of them," the corporation directed that the charters of the guilty groups be "condemned as forfaited" unless at the next "court of Record" their master and wardens should "give in their several lists of their companies." Those who claimed the freedom of their trade were to produce copies thereof under penalty of having their shop windows shut down and of being debarred from using their trades thereafter, within corporation limits.[101] By admitting to their ranks persons who were not free of the city, London leathersellers of the period made it possible for outsiders to enjoy immunities and privileges peculiar to freemen, with the result that when the outsiders were called upon to serve office and do other duties "as ffreemen ought to do," they "do wholly decline the same." As the welfare of the city demanded that the practice be discouraged, the officers of the company were directed to inform themselves and certify to the proper city authorities within "fourteen days next ensuing" the names of all such members "as are not free of both" the company and of the city, and they were further admonished that hereafter whenever "you shall make any person free of your company yt you immediately certifie the name of such person and place of his abode to ye chamberlain for the time being to the end that if he shall be remiss in taking up his freedome of this city that meanes may be used to take up the same." [102]

---

[99] *Egerton MS., No. 1765, B. M.,* f. 160. This was a breach of an act of the assembly which had lately been passed forbidding the practice. The gild authorities, however, resented the indignity and agreed to replevy such goods as should "bee removed." In addition they empowered the master of the gild to sue for recovery and even to proceed "at law if need bee," and the corporation was to bear such charges and costs as should be expended in the business.

[100] *Records,* p. 169. Eight years earlier these Abingdon tailors had been fined for "presumptiously" receiving into their company for excessive sums of money, diverse persons and administering to each the oath of the freedom before they were made freemen of the borough, contrary to an act passed by the "Comon Councell," and for molesting others of their craft, who "cannot buy their freedoms at soe greate a price." Prior to this date, at Salisbury, the shoemakers' fraternity had been summarily dissolved because of the admission by the wardens for a certain fee and a "drink" of an improper person. However, when the company acknowledged the fault of its wardens and requested that they be reinstated, they were "again appointed and licensed to be a company" and endowed with the same orders and constitutions they had before possessed. Hoare, *Wiltshire,* vol. vi, p. 381.

[101] *Council Book,* p. 388.

[102] *Egerton MSS., No. 2383, B. M.,* f. 24.

In 1728, not only were unfree persons found using their trades within the liberties of Durham, but apprentices as well were gaining their freedom by improper gild practice. This objectional procedure the borough authorities tried to stop by imposing a weekly fine of twenty shillings on all intruders, payable so long as they continued to ply their trades within corporate limits.[103]   Seven years earlier, in 1721, the mayor of Wells in Somersetshire charged local gilds with clandestinely admitting into their ranks men who had never properly qualified by serving an apprenticeship within the borough.[104]   In places like Norwich as early as 1622, the authorities had cause to complain that local gilds were not properly enrolling their apprentices or paying a proportionate share of the fees into borough coffers.[105]   In 1672 the "tylers" and "playsterers" of Bristol were binding apprentices to themselves and then turning them over to non-freemen, a procedure forbidden because detrimental to the interests of the city.[106]   Three years later the Derby mercers [107] were taking apprentices fraudulently to the displeasure of the borough.   Because the fraudulent binding of apprentices enabled them to secure their freedom without serving an apprenticeship, at Northampton, in 1702, the assembly forbade freemen thereafter to bind apprentices save in the presence of the mayor, recorder or one of the borough justices.[108]   As a further precaution the indentures were to be made out by the town clerk only, and for a term not less than seven years, while gild masters were to forfeit twenty pounds each time they failed to comply with the rules.   At Bedford, too, "improper apprenticeship" became so serious a menace as to force the authorities of the period to consider the practicability of disfranchising freemen for the offence.[109]

It seems evident that many seventeenth-century boroughs exerted their energies, apparently in good faith, to compel townsmen within their precincts to observe the laws governing apprenticeship. Yet there were others, which as necessity or expediency prompted, so far disregarded such laws themselves as to admit to the freedom either singly or in groups, both handicraftsmen and traders "that never were inhabitants in ye Borrough nor served their apprenticeship to freemen yt were inhabitants." [110]   A practice thus begun at Hertford against the wishes of the freemen (who begged the mayor "to make noe more Straingers freemen by redempcon," because the borough's trade was already impoverished), seems to have been continued in different years of the eighteenth century

---

[103] Fordyce, *History of Durham,* vol. i, p. 214.
[104] *Parl. Papers,* vol. 24, p. 1368.
[105] *Records of Norwich,* vol. ii, p. 382.
[106] *Additional MS.,* 28100, B. M., f. 16.
[107] *Additional MS.,* 6694, B. M., f. 96.
[108] *Borough Records,* vol. ii, p. 325.
[109] *Corporation Records,* Appen., No. i, p. 63.
[110] The early years of the reign of Queen Elizabeth found the city of Bristol admitting to the freedom craftsmen who paid a moderate fee. Latimer, *Bristol in the Sixteenth Century, Newspaper Clippings, B. M.,* No. xvii.

when batches of non-freemen were admitted, as it would appear, for political purposes rather than for economic.[111] The political exigencies of the times had in all probability interfered considerably with the normal working of the apprenticeship laws.[112] Just as the boroughs had to relax the severity of their rules governing the admission of freemen, in order to make room for soldiers who in times of stress had given their services to their country, so in like manner it was felt in 1642 that something should be done to encourage apprentices who already "have or shall voluntarily list themselves to go in this present expedition for the defence of Religion, the preservation . . . of the King and the Kingdome." The following year it was decreed by both the "Lords and Commons in Parliament" that "apprentices unto watermen plying and rowing upon the river of Thames as have been or shall be listed to serve as soldiers . . . shall be secured against their masters . . . from all loss and inconvenience by forfeiture of bonds" and that after this public service "be ended the master of such apprentices shall be commanded . . . to receive them again into their service without imposing any punishment, loss or prejudice for their absence in the defence of the Commonwealth." [113] Later, when invoked, the courts declared that the time spent as a soldier in the Parliament's service must be allowed an apprentice "as if he had continued with his master." [114] Apprentices to other handicrafts, apparently quick to avail themselves of the opportunities thus open to them, took the law into their own hands and eluded gild service. The weavers of Westbury told how in these disordered times apprentices forsook parents and masters under colour of following the wars, and refusing afterwards to serve out their time, set themselves up as weavers, thereby depriving the "ancient weavers" of their accustomed work.[115] At Somerset, the attention of the executive authorities was called to instances where apprentices refused outright to carry out the terms of their "agreement to be bound apprentice" or deliberately ran away from their masters.[116] During these days too, the gilds found themselves obliged to overlook breaches of their rules governing apprenticeship. In 1646 the merchants of Newcastle-upon-Tyne, taking into consid-

[111] Dunlop, *English Apprenticeship*, pp. 121–122, quoted from the *Quarter Sessions Records of Hertford.*

[112] As early as 1407 the commons of the city of London proclaimed themselves aggrieved because strangers were being admitted to the franchise for a small sum of money, "whereas they had obtained their freedom" only after serving a long apprenticeship and paying large sums to their masters. *Letter Book I,* p. 63.

[113] Dunlop, *English Apprenticeship,* p. 104.

[114] *Quarter Sessions Records, North Riding Record Soc.,* vol. v, p. 119.

[115] *Hist. MSS. Rep.,* in Various Collections, vol. i, p. 114.

[116] *Somerset Quarter Sessions Records,* vol. 3, pp. 314, 354. Also *North Riding Quarter Sessions Records,* vol. i, p. 130.

In 1685 at Newcastle-upon-Tyne a butcher's apprentice, who had deserted his master and "gone away with his indentures" was "crossed out of the Cos' books." *Archaeologia Aeliana,* 3rd ser., vol. 14, p. 43.

eration "these distracted times" during which an apprentice living in Rotterdam had neglected to acquire his freedom in the company prior to his marriage, condoned the offense and admitted the offender to membership, although there still remained to his account, thirteen months of service. This same company is known of its own "favour and grace" to have admitted an apprentice still "wanting" eighteen months service.[117] However, even before the tempestuous days of the civil war the gilds had grown lax about enforcing rules governing apprenticeship. In 1629 we find an artisan girdler of London accusing the court of his company of not putting into execution ordinances touching those who "set on worke such as had not served seven years at the art."[118] In 1649 the merchant tailors of Bristol denounced the practice then prevalent in their company of admitting persons who had failed to serve a seven years' apprenticeship. Their company, they said, had, of late years, been exceedingly enlarged by the taking in of strangers by way of redemption and composition, there having been during the past year a "continual adding of such unto this numerous Company."[119] In London during this epoch poor "Working Taylors" besought their company to protect them from the competition of foreigners, who, they asserted, were being allowed to work under a nominal apprenticeship and in some instances without qualification of any sort.[120] A few years later certain silk-weavers of York were assessed a "gratuitee" for taking apprentices contrary to the rules of their gild.[121] In 1656 the glovers of Shrewsbury attributed the impoverishment of their company to the fact that its freedom had been conferred upon many who had not served a due apprenticeship,[122] and later in the century told of brethren among them who had sunk so low as actually to connive at intruders "for fraudulent lucre and gain."[123] Ere long, too, the mercers of the borough had transgressed by taking sons of intruders as apprentices. By the opening of the eighteenth century London pewterers could no longer keep their members from employing workmen who had failed to serve a proper apprenticeship.[124] By that time gildsmen took apprentices without apprising their organisations of the taking. In 1719 the Dublin merchants filed a protest against the many members who "contrary to their oaths and in contempt of the by-laws of this house do take apprentices without causing them to be enrolled in this hall."[125] By 1732 master carpenters of Bristol[126] took apprentices without leave of

[117] *Surtees Soc. Public.*, vol. 93, pp. 139, 183.
[118] Smythe, *History of the Girdlers*, p. 89.
[119] Fox, *Merchant Tailors of Bristol*, p. 19.
[120] Clode, *Memorials of the Merchant Taylors*, p. 20.
[121] *Account of the Company of Silk Weavers of York, MSS. B. M.*, f. 142.
[122] *Trans. Shropshire Archaeol. & Nat. Hist. Soc. Pub.*, vol. x, p. 54.
[123] Hibbert, *Influence & Development of English Gilds*, p. 102.
[124] Welch, *History of the London Pewterers*, vol. ii, p. 176.
[125] *Egerton MS., 1765, B. M.*, f. 61.
[126] Webb, *English Local Government*, ii, ii. p. 450.

the court of the company. Other gildsmen transgressed by taking more apprentices than gild law allowed. By 1617 apprentices among the pinmakers of London were said to have multiplied unduly.[127] By 1629 city girdlers "did exceed in taking of apprentices above their no."[128] By the middle of the century the law regulating the taking of apprentices in accordance with the Newcastle mercantile society's "lawdable and profitable acts" had, it seems, "of late yeares beene too much neglected" and thereby "hath occasioned the number of apprentices soe to abound and consequently the number of merchants soe to increase that the trade is not sufficient to support them."[129] In 1653 the goldsmiths of London found it expedient to limit the number of apprentices members might lawfully take. Three years later city clockmakers protested against the "undue multiplication" of apprentices whereby they said their industry was almost ruined.[130] By 1711 disaster is said to have overtaken the cutlery business in Hallamshire because members of the cutlers' company "do take unto themselves so very many apprentices."[131]

In refusing to limit the number of their apprentices, master gildsmen had to reckon with gild officials who had the enforcing of the rules governing apprenticeship, and with exasperated journeymen whose interest in keeping down the numbers of apprentices led them to combine, so as to coerce masters into complying with the rules.[132] Thus, in 1707, master serge and stuff makers of Bristol told the House of Commons that by combining, journeymen engaged in those industries had prevented masters from taking apprentices without their leave.[133] Not all journeymen succeeded in this way in bringing masters to their terms. When the couchmakers of London complained to the court of aldermen in 1716 of the combination entered into by their journeymen, the masters were advised to retaliate by repealing their by-laws restricting them in the taking of apprentices.[134] Not all masters were so authorised to take the law into their own hands[135] and those who did, rendered themselves liable to being prosecuted by disaffected journeymen.[136]

---

[127] Unwin, *Industrial Organization*, p. 170.

[128] Smythe, *History of the Girdlers' Company*, p. 89.

[129] *Surtees Soc. Pub.*, vol. 93, p. 12. In 1733, "the great number of apprentices taken of late years and the present increase of them" was deplored as being still a very great loss and prejudice to the society, and likely to continue so to be "unlesse restrained." *Ibid.*, p. 13.

[130] Overall, *History of the Clockmakers' Company*, p. 61.

[131] Hunter, *Hallamshire*, p. 219.

[132] *Ibid.*, p. 220. In 1790 master cutlers of Hallamshire called a meeting for the purpose of opposing the "unlawful combination" of their workmen.

[133] Latimer, *Annals of Bristol in 18th Century*, p. 70.

[134] Unwin, *Gilds & Companies of London*, p. 348, who quotes from the London Repertories.

[135] On the contrary, as late as 1731 the court of aldermen were apparently averse to seeing master clothworkers break with their journeymen by calling in foreigners. Unwin, *Gilds & Companies*, p. 348.

[136] In 1749 a club of journeymen painters of London are said to have

Apparently, even at this late date, there were gild masters who were not yet ready to go to such lengths but who, nevertheless, expected their journeymen to accommodate themselves to changed economic conditions. However, journeymen of the period had evidently gotten beyond the accommodating stage, and as gild masters, at least, in the metropolis, had plenty of foreign labour to draw upon, and in addition were practically all-powerful in the councils of the city, they succeeded before long in having passed a city ordinance empowering employers to engage non-free journeymen whenever freemen proved unreasonable.[137] That the feltmakers, at least, needed no second bidding, if they had the first, appears from the admission made two years later to a committee of the House of Commons by a master feltmaker, that he was employing six foreigners to one freeman.[138] In keeping with this admission is the action of the feltmakers three years later, in abolishing the ordinances restraining masters from employing foreigners. It does not appear how the journeymen met this move of the masters, which marked the culmination of years of conflict between them over the question. But struggle as they might to keep gild masters from breaking with the system, elsewhere and in other industries, journeymen struggled to little purpose, either for their own good or for that of gilds in general.[139] So disturbing to the peace of Kingston-upon-Hull became the struggle between journeymen and masters that it led to the withdrawal of borough support from the gilds, hence to their undoing.[140]

Again, during the first half of the century the framework knitters' company, urged on by the journeymen, called one master after another to account for disregarding the laws regulating apprenticeship, until stopped by a parliamentary investigation conducted in 1753 which pronounced the company's by-laws "injurious and vexatious" to the manufacturers and its domination "hurtful

proceeded against a master painter for employing a non-freeman. Webb, *Trades Unions*, p. 59.

[137] Northouck, *London*, p. 370. According to the terms of this act passed in November, 1750, for the licencing of foreigners to work in the city of London, the mayor and aldermen were authorised, after the first day of December next, to grant to any free master who, after using his best endeavours failed to procure a sufficient number of free journeymen able to carry on his business, to employ as many foreigners for such a period of time and under such restrictions as to the said authorities should seem fit and necessary.

[138] Unwin, *op. cit.*, p. 351.

[139] In 1760 because journeymen butchers of Newcastle had refused to work for the wage which had customarily been paid and had combined in order to enhance the price thereof, every brother was given the liberty to employ any person, "notwithstanding any other order issued against such persons . . . as were never admitted freemen of this Company." Twenty-five years later, however, this order seems to have been modified so as to read "no nonfree journeyman to be employed when a freeman is unemployed and willing" to do the work required. *Archaeologia Aeliana, 3rd ser.*, vol. 14, p. 19.

[140] Hadley, *History of Kingston-upon-Hull*, p. 828.

to the trade." [141] In London, as in other places, the day of master capitalists had evidently come. Their concern to increase rather than to limit their output, demanded the erection of factories "wherein it is intended to employ" as many persons as possible, not as few.[142] Masters of this type had nothing to gain from a system which limited their number of employees. Many not having themselves served an apprenticeship to their adopted trade were not interested in employing only those who had served their term. To be sure, there had always been masters of this type both within and just without the English boroughs but their numbers had steadily increased with the passing of the years. For example, at Chester, in 1629, steps were taken to apprehend feltmakers who kept apprentices although they had served no apprenticeship themselves to their art.[143] Nine years later the glovers of London told of the hardship they suffered from the invasion of men and women from different parts of the kingdom, who had served little or no time to the trade yet who worked privately in chambers and took many apprentices.[144] During this time, too, the cordwainers and curriers of Lichfield protested against the numbers of persons "which have shifted abroad in the country and have not orderly served an apprenticeship" in any one place before coming to their city [145] and using one or both industries. In 1698 at Nottingham "Specyall care" was being taken to see that neither a "Burges" nor a "Freaman of the said Towne" should by any chance use a trade "vnto which they haue not served as an apprentice." [146] If a contemporary writer can be credited, by 1656 "not any of the relations to clothing . . . doth observe this rule of apprenticeship notwithstanding it is enjoyned in very strict and penall manner by the Statute Lawes." [147] By the end of the following century, the non-observance of the Elizabethan act had become so universal in the cloth trade in Leeds that masters who had served no apprenticeship were apparently in as good standing as those who had.[148] For that matter, by 1661 the goldsmiths of London were doubtful whether the "statute of the 5 Eliz. will restrain" outsiders from working at their craft, and with some justification when we con-

---

[141] Felkin, *History of Machine-Wrought Hosiery,* etc., p. 80.

[142] Webb, *Trades Unions,* p. 34.

[143] *Harleian MS., B. M.,* f. 23. *"Copie of an Order of Council"* issued to that end, on July 29, of that year.

[144] *Privy Council Register,* 1638, quoted in Unwin, *Gilds & Companies,* p. 330.

[145] *Lancashire & Cheshire Trans.,* vol. x, p. 13.

[146] *Records,* vol. v, p. 397.

[147] Dunlop, *English Apprenticeship,* pp. 105–6. Quoted from *The Golden Fleece, 1656,* by W. S.

[148] Brentano, *History & Development of Gilds* (Toulmin Smith's *English Gilds,* p. 31). According to Professor Brentano in 1796 the trustees of the cloth halls at Leeds admitted masters who had served no apprenticeship. With the adoption of modern machinery the art of weaving no longer required a seven years' apprenticeship and Parliament in the act of 43 George III, c. 136 suspended the Elizabethan law so that clothiers might employ weavers who had served no apprenticeship.

sider the nature of the decisions which were rendered when the question came up for adjudication.[149] From the time of King James I the judges had ruled against the statute and in favour of the common law, according to which a man might exercise any trade whether he had been trained to it or not.[150] In 1669 we find the act being set aside to enable a certain draper to use his trade in a Suffolk town, on the ground that "though not repealed" yet the "Statute . . . has been by most of the judges looked upon as inconvenient to Trade and to the Encrease of Inventions." [151] Fifteen years later it had become a matter of legal knowledge that such "By-laws mett with no favour in Westminster Hall." [152] In 1709 the attorney consulted by the mercers of Derby concerning their power to enforce the apprenticeship service under by-laws which dated from 1675, advised them that in his opinion "Ye Crown cannot originally grant any such privilege to a corporation because ye same tends to ye restraint of trade and traffic," wherefore "any belaw founded thereupon will not be good." [153] How this opinion, which denied to crown, borough and gilds the right to enforce the apprenticeship service, was received in Derby does not appear. But during the first half of the eighteenth century in Newcastle-upon-Tyne, actions to restrain men from using trades to which they had not been apprenticed were brought in the quarter-sessions courts as being contrary not to borough or gild laws, but to the Elizabethan statute of apprenticeship.[154] It is only after the third quarter of the century, that the records of the Newcastle quarter sessions fail to register further proceedings taken under the statute. So it appears that as a means of restraining trade or industry, the apprenticeship system was doomed long before 1814,[155] the year in which the English government swept from the statute-book the clauses of the statute which, for over two centuries, had made apprenticeship a legal requirement.

[149] Prideaux, *Memorials of the Goldsmiths' Company*, vol. ii, p. 139.

[150] *Norris & Trussell, Guardians, and the Weavers of Newbury, Pasch,* 14 *Jacobi.* Hobart 211, p. 369. See also *Parl. Papers, 1884,* pt. i, p. 51.

This decision was rendered in the case of the weavers of Newbury, who in accordance with one of their ordinances allowed in the reign of Queen Elizabeth brought an action of debt of five pounds against a weaver named Staps for using his craft without joining their company. The court, however, ruled that the ordinance in question was allowed subject to the common law which did not forbid any man to use any trade whether he were trained to it or not.

[151] Unwin, (*Industrial Organization*, p. 252. Appen. A, vii) publishes this record from the Privy Council Register, Oct. 29, 1669.

[152] Ferguson, *Boke of Recorde of Kendal*, p. 206.

[153] *Additional MS., 6694, B. M.*, f. 96.

[154] The Merchant Adventurers of Newcastle-upon-Tyne, *Surtees Society Publications,* vol. 93, p. xlv. At Bristol, too, evidently, prosecutions in restraint of trade were taken under the Statute of Apprentices, not under any local custom or gild by-law. Webb, *English Local Government*, vol. ii, pt. ii, p. 449. Quoted from *MS. Sessions Book,* June 20, 1748.

[155] 54 George III, c. 96. Certain gilds kept on enrolling apprentices after the passage of this act. The Shrewsbury mercers recorded their enrollment up to 1835. Hibbert, *Influence and Development of English Gilds*, p. 134.

II

THE LOSS OF GILD POWER OF SEARCH

Along with the loss of gild power to enforce the laws governing apprenticeship went gild supervision of trade and industry in other directions. This was inevitable since a considerable part of gild supervision had to do with enforcing the service. Thus, in making their rounds to see that gild masters made their goods to accord with gild standards, that the "werkhouse" of a candidate for admission was "goode and able or no," [1] that masters used fair weights and true measures,[2] and that they purchased their stocks with due regard to gild requirements, gild supervisors or searchers as they were usually designated, sometimes seized the goods or shut down the shops of men who had not served full time to their trade.[3] They passed upon the fitness of apprentices to be taken into service,[4] saw "whatt apprentyces" masters "kepe," [5] so that only the stipulated number were taken at any one time,[6] that they were properly enrolled in gild records [7] and that none were taken merely to be

[1] In 1490 among the weavers of Kingston-upon-Hull the searchers had to certify as to this before a candidate could "aggre wt the Alderman for the tyme beyng for his upsett." Lambert, *Two Thousand Years of Gild Life,* p. 205.

[2] Searchers of the mercers of Shrewsbury had to "make serche uppon the Occupyers of the said Crafte . . . that none of theym occupie any false Balaunce Weight or measures." *Trans. Shropshire Archaeol. and Nat. Hist. Soc.,* vol. viii, pp. 271–86.

[3] Among the duties of the supervisors of the merchants of Newcastle-upon-Tyne was that of seizing goods unlawfully bought and sold and the "shutting in of unfree shopps." *Surtees Soc. Pub.,* vol. 93, p. 152.

In 1631, among the clockmakers of London, searchers were authorised to seize the goods made by men who had not served full time and to close their shops as well. Overall, *Hist. of the Clockmakers,* p. 15.

[4] If a fourteenth-century master "bower" of York took an apprentice before he had been examined by company searchers he was fined five pounds. *Memorandum Book I,* p. xlvii.

[5] Johnson, *History of the Drapers' Company,* vol. ii, pp. 302–3. This company's "Due Serche" had to be made "4 tymes in the yere att the leaste and oftener yt nede requier."

[6] The search conducted in 1582 by the wardens of the worsted weavers of Norwich disclosed offenders who had more apprentices than they ought to have had. Dunlop, *English Apprenticeship,* p. 89, quoted from *MSS. Court Book of Norwich.*

[7] In 1613 one of the rules of the Merchant Taylors of London authorised their supervisers to search "as well for weights measures, yardes and Ells as for non presenting of apprentices non enrolling of them and of keeping of fforeyns contrary to the Lawes and use of the said city." Clode, *Memorials,* p. 210.

turned over to other masters.[8] The searchers had likewise to testify to borough officials as to the fitness of an apprentice who had served the required term, to set up as a master.[9]

It is evident that gild supervision proved effective in so far as it enforced apprenticeship, and failure to enforce it, led to the breakdown of the gild system as a whole. Of course the Norwich "taillour" who, in 1524, refused to "suffre" the wardens of his craft "to search in his shoppe in causes concernyng the occupation of taillours" was not alone in defying gild authority.[10] But the records tell of the many seventeenth-century craftsmen who denied the right of gild officials not only in Norwich [11] but in other places to search their premises for defective goods. During the first quarter of the seventeenth century, obstructions of one sort or another were frequently put in the way of the wardens of the London goldsmiths as they made their accustomed rounds in search of defective wares.[12] In 1642, the master and wardens of city apothecaries were assailed in a very ill manner when they attempted to search the shop of one of their members.[13] In 1676, at Bristol, the feltmakers' official supervisors were prevented from inspecting certain parcels of felt stored in a member's shop.[14] In 1700 any number of Pontefract merchants either refused outright to permit gild officers to search their shops or interrupted them in the discharge of that office.[15] A year later, a certain member of the London saddlers "did deny the search" threatening to strike the

[8] In 1613 it was agreed by the searchers and the company of silk-weavers of York that thereafter no brother should take an apprentice "uppon sett purpose to turne" him over to another or by any means to defraud the trade. *Account of the Company of Silk Weavers, MS, B M*, fol. 91.

[9] He had in addition to own property to the value of four marks a year. Ordinances of the fullers of York in 1390. York *Memorandum Book*, p. xxx–i.

[10] *Records of Norwich*, vol. ii, p. 160. Ordinances which were drawn up by the Hull glovers in 1499 expressly stipulated the penalty that "any of the sayd crafft" must pay the first, second, and even the third time he presumed to "make resistence agaynst the said sercheours or any of theym in executynge their officery." Punishment for the fourth offence was to be "effter the discresion of the Maire." *Lambert, op. cit.*, p. 216.

[11] In 1615 a Norwich weaver was "presented" by the wardens of his gild for not suffering them to search in his "house" for defective ware, contrary to an order scheduled "in their booke." Dunlop, *English Apprenticeship*, p. 80–1, note, quoted from *MS. Norwich Court Book*.

[12] In 1624, officials of this company reported that they had met with violent resistance from a shop-keeper who displayed suspicious-looking "chains and bracelets of beads linked with gold." Five years later they were frustrated in their search by a gild member who pretended that he could not show his wares because he had no key; and that, in order to escape producing it, he had "stepped out of the shop." Prideaux, *Memorials of the Goldsmiths' Company*, vol. i, pp. 138, 147.

[13] Barrett, *History of the Society of Apothecaries*, p. 60.

[14] Latimer, *17th Century Annals of Bristol*, p. 376. This man, it seems, had resold the goods before they had been approved as marketable, and was in addition contumacious and discourteous to the magistrates when they admonished him for his misdemeanours.

[15] *Booke of Entries*, pp. 375–8.

searchers with a hammer, besides "giveing very abusive words." [16] In 1708, one of the assistants of the city goldsmiths lost the nomination for "Warden" for the ensuing year because "he refused to open his glass or admit Mr. Wardens to take any of his goods in order to try the same." [17] Seemingly gilds of the period suffered no offender to be a law unto himself. In 1701 by order of the court of the London gold and silver wyre-drawers' company, members who resisted the search were to be prosecuted. [18] It was one thing to issue an order of the sort, but another to enforce it, for a few months later this company was consulting the attorney-general to learn whether it could legally prosecute members for transgressing the by-laws under which their search had been conducted.

Long before this epoch, other organisations had begun to question the strength of the authority under which they had been prosecuting their search. As early as 1621 the goldsmiths of London ordered the clerk of the company to "peruse" not alone their charter but the "Act of Parliament" and their ordinances as well, in order to determine "how far" their wardens "have power to search and punish offenders." [19] The reply of the official is not recorded, but by 1661 the company announced its determination to renew its charter and "wherein it is short or defective in power to reform abuses in the trade to have it enlarged," as likewise, "to have such things as shall be agreed on" inserted in an "Acte of Parliament, it being now a favourable time wherein the King's Majesty upon all occasions is willing to graunte the citizens of London anything that can in reason be desired and that he may lawfully graunte." [20] During this epoch, various organisations bestirred themselves to secure an extension of the circuits over which they had been operating, until from a two or three mile area around the city and its suburbs, their powers of supervision were extended to a seven, ten and even a twenty-four mile radius; [21] nor were their efforts at this time devoted merely toward securing a formal confirmation of their powers of search. In 1645 officials of the Newcastle merchants "appointed to seize upon goods foraine bought

---

[16] Sherwell, *History of the Saddlers' Company*, p. 202.
[17] Prideaux, *op. cit.* vol. ii, p. 182.
[18] Stewart, *History of Gold & Silver Wyre-Drawers*, pp. 75, 87.
[19] Prideaux, *Memorials of the Goldsmiths' Company*, vol. i, p. 133.
[20] *Ibid.* vol. ii, p. 137.
[21] In 1636 the London glovers most humbly offered the Lords of the privy Council the reasons why the incorporation for which they had petitioned should be made to comprise seven miles and not three as contended for by city leathersellers. *State Papers Domestic, Charles I*, 377, No. 38. The horners of the same city seem to have had sole control over their industry not only within the liberties but twenty-four miles "on every side next adjoining." Compton, *Hist. of the Worshipful Company of Horners*, p. 7. According to the terms of the letters patent issued to the London clockmakers in 1632, freemen who left London to ply their calling in any part of the Kingdom were still subject to the laws of the company and liable to be proceeded against for default of duties, deceitful workmanship, etc., as though they resided in the said city. Overall, *History of the Clockmakers*, p. 29.

and foraigne sold" were given the "Companies" seale for the further strengthening of their commission in that behalfe." [22] And when, in 1671, the wheelwrights of London found a member using poor materials or "evil and insufficient goods," the goods were seized and fines imposed under a warrant secured from the Recorder of the city.[23] During this same period the warden and searchers of the weavers of Kingston-upon-Hull or a deputy distrained the goods or chattels of a recalcitrant member to recover for penalties owing for the infringement of gild rules, under warrant from the "Maior." [24] However, neither the source from which they derived their power of supervision, the extent of the territory over which they might operate, nor the weight of the authority supposedly inhering in the officials authorised to enforce the office materially strengthened gild control over trade or industry." In 1639 a fine of three "poundes, sixe shillings and eight pence" was assessed upon the person who wilfully resisted such of the assistants, livery, or other of the London clothworkers' company as "once every quarter of a yeare at the leaste" should "goe to search" or oftener "as it shall seeme good to them . . . or any of the Kings Majesties officers brought by them to doe or execute their office in that behalfe." [25] However faithful the execution of office, or whatever the immediate result to the company, it is a matter of record that by the early eighteenth century the clothworkers were appointing a committee to consider "what power the company hath by their charter or otherwise concerning the seizing of cloths which are bad-wrought." [26]

Seventeenth-century gilds losing faith in their power to prosecute the search, naturally grew less zealous in its prosecution. For instance, in 1607, the London goldsmiths called a Mr. Andrew Jones to account for accusing the company of "remissness in the searches." [27] Scarcely twenty-five years after they were incorporated, city clockmakers had become lax in the execution of their search.[28] There were years when, for reasons beyond their control, gilds had perforce to omit the practice. For instance, in 1563 the pewterers of London abandoned their search because of the plague,[29] and the goldsmiths in 1606 "because of the sickness." [30]

---

[22] *Surtees Soc. Pub.*, vol. 93, p. 138. It is interesting to note that as early as 1363, the London saddlers authorised their supervisors to take a sergeant of the chamber with them to any place where "any prove rebellious against them" and "refuse to allow them to search his house or shop in accordance with the rules of the company." Sherwell, *History of the Saddlers*, p. 34.

[23] Scott, *History of the Wheelwrights' Company*, p. 17.

[24] Lambert, *Two Thousand Years*, p. 212.

[25] *Ordinances*, p. 118.

[26] *Parl. Papers, 1884*, pt. ii, p. 675.

[27] Prideaux, *Memorials of the Goldsmiths' Company*, vol. i, p. 109.

[28] Unwin, *Industrial Organization*, p. 245.

[29] Welch, *Pewterers*, vol. i, Introduction, p. vi.

[30] Prideaux, *op. cit.*, vol. i, p. 93. This company refrained from conducting its customary search in the country, in 1597, in consequence, it seems, of

In 1633 "the foulness of the weather" interfered with the gold-smiths carrying on their search in the fair on St. Bartholomew's Day, whereas in 1670, it seems to have been omitted "in regard to the great charge that doth attend the same." [31] Evidently too, the search failed to materialise because of carelessness or indifference on the part of the gild officers charged with its execution. By 1623 the wardens of the Norwich mercers had "omitted to make due search" apparently against the rules of the company which sought to arrest further omissions by imposing a penalty of twenty shillings for dereliction of duty in that direction.[32] Nine years later in London artisan girdlers complained to the court of their company [33] that of recent years the master and wardens failed to take along any of their number on their searches. In 1648 different members of the Newcastle merchant company appointed "for to seaze on all goods foraigne bought and foraigne sould" confessed that "some which are joyned in commission" with them "are very backward to discharge the trust imposed upon them." The fol-lowing year when several non-freemen were discovered keeping their "shopps" open and "vendinge there commodities as free" the offenders were given another chance to "prosicute theire power fourthwith" by "seaseing of goods unlawfully bought and sould and shutting in of unfree shopps." [34] A dozen years later among the weavers of Kingston-upon-Hull, the searcher who "shall refuse to execute the said place" was to forfeit "Tenn Shillings." [35] In 1714 officials of the Newcastle joiners were charged with passing de-fective work for a "gill of ale," with coming into one member's house "in a riotous manner" and without "handshaking" ransack-ing his place, and even with "being drunk" when they came.[36] But whether vigorously or ineffectively prosecuted, gildsmen contrived to escape gild espionage for one reason or another. It appears that

the dearth of coin. Apparently, for the same reason, it "put off" the collec-tion of quarterage. Vol. i, p. 87.

[31] *Ibid.*, vol. i, p. 159., vol. ii, p. 165. Nevertheless the company's wardens were "entreated to make frequent searches by themselves both in the fair and elsewhere amongst goldsmiths in and about" the city of London.

[32] Dunlop, *English Apprenticeship*, p. 85, note i, taken from *MS. Norwich Mercers' Book II.*

[33] Smythe, *History of the Girdlers' Company*, p. 89. The artisans asked the court for leave to search "of their own authority," but were reminded that some of their number had constantly been called upon to accompany the officers on their rounds, and on occasion would again be called, but, "as to giving them libertie . . . to search by themselves" they were told that "the Court neither holds it fitt or convenient." It seems to have been customary for artisan freemen to meet annually at their hall in order, first to choose twenty of their number, and then to present the twenty so chosen to the court of the company. From the twenty the court selected sixteen, known as the yeomanry, and these yeomanry, in their turn, had the appointing of four of the sixteen to attend the master and wardens on their searches for poorly-made wares. Smythe, *op. cit.*, p. 138.

[34] *Surtees Soc. Pub.*, vol. 93, pp. 150, 152.

[35] Lambert, *Two Thousand Years*, p. 209.

[36] *Archaeologia Aeliana*, 3rd ser., vol. v, p. 185.

in 1725 among the pewterers of London, the "searching of Beams and Weights" failed to "answer the End proposed" because the "Day" was "publickly known." [37] Only, whereas sickness, or unfavourable weather, or the lack of funds necessary to finance the search, or the failure of officials to carry on the work, or the discovery by the rank and file of the time set apart for its conduct may serve to explain why the search failed occasionally to materialise on a specific occasion, they scarcely suffice to account for the breakdown of the system as a whole. But then gildsmen of the period had no need to search for a way of escape, gild economy had provided one for those in the best standing. Indeed, as early as 1571 various metropolitan handicraft groups frankly admitted their powerlessness longer to see that gild products were well made as had been the case in the days when gild officials had the "search and punishment of all persons occupying the art." As one way of recovering their earlier control, the dozen and more groups which made the admission urged the adoption of a plan whereby persons free of other companies should henceforth be compelled to observe the ordinances of the handicraft "touching their wares and works made." [38] This proposal for reform furnishes the clue to what appears by that time to have become a serious obstacle in the way of gild supervision in the metropolis. Obviously by the last quarter of the sixteenth century, by no means all London gildsmen who followed a calling belonged to the organisation in control, and for that reason could escape the consequences of wrong-doing. As a goldsmith in Lombard Street put it nearly a century later, in refusing to let the wardens of the goldsmiths make trial of his wares, that, since he was not a member of their company he was "not liable to their search." [39]

It was not only the men in the ranks who evaded the liability. Gild officials used other callings than those sponsored by the company they were chosen to serve, and consequently had become negligent in enforcing their office. For example, in 1633, city girdlers told how of late merchants, dealers in silk and other commodities had joined the company, put down the yeomanry and appropriated the governing power, and being men of other trades neglected to suppress and reform the abuses patent by that time to the members who were really concerned in the art. [40] Conscious of the necessity of suppressing the abuses which had crept into their system,

[37] Welch, *History of the Pewterers' Company,* vol. ii, p. 185. The admission was also made that the present custom of searching "being done now in one day and in October when the days are short, is very troublesome."

[38] Clode, *Early History of the Merchant Taylors,* vol. i, p. 204. In 1549 the municipal authorities of Coventry had issued an order forbidding any inhabitant to "be in felishipp with eny other felishipp or company thenewith that Company and Craft whosse occupacion & Craft he or his seruantes doithe occupie & vse vpon peyne to forfeit xls. for euery monthe that he shall vse hymself contrarie to this acte." *Leet Book,* pt. iii, p. 790.

[39] Prideaux, *Memorials of the Goldsmiths' Company,* vol. ii, p. 142.

[40] Smythe, *History of the Girdlers' Company,* p. 91.

various gilds sought to eliminate them by having handicraftsmen join the organisation in control of the art they practised. In 1605, at the urging of the cooks a city ordinance was passed bidding all cooks in the metropolis to be translated to the cooks' company.[41] A little later the glaziers, among other groups, had a similar edict passed in their behalf.[42] Others took matters into their own hands and brought under their control individuals who used the occupations for which they stood sponsor. In 1619 city apothecaries succeeded in getting an apothecary who belonged to the skinners' company to join their ranks, upon their giving him a week in which "to take his leave of the company of skinners."[43] In 1653, upon the plea that he was unable to ply his calling unmolested by the saddlers, city goldsmiths permitted a freeman of their company, but a saddler by trade, to have himself translated to the saddlers.[44] On the other hand, a saddler of the period who had "left of the profession of a saddler" and "betaken himselfe wholly to the trade of a Baker" was not allowed to leave the saddlers for the bakers' company until he had paid the saddlers the "somme of Tenne Pounds."[45] And the drapers allowed one of their number to join the company in control of the craft he was using on condition that he pay quarterage as of old to the drapers.[46] However, certain companies refused to part with their members on any terms. Indeed, in 1657 the ironmongers would not allow a pinmaker by trade but an ironmonger "by company" to join the newly organised company of pinmakers.[47] Again, half a century after the incorporation

[41] Unwin, *Gilds & Companies of London*, p. 264, quoted from an MS. in the Guildhall in London. According to Professor Unwin the edict was withdrawn in 1614. Yet, according to the London goldsmiths, in 1653, city cooks called the attention of their company to this edict passed by the London common council in 1605, calling for the translation to the cooks' company of the members of other companies who used the occupation of cooks. Prideaux, *Memorials of the Goldsmiths' Company*, vol. ii, p. 33.

[42] From an entry dated 1616 in the records of the glaziers' company, we learn that the committee appointed to inquire into the complaints of the glaziers of that period reported that that "ancient brotherhood" was "much decayed lately by reason that divers persons of other Companies do pursue their trade and take as many apprentices as they please whereas if they were free of the Glaziers they could not take more than one apprentice." Wherefore the committee recommended "that all Freemen of other companies using the trade of a Glazier shall submit to the Search and that apprentices taken by them shall be presented to the Master and Wardens of the Glaziers' Company." Ashdown, *History of the Worshipful Company of Glaziers*, p. 28.

[43] Barrett, *History of the Society of Apothecaries*, p. 4.

[44] Prideaux, *Memorials of the Goldsmiths' Company*, vol. ii, p. 46.

[45] Sherwell, *History of the Saddlers' Company*, p. 156. Occasionally, however, one company allowed a member to transfer himself to another company when it was to its interest to do so. Thus, in 1664 a London goldsmith transferred his membership to the glaziers whose craft he followed, "without a fine" upon his plea that he was "a poor man." Prideaux, *History of the Goldsmiths' Company*, vol. ii, p. 151.

[46] Johnson, *History of the Worshipful Company of Drapers*, vol. ii, p. 167.

[47] Noble, *History of the Ironmongers' Company*, p. 23.

of city clockmakers, their "design to have all clockmakers made free" of their corporation was frustrated by the blacksmiths. Moreover, it cost one clockmaker of the period twenty pounds to quit the clockmakers and as late as 1811 another paid the company fifty pounds for the privilege of betaking himself to the goldsmiths "for very particular reasons." [48] Whereas certain gildsmen allowed themselves the luxury of changing their gild membership, others with reasons probably just as particular kept their membership in two companies. From the start none of the "misterie" of the London clothworkers was "of his own mocion or frowardnes or by the pcuryng of any other psone . . . to go oute of the said Feloushippe to any other misterie." [49] Yet in answering the charges preferred against them by city drapers in 1634, the clothworkers published the fact, that certain clothworkers were free of the merchant adventurers and for that reason were entitled to buy and sell cloth by wholesale and retail. [50] Simultaneous membership in more than one gild had evidently not been eliminated from the gild system. -

Furthermore, while the transfer of a few members from one company to another may have satisfied the individuals or the gilds immediately concerned, it failed to make the gilds as a whole representative of the profession they were organised to serve or their members subservient to gild rule. Recognising the hopelessness of effecting a reform with the membership that they had, certain organisations of the period thought to remedy the situation by having apprentices thereafter bound to members of the company in control of the particular trade or industry they should elect to follow. The London clockmakers had probably this end in view in 1635 in calling the attention of the court of aldermen to the difficulties under which they laboured "being freemen of other companies" and asked for permission to bind their apprentices to themselves, not through the intervention of the companies of which they were free, but through the newly organised company of clockmakers of which they were members. [51] The committee appointed by the court to pass upon the merit of the appeal, favoured it so far as to recommend admitting to citizenship as clockmakers, craftsmen who had gained the consent of the companies of which they were free. The craftsmen who failed to gain their company's assent to their translation were to bind to a freeman the appren-

---

[48] Overall, *History of the Clockmakers' Company*, pp. 118, 39, 113.

[49] *Clothworkers' Ordinances published in 1631*, p. 25. However, in 1587 a member could change his "freedome upon payne of an Hundred Marks," and in 1639 by securing a license, upon what terms is not stated. *Ibid.*, pp. 56, 120. In 1646 the merchants of Newcastle considered it "very distructive to the welfare of this Fellowshipp" that a "taylor" of their "towne" had "altered his copy" and been admitted as a free mercer before "Mr. Mayor and some aldermen." However, he was not to "trade in Mdse" until the justness of his admittance be decided." *Surtees Soc. Pub.* vol. 93, p. 142.

[50] *State Papers Domestic*, 1634, p. 278.

[51] Overall, *History of Clockmakers' Company*, p. 55.

tices who exercised clockmaking, and at the end of their term of service, admit them as citizens and clockmakers. Later, other corporations joined in petitioning the Lord Mayor and aldermen for the passage of an order, enjoining "all persons using their respective trades to present, bind and make free all their apprentices at their respective companies," the apprentices to be subject to the "search and government of that company whose trade they use." [52]   Some companies,[53] notably the glovers [54] and painter-stainers had, evidently, succeeded in securing this concession [55] but by the time that the founders, carpenters, gun-makers and other crafts associated with them asked that similar measures be passed in their behalf, the twelve livery companies had contrived to influence the court of aldermen against granting the concession. The livery companies, however, were willing, that some "expedient as to view and search and the limitation of persons free of other companies . . . be thought on as well to the contentment of those companies as to the weal of the city and citizens." [56]   But on the whole, little seems to have come of any such plan to help the metropolitan gilds. For in 1684 the drapers of the city still attributed the decay of their power to the fact that many who used drapery were free of other companies. And the committee appointed to consider how best to arrest the ruin which threatened to overtake the company, still recommended that all persons who used the mystery be made free of the company and that all apprentices to the trade be bound only to its freemen.[57]   Moreover, the following year certain freemen who had served their apprenticeship to retailing vintners were made free, it seems, by their respective masters of "ye company of Haberdashers." [58]   Again, in 1725, it appears that the goldsmiths had failed to keep goldsmiths "ffree of other companies from binding

[52] Unwin, *Gilds & Companies of London*, p. 341. Professor Unwin quotes from the London Repertories.

[53] In 1631 the paviours petitioned the court of aldermen asking that freemen of the goldsmiths who used the paviours' trade should bind their apprentices to paviours. Prideaux, *Memorials of the Goldsmiths' Co.*, vol. i, p. 153.

[54] In 1650 by an act passed by the common council of the city, glovers who were free of other companies were to present their "intended" apprentices to the master and wardens of the glovers and be bound to one of the company. *Municipal Corp. Com. Report*, 1835, p. 284.

[55] The later a company was incorporated, the more difficult seems to have been the task of bringing under its control persons who practised the mystery accredited to it. In 1587, the clothworkers of London passed an ordinance which bade apprentices of men of other companies who used "clothworkinge" to be bound to one of "ye Company of Clothworkers." *Ordinances*, p. 67. Because framework knitters were "dispersed among other London trade companies and "have not proper government for the management of their own," the framework knitters' company incorporated by King Charles II in 1663, ordered the freemen of the other city companies to bind their children who were framework knitters to members of the framework knitters' company. Felkin, *op. cit.*, p. 70.

[56] Unwin, *Gilds & Companies of London*, p. 341.

[57] *Parl. Papers*, 1885, pt. ii, p. 174.

[58] *Harlein MS., B. M.*, no. 6842, fol. 193.

many apprentices," [59] while as late as 1778, the leathersellers blamed the fraudulent selling of leather goods within city limits to the fact that the persons who practised the trade were free of other companies and consequently made apprentices free of other companies also. In this way, they said, control of the trade had passed out of the hands of the leathersellers' company.[60]

To all intents and purposes, the policy of admitting to membership men who followed diverse callings had been followed too long in the metropolis for a radical reform to be effected at this late date. It seems that the London gild of grocers opened its membership to men who practised other trades, as early as 1376, by "common assent and the payment of a certain fee." [61] By 1403 tradesmen other than mercers gained admittance to city mercers by consent of the whole gild.[62] A charter conceded in 1448 to the haberdashers frankly provided for the admission of persons other than haberdashers.[63] Likewise, by the terms of the charter bestowed upon the Merchant Taylors in 1502, the master and wardens could admit to the fraternity whatsoever persons they saw fit.[64] To the court of the newly incorporated company of clothworkers was given the power to take into their ranks from time to time "by waye of composition" and redemption such "as to them shall seeme meet and convenyent." It is no wonder that by 1587 the company's membership included free persons "of what trade, faculty or mystery they be." [65] In the ordinances drawn up by the drapers in the middle of the sixteenth century, the master and wardens were authorised to admit all "Redempcyoners" without assent or "avise" of any other person and either "gratis" or for such sums as they should decide.[66] The charter incorporating the wheelwrights in 1670, empowered company officials to admit from time to time "such person and persons as they shall thinke fitt and as shall

---

[59] Prideaux, *Memorials of the Goldsmiths' Company*, vol. ii, p. 205.

[60] Black, *History of the Worshipful Company of Leathersellers*, p. 128.

[61] According to an item contained in the ordinances drawn up in that year "none of another mystery shall be received into the company without common assent," and upon the payment of ten pounds at least for his entrance. In addition if the wardens "shall receive any such without common assent they shall pay twenty pounds." Kingdon, *Worshipful Company of Grocers*, pt. i, p. 18.

[62] *Parl. Papers, 1884*, pt. ii, p. 4. In 1404 the company's wardens seem to have admitted a certain pinner, a procedure apparently objected to as contrary to gild ordinances. Whereupon it was ordered that thereafter strangers should not be admitted without the consent of the entire company.

[63] *Parliamentary Papers*, 1884, p. 23.

[64] Clode, *Memorials of the Merchant Taylors*, p. 195. By 1558 records of the London goldsmiths' company reveal the presence of a member who, not being a practising goldsmith, was not "thereafter to be summoned to or be present at the reading of the ordinances." This restriction was to apply also to other members of the sort. Prideaux, *Memorials of the Goldsmiths' Company*, vol. i, p. 59.

[65] *Ordinances of the Clothworkers*, p. 63.

[66] Johnson, *History of the Worshipful Company of Drapers*, vol. ii, pp. 286–7.

desire to become members of the said Societie." [67] There seems thus scarcely a doubt that almost from their start London organisations were admitting to membership persons who had no connexion with the particular trade or industry they were supposed to represent.

Aside from the admission of members by redemption, the heterogeneity of gild membership was due also, in part, to the custom which permitted a son to inherit his father's membership in a gild. It may be that at first sons followed their fathers' calling much as a matter of course,[68] although later admission by patrimony brought into a gild, members with no particular concern in the trade or industry with which the gild was identified. As the London leathersellers [69] phrased it in the first quarter of the seventeenth century, in deploring the conditions prevalent in their ranks by that time, "as the manner of London is,[70] the sonne being free by the fathers copy the company is long since changed to those that know not leather." In 1738 the butchers of Newcastle-upon-Tyne tried to limit their officers to trading "brothers," for the practice of appointing to office brothers who did not follow the trade of a butcher had been found detrimental to the company's interests.[71] Furthermore, the custom still in vogue in the later seventeenth century of compelling a man to belong to a gild if he wished to ply his calling

---

[67] Scott, *History of the Wheelwrights' Company*, p. 13.

[68] It was manifestly not the case by 1396 in York, because of the ten men who gained the freedom of the city in that year "Per Patres," one only seems to have followed his father's business. *The Freemen of York, Surtees Society Publications*, vol. 96, p. 99.

[69] Unwin, *Industrial Organization*, p. 129.

[70] Although thus declared a custom of London, one which proves to have been practised at York as early, at least, as the first year of King Edward I, when the "filius" of one freeman gained the freedom of the city, (*The Freemen of York, op. cit.,* p. 1), it is not evident how early patrimony entitled a son to the freedom of a gild, either in the metropolis or in a provincial borough. Gild records mention the custom as an established fact in the sixteenth century. Thus, by the middle of that century the eldest son born to a free butcher of Northampton seems to have succeeded his father by right of patrimony. By the sixth year of the reign of King Edward VI, "byrthe" seems to have been one way of gaining admission into the merchant gild of Dublin. *Egerton MS.*, 1765, f. 16. By 1560 a man obtained his freedom in the London goldsmiths' company by patrimony. Prideaux, *Memorials of the Goldsmiths' Company*, vol. i, p. 62. In the eighteenth century among the butchers of Newcastle-upon-Tyne, a freeman might enroll his son in the company's books as soon as the child was born, although he could not take up his freedom until he was twenty-one. *Archaeologia Aeliana*, 3rd series, vol. 14, p. 22. Sometimes a son gained admission into a municipality and a gild simultaneously by patrimony. In 1586 the son of a deceased freeman was sworn free of the borough of St. Albans "Of the Company of Mercers by his father's copy." *St. Albans Charters*, p. 14. By 1635, in accordance with "ancient custom" in Kingston-upon-Thames, the eldest son of every freeman living at the time of his father's death was, at the age of twenty-one, admitted a freeman by his father's copy, "to be of the same company his father was of." *Gough MSS., Bodleian Library, Records Relating to Kingston-upon-Thames*, f. 15.

[71] *Archaeologia Aeliana*, 3rd series, vol. xiv, p. 13.

undisturbed in an urban community, probably added little to the effectiveness of gild supervision. A case in point is that of the confectioner who, in 1685, applied to the officials of Newcastle-upon-Tyne for permission to join one of the city companies and take apprentices to help him ply his calling within the liberties. The confectioner in question was accorded liberty to choose the fellow-ship he deemed "most meet" and he elected membership "as a goldsmith" in an organisation which included goldsmiths, plumbers pewterers, glaziers and painters. Upon entering he gave bond that "neither he nor any of his servants shall exercise any of the trades of this Company," but that they would confine themselves to "the trade or art of a confectioner only." [72] However, the fact that a confessed confectioner could gain admittance to a corporation hold-ing together handicrafts with so little in common, proves, doubtless, that the question of supervision played little or no real part in gild polity of that period. Moreover, the pracitce of merging into one gild unrelated groups of craftsmen tended probably to nullify the effectiveness of supervision and to bring the different mysteries to a point where insistence upon uniformity to a common standard seemed neither possible nor profitable. It is true that, upon amal-gamating, various groups provided for the regulation of the sepa-rate interests involved, by appointing separate officials to supervise the work of the separate groups; but whether the results justified the effort expended cannot now be estimated. It is known, how-ever, that fifteenth-century officials of Coventry discouraged the amalgamation of allied interests in the iron industry because of the difficulty under such conditions of placing responsibility for defectively made goods.[73] Of course the more heterogeneous a company, the more difficult the task became of controlling the dif-ferent elements involved; this proved to be the cause of the lack of effort later expended in that direction.

Consequently, no matter how they were recruited, the hetero-geneity of gild membership was a fact, apparently of such long standing and so intertwined with borough and gild custom, that seventeenth-century organisations could do little to make their mem-bership more representative of the particular trade or industry with which they were identified, or to keep their officials loyal to the gild they were elected to serve. Long accustomed to a divided allegiance, gildsmen seem to have lost much of their early "ésprit de corps," often indeed they refused to accept office in one organisa-tion because they belonged to another. In 1732 certain goldsmiths of London had themselves discharged from serving as wardens of the gold and silver wyre-drawers on the ground that they were free of the goldsmiths and therefore exempt from holding office in the other company.[74]

Despite the drawbacks to successful pursuit, seventeenth-century

[72] *Archaeologia Aeliana,* vol. xv, iii, p. 399.
[73] *Supra,* p. 70.
[74] Stewart, *History of the Gold & Silver Wyre Drawers' Company,* p. 88.

charters confirmed gild right of search and many appear to have enforced their right, often to some purpose. Thus, the search conducted by London wheelwrights in 1692 brought to light "wheeles and Carts" made "contrarie to the Rules and Orders" of that company.[75] A year later searchers of the gold and silver wyre-drawers found a quantity of ill-wrought ware which was duly destroyed.[76]   In 1716 felt designated as "not merchantable and deceitful" was seized on the premises of a feltmaker in Dublin and the offender "summoned to show cause" for the deception.[77]   In 1726 wardens of the merchants of Newcastle-upon-Tyne seized goods "foreyn bought and fforreyn sold," apparently regardless of consequences, and the company unanimously agreed to pay the expence of "any action or Suit att law commenced or thereafter to be commenced" against its wardens because of the seizures.[78] In 1773 the tin-plate workers in the city of London maintained their search with considerable diligence,[79] while the first quarter of the nineteenth century found city companies like the saddlers,[80] the goldsmiths and the apothecaries still appropriating as worthless or defective, wares condemned by their respective searchers; but this zealous exercise of the prerogative seems to have been exceptional even among the metropolitan organisations. The clothworkers of the city dubious in 1708 of their right under "their charter and otherwise concerning the seizing of cloths which are badwrought,"[81] by 1749 had become convinced that if they exercised their "right of search," it would no longer tend either to the better skill of the art or mystery or to the profit of the company, and it was consequently abandoned.[82]

This particular company openly repudiated the search, but others of their city, notably the grocers had discontinued its practice years before, for the by-laws which had upheld their right of search had been declared obsolete in 1711.[83] Elsewhere, men who would "no

[75] Scott, *History of the Wheelwrights' Company*, p. 60.
[76] Stewart, *History of the Gold and Silver Wyre-Drawers' Company*, p. 87.
[77] *Royal Society of Antiquaries of Ireland*, vol. 41, ser. 6, pt. i, p. 33.
[78] *Surtees Society Publications*, vol. 93, p. 253.
[79] Unwin, *Gilds & Companies of London*, p. 348.
[80] As late as 1822 sixteen saddles made by a saddler of Holburn, and appropriated by officials of the saddlers' company as worthless, were condemned by a jury of city saddlers and the manufacturer summoned to show cause why the confiscated saddles should not be destroyed. The saddler appeared before the jury and denied the company's right to destroy the saddles in question. His denial, however, failed to save his saddles, which the company caused to be rendered unfit for use. Sherwell, *History of the Saddlers' Company*, p. 142.
[81] *Parliamentary Papers*, 1884, pt. ii, p. 675.
[82] *The City Livery Companies and Their Corporate Property*, p. 159.
[83] *Parliamentary Papers*, 1884, pt. 2, p. 147.
In publishing in 1768 in one of their city papers, an advertisement, offering a reward for the discovery of frauds in their trade (the frauds referring, it is supposed, to smuggled imports of Irish soap and candles), the chandlers and soap boilers of Bristol seem to have given public evidence of their waning power to supervise and control the conditions under which the commodities

serche haue" [84] refused to have it, and there was no power at hand to impose it upon them.[85] Borough authorities of that epoch evidently considered it no part of their office to help gilds "shutt in unfree shops," [86] or to disfranchise handicraftsmen who refused to submit to gild espionage,[87] or compel them to pay gild tribute for breaches of gild law.[88] The search no longer ranked as the laudable custom of earlier, and for old-fashioned gildsmen, apparently happier days. These were the days of new-fashioned gildsmen concerned in keeping from competitors the secrets of the machinery [89] they had installed in their work-rooms, and of independent manufacturers who wanted no officials in their factories prepared to destroy articles not up to the mark, or to delay their export until these bore the stamp of their approval. The survival of a past method of control, gild supervision had no place in the system under which modern products were being manufactured. That system was concerned with removing the obstacles in the way of free trade [90] not in placing them there.

under their jurisdiction were being marketed. Latimer, *Annals of Bristol in the 17th Century*, p. 384.

[84] *Records of Norwich*, vol. i, p. 93.

[85] In 1614 the chief justice of England condemned the charter given the cooks of London on the ground that in allowing the men of the craft unlimited power to search, seize food stuffs and dispose of them as they pleased, they could profit at the expense of their competitors. *Index to Remembrancia*, p. 97.

[86] *The Merchant Adventurers of Newcastle-upon-Tyne, Surtees Society Publications*, vol. 93, p. 158.

[87] Latimer, *Annals of Bristol in the 17th Century*, p. 376.

[88] The wonder is that the gilds contrived to enforce their power of search after the courts had decided that the power to seize defective material under the authority derived from a crown charter was contrary to law. That decision was rendered in 1600 against the London dyers seizing poorly-dyed cloth. *Case of Waltham v. Austin. Parliamentary Papers*, 1884, pt. ii, p. 14.

[89] In 1701 the London gold and silver wyre-drawers got a man to submit to their rule on condition that such of their officers as used "Engines" be kept out of his work-rooms. Stewart, *History of the Gold & Silver Wyre-Drawers Co.*, p. 87.

[90] "The Bristol Chamber of Commerce, Trade and Manufactures" was organised in 1823 for the removal of obstacles which tended to prevent the growth of local trade. *Parl. Papers*, vol. 24, p. 1208.

III

SOME LAST ACTS OF THE GILDS

Whatever the cause may have been, it seems evident that by the middle of the eighteenth century the English gilds had, for the most part, lost their power to control trade as well as industry. Indeed, for many that stage had been reached by the end of the seventeenth century. For example, a minute, dated August 18, 1687, in the court book of the London grocers refers to their organisation as being then merely a "nursery of charities and seminary of good citizens."[1] The merchant taylors seem to have lost their interest in the work-a-day world by 1689, for in that year they went so far as to order their court to "examine of what use and benefit the yeomanry are . . . and what advantage they have brought or damage they have done" to the occupation.[2] Two years later the "Wardens of the Yeomanry" were dispensed with altogether.[3] Again, by the early eighteenth century, city mercers had so far severed their connection with trade as to exclude from the company's courts, its committees and elections, and in addition had declared ineligible to the office of master or wardens, the member who should be "appointed a workman," or be given any employment or "place of profit" in the organisation.[4] Merchant companies in communities like Newcastle-upon-Tyne[5] and Dublin renounced their control over local trade after they realised the futility of expending further effort to enforce it. The mercers of Sandwich, seemingly reluctant to yield their place and power in the community, were forced to do this eventually. Their company spent its last days in contending against unscrupulous officials who were not only withholding money they had collected from members but were also "going to contributors . . . and Diswading them from paying their several contributions" still due the company. In order to attract new members, the company offered its freedom for forty shillings "together with other customary charges," but met with little success in that direction. The last act recorded in the company's history was the choosing of officers for the "Year Ensuing." This leads to the inference that there was not even a meeting for the officers to preside over.[6]

---

[1] *Parliamentary Papers,* 1884, pt. ii, p. 138.
[2] Herbert, *Twelve Great Livery Companies,* vol. ii, p. 409.
[3] *Parliamentary Papers,* 1884, pt. ii, p. 416.
[4] *Charters of Mercers' Company,* p. 95.
[5] *Supra,* pp. 150–1.
[6] *Additional MS., B. M.* No. 27462, ff. 150, 161.

Handicraft organisations like the clothworkers of London also yielded to the inevitable and renounced their powers of control. Still others, notably the glovers of Shrewsbury, made desperate efforts to keep going, but the desperation which inspired the efforts, probably defeated the end the company sought to achieve. In prosecuting interlopers and in merry-making, the company dissipated funds which could never be recouped because gild members refused to pay the penalties attached to the infringing of gild rules. In addition, the misappropriation, by the representatives of a deceased official, of certain sums which had been entrusted to him, helped to bring to an end an especially privileged organisation.[7] Still other companies were kept going a while longer by reducing the fines charged for the infraction of the rules. One instance of the sort is that of the barbers of Oxford,[8] who, in 1771 accepted one pound and one shilling, in settlement of a penalty of ten pounds due from one of their number for "keeping a journeyman beyond the Time without Leaue from the Master."[9] Likewise various metropolitan companies of this epoch "do accept of forty shillings" and even less to encourage persons to enter their ranks.[10] Again, by 1791, the mercers of Shrewsbury[11] had reduced their membership dues from forty to sixteen pounds and eight shillings, and instead of the twenty pounds charged gild members in 1800 the Chester skinners and feltmakers exacted only three pounds and four shillings in 1830.[12] In Ludlow, the stitchmen seem to have reduced gild fees for admission and also the penalties assessed for misdemeanours; yet they failed either to keep their hold over old members or to attract new ones. After the middle of the eighteenth century the quarterly meetings were discontinued for lack of attendance. Apprentices were no longer being enrolled, and the funds, instead of being used to pay the expenses incurred in regulating the trade, furnished feasts for the society, which by the early nineteenth century had evidently become one of good fellows only.[13] Other organisations seem to have disappeared with the demand

---

[7] *Shropshire Archaeol. & Nat. History Soc. Trans.*, vol. x, p. 36.

[8] *Oxford Barbers, MS. Bodleian Lib.*, No. 5, f. 54.

[9] After 1743 the wheelwrights of London are said to have ceased to collect fines for offenses committed against the rules. Scott, *Hist. of the Wheelwrights' Company*, p. 23.

[10] Noble, *History of the Ironmongers' Company*, p. 341.

[11] *Trans. Shropshire Archaeol. and Nat. Hist.*, vol. viii, p. 409.

[12] *Journal Chester and N. Wales Architect., and Historic Soc.*, n. s., vol. 21, p. 92. By the time that the glovers of Chester raised the fee for admission into their company to a point where possible members were deterred from entering (*Parl. Papers*, vol. 26, p. 2635) or the drapers of Shrewsbury refused to admit them on practically any terms (*Ibid.*, vol. 25), the end of the régime of those two gilds for economic good or ill had probably been reached. However, the drapers' was the only one of the Shrewsbury gilds to survive as late as 1898; it had contrived to retain its Hall, its old chest of books and other documents and certain property which it diverted to charitable purposes. *Trans. Shropshire Archaeological & Natural History Society*, vol. viii, 2nd series, p. 175.

[13] *Journ. British Archaeol. Assoc.*, vol. 24, pp. 330–1.

for the product under their domination. Toward the end of the seventeenth century girdles ceased to be the fashion and girdlers had to find other employment for their energies. By 1760 the London girdlers could scarcely find members willing to hold office in the company.[14] In other localities the decline of an industry brought to ruin the organisation invested with its control. With the passing of the clothing industry of Worcester went the city's famous clothing company. By 1711 its members confessed to being "far in debt," a condition they attributed to the admission of strangers to work in Worcester, for previously their company had the exclusive right in this field.[15] Another aspect may be found in the fact that the end of the Nottingham tanners coincided with the disappearance of bark from the neighbourhood.[16] That company appointed its last master in 1808 and thirty years later sold in the borough's market place what remained of its old hall. Still other organisations vanished, leaving no trace of the end. In the "Great Order Books" of the borough of Beverley, ordinances regarding local "Occupations" or craft gilds receive mention only up to 1728.[17] In 1740 the records of the mercers' company of Derby break off abruptly.[18] After the middle of the eighteenth century the gilds of Norwich seem to have ceased from troubling the economic life of the community,[19] while after 1788 no further entries were made in the book of the coopers of Newcastle-upon-Hull.[20] The Bristol organisations silently disappeared during the closing years of the century. The coopers' hall was offered for sale by auction in 1785, and the smiths' one year later. By that time, too, there were not enough weavers in the city to justify their maintaining a hall.[21] Attendance at the meetings of the merchant taylors dwindled rap-

---

[14] Smythe, *History of the Girdlers' Company*, p. 129.

[15] *Trans. Architectural Soc.*, vol. xv, p. 336.

[16] Wylie, *Old & New Nottingham*, p. 288. The sale of the Hall of the bakers of Coventry in 1697 was followed ten years later by the dissolution of the company. *Parliamentary Papers*, 1884, pt. i, p. 16.

[17] *Historical MSS. Commission Report*, Beverley, p. 7.

[18] *Derbyshire Archaeological & Natural History Soc. Journal*, vol. xv, p. 153. By 1680 membership in this company had practically been closed to newcomers. In that year it was resolved that for the future "noe p'son or persons whatsoever of any of the severall Trades now united into the said company of Mercers wch are not at this prsent agreed withall," shall at any time hereafter be admitted "to any composition except such as are prsent traders in this Burrow." The wardens were accordingly instructed to serve notice of the adoption of this resolution so that no person who "shall come and infringe th' libertyes of the said company shall be unwarned of the danger of the penalty the Law provides." *Ibid.*, p. 131. According to an agreement reached by the cordwainers of Coventry at a meeting held in 1747, persons who were unwilling to attend the company were allowed to withdraw, while those who refused to pay the customary assessments were voted out and thereafter excluded altogether. *MS. Coventry Corporation Muniments*, under date of 1748.

[19] Webb, *English Local Government*, vol. ii, pt. 2, p. 537, note.

[20] Lambert, *Two Thousand Years of Gild Life*, p. 295.

[21] Latimer, *17th Century Annals*, p. 470.

idly. In 1787 there were only seven, while in 1815 there was only one member left to attend a meeting.[22] In a sense, it is surprising that the gilds of Bristol maintained a footing so many years after 1703, when, in revising the city ordinances, those levelled at strangers were ordered "left out" altogether by city officials who probably favoured a policy of non-interference with newcomers.[23] Not that the announcement of the policy guaranteed its immediate enforcement; evidently the gilds of Bristol had to be reckoned with. However, when the civic authorities of Kingston-upon-Hull withdrew their support from local gilds the gilds had to go. The only organisations to maintain their hold in the early decades of the nineteenth century were those favoured by the municipalities, since at that late date those bodies only could keep non-freemen from sharing in local trade. For example, in 1821 York succeeded in having declared valid in law the custom that only a freeman might sell by retail within the liberties,[24] although six years later the city's mercantile company failed to prove its corporate right to control local trade in the court of law in which it brought suit against a non-free druggist for setting up in business in York.[25] Moreover by that time the boroughs were evidently averse to having the question aired in the law courts. In 1834 a certain Mr.

---

[22] Latimer, *18th Century Annals*, p. 181. In 1832 this company seems to have been dissolved as appears from a Memorial which was addressed to the "Lords Commissioners of his Majesty's Treasury" by certain individuals who had "under consideration" a Memorial drawn up at an earlier date "respecting certain lands supposed to have escheated to the Crown on the dissolution of the M. Tailors'" company. Fox and Taylor, *Merchant Taylors of Bristol*, p. 141.

[23] Latimer, *17th Century Annals*, p. 495.

[24] *The Mayor of York v. Welbank*, 4 *Barnewall & Alderson*, 438. However, when in 1722, the common council of Deal meditated prosecuting a Scotch pedlar for "selling goods" in the town "on a considerable scale," they were advised that Deal "being a new Corporation lately made and having no prescription to make Bylaws," it was questionable "how far they can make Bylaws to exclude persons not free from using any Trade there." Webb, *Local Government*, vol. i, p. 399, note, quoted from *MS. Records Deal Corporation.* In 1773 an adverse decision of the courts seems to have deprived the corporation of Berwick of its right to prevent non-burgesses from trading within corporate limits. *Ibid.*, pt. ii, p. 510.

In publishing, in 1768, in one of their city papers, an advertisement, offering a reward for the "discovery of frauds in their trade (the frauds referring, it is supposed, to smuggled imports of Irish soap and candles), the chandlers and soap boilers of Bristol gave notice of their powerlessness to control the conditions under which the articles under their jurisdiction were being marketed. Latimer, *Annals of Bristol in the 17th Century*, p. 384.

[25] *The Merchants' Company of York v. Harwood.* According to the decision rendered by Mr. Justice Bayley in that case in 1827, the language of the company's charter was inconsistent with the custom set out. It was a charter of regulations against strangers intromitting without being subject to the control of the company, but was not a charter which compelled every person to become free. Besides the company failed to prove "a custom from time immemorial," which it ought to have proved. Sellers, *The York Mercers and Merchant Adventurers, Surtees Society Publications*, vol. 129, p. 316. Printed from the *York Courant* for April 17, 1827.

Mickleston had the hardihood, not only to sue the borough of Shrewsbury for exacting from him an imposition, or "Tentorshipp," as the record has it, but in addition did "endeavour to make void their charter," whereupon the borough "gave him his burgesship to be quiet." [26] However, when a borough of the standing of Shrewsbury was reduced to such straits, it was apparently time for a higher power to intervene and end a situation which had clearly become impossible for all parties concerned.

Shortly after this Shrewsbury episode, the passing of the Municipal Reform Bill, according to which every inhabitant might keep a shop for the sale of lawful wares and merchandise within any borough, left neither to boroughs nor gilds the right to confer citizenship nor to use a trade or industry within local boundaries. [27] That the mercers of Shrewsbury realised their end had come, is clear from the entry, inscribed in their records under date of 1836, which laconically states that "By the Statute 5 & 6 William 4. cap. 76, entitled 'an act to provide for the regulation of Municipal Corporations in England and Wales,' the privileges of the Company came to an end." [28] However, the property amassed through the centuries which was still at the disposal of the company was not "distributed to the Combrethren" until about forty-two years later, when the company was dissolved for all time. [29] Other companies wound up their affairs during the year which followed the passage of the act. For instance, at two meetings held in 1836, the butchers of Carlisle [30] agreed to divide equally between the company's members or their representatives, the balance of about six hundred pounds left in their treasury after deducting the arrears due from individual members. The barbers of Oxford, however, deferred taking similar action until 1859. In that year, because of "such smallness in the number of members" together with "other circumstances" the dissolution of the company was agreed upon. Accordingly, certain "undersigned" members let it be known that, with the consent of the Vice Chancellor of Oxford University they "Do hereby severally and respectfully agree to dis-

---

[26] Hibbert, *Influence and Development of English Gilds,* p. 155.

[27] 5 & 6 William IV, c. 76, § 14. London was exempted from the operation of the provisions of this act; yet after its enactment, few of the city companies attempted to enforce any of their by-laws in restraint of trade. *Municipal Corporations Commission Report,* 1837, vol. 25, pp. 55, 88, 141, 201, *et passim.*

[28] They had called a halt to their prosecution of foreigners, while awaiting the result of the act then before Parliament. Hibbert, *op. cit.,* p. 136.

[29] *Trans. Shropshire Archaeol. & Nat. Hist. Soc.,* vol. viii, p. 410.

[30] *Municipal Records,* p. 262. The butchers of Newcastle-upon-Tyne were apparently divided on the expediency of selling their corporate property and dividing the proceeds. Indeed a considerable number refused outright to sanction such a proceeding. It was accordingly decided to continue to subscribe as heretofore to such charities as the company had been subscribing to, and to divide among the members any balance left in the treasury at the end of each year. *Archaeologia Aeliana,* 3rd series, vol. 14, p. 10.

solve the company from this time forth and to divide the funds in such manner as may be determined by a majority of the company at any Half Yearly or other meeting." [31]   The hammermen of Ludlow, apparently with no funds left to distribute, drifted on aimlessly for many years after the passage of the act of 1835, until in 1887 only a few members were left to represent the old fraternity. [32]

In this connexion it is worth noting, that while the gilds are usually credited with obstructing local trade and industry, the act, as its name implies, really holds the boroughs responsible for such tactics. "Because of a certain custom," reads this Municipal Corporations Act, "which prevailed in divers cities, towns and boroughs and of certain by-laws made that no person not being free of a city, town or borough or of certain gilds, mysteries or trading companies within the same . . . shall keep any shop or place for putting to show or sale any or certain wares thereafter, notwithstanding any such custom or by-law, every person in any borough may keep any shop for the sale of all lawful wares and merchandises within any borough whatsoever." Moreover the commission appointed to inquire into the conditions which existed in the boroughs prior to the passage of the act, found the trade of a borough like Beverley restricted to freemen when local gilds had evidently ceased from troubling. [33]   Furthermore, non-free shopkeepers and artisans were, from certain accounts, compelled to purchase the freedom of Norwich down to 1835, years after trade organisations are mentioned in corporation records. [34]   The fact that some boroughs had done away with trade restrictions within their precincts long before they were forced by the government to do so, proves possibly that the boroughs realised their rights as well as their responsibilities in the matter. After 1782 the freemen of Maidstone possessed no economic privileges which were denied to outsiders. [35]   In the charter which was conferred upon the borough of Northampton in 1796, all enactments in restriction of trade

---

[31] *MS. Bodleian Library*, No. 5. As late as 1872 a company like the weavers, fullers and shearmen of Exeter still held an annual meeting in their Hall, elected a master and wardens with due formality, but apparently limited their activity to distributing the funds in their treasury to various charitable organisations. Cotton, *The Ancient Gilds of Exeter, Trans. Devon Association*, vol. v, p. 138. The gilds of Chester seem also to have lingered on; the tanners for instance, registered admissions into their gild until 1877. *Historical MSS. Comm. Rep. viii*, p. 403.

[32] *Transactions Shropshire Archaeological & Natural History Soc.*, vol. xi, p. 322.

[33] *Parliamentary Papers*, vol. 25, p. 1457.

[34] Webb, *Local Government*, vol. ii, pt. ii, p. 537, note. After the early years of the nineteenth century the borough of Wokingham in Berkshire made no further effort to enforce such of its bylaws as had given freemen exclusive trade privileges. *Parliamentary Papers*, vol. 23, p. 2939. So too, when the Quarter Sessions court at Newport, in Monmouthshire, were discontinued, anybody in the borough could engage in trade or industry. *Ibid.*, p. 344.

[35] *Parliamentary Papers*, vol. 25, p. 763.

and industry were omitted, it is said, at the request of the corporation.[36]

It had taken a long time for an English borough to put into practise theories current a full century and a half earlier, which advocated the freeing of local trade and industry. Only after experiencing the truth of the declaration enunciated by the courts as early as 1619,[37] to the effect, that corporations in the towns and inferior cities were seldom of good use, but rather disturbed the good government of such communities, did Kingston-upon-Hull rid herself of those disturbers of her peace.[38] Preston evidently learned the lesson in 1772 with the prosecution of "Merchant Baines" and his subsequent withdrawal from the borough's jurisdiction,[39] for thereafter non-freemen were encouraged to ply their trades within the precincts of Preston, to the doubling of her population in something like two decades.[40] Just what part the gilds of Preston played in the process which spelled their ruin does not appear.[41] But the better part of a century elapsed between the time when the executive body of Bristol decided to free local trade and their action upon this decision, by eliminating the trade organisations which stood in the way.[42] Gilds of a borough's own creation were not to be downed in a day or even in a year, or two or three.

[36] *Ibid.*, pp. 1968–69. In 1791 the corporation of Youghal was told that strangers would establish themselves in business in their precincts if certain tolls were abolished; whereupon for a certain period thereafter all goods bought before entering the liberties were declared free from the "Clerk of the Market's dues." Four years later, such bylaws as had prohibited Papists from using local trades and handicrafts were repealed and declared null and void. *Council Book*, p. 535.

[37] *Lansdowne MS., B. M.* 162, f. 195. This was the verdict rendered in the case of the Taylors and Clothworkers of Ipswich, when a remedy was sought for the ills which had overtaken Ipswich's clothing industry, in order that so great an industry might not be concentrated in the hands of one corporation to make "profitt off their ill workmanship."

[38] Later an attempt to revive the gilds of Kingston-upon-Hull was discouraged and her flourishing state compared with stagnant York and Beverley, where business was at a standstill, because in the interest of local gilds, strangers were still excluded from the liberties. Hadley, *History of Kingston-upon-Hull*, p. 829.

[39] Hardwick, *History of Preston*, p. 287.

[40] Wilcockson, *The Preston Gild Merchant*, p. 40.

[41] The Preston mercantile society seems to have paid the cost of prosecuting the Mr. Baines in question. Hardwick, *op. cit.* p. 286. Certain other boroughs evidently failed to realise the ill effects likely to follow further restraint of trade, and in consequence lost out in the economic race. The prosperity of Ripon is said to have departed with the trades and handicrafts which settled in places offering greater opportunity to thrive because free from restrictive regulations.

[42] At Bristol, the year in which the ordinances levelled at strangers were omitted from civic records, by order of city officials, the penalty assessed upon interlopers was raised to twenty pounds upon each conviction. Latimer, *Annals of Bristol in the Eighteenth Century*, p. 21. In 1727 the amalgamated mercers and linen-drapers of the city enforced their monopoly with the help of the city council. Three years later that body upheld local carpenters in prohibiting non-members, whether masters or journeymen, from using that

For gilds which were created by the crown or parliament the process proved even more complicated and therefore slower of accomplishment.[43] The state was less ready than the boroughs to free trade from the clutches of the "societies of merchants and handicrafts" which as early as 1622 were suspected of working for their own "private Gain and particular Advantage," and therefore tended rather to "the hurt of the publique than to its profit." [44] It is true that by 1650 this "suspition" had become enough of a certainty to cause forward-looking state dignitaries to ponder whether it might not be "necessary to give way to a more open and free trade than that of Companies and Societies and in what manner it is fittest to be done." [45] Little, on the whole, seems actually to have been done by the state of that period to free the internal trade of the country.[46] Cromwell and his successors evidently followed the example set them by their predecessors and incorporated industrial organisations [47] in various sections of the realm. Neither did early eighteenth-century authorities free serge and worsted weaving following the finding of the parliamentary committee charged with inquiring into the deplorable conditions complained of by the men engaged in the art. The committee in question found the weavers' allegations true, yet they advised that the trade ought to be free and not restrained.[48] However, economists of that epoch continued to advocate the freeing of trade; one in particular pointedly denounced every sort of restriction of trade as "nought." [49] Another went so far as to hold trade organisations up to derision by propounding a certain set of questions to a supposititious burgess

craft within city limits under pain of paying ten shillings a day. In 1732 a committee was appointed to determine whether the fees charged for admission into city companies were exorbitant, but no action seems to have followed the appointment. *Ibid.* p. 181. Apparently not until 1792 could all residents of Bristol ply their callings in the city unmolested by the authorities. Webb, *Local Government,* ii, pt. 2, p. 449.

[43] On the ground that they were a corporation by prescription, dating from the earliest times, the goldsmiths of London refused the Municipal Corporations Commission the information they asked for in 1833. Prideaux, *Memorials of the Goldsmiths' Company,* vol. ii, p. 319.

[44] Cunningham, *Growth of English Industry & Commerce,* vol. i, p. 217; vol. ii, p. 116.

[45] Inderwick, *Interregnum,* pp. 74–5.

[46] By the passage of the act of 21 James I, c. ix, according to which, any person could sell all or any Welsh cloths, cottons, "Frizes," . . . to any person or persons who, by the laws or statutes of the Realm might lawfully buy such cloths, the state freed trade in Welsh cloth from the restraints which the drapers of Shrewsbury had imposed upon its sale.

[47] A charter incorporating the Needle-makers was issued by Cromwell in 1658, and confirmed by King Charles II in 1664. *Index to Remembrancia,* p. 104. In 1693 William & Mary incorporated the soap-makers and chandlers of Bristol. *State Papers Domestic, William & Mary,* vol. v, No. 269.

[48] Dunlop, *English Apprenticeship,* p. 237. Quoted from *Commons Journals,* vol. 13, p. 783.

[49] This opinion was expressed by Sir Joshua Child in 1708. *Merchant Adventurers of Newcastle-upon-Tyne, Surtees Society Publications,* vol. 93, p. xliii.

of Newcastle-upon-Tyne and eliciting answers couched so as to make membership in an English trade gild appear a hindrance rather than a help to Englishmen of the period.[50] When invoked, the courts upheld free trade as the birthright of every English subject.[51] In addition, the activity of townsmen directed towards downing local by-laws showed which way trade winds were blowing in certain boroughs,[52] where gildsmen, in overriding gild laws, did their part to bring into disrepute laws of their own making.[53] Finally, the many forces working to free trade and industry, forced upon the government the conviction that both trade and industry ought to be free, and the statute directed toward freeing them found its way upon the statute-book.

[50] To the question as to what "you get by your Companies," the burgess was made to answer "the advantage of paying fees for admission, fees for continuance; fines for taking apprentices, fines for employing journeymen, fines for getting a wife" when friendship was needed to buy a frock, and to meet the "expense of repairing the meeting-house." What he got with all these "blessed privileges," was "being plagued with serving on juries," besides "losing" his time and "getting drunk" at elections, not to mention "grumbling at guilds from one seven years' end to another." Collier, "The Poor Burgesses Catechism," Essay on Charters, lect. xiii, p. 97.

[51] Case of the Clothworkers of Ipswich, 12 Jacobi, Godbolt, 2503. The Ipswich clothworkers lost out in this case—one which they had brought against a local tailor who persisted in plying his trade without having joined their company—because, in the finding of the court, the king might make corporations and grant them the right to make ordinances for the government of any trade but that thereby they cannot make a monopoly for that is to take away free trade which is the birthright of every subject.

[52] In the early nineteenth century, Wells was the scene, it is said, of rioting almost nightly when numbers of persons paraded up and down the streets carrying clubs and crying, "Down with the Byelaws." Parliamentary Papers, vol. 24, p. 1368.

[53] By the beginning of the eighteenth century scarcely a meeting of the butchers of Newcastle-upon-Tyne seems to have been held without a quarrel over the collection of debts, which one member owed another, or over purchases made by parties of twos or threes who went into the country for the purpose. Archaeologia Aeliana, series 3, vol. 14, p. 21.

IV

SUMMARY AND CONCLUSION—THE CAUSES OF THE END OF THE GILDS

In the preceding pages we have traced the gradual weakening and the loss finally by the gilds of the chief powers upon which their system rested. In the beginning the different gilds had been organised for the purpose of controlling particular trades and industries, but in order to make such control effective it was found necessary to devise a system of regulation to which all who practised a calling were to conform. Scarcely a quarter of a century after the barbers of Bristol had secured for themselves the "government of their craft," they appeared before city authorities with charges that many "unlearned" were encroaching upon their craft and asked as a means of stopping the practice which they said threatened to destroy their craft, to be allowed to elect annually from among themselves two surveyors whom they might arm with powers sufficient to present to the proper gild officials, "all manner of defaults" which they might discover. It is interesting to note, that chief among such "defaults" they evidently reckoned that of masters taking an apprentice for "less than the term of seven years."[1] Manifestly to keep control over their occupation, these fifteenth-century barbers established a system of inspection, the basis of which they held to be the enforcing of a rigid apprenticeship. Moreover, that seventeenth-century organisations deemed equally essential to their welfare, the enforcement of the service, is evident from appeals for leave to incorporate it as an integral part of their régime. Appeals of the sort were issued not only by a group like London clockmakers, in establishing a new organisation for the purpose of fulfilling their destiny as arbiters of the art of clockmaking[2] but also, by the cutlers of Hallamshire, a company

[1] *Little Red Book*, vol. ii, pp. 135-7. "And if any do the contrary that he be presented by the surveyors of the same craft . . . and be amerced in 20 s. to wit 10 s. to the common profit and 10 s. to the Contribution of the craft above said without any pardon."

[2] Overall, *History of the Clockmakers' Company*, p. 59. When the powers conferred by their crown charter proved ineffectual in preventing unskillful and unscrupulous practice, the company endeavoured to have its members finance parliamentary incorporation, but failed in the endeavour. After the framework knitters had obtained an act of parliament regulating framework knitting—an art not in vogue at the time the Elizabethan act made the seven-years' service a prerequisite to the practice of a trade or industry—the company inserted in its by-laws a provision making apprenticeship a requirement to membership in the craft. Felkin, *History of Machine-Wrought Hosiery and Lace Manufactures*, p. 68.

of established standing,[3] when they asked for parliamentary incorporation in order to prevent their workmen from taking as many apprentices as they considered themselves free to take and for as long a term of years as they pleased. Apparently, no matter what the source of their authority, gilds of the later period could not inculcate in their own members a proper regard for this fundamental requirement of gild economy and consequently failed to impress it upon outsiders.[4]

In the first quarter of the seventeenth century as in the last, master gildsmen themselves not only employed persons who had served little or no apprenticeship to their occupation but they took far more apprentices than gild law allowed,[5] either for their own use or to turn over to others.[6] Likewise, they wilfully neglected to enroll apprentices in gild records, sometimes even refused them their freedom after they had served the required term;[7] nor did gildsmen show a greater respect for gild ruling in other particulars. Evidence is not lacking of brethren so "contentious" as to disregard rules concerned with the making of a masterpiece,[8] or to refuse to hold office,[9] or to pay their gild quarterage[10] or other

[3] Hunter, *Hallamshire*, p. 219.

[4] *Supra*, pp. 157–8.

[5] Although the cutlers of Hallamshire received parliamentary incorporation in 1624 largely to regulate the taking of apprentices, by 1711 the company had cause to complain of freemen taking unto themselves so very many apprentices and turning out vast quantities of wares of all sorts which had to be sold for scarce half the rate at which they were formerly sold, to the ruin of the company. Hunter, *Hallamshire*, p. 219. In 1598 the coopers of Hull were admonished to keep no more than two apprentices at once. Lambert, *Two Thousand Years of Gild Life*, p. 287. In 1683 the court of the wheelwrights' company of London forbade any member not of the Court of Assistants to have or keep more than one apprentice at any one time. Only during the last year of the service of such apprentice could his master take another. Scott, *History of the Wheelwrights' Company*, p. 58.

[6] Already in 1559 the drapers of London had cause to denounce certain members who set apprentices over to other craftsmen, contrary to the ordinances of their company and to its decay. Johnson, *History of the Drapers' Company*, vol. ii, p. 169. By 1672 members of the tylers and plasterers of Bristol were guilty of binding apprentices and then turning them over to non-freemen. *Additional MS.* 28100, *B. M.*, f. 16. A decade later London wheelwrights were frobidden to take a "Turnover" as an apprentice without leave of the Court of Assistants, upon pain of forfeiting ten pounds. Scott, *History of the Wheelwrights' Company*, p. 59.

[7] In 1666 a feltmaker of Shrewsbury was guilty of this offense; whereupon the city officials bade the feltmaker's company admit the apprentice and the mayor gave him "the oath of a Freeman of the said Company." *Shropshire Archaeol. & Nat. Hist. Soc. Trans.*, vol. xi, p. 187. In 1663 a bricklayer of Kingston-upon-Hull was admonished not to "give or sell his Apprentice any part of his tearme in paine of five pounds fyne." Lambert, *Two Thousand Years of Gild Life*, p. 281.

[8] *Index to Remembrancia*, p. 98.

[9] In 1747 among the butchers of Newcastle the penalty for refusing to hold office when elected was two pounds. *Archaeologia Aeliana*, 3rd series, vol. 14, p. 13. At about the same epoch very few of the standing committees of the goldsmiths of London it seems "do of late years attend the business thereof to the great delay and hindrance as well as the prejudice of the

charges for which they were liable or the penalties attached to the infraction of gild law.[11] Many openly worked for, or with non-gildsmen, or employed outsiders instead of gildsmen,[12] and frequently turned out articles made of inferior material.[13] They did not hesitate to open two shops [14] or to replenish their depleted stocks with materials purchased from strangers,[15] or even to "colour" their goods when the opportunity offered itself. In short, gildsmen took advantage of the times no matter how peaceful or "distracted," to disregard most rules considered vital to the maintenance of the system. Moreover, members who thus infringed gild law and order naturally tried to keep the evidence of their lawlessness from gild authorities. For this reason, they denied gild inspectors access to their premises, or assaulted those who contrived to force an entrance, or indeed even sued for "trespass" the organisations which authorised the trespass. No wonder that in these circumstances gild officials lost much of their zeal for enforcing the office of search, which was frequently suspended, too, because funds were lacking, or the times unpropitious, and gradually broke down

company's affairs." Prideaux, *Memorials of the Goldsmiths' Company,* vol. ii, p. 233. In 1811 a barber of Oxford was fined five pounds for the use of the barbers' company for refusing to serve the office of master, after being duly elected, *Bodleian MS.,* f. 92.

[10] In 1679 wheelwrights of London who refused to pay their gild quarterage had their goods seized under warrants issued by the officials of their company. Scott, *History of the Wheelwrights' Company,* p. 56. In 1703 officers of the London glaziers were authorised to prosecute in the Court of Exchequer or other Court at their discretion such "Members as owe Quarteriage." Ashdown, *History of the Worshipful Co. of Glaziers,* p. 70.

[11] In 1632 a "course withall by law" was taken against a city clockmaker "for not paying his Contribution towards the Companies' charter, Ordinaunces and other charges according to his promiss." Overall, *History of the Clockmakers' Co.,* p. 15. In 1735 the bricklayers of Hull were forbidden to employ fellow bricklayers who refused to pay what they owed the company. Lambert, *op. cit.,* p. 282.

[12] An order issued by the Newcastle goldsmiths about the middle of the eighteenth century forbade a goldsmith free of their company to work for or with any person or persons who were not free thereof. *Archaeologia Aeliana,* vol. xv, iii, p. 426.

[13] Smythe, *History of the Girdlers' Company,* p. 87. One of the assistants of that company was found guilty of making children's girdles of poor material and fined for the offense.

[14] In 1788 the barber-surgeons of Shrewsbury took action against a certain Mr. Hulme for opening two shops. *Trans. Shropshire Archaeol. & Natural History Soc.* vol. v, p. 290.

[15] Sentiment seems to have changed considerably since the time when a London alderman was heard abusing strangers for selling fish, saying openly for all who passed to hear, that he preferred to "let a fishmonger in the city make twenty shillings by him than a ribald stranger twenty pence." Riley, *Memorials of London,* p. 469. Indeed, townsmen who could not trade with aliens within the franchises of a city were apt to gravitate outside to meet them on their ground. In 1464 drapers of London were going to "nygh places of the ffraunchises of this Cite that is to say in to Southwark, Westmynster, Saynt Johnsstrete and other places here adjoynaunt . . . to meete with foreyns," a practice which the authorities tried to stop. Johnson, *History of the Drapers' Company,* vol. i, p. 261.

altogether. In addition, if the testimony of sixteenth-century metropolitan gilds can be credited, the system of gild inspection broke down largely because all gildsmen who practised specific callings no longer belonged to the organisation in control and on that ground could claim exemption from its jurisdiction. It seems true that various city companies attempted to end this anomalous condition of affairs by forcing men who practised a specific occupation to join the organisation in control, but no great reform seems to have come of the effort. The custom of admitting to membership or to office, persons who had no real connexion with the particular trade or industry with which the organisation was identified, had evidently become too deeply rooted in gild economy to be eradicated at this late date.[16] In admitting men, apparently at a very early period, by redemption [17] and by patrimony, gild procedure itself furnished a way by which members could evade serving an apprenticeship. This procedure contributed in the end to the causes which brought about the ruin of the system as a whole, by opening up the offices as well as the ranks to men who, not having themselves served an apprenticeship to a calling, naturally had no particular concern in employing only those who filled the requirements in that regard. Then, too, the diversity of interests which were represented in many organisations of the period made more difficult the task of maintaining an effective control over them all. For example, so far as one can judge, the clothworkers of London did not openly condemn their right of search as no longer tending to the better skill of that art until the middle of the eighteenth century. Yet from the company's rise in the sixteenth century there were signs of the obstacles in the way of its power to control the different interests included in the corporation, in spite of its purpose early avowed, of furthering the common interest. Coincident with its rise there was revealed in this particular corporation, admittedly founded for the good of the "handy Trade," [18] a mercantile group, guilty of evading as strenuously as the handicraft groups sought to impose it, a system of inspection considered necessary to the

---

[16] Toward the end of the sixteenth century influence was brought to bear upon parliament to prevent the gilds admitting persons who followed different callings apparently with little result. Strype, *Stow's Survey of London, Book* v, p. 252.

[17] As early as 1344 a "strangeman" could "buy his freedom" in the girdlers' gild of London. Riley, *Memorials*, p. 217. It seems true, however, that redemptioners were sometimes subjected to certain restrictions upon their admission into a gild. According to a rule adopted by the merchant gild of Newcastle-upon-Tyne in 1520, a man "comyng in by redempcon" was neither "to ship woll ne skyn" nor to "have no prentices." A few years earlier "no mane's apprentice comyng in by redempcon" could "brouke no fredom with this Feloship." *The Merchant Adventurers of Newcastle-upon-Tyne, Surtees Society Publications*, vol. 93, pp. 8–10, 15.

[18] The Government of the Fullers, Shearmen and Clothworkers of London as proved by their Charters and Ordinances. *Compiled by a Member of the Court about 1650.*

furtherance of handicraft interests.[19] That the members of other
allied groups were animated by different aims and ambitions has
already been gathered from the accounts of their activities left by
many organisations of that epoch. In fact, the metropolitan gilds
had undoubtedly become honey-combed with classes [20] each one of
which was more concerned with advancing its own particular interests, than of cooperating for the good of the whole body and often
they lacked a court of appeal where individual members could be
assured of an unprejudiced hearing for the redress of their grievances. This, at least, seems to have been the burden of the complaint voiced by the clockmakers about a quarter of a century after
their incorporation, at which time the freemen proclaimed their
condition to be worse than "ever before they were given their
charter." For then they said "such as were agrieved sought their
remedy by the law of the land and ye customs of this citty, but
since the power hath bin in the Courte of Assistants all manner of
evils have flowed in upon us, as may appear by theis particulars." [21]

[19] Unwin, *Industrial Organization*, pp. 122–3.
[20] The freemen at large no longer had any voice in the enacting of ordinances or in the electing of officials as had been the case in former days.
Thus, by 1493 a brotherhood in the clothing or livery had come into control
of the London drapers' company, from whose ranks gild masters and wardens
were drawn and who could therefore dominate the yeomanry or "Broderhode
oute of the clothing." Herbert, *Twelve Great Livery Companies,* vol. i,
p. 406. On the other hand, among the goldsmiths, the yeomanry was not
organised into a separate group until 1542. At an assembly held in that
year it seems that the young men out of the livery asked Mr. Aldermen and
the Court "to have a yeomanry of this Company." The request being
granted, the young men were ordered to come into court and to present the
names of six to serve as wardens of such yeomanry. Prideaux, *Memorials
of the Goldsmiths' Company,* vol. 1, p. 51. By 1647 among the London pewterers, the yeomanry were allowed to be present at the quarterly courts while
the ordinances were being read and the result of the search announced.
After that they appear to have retired. Welch, *History of the Pewterers'
Company,* vol. ii, p. 112. In time the liverymen lost control of the government of the gild and of the election of the chief officers. Those powers
passed into the hands of the master, wardens and court of assistants.
[21] Overall, *History of the Clockmakers' Company,* pp. 60–1. One wonders
how far back the clockmakers dated this halcyon period. As late as 1627
they were still members of the blacksmiths' company, and subject presumably
to its governing body, which, by that time seems to have been a court of
assistants. *Ibid.,* p. 2. It is evident that by 1540, about thirteen years after
its incorporation, a court of assistants was in control of the clothworkers'
company. Unwin, *Industrial Organization,* p. 45. Later assistants to the
number of twelve seem to have constituted a court of the company. *The
Government of the Fullers, Shearmen and Clothworkers,* p. 14. Tracing the
beginnings of these courts of assistants, we find that as far back as 1376,
annually after their dinner, the assembled company of grocers of London
elected two masters and in addition six other members to give "assistance
and advice" to the two masters. Kingdon, *The Worshipful Company of
Grocers,* pt. i, p. 21. In 1521 the London drapers drew up a "Bill" contain-
ing the names of such as they were pleased "to elect and name to be assistants and of their Councell"; (Johnson, *History of the Worshipful Company
of Drapers,* vol. ii, p. 55, Note 1.) By 1550, their ordinances were passed
not by the whole "fellyship" nor by the livery, but by the master, wardens

Foremost in the list of particulars, appears the charge that the governing body abetted strangers and foreigners "whereas the charter was in especiall manner procured for ye restraint" of all such. Next they denounced the court's method of binding apprentices to freemen for foreigners, thereby enabling apprentices to become freemen as if they had served their whole time with freemen. Finally, they accused the court of disregarding the "Order which hath bin often renewed for restraining the multiplicity of Apprentices," and permitting apprentices to multiply until "the trade is almost ruined." A similar antagonism of purpose is discernible in the government of most corporations of the period. It had, seemingly, become part of gild procedure that officials being merchants and "not skylfull in the handycrafte," failed to uphold handicraft interests, or "being men of other trades" neglected to suppress and reform "abuses" practised in the one most concerned, or being foreigners showed themselves "in no wayes capable to judge of an art."

The cleavage was scarcely less pronounced between masters and men than between the different master classes. There seemed little chance of reconciling free journeymen of the seventeenth century to the fact that masters refused them work while they gave it to unfree journeymen,[22] or to those from the country,[23] or extracted from them a pledge not to set up for themselves,[24] or denied them

and the Court "of their sole authority." *Ibid.,* vol. ii, p. 51. In accordance with the regulations which were drawn up by the tailors of Shrewsbury in 1563, the whole gild elected two wardens, who in their turn nominated four assistants "for advising them in the Government of the Gild." Hibbert, *Influence and Development,* p. 104. According to the terms of the charter which King Charles I conceded to the Merchant Adventurers of Bristol, the power of making ordinances was restricted to the master, wardens and assistants. *Parliamentary Papers,* vol. 24, p. 1204.

[22] In 1678 six journeymen appeared before the court of the London feltmakers' company charging a master with employing foreigners and refusing work to freemen. Unwin, *Industrial Organization,* p. 217. In 1507 the shearmen of that city had, apparently, in good faith attempted to protect their journeymen by forbidding any householder from henceforth to set any stranger to work so long as he "may have a free Journeyman that hath been apprentice in the same city at the same craft to doo hym svice." *Ordinances of the Clothworkers' Company,* p. 12. Again, by 1680, at Chester, brethren of the bricklayers' society were selling bricks to journeymen bricklayers who were not free, thereby enabling the journeymen to "lay said Bricks as of themselves and for their own profit and not as journeymen or servants to any Brother" of the company. *The Bricklayers' Company of Chester, Journal Chester & N. Wales Archaeol. & Historic Soc.,* n. s., vol. xxii, p. 71. A century later, in 1785, butchers dwelling in Newcastle were not to employ non-free journeymen when freemen were unemployed and willing to do their work. *Archaeologia Aeliana,* 3rd ser. vol. 14, p. 19.

[23] Journeymen clothworkers during the reign of King Charles II brought this charge against gild masters. Unwin, *op. cit.,* p. 199. In 1636 the Salisbury corporation passed a resolution forbidding freemen or shopkeepers to "put out work out of the city" if it could be done within. Haskins, *The Ancient Trade Guilds & Companies of Salisbury,* p. 389.

[24] By act of 28 Henry VIII, c. 5, gild officials were forbidden to exact from journeymen a pledge not to set up for themselves.

membership in their gilds or took more apprentices than gild law allowed.[25] Apprentices, in their turn, could scarcely be expected longer to sympathise with the policy of masters who broke faith with them by neglecting to enroll them in gild,[26] and even in borough records,[27] or who refused them their freedom after they had faithfully served their term,[28] or charged them such exorbitant fees for entry as to make gild mastership practically impossible for them forever after.

Masters, of course could prefer charges equally grave against journeymen and apprentices. Journeymen, they averred, combined to raise wages,[29] or to shorten their working hours,[30] or took service with men of rival corporations when their own needed workmen,[31] or refused to pay their gild quarterage,[32] or to take up their

[25] *Supra,* p. 158.

[26] In 1677, members of the skinners and feltmakers of Chester were evidently neglecting to enrol their apprentices in the company's books. According to an order issued in that year, the company's stewards were to go through the books each month to "ascertain what apprentices were kept which were not so in rowled," and for each omission, the stewards were to be fined twelve pence. *Journal Chester & North Wales Architect. Archaeol. & Historic Soc.,* n. s., vol. 21, p. 112.

[27] By 1490 gild masters were evidently not enrolling their apprentices in the books of the "Comen Chamber" in Canterbury as they were called upon to do by law. *Historical MSS. Commis. Report,* ix, p. 173. Ordinances which were drawn up by the drapers of London under date of 1541, provided for the swearing in of apprentices in "the house" of the drapers after their "termys ende," before they were made free in the Chamber of London. Johnson, *op. cit.,* vol. ii, pp. 286–7.

[28] In 1757 among the Newcastle butchers, masters were bound to give notice to the stewards within a week of the expiration of the apprentice's term; whereupon said apprentice was to take up his freedom at the next meeting day. *Archaeologia Aeliana,* 3rd ser., vol. 14, p. 23. *Shropshire Archaeol. & Nat. Hist. Soc. Trans.,* vol. viii, p. 270. Apprentices could escape serving their apprenticeship to a master to whom they had once been bound. Thus, in 1607, we find a goldsmiths' apprentice asking to be turned over to another master because the master whom he had been serving had served a term in Newgate for clipping gold, and had thereby tarnished his reputation. Prideaux, *Memorials of the Goldsmiths' Company,* vol. 1, p. 160. In 1728 several apprentices bound to a master who had died insolvent without having provided for them, were discharged from their "several and respective" apprenticeships. *Quarter Sessions Records, North Riding Record Society,* vol. viii, p. 183.

[29] Welch, *History of the Worshipful Company of Pewterers,* vol. 1, p. 196.

[30] Journeymen clothworkers were charged with this offense in 1639. Unwin, *Industrial Organization,* p. 79.

[31] In 1559 the London clothworkers warned their journeymen to "beware with whom they dyd make any covenant for their service." *Ibid.* p. 119.

[32] No journeyman was to be "sett at worke" in 1680 by the bricklayers of Chester "untill hee bee" enrolled in the Company's book kept for that purpose; every journeyman was to pay at his entrance one shilling and at every quarter-day afterwards six pence, to the use of the company. *The Bricklayers' Company of Chester, Journal Chester & N. Wales Archaeological & Historic Society,* n. s., vol. xxii, p. 70. In 1681 journeymen feltmakers of London who refused to pay their quarterage were prosecuted by the feltmakers' company. Unwin, *Industrial Organization,* p. 247.

freedom,[33] preferring to work secretly in chambers;[34] indeed, they often went so far as to dictate to masters in the taking of apprentices.[35] Apprentices, in effect, they accused of wasting their masters' time in rioting; of demanding unreasonable wages;[36] of deserting during times of war,[37] or even peace;[38] of refusing to serve them after coming "out of their terms" and taking upon themselves rather "a mansion or shop" of their own;[39] or of setting up in business before they took up their freedom, of failing thereby to "unite and conform themselves"[40] to their respective trade companies.[41]

[33] Seventeenth-century journeymen wheelwrights evidently refused to take up their freedom in the company. Whereupon a fine was imposed upon the member who employed a journeyman who was not free. Scott, *History of the Worshipful Company of Wheelwrights,* p. 54. By that time journeymen wheelwrights seem to have set up an organisation of their own, a fact which may account for their failure to take up their freedom in the gild of the master wheelwrights. It may also explain why, in 1740, journeymen were excused from paying quarterage to the wheelwrights' company. *Ibid.,* p. 24. It is noteworthy that in 1670 a journeyman paid six pence per quarter "to the use of the said fellowship" while a master paid six shillings. *Ibid.* p. 17. When master glovers of Kingston-upon-Hull paid eight pence, every "hyred man" had to pay four. Lambert, *Two Thousand Years,* p. 216. By 1635 at Kingston-upon-Thames a free householder was obliged to pay eight pence to the use of his company and a journeyman taking wages four pence. *Genealogical Magazine,* vol. iii, p. 342. Among the cutlers, painter-stainers and stationers of Dublin in 1675 every journeyman employed by a brother had to be registered and the employer was to keep out of his journeyman's wages for the use of the corporation, one shilling per quarter or be himself amerced two shillings and six pence every time he neglected to do so. *Dublin Corporation Records, Egerton MSS., B.M.,* no. 1765, f. 167. In 1587 among the clothworkers of London every "Journeyman being of the sayd art" like every householder paid quarterly for his "quarteredge Sixe Pence of lawful English money." Unwin, *op. cit.,* p. 84.

[34] Clode, *Memorials of the London Taylors,* p. 211.

[35] Latimer, *Annals of Bristol in the 18th Century,* p. 70. By 1518, the combinations entered into by the journeymen of Coventry proved disturbing to the city's peace and provoked from the Leet an order which forbade journeymen of whatever "occupacion or craft so euer" they happened to be, "to make" any by-law or assembly or to hold "metynges" at any place "by ther somner without licens of maister Meire and the maister" of his occupation. *Leet Book,* p. 656. It is interesting, too, to note the restrictions which were placed upon journeymen by the gilds. By 1490 journeymen weavers of Kingston-upon-Hull were not at the "eleccon day to gyff any voyce to the chesyng" either of an alderman or of any other officer. Lambert, *Two Thousand Years of Gild Life,* p. 205. By 1587, journeymen clothworkers of London were summoned to come to the Hall of the company four times a year, "to heare speciallie" that "which belongeth to them and that done they may departe." *Clothworkers' Ordinances,* p. 93.

[36] Stewart, *History of the Gold and Silver Wyre Drawers,* p. 90.

[37] *Hist. MSS. Comm. Rep. in Various Collections,* vol. I, p. 114.

[38] *Somerset, Quarter Sessions Records,* vol. 3, p. 288.

[39] Unwin, *Gilds and Companies of London,* p. 226.

[40] This was the grievance which certain master gildsmen of Coventry had against their apprentices by 1670. Webb, *Local Government,* vol. ii, p. 249, quoted from *MS. Records, Corporation of Coventry.*

[41] Undoubtedly, apprentices owed certain obligations to the gild in control of the occupation they used, which they were required to meet. According

Taken all in all, charges such as these tend to show that men as well as masters were breaking with a system with which they had lost sympathy. Of course, the advantage lay with the masters who, by this time, had probably plenty of outside labour to draw upon. Only, in drawing upon it, they had to reckon with both exasperated journeymen and apprentices who were determined to use every method known to labour to keep their hold over trade and industry. They placed such obstructions as they could in the way of foreign workmen who were procured to take their places, and when peaceful means failed, resorted to violence, until borough authorities were obliged to intervene in the interest of local peace and order, and to end a situation which had grown intolerable for all concerned. Thus, when the gilds of Kingston-upon-Hull failed to serve the interests for which they had been created, the gilds had to go.[42] Not all the boroughs were able or even inclined to go this far on their own initiative, even though they were rapidly losing patience with the tactics pursued by gildsmen within their boundaries. Manifestly, later-day gildsmen showed as little respect for borough ruling as for gild when their economic interests clashed and when it came to a choice between the two did not hesitate to serve the company to which they were "sworn" rather than the borough.[43] Gildsmen not only refused to hold office,[44] but deliber-

---

to a ruling adopted in the twentieth year of the reign of King Edward IV, an apprentice could gain the freedom of the merchant gild of Newcastle-upon-Tyne provided that he duly "observe and kepe all maner gud ordinances and acts maid . . . in the courtes," and in addition contribute to the "comon box at his entering" as well as at the end of his "foresaid termes" of service, the sum specifically designated for the privilege. *The Merchant Adventurers of Newcastle-upon-Tyne, Surtees Society Publications,* vol. 93, p. 1. In Elizabethan days every bricklayer's apprentice born within the borough of Kingston-upon-Hull had "for his parte" to pay three shillings to the bricklayers' gild, while one born elsewhere paid five shillings. Lambert, *Two Thousand Years,* p. 278. Among seventeenth-century clockmakers of London, an apprentice who had served his term and been admitted a free-man of the company, attained to mastership after he had served two additional years as a journeyman and produced his masterpiece. Overall, *History of the Clockmakers' Company,* p. 30.

[42] Hadley, *History of Kingston-upon-Hull,* p. 828. For instance, in 1598, local bricklayers were authorised to "make any orders for good government and rule to be kept among themselves" in regard to their craft, provided that the same tend "nott to the hurt of the comon weale of this towne" nor to contravene the "lawes of this land." Lambert, *op. cit.* p. 274.

[43] In 1614 two members of the Chester mercers' and ironmongers' company from "daie to daie . . . walked all daie" before the shop of an interloper so as to "forbidd and inhibit all that came to the said shopp" from buying any wares there. Nor would they depart "upon their oathe" when ordered by the mayor so to do, but answered that they were "sworn to their Company" and so "they walked and remayned and plaied their wilful parte." *Harleian MS. B.M.,* 2054, ff. 89–90.

[44] In 1682 two Shrewsbury burgesses were fined ten pounds each, for "refusing to accept of the places of Assistant and this," the corporation ruled was "to be a precedent for the future." *Shropshire Archaeol. & Nat. Hist. Soc. Trans.,* vol. xi, p. 192.

ately absented themselves from a "Comen Hall" [45] or from borough courts when summoned to attend.[46] They neglected to keep "in sufficient reparacons" certain bridges [47] or perform other services for which they were responsible,[48] or to pay the penalties attached to the infraction of borough law,[49] or the sums due for charters which authorised their being,[50] even laying themselves open to being prosecuted "for not shewing their composition to Mr. Mayor upon his demand as usually hath been done." [51] They squandered "idly" for private purposes, sums of money collected from non-free traders which were supposed to go to help the poor.[52] They had no scruples against letting houses and shops to non-freemen [53] or against "colouring" strangers' goods as being their own or entering them free of duty.[54] They made men free of their organisations without acquainting borough officials with the fact [55] or imposed upon the latter by "bringing up a person to be made a Burgess" as being an "apprentice when he was not." [56] They elected outsiders to serve as gild wardens,[57] failed to meet the expences incidental to the prosecution of intruders or to furnish the funds or the labour required to put through borough enterprises. In other words the gilds failed frequently to meet the obligations which they owed to their respective boroughs while demanding from the boroughs, unfailing support for their restrictive trade policy.

[45] At Stratford-on-Avon in 1586 two aldermen were chosen to be aldermen in the places of John Wheler and John Shaxspere "for that Mr. Wheler dothe desyre to be put owt of the companye and Mr. Shaxspere dothe not come to the halle when they be warned, nor hathe not done of longe tyme." Halliwell, *Stratford Council Book A.*, p. 82.

[46] In 1776 the cordwainers of Boston refused to attend the court of Pie Poudre. Thompson, *History of Boston*, p. 158.

[47] During the first half of the seventeenth century several craft companies of Leominster were fined for dereliction of duty in this respect. Townsend, *History of Leominster*, pp. 303–4.

[48] At Shrewsbury such innkeepers, victuallers and alehouse-keepers as refused to pay their assessment for the entertainment of the "Counsell of the Marches" in 1587, were ordered "to be discharged by Mr. Bailiffs of victualling hereafter." *Shropshire Archaeol. & Nat. Hist. Soc. Trans.*, vol. xi, p. 156. And in 1642 several burgesses were disfranchised for not paying borough assessments. *Ibid.*, p. 181.

[49] In 1613 the wardens of the Boston cordwainers were directed to pay quarterly all penalties incurred by their company. Thompson, *History of Boston*, p. 158.

[50] At Kinsale, in 1687, it was determined to sue for breach of promise the masters of such companies as refused to pay the sums they promised for their charters. *Council Book*, p. 179.

[51] *Shropshire Archaeol. & Nat. Hist. Soc. Trans.*, vol. xi, p. 185.

[52] Caulfield, *Council Book of Kinsale*, p. lxx. To prevent a repetition of this offense, the Kinsale companies were thereafter to support their own poor "as far as the money will reach," or forfeit their charters.

[53] Hoare, *Salisbury*, vol. vi, p. 384.

[54] *Annals of Bristol in the 17th Century*, p. 346.

[55] May, *History of Evesham*, p. 341.

[56] *Nottingham Records*, vol. vi, p. 25.

[57] *Shropshire Archaeological & Natural History Society Trans.*, vol. xi, p. 195.

In spite of this long list of counts in the indictment of the gilds, they cannot be accused of failing the boroughs necessarily with malice aforethought. A considerable expenditure of time, energy, and money could alone have kept out the numbers of outsiders constantly on the alert to get into the boroughs, and after all, those on the inside were at best only human. In the days of good Queen Bess, foreign bakers, it seems, were baking at Oswestry "not regarding the keepinge of th' assise thereof, ne yet whether the same be good and holesome," mainly because the persons who were "bounde" by the laws of this realme, neglected "to look ynto and to see aull suche personnes as shall offend dewlie punisshed." [58] About the same epoch, evidently, with the connivance of Winchester townsmen, foreigners were selling various commodities by "retayle" within their houses.[59] After having once secured a footing, intruders were not easily gotten out even by "any legal course" a method which experience was teaching seventeenth-century gildsmen to be both tedious and costly and not lightly to be undertaken.[60] Besides an organisation courageous or desperate enough to bring suit against an unusually aggressive outsider who had invaded their market, sometimes found itself obliged to admit others in order to obtain the funds with which to meet the expenses incidental to such prosecution, thereby defeating the end the suit was brought to further.[61] To seventeenth-century gildsmen, as to their brethren of an earlier age, the condoning of trading by outsiders proved a convenient source from which to fill gild exchequers. These, at this stage, often lacked the wherewithall to meet the ordinary demands made upon them.[62] Again, individual gilds may, at certain times, have

[58] Price, *History of Oswestry*, p. 70.

[59] Bailey, *Winchester*, p. 58. From early times aliens had been forbidden to engage in retail trade within the boroughs. Thus in the letters patent conferred upon the London fishmongers by King Edward III, foreigners were not to sell fish within the city but "but only wholesale" as it had been in the time of his grandfather. *Letter Book H.*, p. 447. Later, we find exceptions being made in the case of such aliens as secured a license from the mayor of the borough in which they expected to trade. In fact, by the terms of the charter conceded to a borough like Leicester, in 1599, foreigners could sell other than "in grosse" only in fair time unless especially licensed by the mayor. Bateson, *Records of the Borough*, vol. iii, pp. 43-4.

[60] *Supra*, pp. 147–9.

[61] This seems to have been the situation in which the merchant taylors of Bath found themselves toward the end of the eighteenth century. *Supra*, p. 153.

[62] In 1643, the court of the London clothworkers' company, "Taking into their sad and serious consideration the many great pressing and urgent occasions which they have for money, as well for the payment of their debts as otherwise, and considering the danger this city is in by reason of the great distractions and civil wars of this kingdom, have thought fit and so ordered that the stock of plate which this Company hath shall be forthwith sold at the best rate that will be given for the same." *The City Companies*, p. 159. A decade later, city pewterers confessed to being not "Very well able to undergoe" certain expenditures incidental to the conduct of their business. In 1655, the merchants of Dublin testified that the stock of "this Guild is but little by reason of the many disbursements and small receipts." *Dublin*

let in strangers in order to meet a demand for articles which they could not supply.[63] This may explain why in 1611 feltmakers and haberdashers of Bristol conceded to foreigners the right to sell hats and caps in their city on one week day.[64] Still other corporations allowed their members to employ outsiders who could teach them new processes of manufacture. For instance, to all such brethren as would undertake to learn the art of cabinet making, inlaying and "phinearing," the joiners of Newcastle-upon-Tyne in 1711 conceded liberty to hire or set at work foreign journeymen "in cabinet work only."[65] As a matter of fact, in their most halcyon days, the gilds were more or less dependent upon outside labour. In 1518, members of the amalgamated gild of shoemakers, curriers and cobblers of Canterbury were known to have "moo jornymen beyng aliants then jornymen beyng englesshemen."[66] Gild by-laws frequently provided a way by which members could engage non-freemen. As early as 1452, a license secured from the "wardeyns and the xii persones of the more partie" thereof enabled a man of the "crafte" of shearmen of London to employ "any foren man."[67] Indeed, where the gilds failed to make some such provision for the employment of aliens, the community took it upon itself to do so. In 1635 it appears that the gilds of Kingston-upon-Thames lacked sufficient freemen to do freemen's work and were consequently obliged to sanction the employment of foreigners.[68] Moreover, local gilds might prohibit alien workers from setting up business in their communities, but they had always to take into account those whom local executives licensed for that purpose. In 1490, an "alian" could defy the incorporated weavers of Kingston-upon-Hull if he had a "licence of the mayr for tyme beyng."[69] In the early days of the reign of Queen Elizabeth, a stranger, "denison or English not being a freeman of" the "towne" of Sandwich[70] could keep "any open shoppe" by securing a license "in writing" from the mayor, and a century later foreigners not free of the local merchant gild were being licensed to trade in the liberties. At Oswestry too, during this time a foreigner could ply

Merchant Guild, Egerton MS., B. M., 1765, f. 42. In the last decade of the century, because of "the pr'sent warr taxes and decay of Trade occasioned thereby," the London skinners retrenched by keeping their court that year in a private manner." Wadmore, *History of the Worshipful Company of Skinners,* p. 60.

[63] In 1678 the mercantile company of Newcastle-upon-Tyne was confronted with the problem of keeping the local market supplied since it had prohibited peddlars from setting up their booths upon the "Sandhill." *Surtees Soc. Pub.,* vol. 93, xli, pp. 220–223.

[64] Latimer, *17th Century Annals of Bristol,* p. 26.

[65] *Archaeologia Aeliana,* 3rd Series, vol. v, p. 176.

[66] Civis, *Canterbury,* Supplement No. xx.

[67] *Ordinances of the Clothworkers' Company,* p. 150.

[68] *The Genealogical Magazine,* vol. iii, p. 341.

[69] Lambert, *Two Thousand Years of Gild Life,* p. 206.

[70] A printed paper called the *Advertiser,* dated May, 1883, attached to *Additional MS.,* 27462, B. M.

his trade and keep a shop if he were licensed by the mayor and his associates.[71]

Naturally seventeenth-century boroughs could not let the limitations of the gilds hinder their growth and development. When local gilds failed to provide sufficient money to pay for the upkeep of a borough, the authorities secured it by selling their cherished trade privileges to the aspirant willing to pay the price demanded.[72] By admitting a distinguished stranger, one borough obtained funds to help the poor;[73] another "made" burgesses in order to pay for the repairing of gates or walls.[74] By the last quarter of the century, Salisbury evidently maintained a "committee of revenue," not the least of whose activities had to do with admitting outsiders to free citizenship.[75] Kinsale, too, at this time, kept a list of her non-free inhabitants, and as the need arose had a special committee, which she maintained for the purpose, offer to sell the borough's freedom to persons who should be judged "fit to be made free."[76] The "Hall," which was held at Nottingham, in 1728, seems to have been "resolved into a committee to consider of fit persons to whom this corporacion may sell or give their freedom and for what consideration."[77] To most boroughs at this stage, the consideration to be had, evidently demonstrated a candidate's fitness for citizenship, not his previous condition of servitude. Likewise, when the gilds of London or Bristol failed to provide a sufficient number of workmen to meet the demand, outsiders were admitted to make up the shortage. When a local market wanted commodities which the merchants in control could not provide, aliens were allowed in who could. In times of stress, burghal necessity evidently knew no gild law. When the Chester weavers attempted to interfere with foreign weavers whom the civic authorities had admitted to establish the manufacture of Shrewsbury cloth in their city, they learned that "the corporation will not allow this interference." The corporation was, evidently, as good as its word and the city weavers had to see the foreigners weave their kind of cloth in Chester.[78] By threatening to let country bakers furnish citizens with bread thereafter, city officials of Bristol brought her defiant bakers to terms in 1616.[79] Sooner or later the boroughs were forced to favour outsiders, even at the expense of free gildsmen, out of regard for their wealth as a whole rather than the "community or franchise"

[71] Price, *History of Oswestry,* p. 67.
[72] By 1563 all "unfraunchest artificers within the city" of Lincoln could secure the "fraunchesse for so much money as the mayor and his brethren shall agree unto, any act, law or ordinance to the contrary notwithstanding." *Historical MSS. Commission Report,* Lincoln, p. 55.
[73] Hoare, *Wiltshire,* vol. vi, p. 473.
[74] *Shropshire Archaeol. & Nat. Hist. Soc. Trans.,* vol. xi, pp. 169, 174.
[75] Hoare, *Wiltshire,* vol. vi, p. 473.
[76] Caulfield, *Council Book of Kinsale,* lxx.
[77] *Records,* vol. 6, p. 122.
[78] *Supra,* p. 145.
[79] Seyer, *History of Bristol,* vol. II, p. 268.

of some particular craft or mystery, which, however important it may have seemed to its own members, to a borough was only "one particular company." Because in 1615 the clothiers of Coventry were "very much hyndered by reason that theyre clothes are not sufficiently milled, thicked and burled to theire content," it was enacted by the Leet that foreign "Walkers or Fullers may resort to the City and work without molestation." [80] The admission of strangers to Worcester probably contributed to ruin the clothiers' company, once supreme in the local clothing industry. [81] The privileged company of ironmongers of Evesham lost out when city authorities refused to support their restrictive policy. [82] And when eighteenth-century blacksmiths of Doncaster made such "illuse" of their privileged position as unduly to harass outsiders, the borough corporation wittingly espoused the cause of outsiders. [83]

Of course, at some time in their history, the boroughs were obliged to take into account the cause of outsiders who dwelt within their borders. Every community of consequence had a certain number of inhabitants who could not meet the requirements demanded of freemen, but yet had a certain status which they were taxed to support. Since a borough grew by annexing adjacent territory, it naturally annexed tenants for whom a place had to be made in community life, pending their rise to the rank of freemen. [84] In fourteenth-century Bristol, persons who had not the "means" or who would not pay the ten pounds charged for the franchise were received as "portmen" by paying a fine to the communalty, "at the discretion of the mayor and his associates for the time being." [85] According to a decree issued by the authorities of Leicester [86] in 1467, shopkeepers, who did not belong to the "Chapman Gild," [87] paid an annual tax to the borough. In 1582 a trader who was "not able to be a burgess" of Beverley, contributed six shillings a year to the merchants' gild instead of the ten charged burgesses. [88] In 1716 at Hartlepool "ye accustomed sess of five shillings for

[80] Fretton, *Memorials of Coventry Gilds,* p. 13.
[81] *Architectural Society Trans.,* vol. xv, p. 336.
[82] *Parl. Papers,* vol. 23, p. 56.
[83] *Records,* vol. iv, p. 206.
[84] The land which was enclosed by the borough of Liverpool in the first decade of the fourteenth century as in the last, is said to have been tenanted by many persons who were not burgesses. Muir, *History of Liverpool,* pp. 20–21.
[85] *Little Red Book,* vol. ii, p. 48.
[86] Nichols, *County of Leicester,* vol. i, p. 376.
[87] In Shrewsbury non-burgesses were known as tensers. This appears from an item picturing life in that borough in 1499 when for some reason the "burgesses and Tensaors . . . did vary." Hibbert, *Influence and Development of English Gilds,* p. 151, Appendix i. So too, every "Tensure" dwelling in Worcester a little later in the fifteenth century was "set" a reasonable fine "after the discression" of the aldermen; and after the "tensure" had dwelt within the city a year or more and "hath sufficiaunt to the valor of xls or more," he was given a "resonable tyme" to be made a citizen, "and iff he refuse that" he had "yerely" to pay to the "comyn cofre xld." *Ibid.,* p. 154.
[88] *Hist. MSS. Com. Rep. Beverley,* p. 84.

every freemen and two shillings and six-pence for every unfreeman or inhabitant in ye said corporation, being time immemorial yearly due and paid to ye mayor" was collected and diverted to the repairing of a local church.[89] Unquestionably, therefore, non-freemen paid their quota of the yearly taxes that were levied by communal authorities for the privileges they enjoyed.[90] This fact free gildsmen were fond of ignoring when they wished to belittle the part played in their community by non-freemen. Apparently the "ffreemen" of Coventry did this in 1616, when they complained of the "manie straungers, forreyners" in their citie and suburbs," who not being freemen, "beareth no burden and yet use the trades of malting, brewing and victualing, to the hindrance and damage of many of the poore Citisens, ffreemen of this Citie" who used those trades, many "having spent a good part of theire estates in the necessarie charg of the support and maintenaunce" of the city.[91] Perhaps the strangers would have told a different tale regarding their activities.

Eighteenth-century cutlers, painter-stainers and stationers of Dublin, for their part, did not deny that non-freemen shared the burden of maintaining their city. While they insisted that their failure to take part as a "corporation" in a civic ceremony was due to a lack of funds, the above-named gildsmen contrasted the hardship they suffered in meeting the obligations which devolved upon them as freemen, with the indulgence and protection accorded nonfreemen or "Quarter Brethren" as they were known in Dublin. The free gildsmen attributed the discrimination in favour of non-freemen to some "secret influence." This, they alleged, "not only partially exempted non-freemen from paying their customary contributions towards the support of the city, but also prevented the passage "into a law" of a certain "Quarteridge Bill" which the gildsmen favoured as being "Salutary" as well as "necessary." [92] The central

---

[89] Sharp, *History of Hartlepool*, p. 77. At a court held in 1663 at Totnes, diverse shopkeepers "compounded for opening their shop windows and using the Liberties of the Town not being free." *Devonshire Association for Advancement of Science*, vol. xii, p. 323.

[90] Under an order issued by the mayor of Chester in 1602, "forreners" in the city who used the occupations of "Lynnen" drapers, brickmakers, and "bricklaiers" were, in conjunction with the freemen of the bricklayers' company, to contribute to the charge of setting forth the "showe" or "Watch at Mydsomer," as had been customary. *The Bricklayers' Company of Chester, Journal, Chester & North Wales Archaeol. & Historic Soc.*, n. s., vol. xxii, pp. 77–8.

[91] *Leet Book*, pt. iii, p. 838. At about the same time the freemen of Hereford brought practically the same charge against foreigners in their borough. *Hist. MSS. Comm. Rep.*, xiii, appen. iv, p. 340. In 1413 coopers of Beverley brought to the attention of the authorities the fact that, while they were heavily taxed, many coopers who dwelt in the country came into Beverley and yearly, indeed, almost continuously, worked and pocketed their profits without paying anything toward the charges of the borough. *Hist. MSS. Com. Rep., Beverley*, p. 97.

[92] *Dublin Corporation Records*, Egerton MS., B. M., 1765, fol. 181. In the previous century, about 1678, the threatened descension of "Protestant strangers to come from points beyond the seas, here to exercise manual occupations

authorities were also charged with favouring aliens at the expense of Englishmen. Over a century earlier, on April 17, 1627, to be exact, the London clockmakers called the attention of the king and his council to the suffering entailed upon them because of the "intrusion of clockmakers, straingers, who contrary to ye Statutes and Lawes of this Kingdome doe use theire trades here with more freedome then his Maties freeborne subjects and that the said straingers have obteyned a warrant under his Maties Privye Seale for using of theire Trades." [93] And his Majesty's freeborn subjects bestirred themselves to enlist the support of the mayor, commonalty and citizens of the city to procure a "stay of" the "Patent" which had been bestowed upon the "ffrench Clockmakers."

Yet in the nature of things "regarde to their private and perticular gaine" led "foreyns" by "sundrie meanes" to "seeke" for more trade [94] than they were entitled to. During the reign of Queen Elizabeth certain strangers were admitted into the borough of Sandwich "there to use such trades as Englishmen" at the time did not use. Scarcely a quarter of a century later, however, the strangers "not regarding their then agreement . . . of a gredie desire to enrich themselves and to encroach all manner of trades into their own hands" were keeping open shop and using "all occupations" which the English inhabitants used.[95] Apparently, neither collectively nor individually were aliens of that epoch readier than Englishmen to play the industrial game according to prescribed rules. So too, during the first quarter of the seventeenth century, strangers "not keeping scot and lot" in Shrewsbury brought malt into the borough and sold it in shops and houses instead of in the open market as prescribed by law,[96] while in Kingston-upon-Thames they kept shop and offered their wares for sale on days other than those set apart as fair days.[97] In 1629, diverse persons boarding at Preston seem to have taken advantage of the "woeful" plague to "sett up and take upon them to exercise and imploy themselves" in established occupations to the undoing of "very neere eighty

---

without let or molestation" influenced the goldsmiths of London to oppose a bill then "depending" in Parliament to effect their entry into the Kingdom. Prideaux, *Memorials of the Goldsmiths' Company*, vol. ii, p. 170. By a decree issued by the Star Chamber in 1528 and ratified by a parliamentary act which was passed the following year, aliens in London were obliged to contribute as much to the quarterage paid by the city companies, as the companies levied upon them. Unwin, *Gilds and Companies of London*, p. 249.

[93] Overall, *History of the Clockmakers' Company*, p. 2.

[94] This accusation was brought against "merchant straungers" at Newcastle in 1599 for taking away the "speciall, occupie and vente of some kynde of merchandizes, not onlie in deallinge and bargayninge within this towne but also in transportinge and cheiflie for the buyinge, caringe away and shippinge forth from hence great quantities of leade and other comodities." *Merchant Adventurers, Surtees Soc. Pub.*, vol. 93, p. 31.

[95] Printed in the *Sandwich Advertiser* of May, 1883, attached to *Additional MS. No. 27462, B. M.*

[96] *Shropshire Archaeol. & Nat. Hist. Soc. Trans.*, vol. xi, p. 172.

[97] *Genealogical Magazine*, vol. iii, p. 341.

poore" members of the local mercantile fraternity who managed to survive the grievous visitation.[98] During these days, too, London stationers openly charged "Ffrenchmen and straungers beinge Denizens" with having an "excessive nomber of apprentices."[99] According to the "cordwayners" of Leicester about 1640 "divers of ye coblers in this Borough" though not freemen "doe keep open Shopps make wares take apprentices and doe covenant to teach them ye trade of a Shoomaker in back houses contrary to ye statute to the damage to the people of this Nation ye great impoverishing and allmost undoing of" the members of the cordwainers' company.[100] In 1703 Bristol merchants objected to letting "one foreigner" deal "with another."[101]

And no matter how indulgent to free gildsmen may have seemed the treatment accorded outsiders in various communities, the individual outsider saw little favour to him in a system which kept him outside in whole or in part unless he paid the exorbitant sum asked for the privilege of using undeterred a trade or industry within borough precincts. Thirty-five pounds seems a considerable sum to have paid to open a shop at Bristol in 1699,[102] or thirty at Guildford in 1740,[103] not to mention the fifty pounds demanded for the privilege at Abingdon in 1695.[104] No wonder that, as the years brought enlightenment, the desire for either borough or gild freedom appealed less and less to outsiders who wanted a chance to work without subscribing to the rules of some particular "howse" or of being haled into court by gild officials for working in defiance thereof. Only, no law compelled newcomers to live within the boroughs or corporate towns. They had always the alternative of settling outside, where free from the restraints which hemmed in gildsmen, they could defy borough and gild authorities alike, while pursuing the tenor of their own way. In 1629 alien needle-makers who lived without the limits of London refused to appear before the city authorities when summoned during the course of an inquiry then being conducted into the methods employed in making needles, on the ground that they were aliens, not freemen and so outside the jurisdiction of city officials.[105] To the demand of a committee

---

[98] Abrams, *Memorials of Preston Guilds*, p. 41.

[99] Quoted from Dunlop, *English Apprenticeship*, p. 89, note 1.

[100] These Leicester cordwainers also objected to the admission into the borough of alien curriers on the ground that there were "Fower Curriers which bee freemen of this Borough and which are sufficient to doe and supply the worke of this Towne, and that there is noe wannt or neede of any stranger or farrowner here." Stocks, *Records of the Borough of Leicester*, pp. 388, 416.

[101] Latimer, *Annals of the Eighteenth Century*, p. 21.

[102] Latimer, *Merchant Venturers of Bristol*, p. 170.

[103] Stevens, *Surrey Archaeological Collection*, vol. ix, p. 336.

[104] *Selections of the Municipal Chronicles*, p. 182. In 1671 the Eastland Company refused to lower their redemption fee from twenty pounds to five, as was suggested by the Council of Trade, on the ground that "a smaller one would cumber the body with unskilful members." *Camden Society*, p. xlix.

[105] *Index to Remembrancia*, p. 104.

of the Newcastle mercantile company that he secure their license or give up trading, a man who lived at the "Blackgate" returned for answer in 1789, that he "lived without the liberties of the town and is therefore exempt" from obedience to their laws.[106] From their point of vantage at Wandsworth, Battersea and Lambeth,[107] where plenty of country labour was to be had for the taking, the Huguenot hatters who migrated to England in 1685 contrived apparently to prosper at the expense [108] of feltmakers within the city, who were obliged to work according to gild regulations. Nonfreemen residing within a borough discovered that they could work more freely outside and still find a market for their goods within the boroughs. In the early eighteenth century non-free tailors seem to have deserted Bath for adjoining villages,[109] where they plied their calling and disposed of their finished product at the borough's market, and thereby forced local tailors, who were unable to compete with them, out of business.[110] Master manufacturers, finding it practically impossible to work under conditions which the gilds were imposing, moved to where they could manufacture goods in accordance with ideas of their own. For instance, disaffected framework knitters of this epoch left London, set up their frames in Nottingham and defied the framework knitters to do their worst. The company took up the challenge and did its worst, but what it did reacted upon the company rather than upon the recalcitrant masters and in the end proved the company's undoing.[111] By that time, free gildsmen within the boroughs were, seemingly, under a two-fold disadvantage. They could neither compete with outsiders who worked according to rules of their own ordering, nor meet free traders on their ground by disregarding the rules of the company to which they were pledged. The feltmakers of London

---

[106] *Surtees Soc. Pub.*, vol. 93, p. 267.

[107] Unwin, *Industrial Organization*, p. 219.

[108] From early times handicraftsmen within the cities and corporate towns had had to compete with those who, settled on the outskirts, managed to obtain work which the city men claimed as theirs by right. By 1381, the fullers of Bristol protested against city merchants sending their cloth to villages round about to be fulled. *Little Red Book*, vol. ii, p. 15. By 1439 cloth was being taken outside the limits of Oxford to be woven. *Calendar of Patent Rolls*, 18 Henry VI, vol. iii, pt. i, p. 347. In 1634 the clothworkers of the city of London said they had not enough work to pay the charges imposed upon them because workmen in the country had taken to making Spanish cloth. *State Papers Domestic*, 1634, f. 106, p. 278. In 1705, according to the London pewterers, countrymen were taking advantage of them by striking "London" on their wares. Welch, *History of the Pewterers' Company*, vol. ii, p. 175.

[109] According to Adam Smith, persons in his day, desirous of having their work "tolerably done," had it done in suburbs where workmen had no exclusive privileges and so had nothing but their character to depend upon. *Wealth of Nations*, vol. i, p. 131.

[110] Dunlop, *English Apprenticeship*, p. 126, quoted from Schickle, *Guild of the Merchant Taylors in Bath*.

[111] Felkin, *History of the Machine Wrought Hosiery & Lace Manufacture*, pp. 74-5.

found it impossible to do this and uphold the traditions of the system so that in the end they let the system go.[112]

The system was doomed, too, in a community like Worcester,[113] when, free townsmen withdrawing themselves from the liberties, settled in country districts, plied their trade and sold the product in the city market "toll-free under colour of their freedom." For that matter, the system went in Newcastle-upon-Tyne, when in defiance of the merchant gild, outsiders contrived to sell commodities they had purchased on the outside, and to order more from the same source when those in stock were disposed of; nor was the isolated free trader alone in bringing into disrepute Newcastle's long-cherished gild of merchants. In time, organised bakers and brewers denied the right of the merchants to seize as forfeit certain supplies of grain which they had bought through an agency other than that of the merchants. Moreover they made good their stand in the court in which the merchants defended their right of seizure, but from whose verdict the merchants realised there was no appeal.[114] Only if the Newcastle bakers and brewers could thus deny the monopolistic right of a rival group, another rival group could, in its turn, deny those put forward by bakers and brewers. Producers could scarcely claim a protection they denied consumers, or consumers claim one, denied producers, or, as it were, enjoy the

[112] Unwin, *Industrial Organization*, p. 218.

[113] Green, *History and Antiquities of Worcester*, vol. ii, Appendix, xcviii. The city fathers tried to stop the exodus by threatening to deprive of their privilege of citizenship, those who dwelt without the liberties for a year and a day, for so long a time as they should so dwell. Of course, for one reason or another, townsmen had, from early times withdrawn from the towns into adjacent districts. For instance, in the middle of the fourteenth century the mayor, aldermen and commonalty of London petitioned the king and his council for the restitution of the city's franchises. The loss of these, they averred had driven many to leave the city and settle in Westminster, St. Martin le Grand and elsewhere. *Letter Book G*, p. 185. By the middle of the sixteenth century, craftsmen from the towns had set up in country districts in the Feate and Mistery of clothmaking. 4 & 5 Philip & Mary, c. 5. And by Queen Elizabeth's day, the weavers of York had fled to adjoining places to avoid paying their quota for the city's support. Sellers, "*York in the Sixteenth and Seventeenth Centuries,*" *English Historical Review*, vol. xii, p. 439.

[114] In their plea, the Newcastle merchants contended that time out of mind there had been in their city a custom to the effect, that, if any person other than one of their number bought or sold at any granary or other place within the city, of or to an outsider, any corn imported or stored in any granary or place other than theirs, the corn was to be forfeited to the use of the merchant adventurers and might be seized by the company's wardens or one of its members. The defendants, however, in their turn asserted, that, if any such custom had ever existed, it was unreasonable as "tending to a monopoly" of corn; that if any seizures of the sort had been made, they had been made from persons who could not afford to bring suit against their more powerful competitors; and that the circumstances surrounding the seizures differed from those in the present case. However, it is noteworthy, that the "Barons" of the Exchequer who heard the case, dismissed the complainants' bill with costs. The *Merchant Adventurers of Newcastle-upon-Tyne*, Surtees Society Public., vol. 93, p. 255.

privileges of an insider of the system in one aspect of their business and an outsider in another. So the system broke down from within as well as from without.

Outsiders,[115] whether within or just without the boroughs, countenanced or opposed by state, borough or gilds, whether of the system as a whole or of some particular group only, gradually won for English economic society as a whole complete freedom of trade and industry. In much earlier times free-thinking individuals had sought to throw off the restrictions which the system sought to impose upon them. A fourteenth-century tanner might assert his right as a freeman of London [116] to trade as he pleased but he had to make good his assertion by proving his right. The tanner in question failed evidently to do this before the jury of established gildsmen whom he selected to pass upon his claim and from whose decision there seems to have been no question of appeal. But the cause of free traders of the seventeenth and eighteenth centuries was no longer left to the decision of gild tribunals.[117] Their cases

[115] In this connection it should be borne in mind that an outsider of a specific gild was not necessarily an outsider of the system as a whole. About 1570, the drapers and hosiers of Chester accused a freeman of their city, although not of their gild, of having, by some means, obtained possession of their books and other records of their activities, and with the knowledge derived therefrom, had embarked upon the business of selling all sorts of woollen cloth, to their "extreme prejudice." *Harleian MS.,* 1996, f. 7. Again, in 1648 the merchant adventurers of Newcastle-upon-Tyne bade their "Governor and Wardens" to "goe to councell there to advise what may be done against free men of this towne, which are not free of this Company that sell by wholesale or retayle any kind of merchandize to foriners, that they may be likewise proceeded against according to law." *The Merchant Adventurers of Newcastle-upon-Tyne, op. cit.,* vol. 93, p. 150.

[116] *Letter Book H,* p. 93. *Supra,* p. 64, note 47.

[117] The gilds had always been averse to having disputes between their members settled in courts outside of their jurisdiction. Even after the passage of the act of 19 Henry VII, c. 7, which forbade the gilds, under penalty, to "take upon them to make any acts or ordinances to restrain any person or persons to sue to the King's Highness, or to any of his Courts, for due remedy to be had in their causes, nor put nor execute any penalty or punishment upon any of them for any such suit to be made," gild ordinances continued to prohibit their members from suing, molesting or troubling one another without license of the wardens of their gild (Noble, *History of the Company of Ironmongers,* p. 131), or from taking disputes to the common law until their gild wardens had heard them (*Corvisors and Curriers of Lichfield, Lancashire & Cheshire Trans.,* vol. x, p. 13). Again in 1621, the apothecaries of London commanded one of their members, under penalty of paying a heavy fine, to "stay a suit" which he had already instituted in the Sheriffs' court against a fellow-gildsman, without leave of the master and wardens, for a "pretended debt of five pounds." This, they averred, was "contrary to the ordinances in that behalf made and approved by the Lord Chancellor or the Lord Treasurer and the Chief Justice of England." Barrett, *History of the Apothecaries' Society,* p. 16. The gilds were often able to defy the letter as well as the spirit of this law of King Henry VII by reason, seemingly of the support given them by borough authorities. For example, if the records of the London goldsmiths can be credited, in 1495. the mayor of their city issued a "Bill" which forbade a person of any craft to sue another until he had complained to the wardens. Prideaux, *Memorials*

were heard and judged in the higher tribunals of the kingdom where free trade was conceded to them as their birthright,[118] or on the basis of their right derived from Magna Charta,[119] or of their liberty as citizens under the common law to work freely.[120] Upheld by the spirit of the age [121] which condemned restraints of trade, with their ranks recruited by disaffected gildsmen who, in breaking down the monopoly of competing gildsmen, inevitably undermined the foundations upon which their own were built, free traders together gained the day, necessarily at the expense of the protected trades and handicrafts.

However, in the last analysis, outsiders won out all along the line only because the gild system could not consistently be carried out as originally conceived by state, borough or even the gilds for that matter. Instituted primarily to exclude outsiders, almost from the start the system had somewhere to make room for them. To the state and the boroughs, aliens were almost as valuable in their way as the gilds were in theirs. The gilds protected and developed home trade and industry and could be counted upon to divert a

---

of the Goldsmiths' Company, vol. i, p. 32. Again, in 1514, the governors of Beverley conceded to every carpenter "being brother with the carpenters," liberty to occupy different processes in wood work, "without accounting to the Bowers," on condition that they withdraw "their suit in London." *Historical MSS. Commis. Rep., Beverley,* p. 99. Later in the century, in 1591, the corporation of Exeter imposed a fine upon one freeman "for suing another freeman at Westminster out of the Jurisdiction of this Court contrary to his Oath." Izache, *Exeter,* p. 139.

[118] *Case of the Clothworkers of Ipswich,* 12 Jacobi, *supra,* p. 184.

[119] *East India Company vs. Thomas Sands,* decided in 1684, printed in Anderson, *Commerce,* vol. ii, p. 566.

[120] *Norris and Weavers of Newbury vs. Staps,* 14 Jacobi, *supra,* p. 161. Although the economic privileges of the gilds were successfully disputed in sixteenth-century courts of law, yet in general the sentiment which favoured gild dominance seems to have triumphed over that aroused against it. It is a matter of record that the commissioners of trade appointed in 1622 to inquire into the decay of the cloth industry decided that the companies should be maintained. *Historical MSS.* Commis. Report, iv, Appen., p. 312. Furthermore the act of James I of 1624 (21 James I, c. 3, sec. ix) which destroyed monopolies, maintained the gilds in power by exempting "Corporacions Companies or Fellowshipps of Any Art, Trade, Occupation or Mistery," from the operation of its provisions. Even the gilds whose restrictive policy had been condemned in courts of law contrived to live on far into the eighteenth century. Thus, although the weavers of Newbury lost the case they had instituted against the weaver Staps as cited above, on the ground that the common law did not forbid a man to use a trade whether or not he had been trained to it, the company apparently held its ground in Newbury until 1792, when it renounced its right to monopolise the weaving industry in the borough, *Supra,* p. 153. By that time, too, free traders in other communities had verdicts rendered in their favour on the principle that every man had a right naturally and legally to use any trade he found profitable. 1, *Burrows Rep.* p. 3.

[121] In his "Englands Grievance Discovered in Relation to the Coal Trade" of Newcastle-upon-Tyne, written in 1655, Ralph Gardiner pleaded for a "revival of that never to be forgotten Statute 11 Richard II, c. 7, for a free Trade to all, which voided all monopolies and charters as being the greatest grievance in a Commonwealth," p. 33.

goodly part of the wealth gained by their enterprise and initiative to further state [122] and borough interests, but aliens in ever-increasing numbers introduced new ideas and industries into England and helped thereby to increase her power and prosperity both at home and abroad. So, to the end that the energies of gildsmen and aliens might secure play free enough to permit each to fulfill its destiny in the development of the whole economic scheme, a course of expediency rather than of consistency was entered upon and ordered as the interests of the one side or of the other dictated. In pursuing this policy, the state appears as ready to favour an alien group with some new concession which made for free trade, as to propitiate boroughs and gilds by confirming certain powers they enjoyed in restraint of trade, when these seemed in danger of being nullified because of a newer concession allowed an alien group. For instance, shortly after King Edward III and his council conceded to merchant strangers the right to trade freely throughout English cities and privileged boroughs, their charters or customs to the contrary notwithstanding,[123] assurance was given the citizens of London that the liberties guaranteed them in Magna Charta were not to be interfered with.[124] So the force of practically every law, charter or gild ordinance was impaired by the inclusion of a clause which protected, in one way or another, certain privileges conceded to an established group. The Elizabethan act of 1563 itself exempted not only the London companies but a company like the worsted weavers of Norwich from the operation of the apprenticeship clauses, in order that previous liberties bestowed upon them might not be prejudiced.[125] Again, the charter granted by King Edward VI to the Bristol Merchant Adventurers, expressly stipulated that the ordinances drawn up by that society should in no wise prejudice the privileges or rights claimed by any person or body by virtue of an earlier grant.[126] Ordinances were conceded to some gild group on condition that they impugned neither the prerogatives of the crown, the laws of the realm, nor the customs of the particular city or borough in which the gild had its being.[127]

It would seem as if to English craftsmen the mere presence of aliens was an affront, no matter what the justification of their

---

[122] The hundred shillings which were contributed by the gilds of the fourteenth century to support the wars of the English kings (Sherwell, *Hist. of the London Saddlers*, p. 37) had become as many pounds sterling in the eighteenth century, for in 1798 the mercers of Shrewsbury agreed to pay annually one hundred pounds to the government "during the continuance of the war" which was then being waged. Hibbert, *Influence and Development*, p. 108.   And in 1815 the London goldsmiths subscribed the sum of two hundred guineas towards the "relief of the sufferers in the glorious battle of Waterloo." Prideaux, *Memorials of the Goldsmiths' Company*, vol. ii, p. 316.
[123] *Statute of York* passed in 1335.
[124] Norton, *Commentaries*, p. 363.
[125] 5 Elizabeth c. 4, sec. xxvii.
[126] Latimer, *Merchant Venturers of Bristol*, p. 45.
[127] *Lansdowne MSS.*, No. 28. Controversy between the London haberdashers and the feltmakers.

coming or how limited the sphere of activity allotted them in the place of their abode. For aliens were not admitted to work according to their own sweet will. The state was careful to limit them to the special field they were introduced to develop with due regard to the rights of the gild group already on the ground and of the particular borough which had to make room for the newcomers, and to secure for them something like a fair field in which to pursue their calling within borough limits. There was a fourteenth-century mayor of London who took up the cudgels for certain "cobelers from beyond the sea" when he learned they were being interfered with by city cordwainers so that they could no longer gain a living as they had gained it "beforetime" and as the King had decreed should again be permitted them. The city executive, it seems, "after due consideration" of the matter involved in the controversy, had summoned twelve cordwainers and an equal number of cobblers, six of them aliens and six Englishmen, who between them were to settle the points at issue. In this way, so the account reads, the king's decree was satisfied.[128] Satisfying the king's decree in this particular instance may have resulted in an adjustment of the controverted points which was acceptable to both sides involved, but the task of reconciling the interests of native and foreign-born subjects in other ages and in other fields of endeavour was not always effected so amicably. On the whole, alien craftsmen were no readier than the English to abide by the terms to which they had subscribed at the time of their entry into a borough. In 1613 there was trouble between the citizens of Norwich and certain Dutch strangers, when the latter, contrary to the agreement entered into at their admission into the city, began to work at handicrafts which the citizens had established in Norwich many years before.[129]

The boroughs,[130] handicapped in the exercise of their authority by the greater power which inhered in the prerogatives of the crown and the laws of the land, were bound by their charters [131] to provide good rule and government for all classes of inhabitants,

---

[128] Riley, *Memorials of London,* p. 540.

[129] Blomefield, *History of Norwich,* vol. iii, p. 364.

[130] In 1705 the mayor of Winchester could not get a court of justice to uphold the monopoly of the men of the borough. *The Mayor of Winton vs. Wilks, 2 Raymonds' Reports,* 1129. Later in the century the corporation of Berwick seems to have been deprived of its power to prevent non-burgesses from trading within local precincts. Webb, *Local Government,* vol. ii, p. 510. In the case of Rex vs. Kilderby which was tried in the twenty-first year of King Charles II, the defendant was indicted for exercising woollen drapery without having served an apprentice to that trade. Although he pleaded that as a citizen of London he was entitled under the charter of Henry III to trade freely anywhere without let or hindrance, his plea was overruled because in the opinion of the court, the statute 5 Elizabeth, c. 4, took precedence over the charter. 1 *Saunders,* 311. In Chapter IV of his *Historical Essays on Apprenticeship,* Dr. Jonathan F. Scott discusses this and other cases of the sort.

[131] Nicholson, *History of Kendal,* p. 146.

English and aliens alike, and something like equitable working conditions. In granting franchises to some gild group "as moche as in them is" [132] or to endure only so long as they served the common welfare, the boroughs fully admitted the limitations [133] to their power in the state as well as their liability to the wards under their protection. And subject to a state which shaped its policy to accord with the needs of the times,[134] with a population in which as time passed the numbers of freemen [135] failed, apparently, to increase in proportion to the "aliantes" whether they happened to be "Denyzones [136] or Forreyners," obliged to order their own affairs so as to bring the greatest good to the greatest number or lose out in the economic race, the boroughs, in dealing with the gilds, drifted into an expedient rather than a consistent line of action. They seemed equally ready to confer charters anew for gild asking as to declare those previously granted "vacated and made void" in order, apparently, to force gilds to "treat" with them for new.[137] They shared with local gilds as much of the fees that they collected from newly-created freemen as the gilds were entitled to, or with-

---

[132] Lambert, *Two Thousand Years of Gild Life*, p. 264.

[133] In proceeding against non-freemen who plied their callings in the city under the statute of apprentices rather than under her by-laws, Newcastle-upon-Tyne's executives revealed their realisation of the city's limitations in that direction. *Supra*, p. 161. By 1826 the representative of one borough frankly acknowledged the precariousness of the tenure under which most of the municipalities exercised the authority they derived from the crown. They can neither "assume their Franchises," he said, "nor discharge their duties without running the risk of being involved in legal proceedings of doubtful issue." Webb, *Local Government*, ii, p. 399, *Note*..

[134] A sixteenth-century House of Commons might prohibit the use of the gig-mill, but its eighteenth-century successor refused even to receive a petition which was addressed to it in protest against the introduction of the spinning-jenny. Webb, *Trade Unionism*, p. 44, quoted from the *House of Commons Journal*, vol. 36, p. 7, Nov. 1, 1776.

[135] By 1703 in Norwich, according to Mr. Webb, a "class of persons of considerable estates" who had not taken up their freedom in the city were engaged in trades which had been recently introduced. And a century later the resident freemen, he says, numbered about twenty-five hundred, which represented about one-fifth of the householders of the city. *Local Government*, vol. ii, 2, pp. 536–7: Again of a population of 3442 credited to Totnes in 1831 only ninety-seven seem to have been registered freemen. *Parl. Papers*, vol. 23, p. 642. By 1771 only such freemen were admitted to the freedom of Liverpool who could claim it "by right," with the result that the body of freemen became a privileged minority of the inhabitants. Muir, *History of Liverpool*, p. 170. In 1832 Winchester seems to have boasted only sixty-seven freemen. *Parl. Papers*, vol. 24, p. 898.

[136] In gild "parlance," denizens no less than foreigners ranked as aliens. *Clothworkers' Ordinances, 1587*, p. 78. In 1507 rules were promulgated by the London merchant taylors for the guidance of "foreyns straungers" as well as for "fforeyns denizens." Clode, *Memorials of the Guild*, p. 211.

[137] In 1675 the constitutions of the different gilds of Salisbury were declared from "henceforth vacated and made void," and the committee of revenue was commanded to send for the wardens of the gilds and treat with them for new ones. Hoare, *Salisbury*, vol. 6, p. 475. In 1687, the masters of the trade and artisan gilds of Kinsale were bidden to bring in their charters by a certain day and take out new charters. *Council Book*, p. 174.

held their share altogether when it seemed to be expedient.[138] They admitted newcomers openly for purposes of their own,[139] or "in secrete-wise"[140] unbeknownst to the gilds that had a right to know,[141] or refused them admission on practically any "termes whatsoever."[142] In the interest of free gildsmen, work that had been undertaken by persons who employed non-freemen was ordered to be pulled down and rebuilt by freemen.[143] Again in the interest of non-gildsmen, gild ordinances once cheerfully sanctioned were at another not allowed under any conditions,[144] while still others, which were prohibited on an earlier occasion, later on were readily espoused.[145] And when the political interests of the boroughs demanded the creation of freemen ad libidem,[146] the economic interests of the gilds which depended upon the limitation of freemen, went by the board.[147]

[138] When a certain Mr. Thompson was made a freeman of Ripon, "it was moved and voted whether the company of apothecarys should have ten pounds, a part of his fine or not." The motion, however, was "carryed in the negative." *Millenary Record*, p. 101.

[139] In 1581, in order to meet the expense incidental to acquiring a new charter Bristol admitted to burgess-ship many who had been trading in the city as "foreigners." Latimer, *Bristol in the Sixteenth Century, Newspaper Clippings, B. M.*, No. xi.

[140] During the sixth year of the reign of King Edward VI, this practice was prohibited in Worcester and burgesses were thereafter to be made "openly before sufficient record." Green, *History of Worcester*, vol. ii, Appen. xcvii.

[141] As early as the sixth year of King Edward II, the mayor and aldermen of London were forbidden to admit to the freedom any persons without the assent of the craft which they intended to pursue. Riley, *Memorials*, p. 151. Likewise, in 1613, the civic body of Salisbury was not supposed to admit handicraftsmen without the knowledge of the company to which they belonged. Dunlop, *English Apprenticeship*, p. 81.

[142] At Ripon in 1698 a certain tanner met with this curt refusal upon his asking to be admitted for a reasonable sum. *Millenary Record*, p. 81.

[143] Such an order was issued by the authorities of Newcastle-upon-Tyne in 1781, apparently, in the interest of free joiners in the city. *Archaeologia Aeliana*, 3rd ser., vol. v, p. 187.

[144] In the days of Queen Elizabeth the borough of Kingston-upon-Hull refused to sanction an ordinance drawn up by local bricklayers for the purpose of prohibiting any of the brotherhood to "hier" or "retayne" in his employ "anie laborer to worcke by daie or otherwaise" who was not a "townesman." Lambert, *Two Thousand Years*, p. 278.

[145] In 1729 the haberdashers of Shrewsbury received permission to elect as wardens of their company, non-burgesses (Hibbert, *Influence and Development of English Gilds*, p. 100), when twenty-nine years earlier a non-burgess who presumed to act as warden of a local company did so under a heavy penalty. *Shropshire Archaeol. & Nat. Hist. Soc. Trans.*, vol. xi, p. 199.

[146] The mayor of a borough sometimes took it upon himself to "make" burgesses. This is evident from an order promulgated in fifteenth-century Bristol, which decreed that no stranger, who dwelt without the liberties be made a burgess by the mayor, without the assent of the sheriff and the forty men who, at that time "have rule over" Bristol. *Little Red Book*, vol. ii, p. 62. Again, in 1561, at Carlisle, a law was enacted which forbade the mayor to make "outmen" freemen without the advice of the most part of the city council and four of every occupation. *Historic Towns, Carlisle*, pp. 193-4.

[147] On October 13, 1761, in Durham, the mayor together with certain

The gilds, accustomed to compromise in one way or another with outsiders for purposes of their own,[148] contenting themselves by securing the best terms for the favours with which they parted,[149] had no recourse except to accede to the alteration or even the revocation of their by-laws passed at an earlier age and to the insertion of such new as to their boroughs seemed fitting or necessary. Many indeed wise enough to read the signs of the times, themselves gradually renounced [150] some of their privileges and in certain instances, even all of them, thus acquiescing in a fate which was finally forced upon less amenable brethren. For the course of one gild as of all was finally run when borough interests called a halt to their proceeding, a point not reached simultaneously by all the gilds even in the same borough.

aldermen and members of the common council drew up a by-law, which changed the way of admitting new freemen into the city, and scarcely three weeks later they actually admitted to the freedom under this by-law about two hundred and sixty-four persons despite the objections raised against the procedure by the wardens of various trade companies. Fordyce, *History of Durham*, vol. i, p. 215. In 1780 as many as five hundred outsiders were admitted to Bedford, in the interest, it appears, of a certain Sir Robert Barnard, who became the recorder of the borough and loaned it a considerable sum of money. *Schedule of the Records and Other Documents of Bedford*, p. 22.

[148] In 1646 the merchant gild of Dublin accorded interlopers who had opened shops in the city, a license which allowed them to ply their trade for a stipulated period. *Supra*, p. 196. In the eighteenth century we find the mercantile fraternity of Newcastle-upon-Tyne licensing certain traders for so much a year. *The Merchant Adventurers of Newcastle-upon-Tyne, Surtees Society Pub.*, vol. 93, pp. 262–3.

[149] By 1515 admittance into any of the Newcastle companies could be purchased for a fee. *Archaeologia Aeliana*, 3rd series, vol. vii, p. 85. In that same year the wardens of the London goldsmiths decided to admit into their company a Salisbury merchant and "take from him all that they can get." Prideaux, *Memorials of the Goldsmiths' Company*, vol. i, p. 38. In 1668, the amalgamated drapers, dyers, apothecaries and barber-surgeons of Ripon evidently proceeded on this principle, and when a certain John Wood refused to pay the hundred pounds which the company demanded for leave to set up as an apothecary, the sum was reduced to fifty pounds. Upon his refusal to pay this sum, it was further reduced to twenty-five pounds; of this, he seems to have paid ten pounds and given security for the balance. *Millenary Record*, p. 69. Again, men who could only afford to pay part of the regular fee charged for admittance into a gild were often admitted as a half-brother (*Trans. Shropshire Archaeol. & Nat. Hist. Soc.*, vol. viii, p. 314), or as a quarter brother (*Feltmakers of Dublin, Royal Soc. of Antiq. of Ireland*, vol. 41, ser. vi, p. 30), or as happened among the silk weavers of York as a "contribetter." *Silk Weavers of York, MS., B. M.,* f. 266.

[150] A by-law drawn up in 1675 by the cutlers, painter-stainers and stationers' company of Dublin, which insisted that no brother sue another in any court "without leave first had from the master in Writing," provided that the debt was less than forty shillings, not quite a century later was condemned as being "well calculated for the maintenance of good Brotherhood but cannot be enforced by any authority of the Guild." *Dublin Corporation Records, Egerton MS.*, 1765, *B. M.,* f. 168. An act passed in 1573 by the merchant company of Newcastle-upon-Tyne, according to which "freemens sonnes and apprentices only" were to be "sett on worke aboote any affair of merchandize beyonde see," was repealed in 1771. *The Merchant Adventurers of Newcastle-upon-Tyne, Surtees Soc. Pub.*, vol. 93, p. 72.

BIBLIOGRAPHY

LIST OF MANUSCRIPT SOURCES CONSULTED IN THE BRITISH MUSEUM

Additional *MSS.* No. 8935. *Charter to the Tailors and Drapers of York with Counsel's Opinion in a Case Touching their Privileges.* 14 Charles II.

6694. *The Case of the Company of Mercers in Derby.* 14 Charles I.

28000. *The Tylers and Plaisterers of Bristol.* 1672.

10407. *Accounts and Memorandum Relating to the Company of Silk Weavers of York between 1611 and 1700.*

27462. *Register of the Minutes and Accounts of the Company of Mercers, Linen-drapers, Woollen-drapers and Merchant Taylors of Sandwich, Co. Kent.* 1655-1772.

8935. *Case of York Drapers & Taylors.*

BELL, JOHN. *Collection for History of Newcastle-upon-Tyne. Miscellaneous Papers.*

EGERTON *MSS.* No. 1765. *Dublin Corporation Records. The Merchants' Guild,* 1438–1824. Wm. Monck Mason.

Corporation of Cutlers, Painter-Stainers & Staconers or Guild of St. Luke the Evangelist.

Corporation of Bricklayers and Plaisterers.

2383. *Papers Relating to the London Leathersellers' Company.* 1694.

HARLEIAN *MSS.* No. 1996. f. 9. *Chester Drapers and Hosiers form a Gild Alliance.*

f. 23. *Copie of Order of Council of 1629 to Apprehend Feltmakers for keeping Apprentices not having themselves served an Apprenticeship.*

f. 34. *Chester Inn-keepers and Ale-sellers beg for Protection from Brewers in the Sale of Beer and Ale.*

f. 40. *A Company of "Marchant" Drapers and Hosiers of Chester opposed to non-members selling "woollen Cloathes."*

f. 42. *Ironmongers and Mercers of Chester form one Body Corporate by 1606.*

f. 46. *Privy Council notified of Diverse Riots and Disorders in Chester because Merchants exercised Trade of Ironmongers.*

f. 68. *Seventeenth-century Mercers of Chester claim exclusive right to handle silk.*

f. 193. *London Freemen apprenticed to Vintners made free of Company of Haberdashers.*

f. 546. *Occupation of Linen-drapers not made whole Occupation of itself until 6 Edward VI.*

2054. f. 37. *The Trade of "Merceries" as constituted in the Beginning.*

f. 46. *Chester "mersers" declared "free" of the Merchant Adventurers.*

f. 47. *Linen-drapers of Chester opposed by the Silk-weavers.*

f. 56. *Amalgamated Company of Mercers of Chester.*

f. 68. *The Trade of Linen-drapers of Chester outlined in 1634.*

f. 89. *Tactics pursued by the Mercers and Iron-mongers of Chester against an Interloper.*

2104. f. 44. *Chester Company of Ironmongers pay "weeklye" Sum toward "makinge of Haven."*

f. 62. *Inn-keepers and Victuallers of Chester oppose Brewers in the brewing of Beer and Ale to sell in City.*

6842. f. 193. *London Freemen who had served Apprenticeship to Vintners made free of Haber-dashers' Company.*

LANSDOWNE *MSS.* No. 22. *Complaint of the Devonshire Shoemakers to the Council against the Tanners, 1576.*

38. *Declaration made by Lord Mayor and Aldermen against putting into execution a Patent granted the Tallow Chandlers, 1583.*

63. *Articles agreed to by Company of Cordwainers on Conditions to be performed by the Curriers, 1590.*

71. *Reasons to further Suit of the London Skinners notwithstanding the Murmurs of the Merchants, 1592.*

106. *Petition of Plaisterers against attempts of London Painters to ingross all Painting and Colouring.*

154. *Abstract of Sinister and Hard Dealings of the Marchaunts adventurers against the poore clothworkers, 1599.*

162. *Report in a Cause between the Town of Ipswich and the Corporation of Tailors and Clothworkers, 1619.*

TITUS *MSS.* No. IV. f. 36. *Plaisterers of London object to having Painters engross Colouring as well as Painting in the City.*

MANUSCRIPTS IN THE BODLEIAN LIBRARY, OXFORD

GOUGH *MSS.* *Records Relating to Kingston-upon-Thames, Surrey, 1714.*

———————— *Collections for a History of Lincoln.*

Old Order Book of Oxford Barber's Company, 1846.

MANUSCRIPTS IN MUNIMENT ROOM, GUILD HALL, COVENTRY

MSS. *Book of the Taylors and Clothworkers' Company.*

Agreement reached by the Cordwainers in 1747 with Persons unwilling to attend the Company.

BOOKS AND ARTICLES

NOTE.—The list which follows includes the books and articles consulted during the progress of this investigation which extended over a period of many years. Many of the books are now so well known, and so frequently used by students of the history of the English gilds, as to need no special introduction at this time. It seems, however, timely to call attention to the valuable material on the subject, which is to be found in the English periodicals and the transactions of the various archaeological societies and the like. For instance, the records of the amalgamated gild of mercers, ironmongers and goldsmiths of Shrewsbury, presented to the Shropshire Archaeological Society by one of the gild's few surviving members, and in 1884 contributed to the society's transactions by the Rev. W. A. Leighton as one of "The Guilds of Shrewsbury," in vol. viii, contain much of interest and value from which to draw conclusions on the internal economy of this species of gild. The publication, in more recent years, by the Surtees Society under the editorship of Miss Maud Sellers, of the records of the gilds of York, enables students to learn something of the development of the gilds in that city. We, in America, are greatly indebted to English scholars who, from time to time, render accessible records of institutions, which we find interesting subjects of study.

ABRAMS, W. A. *Memorials of the Preston Guilds.* Preston, 1882.
ADNIT, H. W. "The Orders of the Corporation of Shrewsbury, 1511–1735." *Shropshire Archaeological and Natural History Society Transactions.* Vol. xi. 1888.
AMERY, J. S. "The Accounts of the Receiver of the Corporation of Totnes." *Transactions Devonshire Association for Advancement of Science.* Vol. xii. Plymouth, 1880.
ANDERSON, ADAM. *Historical and Chronological Deduction of the Origin of Commerce.* 4 vols. London, 1787–1789.
ARMSTRONG, CLEMENT. *A Treatise concerninge the Staple and the Commodities of this Realme.* Printed in Reinhold Pauli's *Drei Volkswirthschaftliche Denkschiften.* Göttingen, 1878.
ASHDOWN, CHARLES HENRY. *History of the Worshipful Company of Glaziers of the City of London, otherwise the Company of Glaziers and Painters of Glass.* London, 1919.
ASHLEY, W. J. *An Introduction to English Economic History and Theory.* 2 vols. London and New York, 1888–1893.
ATKINS, S. E., and OVERALL, W. H. *Some Account of the Worshipful Company of Clockmakers of the City of London.* London, 1881.
ATKINSON, REV. J. C. "Quarter Sessions Records." *The North Riding Record Society.* Vol. ix. London, 1892.
BACON, NATHANIEL. *The Annalls of Ipswche. The Lawes, Customes and Governmt of the Same.* Edited by William H. Richardson. Ipswich, 1884.
BAILEY, CHARLES. *Transcripts from the Municipal Archives of Winchester.* Winchester and London, 1856.
BALLARD, ADOLPHUS. *Chronicles of the Royal Borough of Woodstock.* Oxford, 1896.
——*Notes on the History of Chipping Norton.* Oxford, 1893.
BARNEWALL, RICHARD VAUGHAN and ALDERSON, SIR EDWARD HALL. *Reports*

of Cases Argued and Determined in the Court of King's Bench. 5 Vols. London, 1818–1822.

BARRETT, C. R. B. *History of the Society of Apothecaries of London.* London, 1905.

BATESON, MARY. *Records of the Borough of Leicester. Being a series of extracts from the Archives of the Corporation of Leicester, 1103–1603.* 3 Vols. Cambridge University Press. 1899–1905.

BAZELEY, WILLIAM. "The Guilds of Gloucester." *Bristol and Gloucestershire Archaeological Society Transactions.* Vol. xiii. 1888.

BEESLEY, ALFRED. *The History of Banbury.* London, 1841.

BEMROSE, H. A. "The Derby Company of Mercers." *Derbyshire Archaeological and Natural History Society Journal.* Vol. xv. 1893.

BENHAM, W. G. *Red Paper Book of Colchester.* Colchester, 1902.

BENNETT, JAMES. *The History of Tewkesbury.* Tewkesbury, 1830.

BERRY, HENRY F. "Records of the Dublin Gild of Merchants, Known as the Gild of The Holy Trinity." *Journal of the Royal Society of Antiquaries of Ireland.* Fifth Series. Vol. 10. 1900.

—— "The Ancient Corporation of Barber-Surgeons or Gild of St. Mary Magdalene, Dublin." Vol. 33, pt. iii. 1903.

—— "The Dublin Gild of Carpenters, Millers, Masons and Heliers in the Sixteenth Century." Vol. 35, pt. iv. 1905.

—— "Records of the Feltmakers' Company of Dublin." Sixth Series. Vol. 41. 1911.

BICKLEY, F. B. *The Little Red Book of Bristol.* 2 vols. Bristol, 1900.

BLACK, W. H. *History and Antiquities of the Worshipful Company of Leathersellers of the City of London.* London, 1871.

BLOMEFIELD, FRANCIS. *An Essay towards a Topographical History of the County of Norfolk.* 11 vols. *History of Norwich.* Vol. iii. London, 1805–1810.

BOYLE, J. R. *The Early History of the Town and Port of Hedon.* Hull and York, 1895.

—— "The Goldsmiths of Newcastle-upon-Tyne." *Transactions Society of Antiquaries of Newcastle. Archaeologia Aeliana..* Vol. xv, pt. iii. 1887.

—— and DENDY, F. W. *Extracts from the Records of The Merchant Adventurers of Newcastle-upon-Tyne.* Surtees Society Publications. Vols. 93, 101. 1895–1899.

BOYS, WILLIAM. *Collections for an History of Sandwich in Kent.* Canterbury, 1792.

BOWMAN, T. *History of Richmond, in the County of York.* Albion Press, 1814.

BRAND, JOHN. *The History and Antiquities of the Town and County of Newcastle-upon-Tyne.* London, 1789.

CAULFIELD, RICHARD. *Council Book of the Corporation of the City of Cork.* Guildford, 1876.

—— *The Council Book of the Corporation of Youghal.* Guildford, 1878.

—— *Council Book of the Corporation of Kinsale, 1652–1800.* Guildford, 1879.

CHALLENOR, BROMLEY. *Selections from the Municipal Chronicles of the Borough of Abingdon.* Abingdon, 1898.

Charters, Ordinances and Bye-Laws of the Mercers' Company. London, 1881. Privately printed.

CHÉRUEL, PIERRE ADOLPHE. *Histoire de Rouen pendant L'Epoque Communale, 1150–1382.* 2 vols. Rouen, 1843.

CIVIS. *Minutes collected from the Ancient Records and Accounts in the Chamber of Canterbury.* Canterbury, 1801–1802.

CLODE, C. M. *The Early History of the Guild of Merchant Taylors of the Fraternity of St. John the Baptist, London.* 2 vols. London, 1888.

—— *Memorials of the Guild of Merchant Taylors of the Fraternity of St. John the Baptist in the City of London.* London, 1875.

Clothworkers Company of London, Charters, etc., 1480–1688. London, 1881.

The Government of the Fullers, Shearmen and Clothworkers of London, as proved by their Charters and Ordinances. Compiled by a member of the Court about 1650.

Ordinances of the Clothworkers' Company; together with those of the Ancient Guilds or Fraternities of the Fullers and Shearmen of the City of London. Transcribed from the Originals in the Possession of the Company. 1881.

COATES, CHARLES. *The History and Antiquities of Reading.* London, 1802.

COLLIER, C. "Andover and its Neighbourhood." *Wiltshire Archaeological and Natural History Society Magazine.* Vol. xxi. 1884.

COLLIER, JOHN. *An Essay on Charters.* Newcastle, 1777.

COLLINS, FRANCIS. *Register of the Freemen of the City of York from the City Records.* Vol. i. 1272–1558. *Surtees Society Publications.* Vol. 96. Durham, 1897.

COMPTON, CHARLES HENRY. *History of the Worshipful Company of the Horners of London.* London,, 1902.

COTTON, WILLIAM. *An Elizabethan Guild of the City of Exeter:* an Account of the Proceedings of the Society of Merchant Adventurers. Exeter, 1873.

—— "Some Account of the Ancient Guilds of the City of Exeter." *Devonshire Association for Advancement of Science Transactions.* Vol. v. 1872.

CREIGHTON, MANDELL. *Carlisle* (Historic Towns). London, 1889.

CROFTON, H. T. "Manchester Gilds and the Records of the Lichfield Corvisors." *Lancashire and Cheshire Antiquarian Society Transactions.* Vol. x. 1893.

CRUDEN, R. P. *The History of the Town of Gravesend.* London, 1843.

CUNNINGHAM, WM. *Growth of English Industry and Commerce.* 3 vols. London, 1910.

—— "On the Laws of the Mercers' Company of Lichfield." *Transactions of Royal Historical Society.* New Series. Vol. vii. 1893.

DALLAWAY, JAMES. *A History of the Western Division of the County of Sussex.* 2 vols. Chichester, vol. i. London, 1815–1830.

DALTON, MICHAEL. *The Country Justice.* London, 1742.

DAVIES, J. SILVESTER. *A History of Southampton.* Southampton, 1883.

DENDY, FREDERICK WALTER. *Extracts from the Records of the Merchant Adventurers of Newcastle-upon-Tyne.* *Surtees Society Publications.* Vols. 93, 101. Durham, 1894–1899.

—— "The Struggle between the Merchant and Craft Gilds of Newcastle-upon-Tyne, in 1515." *Transactions Society of Antiquaries of Newcastle. Archaeologia Aeliana.* 3rd series. Vol. vii. 1910.

DITCHFIELD, J. H. "The Guilds of Reading." *The Reliquary.* New series. Vol. iv. 1890.

DODDS, EDWIN. "The Records of the Gateshead Company of Drapers, Tailors, Mercers, Hardwaremen, Coopers and Chandlers." *Supplement to "Northern Notes and Queries."* Newcastle-upon-Tyne, 1907.

DRAKE, FRANCIS. *Eboracum: or the History and Antiquities of the City of York.* 2 vols. York, 1788.

DRINKWATER, THE REV. C. H. "Shrewsbury Trade Guilds." The Glovers' Company. *Shropshire Archaeological & Natural History Society Transactions.* Vol. x. 1887.

—— "Petition of Cordwainers of the Town of Salop in 1323–1324." Second series. Vol. vi. 1894.

—— "The Shrewsbury Drapers' Company Charter, Jan. 12, 1461–1462." Vol. viii. 1896.

—— "7 Shrewsbury Gild Merchant Rolls of the 14th Century." Third series. Vol. iii. 1903.

—— "A Burgess Roll and a Gild Merchant Roll of 1372." Vol. iv. 1904.

DUNLOP, O. JOCELYN, and DENMAN, RICHARD D. *English Apprenticeship and Child Labor.* London, 1912.

EARWAKER, J. P. *The Court Leet Records of the Manor of Manchester, 1562–1846.* 12 vols. Manchester, 1884–1890.

EMBLETON, DENNIS. "The Incorporated Company of Barber-Surgeons and Wax and Tallow Chandlers of Newcastle-upon-Tyne." *Transactions Society of Antiquaries of Newcastle. Archaeologia Aeliana.* New series. Vol. xv. 1891.

England, Public Records of:
—— *Calendar of Patent Rolls.* In progress.
—— *Calendar of State Papers Domestic,* 1634–1693. Rolls series. 59 vols. London, 1856–1895.
—— *Great Rolls of the Exchequer commonly called The Pipe Rolls.* Pipe Roll Society Publications. London, 1884–1913.
—— *Historical MSS. Commission Publications,* 1870–1899.

MSS. of

Axbridge	*Report*	iii,
Bury St. Edmunds	"	xiv, App. viii
Canterbury	"	ix,
Chester	"	viii,
Coventry	"	xv,
Gloucester	"	xii, App. ix
Hereford	"	xiii, " iv
Ipswich	"	ix, " i
Kendal	"	x, " iv
Lincoln	"	xiv, " viii
Lynn	"	xiii, " iv
Reading	"	xi, " vii
Rye	"	xiii, " iv
Sandwich	"	v,
Shrewsbury	"	xv, App. x

Worcester Report on MSS. in *Various Collections.* Vol. i, 1901.
Independent Publications.
Beverley 1900.
Exeter 1916. See under Wylie, J. H.

—— *Report of Commissioners Appointed to Inquire into the Municipal Corporations of England and Wales. Parliamentary Papers.* Vols. xxiii–xxvi. 4 vols. London, 1835.
—— *Reports upon Certain Boroughs. Parliamentary Papers.* Vol. xxxv. 1837.
—— *Second Report of the Commissioners on Municipal Corporations* (London and Southwark). *Parliamentary Report.* Vol. xxv. 1837.
—— *Report and Appendix. City of London Livery Companies' Commission. Parliamentary Papers.* Vol. xxxix, 5 pts. London, 1884.
—— *Rotuli Parliamentorum.* 6 vols. London, 1767–1783.
—— *Rymer, Thoma. Foedera.* 20 vols. London. 1704–1735.
—— *Statutes of the Realm.* Record Commission. 9 vols. London, 1810–22.
FELKIN, WM. *History of the Machine-Wrought Hosiery and Lace Manufactures.* London, 1887.
FERGUSON, R. S. *The Boke of Recorde of the Burgh of Kirkby, Kendal. Cumberland and Westmoreland Antiquarian and Archaeological Society* Extra series. Vol. 7. Kendal, 1892.
—— and NANSON, W. *Some Municipal Records of the City of Carlisle. Cumberland and Western Antiquarian and Archaeological Society.* Carlisle and London, 1887.
FIRTH, JAMES F. *Coopers Company of London. Historical Memorandum, Charters, Documents and Extracts from the Records of the Corporation.* London, 1848.
FORDYCE, WILLIAM. *The History and Antiquities of the County Palatine of Durham.* 2 vols. Newcastle, 1857.
FOSBROKE, T. D. *An Original History of the City of Gloucester.* London, 1819.
FOX, FRANCIS F. "Some Account of the Ancient Fraternity of Merchant

Taylors at Bristol with Manuscripts of Ordinances and other Documents." *Archaeological Journal.* Vol. xxxviii. 1881.

—— and TAYLOR, JOHN. *Some Account of the Guild of Weavers in Bristol.* Bristol, 1889.

FRETTON, WM. GEORGE. *Memorials of the Fullers' or Walkers' Guild Coventry.* Coventry, 1878.

GARDINER, RALPH. *England's Grievance Discovered in Relation to the Coal Trade of Chriton.* London, 1655.

GIBBS, A. E. *The Corporation Records of St. Albans.* St. Albans, 1890.

GIBBS, ROBERT. *A History of Aylesbury with its Borough and Hundreds.* Aylesbury, 1885.

GIRAUD, F. F. "Faversham Town Charters." *Kent Archaeolgical Society, Archaeologia Cantiana.* Vol. ix. London, 1874.

GODBOLT, JOHN. *Reports of Certain Cases Arising in the Several Courts of Record at Westminster in the Reigns of Elizabeth, James and Charles, 1575–1638.* London, 1652.

GOLDNEY, F. H. *Records of Chippenham.* London, 1889.

GREEN, VALENTINE. *The History and Antiquities of the City and Suburbs of Worcester.* 2 vols. London, 1796.

GRIBBLE, J. B. *Memorials of Barnstaple.* Barnstaple, 1830.

GROSS, CHARLES. *Gild Merchant.* 2 vols. Oxford, at the Clarendon Press, 1890.

GUILDING, J. M. *Reading Records.* 4 vols. London and Oxford, 1892–1896.

GURNEY, HUDSON. "Extracts from Proceedings of the Corporation of Lynn Regis, in Norfolk." *Archaeologia.* Vol. xxiv. 1832.

HADLEY, GEORGE. *A New and Complete History of the Town and County of Kingston-upon-Hull.* Kingston-upon-Hull, 1788.

HALLIWELL, J. O. *Council Book of Stratford-upon-Avon.* 1864.

HARDWICK, CHARLES. *History of the Borough of Preston and its Environs.* Preston, 1857.

HARDY, W. J. *Records of Doncaster.* 4 vols. Doncaster, 1899–1903.

HARRIS, MARY DORMER. *The Coventry Leet Book or Mayor's Register.* 3 parts. 1907–1909.

—— *Life in an Old English Town* (Coventry). (Social England Series.) London, 1898.

HARRISON, WILLIAM. *Ripon Millenary: a Record of the Festival and a History of the City.* Ripon, 1892.

HARTSHORNE, C. H. *Historical Memorials of Northampton.* Northampton, 1848.

HARWOOD, THOMAS. *The History and Antiquities of the City of Lichfield.* Gloucester, 1806.

HASKINS, CHARLES. *The Ancient Trade Guilds and Companies of Salisbury.* Salisbury, 1912.

HAZLITT, W. C. *The Livery Companies of the City of London.* 1892.

HEDGES, J. K. *The History of Wallingford.* 2 vols. London, 1881.

HERBERT, WILLIAM. *History of the Twelve Great Livery Companies of London.* 2 vols. London, 1837.

HEWINS, W. A. S. "The Regulation of Wages by the Justices of the Peace." *Economic Journal.* Vol. viii. 1898.

HIBBERT, FRANCIS AIDAN. *Influence and Development of English Gilds, as Illustrated by the History of the Craft Gilds of Shrewsbury* (Cambridge Historical Essays). 1891.

HILLS, GORDON M. "On the Ancient Company of Stitchmen of Ludlow. Their Account Book and Money-Box." *Journal of British Archaealogical Association.* Vol. xxiv. 1868.

HINDERWELL, THOMAS. *The History and Antiquities of Scarborough.* Scarborough, 1832.

HOARE, R. C. *The Modern History of South Wiltshire.* 6 vols. London, 1822–1843.

HOBART, SIR HENRY. *The Reports. Court of King's Bench.* First American from Fifth English Edition. Boston, 1829.

HODGSON, J. C. *History of Morpeth*. Newcastle-upon-Tyne, 1832.
—— "An Account of the Customs of the Court Leet and Court Baron of Morpeth with the Court Roll of 1632." *Society of Antiquaries of Newcastle. Archaedlogia Aeliana.* New series, pt. iii. Vol. xv. 1892.
—— "The Company of Saddlers of Newcastle-upon-Tyne." Third series. Vol. xix. Kendal, 1922.
HOLMES, RICHARD. *The Booke of Entries of the Pontefract Corporation.* Pontefract, 1882.
HOOPER, J. H. "The Clothiers' Company, Worcester." *Reports and Papers, Associated Architectural Societies.* Vol. xv. 1880.
HOPE, R. C. "Ordinances of the Goldsmiths of Norwich." *Reliquary.* New series. Vol. iv. 1890.
HUDSON, W. and TINGEY, J. C. *The Records of the City of Norwich.* 2 vols. Norwich, 1906–10.
HUDSON, WILLIAM. *Leet Jurisdiction in the City of Norwich. Selden Society Publications.* Vol. v. London, 1892.
HUNTER, JOSEPH. *Hallamshire.* London, 1869.
HUTCHINS, B. L. "The Regulation of Wages by Guilds and Town Authorities." *Economic Journal.* Vol. x. 1900.
HUTCHINS, JOHN. *The History and Antiquities of the County of Dorset.* Edited by William Shipp and J. W. Hodson. 4 vols. Westminster, 1861–1870.
INDERWICK, FREDERICK A. *The Interregnum.* London, 1891.
IZACKE, RICHARD. *Antiquities of the City of Exeter.* London, 1677.
JOHNSON, ARTHUR, HENRY. *History of the Worshipful Company of the Drapers of London.* 2 vols. Oxford, 1914–1915.
JOHNSON, RICHARD. *The Ancient Customs of the City of Hereford.* London, 1882.
JONES, LLEWELLYN. "The Antiente Company of Smiths and Others Commonly called 'Hammermen,' Ludlow." *Shropshire Archaeological and Natural History Society Transactions.* Vol. xi. 1888.
JUPP, EDWARD BASIL. *An Historical Account of the Worshipful Company of Carpenters of the City of London.* London, 1848.
JUPP and POCOCK. *Historical Account of the Worshipful Company of Carpenters.* London, 1848.
KEMP, THOMAS. *The Book of John Fisher, Town Clerk and Deputy Recorder of Warwick.* Warwick, 1900.
—— *The Black Book of Warwick.* Warwick, 1898.
KERRY, CHARLES. "Discovery of the Register and Chartulary of the Mercers' Company, York." *The Antiquary,* vol. xxii. 1890.
KING, A. J. and WATTS, B. H. *The Municipal Records of Bath.* London, 1885.
KING, EDWARD. *Old Times Re-visited in the Borough and Parish of Lymington, Hants.* London and Lymington, 1879.
KINGDON, JOHN ABERNETHY. *Facsimile of MS. Archives of the Worshipful Company of Grocers of the City of London.* 2 pts. London, 1886.
KITE, EDWARD. "The Guild of Merchants, or three Trading Companies Formerly existing in Devizes." *Wiltshire Archaeological and Natural History Society Magazine.* Vol. iv. 1858.
KRAMER, STELLA. *The English Craft Gilds and The Government. Studies in History, Economics and Public Law.* Vol. xxiii. Columbia University Press. New York, 1905.
LAMBERT, GEORGE. *History of the Worshipful Company of Patten-Makers.* London, 1890.
LAMBERT, J. MALET. *Two Thousand Years of Gild Life, with a full Account of the Gilds and Trading Companies of Kingston-upon-Hull.* Hull, 1891.
LAMOND, ELIZABETH. *Introduction and Notes to Hales' Discourse of the Common Weal.* Cambridge, 1893.
LATIMER, JOHN. *Annals of Bristol in the Seventeenth Century.* 1900.

LATIMER, JOHN. *Annals of Bristol in the Eighteenth Century.* 1893.
—— *History of the Society of Merchant Venturers of the City of Bristol.* 1903.
—— "The Mercers' and Linen Drapers' Company of Bristol." *Bristol and Gloucester Archaeological Society Transactions* Vol. 26, pt. ii, 1903.
—— *Bristol in the Sixteenth Century. Newspaper Clippings in the British Museum.*
LAW, MISS ALICE. "The English Nouveaux-Riches in the Fourteenth Century." *Transactions Royal Historical Society.* New series. Vol. ix. 1895.
LEACH, ARTHUR F. *Beverley Town Documents (Selden Society Publications).* London, 1900.
LEIGHTON, THE REV. W. A. "The Guilds of Shrewsbury." Extracts from the Records of the Barber-Surgeons. *Shropshire Archaeological and Natural History Society Transactions.* Vol. v. 1882-3.
—— "The Guilds of Shrewsbury." The Gild of Mercers, Ironmongers and Goldsmiths. Vol. viii. 1884-5.
MACKENZIE, E. *An Historical, Topographical and Descriptive View of the County of Northumberland and of Parts of the County of Durham.* 2 vols. Morpeth, vol. ii. Newcastle, 1825.
MADOX, THOMAS. *The History and Antiquities of the Exchequer.* 2 vols. London, 1759.
MARKHAM, CHRISTOPHER A. *The Liber Custumarum.* Northampton, 1895.
MARKHAM, C. A. and COX, J. C. *The Records of the Borough of Northampton.* 2 vols. Northampton, 1898.
MAY, GEORGE. *The History of Evesham.* Evesham, 1834.
MILBOURN, THOMAS. *The Vintners' Company. Their Muniments, Plate and Eminent Members.* London, 1888.
—— "Biographical Notices of Some Eminent Members of the Vintners' Company." *Transactions of the London and Middlesex Archaeological Society.* Vol. iii. 1871.
MONEY, WALTER. *The History of the Ancient Town and Borough of Newbury in the County of Berks.* Oxford and London, 1887.
"The Guild or Fellowship of the Clothworkers of Newbury." *Journal British Archaeological Association.* New series. Vol. ii. 1896.
MORRIS, R. H. *Chester in the Plantagenet and Tudor Periods.* Chester, 1893.
MUIR, RAMSAY. *A History of Liverpool.* London, 1907.
NICHOLL, JOHN. *Some Account of the Worshipful Company of Ironmongers of London.* London, 1851.
NICHOLS, JOHN. *The History and Antiquities of the County of Leicester.* 4 vols. Leicester, 1795-1815.
NICHOLS, J. GOUGH. "The Muniments of the Vintners Company." *Transactions of the London and Middlesex Archaeological Society.* Vol. iii. London, 1870.
—— "Records of the Mercers and other Trading Companies of London." *London and Middlesex Archaeological Society Transactions.* Vol. iv. London. 1869.
NICHOLSON, CORNELIUS. *The Annals of Kendal.* London and Kendal, 1861.
NOBLE, T. C. *A Brief History of the Worshipful Company of Ironmongers.* London, 1889.
NORTON, GEORGE. *Commentaries on the History, Constitution, and Chartered Franchises of the City of London.* London, 1869.
OVERALL, H. W. and H. C. *Analytical Index to the Series of Records Known as the Remembrancia, 1579-1664.* London, 1878.
OVERALL, WM. H. "Some Account of the Ward of Vintry and the Vintners Company." *Transactions of the London and Middlesex Archaeological Society.* Vol. iii. London, 1870.
PHILLIPS, WILLIAM. "The Shrewsbury Company of Drapers." *Shropshire Archaeological & Natural History Society Transactions.* 3rd Series. Vol. v., Miscellanea, iii. 1905.

PICTON, JAMES A. *Selections from the Municipal Archives and Records of Liverpool from the 13th to the 17th Centuries.* Liverpool, 1883.

PRICE, WILLIAM. *The History of Oswestry from the Earliest Period.* Oswestry, 1815.

PRIDEAUX, SIR WALTER SHERBURNE. *Memorials of the Goldsmiths' Company.* 2 vols. London, 1896.

POOLE, BENJAMIN. *Coventry: its History and Antiquities.* London and Coventry, 1870.

PULLING, ALEXANDER. *The Laws, Customs, Usages and Regulations of the City and Port of London.* London, 1854.

RAYMOND, LORD ROBERT. *Reports of Cases adjudged in the Courts of King's Bench and Common Pleas, 1694–1732.* London, 1790.

REDFERN, FRANCIS. *History and Antiquities of the Town and Neighbourhood of Uttoxeter.* London, 1886.

REDSTONE, V. B. "St. Edmundsbury and Town Rental for 1295." *Proceedings of the Suffolk Institute of Archaeology and Natural History.* Vol. xiii, pt. 2. 1908.

REINHOLD, PAULI. *Drei Volkswirthschaftliche Denkschriften aus der Zeit Heinrichs VIII von England.* Göttingen, 1878.

RILEY, H. T. *Memorials of London and London Life in the XIII, XIV, and XV Centuries.* London, 1868.

Munimenta Gildhallae Londoniensis. Rolls Series. 4 vols. 1859–1863.
Liber Albus. Vol. I. 1859.
Liber Custumarum. 2 vols. 1860.

ROBSON, JOHN STEPHENSON. "Some Account of the Incorporated Company of Free Joiners of Newcastle-upon-Tyne." *Society of Antiquaries, Archaeologia Aeliana.* Third Series, vol. v., 1909.

ROPE, IRENE MARY. "The Earliest Book of the Drapers' Company of Shrewsbury." *Shropshire Archaeological & Natural History Transactions,* Fourth Series, vol. iii. 1913.

ROSEDALE, H. G. "The Horners' Company." *Proceedings of the Society of Antiquaries of London,* 1909.

ROWSELL, R. F. "The Ancient Companies of Exeter." *The Western Antiquary.* Vol. iv. 1885.

RUSSELL, J. M. *The History of Maidstone.* Maidstone, 1881.

RUSSELL, W. H. "The Laws of the Mercers' Company of Lichfield. *Royal Historical Society Transactions.* New Series. Vol. vii. 1893.

SAUNDERS. SIR EDMUND. *The Reports of Cases in the Court of King's Bench in time of King Charles II.* (1666–1672). 2 vols. First American edition from the third London edition. 1807.

Schedule of the Records and Other Documents of the Corporation of Bedford. Printed by Order of the Corporation. Bedford, 1883.

SCOTT, JAMES B. *A Short Account of the Wheelwrights' Company.* London, 1884.

SCOTT, JONATHAN FRENCH. *Historical Essays on Apprenticeship and Vocational Education.* Ann Arbor, Michigan, 1914.

SELLERS, MAUD. "York in the Sixteenth and Seventeenth Centuries." *English Historical Review.* Vol. xii. 1897.

—— *The Acts and Ordinances of the Eastland Company of York.* Edited for *The Royal Historical Society from Original Muniments of the Merchant Adventurers of York.* London, 1906.

—— *The Merchant Adventurers of York.* Handbook for the British Association Meeting Held at York, 1906. Edited by Mr. George Auder.

—— *The York Memorandum Book.* Part I. 1376–1419. *Surtees Society Publications.* Vol. cxx. 1912.

—— *Memorandum Book.* Part II. 1388–1492. Vol. cxxv. 1915.

—— *The York Mercers and Merchant Adventurers.* Surtees Society Publications. Vol. cxxix. 1918.

SEYER, SAMUEL. *Memoirs, Historical and Topographical of Bristol.* 2 vols. Bristol, 1821–23.

SHARP, CUTHBERT. *History of Hartlepool.* Hartlepool, 1858.

SHARPE, REGINALD R. *Calendar of Wills Proved and Enrolled in the Court of Hustings.* Pt. i, 1258–1358. Pt. ii, 1358–1688. London, 1890.

—— *Calendar of Letter Books Preserved Among the Archives of the City of London.* 1275–1314. 4 vols. 1899–1902.

SHERWELL, J. W. *A Descriptive and Historical Account of the Guild of Saddlers of the City of London.* London, 1889.

SIMPSON, FRANK. "City Gilds or Companies of Chester with Special Reference to the Barber-Surgeons." *Journal of the Architectural, Archaeological and Historic Society for County and City of Chester and North Wales.* New Series. Vol. xviii. 1911.

—— "City Gilds of Chester." The Smiths, Cutlers and Plumbers' Company. Vol. xx. 1914.

—— "The Bricklayers' Company of Chester." Vol. xxii. 1919.

SIMPSON, ROBERT. *The History and Antiquities of the Town of Lancaster.* Lancaster, 1852.

SKEEL, MISS C. A. J. "The Bridgnorth Company of Smiths." *English Historical Review,* April 1920.

S., L. B. *The City Livery Companies and their Corporate Property.* London, 1885.

SMITH, ADAM. *An Inquiry into the Nature and Causes of the Wealth of Nations.* (Edwin Cannan Edition). 2 vols. Methuen & Co., London, 1904.

SMITH, LUCY T. "The Bakers of York and their Ancient Ordinary." *Archaeological Review.* Vol. i. London, 1888.

—— "Ordinances of the Companies of Marshals and Smiths of York." *The Antiquary.* Vol. xi. London, 1885.

SMITH, J. TOULMIN. *English Gilds. Original Ordinances of more than 100 early English Gilds. Early English Text Society Publications.* London, 1870.

SMITH, WILLIAM. *Old Yorkshire.* 5 vols. London, 1881–84.

SMYTHE, W. D. *An Historical Account of the Worshipful Company of Girdlers of London.* London, 1905.

STEVENS, D. M. *The Records and Plate of the Borough of Guildford.* Surrey Archaeological Collections. Vol. ix. London, 1888.

STEVENSON, W. H. *Calendar of the Records of the Corporation of Gloucester.* Gloucester, 1893.

—— *Records of the Borough of Nottingham.* 6 vols. Nottingham, 1882–1900.

STEWART, HORACE. *History of the Worshipful Company of Gold and Silver Wyre-Drawers and of the Origin and Development of the Industry.* London, 1891.

STOCKS, HELEN. *Records of the Borough of Leicester. Extracts from Archives, 1603–1688.* With the Assistance of W. H. Stevenson. Cambridge University Press, 1923. Continuation of the Volumes edited by Mary Bateson.

STOKES, ETHEL AND REDSTONE, LILIAN. "Calendar of The Muniments of the Borough of Sudbury." *Proceedings of the Suffolk Institute of Archaeology & Natural History.* Vol. xiii, part 3. 1909.

STRYPE, JOHN. *A Survey of the Cities of London and Westminster, and the Borough of Southwark,* etc. by John Stow. 2 vols. London, 1754–55.

TATE, GEORGE. *The History of the Borough, Castle and Barony of Alnwick.* 2 vols. Alnwick, 1866–69.

THOMPSON, A. HAMILTON. "On a Minute-Book and Papers formerly belonging to the Mercers' Company of the City of Durham."

—— "The Ordinary of the Company of Goldsmiths, Plumbers, Pewterers, Potters, Glaziers and Painters, in the City of Durham." *Transactions Society of Antiquaries of Newcastle, Archaeologia Aeliana.* Third Series. Vol. xix. 1922.

THOMPSON, PISHEY. *The History and Antiquities of Boston.* Boston, 1856.

TIGHE, R. R., and DAVIS, J. E. *Annals of Windsor.* 2 vols. London, 1858.

TOMLINSON, JOHN. *Doncaster from the Roman Occupation to the Present Time.* Doncaster, 1887.

TOWNSEND, G. F. *The Town and Borough of Leominster.* Leominster and London, 1863.

TURNER, EDWARD. "The Merchant Gild of Chichester." *Sussex Archaeological Association.* Vol. xv. 1863.

TURNER, WM. H. *Selections from the Records of the City of Oxford,* 1501–1583. Oxford and London, 1880.

UNWIN, GEORGE. *Industrial Organization in the Sixteenth and Seventeenth Centuries.* London, 1902.

—— *The Gilds & Companies of London. Antiquary's Books.* Methuen & Co. London, 1909.

WADMORE, J. F. *Some Account of the History and Antiquity of the Worshipful Company of Skinners,* London. London, 1876.

WAINWRIGHT. THOMAS. *Barnstaple Records.* 2 vols. Barnstaple, 1900.

WALFORD, CORNELIUS. *Gilds: their Origin, Constitution, Objects and Later History.* London, 1888.

WARBURTON, J., WHITELAW, J. and WALSH, R. *History of the City of Dublin.* 2 vols. London, 1818.

WARDELL, JAMES.—*The Municipal History of the Borough of Leeds.* London and Leeds, 1846.

WAYLEN, JAMES. *A History, Military and Municipal of the Town of Marlborough.* London, 1854.

WEBB, SIDNEY and BEATRICE. *English Local Government from the Revolution to the Municipal Corporations Act.* London, 1906–8.

—— *History of Trade Unionism.* London, 1894.

WELCH, CHARLES. *History of the Pewterers of London.* 2 vols. London, 1902.

WILCOCKSON, I. *Authentic Records of the Guild Merchant of Preston.* Preston, 1822.

WILLIAMSON, GEORGE C. *Guildford in The Olden Time.* London, 1904.

WILLIS, BROWNE. *The History and Antiquities of the Town, Hundred and Deanery of Buckingham.* London, 1755.

WILSON, J. "The Cordwainers and Corvesors of Oxford." *Archaeological Journal.* Vol. vi. 1849.

WODDERSPOON, JOHN. *Memorials of the Ancient Town of Ipswich in the County of Suffolk.* Ipswich and London, 1850.

WRIGHT, THOMAS. "On the Municipal Archives of the City of Canterbury." *Archaeologia,* vol. 31. *Society of Antiquaries of London.* London, 1846.

WYLIE, J. H. *Report on the Records of the City of Exeter. (Historical MSS. Commission.)* London, 1916.

WYLIE, WM. H. *Old and New Nottingham.* London, 1853.

YOUNG, SIDNEY. *Annals of the Barber-Surgeons of London.* London, 1890.

INDEX